Complementarity and the Exercise of Universal Jurisdiction for Core International Crimes

Morten Bergsmo (editor)

2010
Torkel Opsahl Academic EPublisher
Oslo

This and other books in the FICHL Publication Series may be openly accessed and downloaded through the Forum website (www.fichl.org). Printed copies may be ordered at www.amazon.co.uk. This book was first published on 1 August 2010.

ISBN 978-82-93081-14-2

To Nora Helene Bergsmo

PREFACE

The Forum for International Criminal and Humanitarian Law seeks to contribute to scholarship and practice. To this end, it not only organizes seminars and other activities, but it also promotes seminar findings and other publications through this Publication Series. The present volume grew out of a mini-seminar organized by the Forum in Oslo on 4 September 2009. The chapters by Jo Stigen, Pål Lønseth and Wolfgang Kaleck *et al.* are based on the papers they presented at that seminar. The other contributors to this anthology were specifically invited by the Forum to submit a text.

Complementarity and the Exercise of Universal Jurisdiction for Core International Crimes is published as one of the early volumes of the Torkel Opsahl Academic EPublisher. Its publication reinforces the open access programme of the Forum, which aspires to place high quality texts on an Internet-based platform that is equally accessible to all. The book can be freely read, printed or downloaded from the Forum Internet site (www.fichl.org). It can also be purchased through Amazon as a regular printed book. Firmly committed to open access, the Forum and the EPublisher do not charge for these authorized printed versions of their books.

We thank Gordana Višković for her professional Bosnian/Croatian/ Serbian language assistance. We also place on record our appreciation to the Hoover Institution of Stanford University for its support at the end of the editing process.

Morten Bergsmo
Publication Series Co-Editor

Alf Butenschøn Skre
Senior Editorial Assistant

Mats Benestad
Editorial Assistant

TABLE OF CONTENTS

1

Between Territoriality and Universality: Room for Further Reflection

Morten Bergsmo*

The complementarity principle on which the International Criminal Court (ICC) is based entails that the Court can only investigate and prosecute core international crimes (war crimes, crimes against humanity and genocide) when national jurisdictions are unable or unwilling to do so genuinely. The principle is analyzed extensively in the following chapters in this book, in particular by Rod Rastan, Jo Stigen and Cedric Ryngaert, all three of whom are leading international experts on the topic. The ICC complementarity regime reflects a realization by states that it is preferable that such crimes are investigated and prosecuted in the country where they occur or in the state of nationality of the suspects – that is, in the states most directly affected by the armed conflict, attack against the civilian population or manifest pattern of serious international crimes. It was created as an admissibility principle for cases to come before the ICC.

Universal jurisdiction, on the other hand, is a jurisdictional basis of last resort which a number of national criminal justice systems provide for, when core international crimes can not be prosecuted on the basis of the principle of territoriality (in the state where the crimes occurred), active nationality (in the state of the alleged perpetrator) or passive national-

---

* **Morten Bergsmo** is Researcher, University of Oslo, Faculty of Law; Visiting Fellow, Stanford University (2010-11); Visiting Professor, Georgetown University (2010 Fall); and ICC Consultant and Co-ordinator of the ICC Legal Tools Project (2006-). He was formerly Visiting Scholar, UC Berkeley (2010 Spring); Senior Researcher, PRIO (2006-09); Special Adviser to the Office of the Director of Public Prosecution of Norway (2007-08); Senior Legal Adviser and Chief of the Legal Advisory Section, ICC Office of the Prosecutor (2002-05); Co-ordinator of the establishment of the ICC Office of the Prosecutor (2002-03); Legal Adviser, ICTY (1994-2002); and Legal Adviser, UN Commission of Experts for the Former Yugoslavia established pursuant to Security Council resolution 780(1992) (1993-94). He represented the ICTY to the UN negotiation process to establish the ICC (1996-2002). He founded and directs the capacity building platform *Case Matrix Network* (www.casematrixnetwork.org) and the *Forum for International Criminal and Humanitarian Law* (www.fichl.org).

ity (in the state of the victim). Universal jurisdiction is discussed in depth in later chapters of this volume, especially by Judge Fausto Pocar and Magali Maystre, and Christopher K. Hall. In its pure form, universal jurisdiction enables the prosecution of core international crimes committed in a foreign state, by a foreign citizen, against foreign victims, when neither has a personal link to the forum state.

This book has a focus on the relationship between the principles of complementarity and universal jurisdiction. Territorial states are normally affected most strongly by core international crimes committed during a conflict or an attack directed against its civilian population. Most victims reside in such states. Most damaged or plundered property is there. Public order and security are violated most severely in the territorial states. It is also on their territory that most of the evidence of the alleged crimes can be found. There are, in other words, obvious policy and practical reasons why states should accord priority to territoriality as a basis of jurisdiction for core international crimes.

But is there also an obligation for states to defer the exercise of universal jurisdiction of core international crimes to investigation and prosecution of the same crimes by the territorial state? If not, should there be such an obligation? On which legal basis could it be constructed *de lege ferenda*? At what stage of the criminal justice process and pursuant to which criteria should forum states defer to territorial states? Would there be a difference between the various core international crimes? What – if any – is the impact of the principle of complementarity in this context? How does it affect existing notions of subsidiarity? These are among the questions discussed in this anthology.

In the next chapter of the anthology, Joseph Rikhof provides a detailed overview of the contemporary practise of prosecution of core international crimes at the national level. He shows that the number of national prosecutions is much higher than what is frequently perceived. He distills several key conclusions from the extensive national case law and makes comparisons with the international jurisprudence.

In chapter 3 Rod Rastan analyzes the main dimensions of the complementarity principle based on early judicial pronouncements by the ICC and public policies of its Office of the Prosecutor. He explains that the complementarity principle can be understood in two ways: "as an admissibility principle governing case allocation between competing jurisdictions, and as a burden sharing principle for the consensual distribution of caseloads". Rastan offers a comprehensive statement on complementarity seen from his perspective working in the ICC Office of the Prosecutor, one important actor in the emerging system of criminal justice for atrocities.

Combined, the chapters of Rastan and Rikhof provide a broadly-based overview of the practise of states with regard to the investigation and prosecution of core international crimes, and the legal scope of the complementarity principle in the ICC Statute. This further elaborates the stage for the subsequent chapters in the book.

In chapter 4 Jo Stigen argues that a subsidiarity principle for universal jurisdiction, requiring the forum state to first offer the case to the territorial state and the suspect's home state, "is in the process of being developed". After first surveying relevant international law instruments and national jurisprudence, he discusses how the ICC's complementarity principle might contribute to the development and refinement of a subsidiarity principle. This chapter goes to the heart of the theme of the anthology. Stigen concludes that, while "currently not amounting to a duty under international law", it is a right of the forum state to offer the case as a matter of policy to the territorial state or the suspect's home state when that state is willing and able to carry out genuine proceedings.

Pål Lønseth addresses the preëminence of the principle of territoriality in chapter 5. As a former public prosecutor of core international crimes cases in Norway, he addresses some reasons why it is preferrable that such crimes be prosecuted in the states directly affected by the crimes. He also points out that the scenario of concurrent or competing criminal jurisdictions for core international crimes remains exceptional. The main rule is still that no jurisdiction wants to pursue criminal responsibility for such crimes, and that impunity therefore reigns too often.

In chapter 6 Cedric Ryngaert provides a careful analysis of arguments for and against the applicability of the principle of complementarity for core international crimes in the horizontal relationship between sovereign states. He presents and critically analyses recent case law and legislative developments in national jurisdictions. He points out that it is crucial for the legitimacy and viability of universal jurisdiction that the territorial or national state "is accorded the first right of way to prosecute, and that due respect is shown for ongoing local prosecutorial efforts". But Ryngaert concludes that although there are strong normative arguments in favour of a principle of horizontal complementarity, "admittedly it may not yet have crystallized as a norm of customary international law given the dearth of pertinent state practice". Implementing horizontal complementarity is challenging, he notes, in particular with reference to "an overly policy-based horizontal complementarity analysis". He warns of the danger that prosecutors may use subsidiarity as an excuse not to prosecute. Moreover, he cautions against weak horizontal complementarity analyses – inadequate assessments of investigation and prosecution in the territorial state or state of nationality of the suspect – which can lead to jurisdictional overreach. Such overreach can undermine political support for the legislative basis and use of universal jurisdiction.

Christopher K. Hall offers a broad overview of legislation and case law relevant to the exercise of universal jurisdiction by national criminal justice systems in chapter 7 of this volume. He also refers to "the judicially created requirement in a handful of states of the misnamed concept of horizontal 'complementarity' or the equally misapplied concept of 'subsidiarity' before national courts are permitted to exercise universal jurisdiction" as "[o]ne particularly disturbing obstacle to the exercise of universal jurisdiction with regard to crimes under international law". Hall offers a resounding defence of the practise of universal criminal jurisdiction for core international crimes. It represents a clear statement of the position of many non-governmental organizations and other actors in the community of criminal justice for atrocities.

In chapter 8, the authors Florian Jessberger, Wolfgang Kaleck and Andreas Schueller provide an analysis of concurrent criminal jurisdiction for core international crimes under international law. They consider which universal standards of investigation have to be met and the relevancy of the *ne bis in idem* principle in inter-state relations. They argue that the complementarity principle does not exist on the state-to-state level, "where concurrent jurisdiction with conditional subsidiarity prevails". It is only as "a matter of policy that the territoriality principle is favoured over the universality principle once there is an investigation concluded". They argue that the standard in article 17 of the ICC Statute can serve as a guiding principle in inter-state relations, but it is necessary to make a "positive determination whether another state is genuinely conducting an investigation or prosecution" also at that level.

In the final chapter 9, Judge Fausto Pocar and Magali Maystre first present a comprehensive analysis of the origins, complexity and limits of the principle of universal jurisdiction. They move on to discuss the application and effectiveness of universal jurisdiction as a contemporary prosecution mechanism, with particular emphasis on Belgium and Spain. They argue that the bell has not tolled for the end of universal jurisdiction and explore how the goal pursued by universal jurisdiction "could be better enforced through the principle of complementarity". They develop ideas on how the ICC's complementarity principle can motivate states to exercise universal jurisdiction for core international crimes. They suggest that states exercising universal jurisdiction have priority over the ICC and that "[s]trengthening a reverse form of cooperation from the Court to national courts should be part of the ICC and its Prosecutor's policy. Promoting legal empowerment of domestic jurisdictions, including those exercising universal jurisdiction, should be encouraged by the ICC and its Prosecutor". Pocar and Maystre conclude their comprehensive chapter by observing that the main challenge for criminal justice for atrocities is to enhance a "more pragmatic and homogenous implementation of the principle of universal jurisdiction. Positive and proactive implementation of the principle of complementarity, as well as cooperation of states with the Court and of the Court with states, must be encouraged and strengthened. A mechanism of transfer of cases from the Court to domestic courts exercising universal jurisdiction should also be envisaged".

This anthology focuses on the impact of the relatively new principle of complementarity enshrined in the ICC Statute on jurisdictional principles for core international crimes. The book seeks to stimulate further, in-depth analysis of the relationship between the principles of territoriality and active nationality, universality, and complementarity or subsidiarity. The rise of the ICC and its standard of complementarity has so far not been matched by a strengthening of the exercise of universal jurisdiction. Several authors in this volume point to the danger that horizontal complementarity or subsidiarity may be used by national criminal justice systems as an excuse not to prosecute. As such, subsidiarity can further undermine universal jurisdiction. But it is also argued that only by respecting the primary role of territorial and active nationality jurisdictions – by, for example, ensuring professional assessments of ongoing national investigations and prosecutions – will universal jurisdiction preserve its legitimacy over time.

We may benefit from further research and discussion on these dilemmas and relevant underlying conflicts of reasonable interests. Some wider perspectives should also be taken into consideration. For example, when the *ad hoc* internationalised criminal jurisdictions have completed their operations in a few years and the ICC represents international criminal justice for atrocities, the complementary nature of the ICC will lead to a shift of emphasis to how national ability to investigate and prosecute core international crimes can be strengthened. Such development of national capacity does not happen over night, especially not in territorial states directly affected by conflict and socially disruptive crimes. What, if any, should be the impact of this scenario on the use of subsidiarity in forum states?

Furthermore, for the younger generations of legal scholars there are other future-oriented issues waiting to be explored, such as the effect of the predictable broadening of the catalogue of core international crimes on the tension between subsidiarity and universal jurisdiction. As it stands in August 2010, the established crime of aggression may be the first addition to the list of such crimes in the context of the ICC. But later additions could include crimes of international terrorism and even serious international environmental crimes where the application of the notion of *hostes humani generis* (that the perpetrators are considered the enemies of all mankind) may not always be entirely clear.

2

Fewer Places to Hide? The Impact of Domestic War Crimes Prosecutions on International Impunity

Joseph Rikhof[*]

> *Ending impunity by perpetrators of crimes of concern to the international community is a necessary part of preventing the recurrence of atrocities.*[1]

2.1. Introduction

This chapter will examine the developments in the domestic arena to achieve a higher level of accountability for international crimes. After examining the historical and international context, it will look at a number of mechanisms, which have been utilized to accomplish this goal. The first level of examination is to determine how countries have adjusted their legislation to ensure that it is possible to prosecute international criminals especially in the wake of the high number of ratifications of the Rome Statute.[2] Then the focus will shift to the recent trend of war crimes prosecutions, including prosecutions based on territorial jurisdiction by the country where the crimes occurred, or active nationality jurisdiction where perpetrators were nationals of the prosecuting country or based on universal jurisdiction where there is no link between the location of the

---

* **Joseph Rikhof** is Senior Counsel at the Crimes against Humanity and War Section of the Canadian Department of Justice and Part-time Professor, International Criminal Law, University of Ottawa. The opinions expressed in this article are of the author and do not necessarily represent the positions of the Department of Justice or the government of Canada. The author wishes to thank Emily Dwyer for the research carried out for this article.

1 Chautauqua Declaration, signed by the prosecutors of the Nuremberg International Military Tribunal, the International Criminal Court, the International Criminal Tribunal for the Former Yugoslavia, the International Criminal Tribunal for Rwanda, the Sierra Leone Special Court and the Extraordinary Chambers of the Courts of Cambodia, 29 August 2007; see http://www.asil.org/chaudec/index_files/frame.htm.

2 110; see http://www.icc-cpi.int/about.html.

crime and the country bringing the prosecutions except for the fact that in most cases the perpetrator has fled to the country in question. The overview of the various mechanisms will conclude with an assessment of the application of international criminal law in the various countries by looking at developing trends in domestic prosecutions as well as discussing emerging legal issues pertaining to the notion of universal jurisdiction and the elements of the international crimes of genocide, war crimes and crimes against humanity.

2.2. Historical and International Context

Both the development of the legal parameters of law dealing with international crimes and the application of this law by both international and national institutions has known historical ebbs and flows. A major impetus was received after the Second World War until about 1950 after which very little happened until the mid-1990s even though conflicts in which international crimes occurred continued unabated during this time period.

Most of the law of war crimes and crimes against humanity was developed in the immediate aftermath of the Second World War and consisted of the instruments setting up the two international military tribunals in Nuremberg and Tokyo, the legislative authority enabling domestic courts to deal with war criminals in Europe and Asia, the caselaw developed by these tribunals and courts[3], the adoption of the

[3] The most important cases have been described in a variety of law reports; the proceedings and the verbatim judgments of the Military Tribunals in Nuremberg have been reported very extensively in the 15 volumes of the *Trials of War Criminals before the Nuernberg Military Tribunals*, the so-called Green Series (see also http://nuremberg.law.harvard.edu/php/docs_swi.php?DI=1&text=nur_13tr). There has also been the Law Reports of Trials of War Criminals for all proceedings including the Nuremberg Tribunals, which is a 15 volume compilation of summaries and case comments of important decisions selected and prepared by the United Nations War Crimes Commission (see also http://www.ess.uwe.ac.uk/genocide/war_criminals.htm). The judgment of the Nuremberg International Military Tribunal is reported in Volume XXII of the *Trial of the Major War Criminals before the International Military Tribunal, Nuremberg, 14 November 1945 - 1 October 1946* which was published at Nuremberg in 1949 and is also known as the Blue Series (see also http://www.yale.edu/lawweb/avalon/imt/imt.htm). There has also some reporting of war crimes trials in *Annual Digest and Reports of Public International Law Cases*, which changed its name in 1950 to *International Law Reports*.

1948 Genocide Convention and the passing of the Geneva Conventions which regulated the conduct of war, including its violations.[4] Virtually all the important principles for this area of law can be traced back to this time period with some other important cases, such as the Menten case in the Netherlands[5], the Barbie, Papon and Touvier cases in France[6] and the Eichman trial in Israel[7] adding refinements to those principles. When international criminal law was examined by Canadian[8], Australian[9] and British criminal courts[10] in the 1980s and 1990s, a direct linkage was made between the post WWII law and the cases before them. This was not only done because the persons who had been investigated by the Canadian, British and Australian governments had committed their acts during the Second World War, but also because there was no new law to speak of in the interim.

However, there has been an explosion of new developments internationally in the area of war crimes law in the last 15 years. There

4 There are four Geneva Conventions, namely the Geneva Convention for the Amelioration of the Condition of the Wounded and Sick in Armed Forces in the Field (Geneva I); Geneva Convention for the Amelioration of the Condition of Wounded, Sick and Shipwrecked Members of Armed Forces at Sea (Geneva II); Geneva Convention relative to the Treatment of Prisoners of War (Geneva III); and Geneva Convention relative to the Protection of Civilian Persons in Time of War (Geneva IV). The war crimes provisions of the 1949 Geneva Conventions have been supplemented by the 1977 Additional Protocol I, articles 11 and 85. For a discussion of the post WWII case law, see Joseph Rikhof, "War Crimes, Crimes against Humanity and Immigration Law", *Immigration Law Reporter* (2nd), 1999, vol. 19, at 30-46.

5 *International Law Reports*, vol. 75, 331.

6 See *International Law Reports*, vol. 78, 123 for the Barbie case; http://www.trial-ch.org/en/trial-watch/profile/db/facts/maurice_papon_188.html for the Papon case and http://www.trial-ch.org/en/trial-watch/profile/db/facts/paul_touvier_124.html for the Touvier case.

7 *International Law Reports*, vol. 36, 1.

8 The Finta case; for the Supreme Court of Canada decision see [1994] 1 S.C.R. 701.

9 There have been three criminal prosecutions in Australia, namely the cases of Berezovsky, Wagner and Polyukhovich; the decision of the High Court of Australia in the last case can be found in Australian Law Reports, vol. 101, 545, 1991, 172 CLR 501 and *International Law Reports*, vol. 91, 1.

10 There has been one prosecution in the United Kingdom, namely the Sawoniuk trial which has been the only successful prosecution of a WWII perpetrator based on universal jurisdiction; for an assessment, see *Yearbook of International Humanitarian Law (YIHL)*, 1999, vol. 2, Part III, "National Decisions".

have been the International Criminal Tribunals for the Former Yugoslavia (ICTY)[11] and Rwanda (ICTR)[12], which were established in 1994 and 1995 respectively. These tribunals have their own Trial Chambers and a shared Appeals Chamber. The decisions of the Chambers of the two tribunals have greatly contributed to the development of the international law of war crimes, genocide and crimes against humanity. As of 14 March 2010, the ICTY has indicted 161 persons, the cases of 116 of those have been completed resulting in convictions and sentences of 62 persons in 48 separate trial processes[13] plus 11 acquittals, while it also has transferred eight cases involving 13 persons to national jurisdictions, all to Bosnia and Herzegovina except two to Croatia and one to Serbia[14]. The ICTR has indicted 90 persons of whom 75 have been arrested and 40 convicted in 32 judgments[15] (plus another seven have been acquitted) while transferring three persons to national jurisdictions, one to the Netherlands and two to France[16].

Apart from the activities of the two *ad hoc* tribunals, there has been a lot of work done under the auspices of the United Nations to establish a permanent international criminal court. The Statute of the International

11 The official name is "The International Tribunal for the Prosecution of Persons Responsible for Serious Violations of International Humanitarian Law Committed in the Territory of the Former Yugoslavia since 1991" and was established on 25 May 1993 as the result of Security Council Resolution 837 (UNDOC S/RES/827 (1993)).

12 The official name of the tribunal is "The International Criminal Tribunal for the Prosecution of Persons Responsible for Genocide and Other Serious Violations of International Humanitarian Law Committed in the Territory of Rwanda and Rwandan citizens responsible for genocide and other such violations in the territory of neighbouring States, between 1 January 1994 and 31 December 1994" and was established by Security Council Resolution UNDOC S/RES/955 on 8 November 1994.

13 See http://www.un.org/icty/glance-e/index.htm, under "Key Figures".

14 Namely Janković, decided by both the Trial and Appeal Chamber; Stanković, both TC and AC; Todović/Rašević, both TC and AC; Mejakić/Gruban/Knežević/Dušan Fuštar, TC and AC; Ademi/Norac, TC; Ljubičić, TC and AC; Kovačević, TC and AC, and Trbić, TC, all to BiH except two to Croatia (Ademi/Norac) and one to Serbia (Kovačević).

15 See Report on the Completion Strategy of the International Criminal Tribunal for Rwanda, 21 November 2007, paragraph 60.

16 Bagaragaza, TC and AC to the Netherlands (however, this transfer has been cancelled, see footnotes 48, 132 and 133); Bucyibaruta, TC and Munyeshyaka, TC, to France.

Criminal Court, which was adopted on 17 July 1998[17], contains definitions of genocide, crimes against humanity and war crimes, which can be considered the most contemporary formulation of the international law pertaining to these crimes. The court started operating on 1 July 2002 and has indicted 14 persons, five leaders of the Lord Resistance Army for the Ugandan situation (two of whom have died since the approval of the indictment), four Sudanese persons in respect to the Darfur situation (including the head of state of Sudan while another is in custody), one for the situation involving the Central African Republic who is in custody, and four from the Democratic Republic of the Congo (DRC) regarding war crimes committed in the Ituri region of that country; three of the four indictees for the last situation are in custody at the ICC. The first trial before the ICC was supposed to start on 23 June 2008, but the proceedings were stayed on 13 June 2008 due to irregularities in the prosecution case, which was upheld by the Appeals Chamber on 21 October 2008; however, on 18 November 2008 the stay was lifted and the trial has begun on 26 January 2009. The second trial started on 24 November 2009.

The United Nations has also been instrumental in establishing five hybrid tribunals for dealing with international crimes[18], namely the Special Panel for Serious Crimes of the Dili District Court in East Timor (and its Court of Appeal), the Special Court for Sierra Leone (with a Trial Chambers and an Appeals Chamber), the Extraordinary Chambers of the Courts of Cambodia, the War Crimes Chamber of the state court of Bosnia and Herzegovina and the courts in Kosovo. These courts have a mixed membership of local and international judges.[19]

The Special Court for *Sierra Leone* was established on 16 January 2002 as a result of an agreement between the United Nations and the

---

17 The Statute can be found in I.L.M, vol. 37, 999 and on the United Nations website at http://un.org/law/icc. The ICC's own website is http://www.icc-cpi.int/; 110 countries have ratified the Statute at the time of writing.

18 The United Nations has also established a sixth tribunal based on an agreement with a national state with international aspects, namely the Special Tribunal for Lebanon, but this tribunal does not have same jurisdiction as the other three tribunals (see article 1 of the Agreement which is attached as an Annex to Security Council Resolution 1757 (2007), 30 May 2007).

19 Generally see http://www.pict-pcti.org/courts/hybrid.html and Sarah Williams, *Hybrid and Internationalised Criminal Tribunals,* Hart, 2009.

government of Sierra Leone and has jurisdiction over the international crimes of crimes against humanity, violations of common article 3 of the Geneva Conventions and other serious violations of international humanitarian law, all defined in the same manner as in the ICC Statute. The Special Court has indicted twelve persons (two of which have died since the indictment against them had been approved while the whereabouts of one is uncertain[20]) resulting in four trials of which three involving eight indictees have been completed at the Trial Chamber level, namely the so-called AFRC, CDF and RUF cases[21] while the Appeals Chamber issued judgments in the AFRC case on 22 February 2008, in the CDF case on 28 May 2008, and the RUF case on 26 October 2009; all convicted persons were transferred on 31 October 2009 to Rwanda to serve their sentences.

The Law on the Establishment of the Extraordinary Chambers of the Courts of *Cambodia* was the result of an agreement between the United Nations and the government of Cambodia and was adopted in Cambodia on 2 January 2001, providing jurisdiction over genocide, crimes against humanity and grave breaches of the 1949 Geneva Conventions in the same manner as the ICTY/ICTR Statutes.[22] It has started to operate in 2006[23] and five persons are in custody[24] of whom one has been indicted for war crimes and crimes against humanity[25] whose trial started on 17 February 2009 while the others have been indicted for war crimes, crimes against humanity and genocide. Like the Sierra Leone Special Court it can be seen as a nationalized international tribunal in that it was established with involvement of the international community and has an international presence at all levels of the judicial process, but is

20 See http://www.sc-sl.org/cases-other.html.

21 The website is http://www.sc-sl.org/.

22 It also allows for the possibility of civil suits and such a claim concerning rape and sexual abuse was filed on 3 September 2008.

23 The Law can be found at http://www.eccc.gov.kh/english/law.list.aspx; see also in general http://www.eccc.gov.kh/ and http://www.unakrt-online.org/.

24 *International Justice Tribune* (*IJT*), Issue 78, 19 November 2007, page 1; for a general assessment of the progress at the ECCC, see the 15 May 2008 report by the NGO Open Society Justice Initiative at http://www.justiceinitiative.org/db/resource2?res_id=104086.

25 On 8 August 2008, see http://www.eccc.gov.kh/english/cabinet/courtDoc/115/Closing_order_indicting_Kaing_Guek_Eav_ENG.pdf.

apart from that aspect an extension of the regular Cambodian court system.[26]

The *East Timor* Special Panels came into being on 6 June 2000 as a result of the promulgation of its constituting instrument by the United Nations Transitional Administration in East Timor (UNTAET) rather than an agreement between the United Nations and a national government. They have jurisdiction over the international offences (in addition to serious ordinary criminal matters) of genocide, war crimes and crimes against humanity, the contents of which are almost identical to the description of these crimes in the ICC Statute. The panels finished their mandate on 20 May 2005 after having convicted 84 defendants and acquitted three in 60 trials (arising out of 95 indictments covering 440 people); the Court of Appeal of East Timor heard seven cases with six other ones pending.[27] These panels are internationalized domestic courts in that the only international aspect is the fact that they had international personnel in the judiciary and the office of the prosecution to ensure that the transition from a conflict situation to a peaceful society was as efficient as possible.[28]

There is another internationalized domestic court in *Bosnia and Herzegovina* (BiH) which is a joint initiative of the ICTY and the Office of the High Representative in Bosnia and Herzegovina (OHR) and which

26 For an appraisal, see Sylvia De Bertodano "Problems Arising from the Mixed Composition and Structure of the Cambodian Extraordinary Chambers", *Journal of International Criminal Justice* (*JICJ*), 2006, vol. 4, no. 2, 285-293.

27 The authorizing documents can be found at http://www.un.org/peace/etimor/UntaetN.htm, specifically http://www.un.org/peace/etimor/untaetR/Reg0015E.pdf, while the decisions of the Dili District Court and the Court of Appeal are available at http://www.jsmp.minihub.org/trials.htm and at http://socrates.berkeley.edu/~warcrime/ET.htm; see also *Yearbook of International Humanitarian Law* (*YIHL*), vol. 9, 2006, 578-601; for an review of this institution, see "Justice Abandoned, An Assessment of the Serious Crimes Process in East Timor", by the ICTJ, June 2005 at http://www.ictj.org/images/content/1/2/121.pdf; for an assessment ten years after the establishment of this institution, see www.amnesty.org/en/news-and-updates/report/no-justice-timor-leste-ten-years-after-independence-vote-20090827.

28 For an academic examination of the hybrid tribunals (*i.e.*, institutions with international and domestic aspects), see Cesare P. R. Romano, André Nollkaemper and Jann K. Kleffner (eds.), *Internationalized Criminal Courts: Sierra Leone, East Timor, Kosovo, and Cambodia*, Oxford, 2006.

started on 9 March 2005.[29] It has jurisdiction for genocide, war crimes and crimes against humanity. Since its inception until June 2008, Chamber I of this court, the war crimes chamber, has indicted 84 persons for involvement in international crimes in 48 cases, including 11 which had been transferred from the ICTY as part of its completion strategy and has convicted 28 persons in 33 trial judgments including seven which had been transferred from the ICTY while it has acquitted five persons.[30] One person who had been convicted was acquitted on appeal by the Appellate Chamber of the Court of Bosnia and Herzegovina on 13 August 2008, namely Radmilo Vukovic, while another had its sentence reduced, namely Marko Samardzija. Virtually all these convictions have been based on war crimes although this number encompasses the conviction of seven persons (and the acquittal of four others) on 29 July 2008 for the crime of genocide, a first, as a result of their involvement in events in July 1995 around Srebenica.[31]

On 29 September the court convicted four ethnic Serbs and one Croat for crimes against Muslim civilians and prisoners during the country's 1992-1995 war; in a joint trial of four former prison officials, it sentenced Sreten Lazarević to ten years in jail for inhuman treatment of Muslim prisoners in the eastern town of Zvornik. Lazarević (55) then served as deputy head of the prison. Three guards, Dragan Stanojević, Mile Marković and Slobodan Ostojić, were also found guilty for crimes against civilians. The same court jailed a former Bosnian Croat soldier for

---

29 See Tarik Abdulhak, "Building Sustainable Capacities - From an International Tribunal to a Domestic War Crimes Chamber for Bosnia and Herzegovina", in *International Criminal Law Review*, 2008, vol. 9, no. 2, pp. 333-356.

30 The English website of the court can be found at http://www.sudbih.gov.ba/?opcija =sadrzaj&id=3&jezik=e, while the website of the Prosecutor's office is at http:// www.tuzilastvobih.gov.ba/?jezik=e; see also *IJT*, Issue 80, 17 December 2007, pp. 3-4. There have also been another 154 indictments since 2004 in other courts in BiH (at the district and cantonal level) of which 122 have resulted in convictions; see the website of the OSCE at http://www.oscebih.org/human_rights/warcrimes.asp?d=1 and the 2007 Annual Report of the Humanitarian Law Centre at http://www.hlc-rdc.org/uploads/editor/Godisnji_izvestaj_engleski.pdf, pp. 40-44, as well as the February 2007 and 10 July 2008 Reports by Human Rights Watch at http://hrw.org/repo rts/2007/ij0207/ij0207webwcover.pdf and http://www.hrw.org/english/docs/2008/07/ 10/bosher19272.htm and a report by the ICTJ in 2008 at http://www.ictj.org/images /content/1/0/1088.pdf. See also *YIHL*, 2006, vol. 9, 445-449 and 452-463 and *YIHL*, 2008, vol. 11, 421-437.

31 See http://www.trial-ch.org/en/trial-watch/profile/db/facts/brano_dzinic_509.html.

8 1/2 years after he pleaded guilty to war crimes against Muslim civilians in 1993.

On 22 October 2008, Marko Škrobić was found guilty of war crimes against civilians and sentenced to ten years imprisonment. On 23 October 2008, Vaso Todorović was sentenced to six years imprisonment for crimes against humanity in Srebrenica after a guilty plea. On the same day, the appeals chamber of Bosnia's war crimes court said a convicted former Bosnian Serb soldier should not have been sentenced for war crimes, only crimes against humanity; the court reduced 72-year-old Marko Samardžija's previous 26 year sentence to seven years.

On 6 November 2008, the trial court found Mladen Blagojević guilty because, as a part of the widespread and systematic attack by the Army and Police of the Republika Srpska (RS) directed against the Bosniak civilian population of the UN safe area, he committed crimes against humanity and was sentenced to seven years imprisonment. Zdravko Božić, Zoran Živanović and Željko Zarić were acquitted on all counts. On 28 November 2008, a Bosnian Croat, Zrinko Pinčić, was sentenced to nine years for the sexual abuse of a woman during the 1992-1995 war in Konjic municipality.

On 16 December 2008, the Appeals Council of the State Court of Bosnia and Hercegovina acquitted former Croat Defence Council (HVO) officer Krešo Lučić of crimes against humanity and quashed a court of first instance verdict which sentenced him to six years imprisonment. The Appeals Council found that the prosecution had not proven Lučić's command responsibility for war crimes committed in Kreševo municipality in central Bosnia.

On 20 February 2009[32], the Court of Bosnia and Herzegovina (BiH) handed down the first instance verdict in the Marko Radić case. The accused Marko Radić, Dragan Šunjić, Damir Brekalo and Mirko Vračević were members of the Croatian Defense Council (HVO), and were found to have taken part in a widespread and systematic attack directed against the Muslim civilian population, including children, women, and elderly people, of the Mostar Municipality, from July 1993 to March 1994. The defendants were all found guilty of persecution as a crime against humanity as well as murder, unlawful confinement, torture, sexual violence and other inhumane acts such as forced labor, harassment,

[32] For the results in 2009, see http://www.bim.ba/en/199/10/24722/.

humiliation or other psychological abuses. They were sentenced to 25, 21, 20 and 14 years imprisonment respectively.

The day before, the same Court of BiH rendered a first instance verdict against Miodrag Nikačević, a member of the Armed Forces of the Republika Srpska, sentencing him to 8 years imprisonment for rape, and unlawful detention (crimes against humanity) committed in the Foča area at the KPD detention facility.

On 5 May 2009, the Appellate Chamber of the Court of Bosnia and Herzegovina rendered a second-instance verdict, sentencing Mirko Pekez to 14 years imprisonment and Milorad Savić to 21 years for their participation in the shooting of a group of Bosniak civilians in Jajce Municipality in 1992. The former members of the reserve police forces had in first instance been sentenced to 21 years imprisonment each, while Mirko Pekez had been sentenced to 29 years imprisonment. The indictment had alleged that on 10 September 1992, the three men, "acting as an organized group of armed people", and after having made a joint plan, gathered 29 Bosniak civilians, including women, children and the elderly, from Ljoljići and Čerkazovići villages, in Osoje village and then took them to Tisovac, where they shot them. On this occasion, 23 people, including four minors, were killed. On 12 June 2009, Novak Djukić was found guilty of the shelling of Tuzla in May 1995 and sentenced to 25 years in prison while on 2 July 2009 a former Serb policeman, Damir Ivanković, was given 14 years in jail for crimes against humanity in a massacre of more than 200 Muslims and Croats early in the country's 1992-95 war.

On 16 October 2009, the first-instance verdict the Court of Bosnia and Herzegovina pronounced Milorad Trbić guilty of genocide committed as part of a joint criminal enterprise in Srebrenica and sentences him to 30 years in prison. Trbić, former Assistant Commander for Security with the Zvornik Brigade of the Republika Srpska Army (VRS), was pronounced guilty of having participated, through a joint criminal enterprise together with Ljubiša Beara, Vujadin Popović and Drago Nikolić from 10 July to 30 November 1995, in operations consisting of capturing, detaining and "executing without trial" followed by burying and hiding the bodies of killed Bosniaks from Srebrenica.

The court hopes to process 10,000 war crimes cases over the next 15 years, it was announced in January 2009.

On 4 December 2009, the Appellate Chamber of the Court of Bosnia and Herzegovina acquitted Miladin Stevanović of charges that he committed genocide in Srebrenica in July 1995. The Appellate Chamber confirmed the first-instance verdict by which Stevanović was acquitted of charges that he participated, as a member of the Second Special Police Squad from Šekovići, in guarding the road leading from Bratunac to Konjević polje and capturing men from Srebrenica on 12 and 13 July 1995. Stevanović was acquitted of the charges that he participated in the shooting of about 1,000 Srebrenica residents in Kravica Agricultural Cooperative, in Bratunac Municipality, on 13 July 1995.

On 24 December 2009, after accepting the guilt admission agreement, the Trial Chamber sentenced Stojan Perković to 12 years in prison for crimes committed in Rogatica area. Perković was sentenced for participation in a broad and systematic attack against non-Serb civilians in Rogatica. As part of the attack, he participated in the murder, beating, persecution and forcible disappearance of civilians in Surovi, Mesići and Varošiste villages.

On 4 February 2010, the Appellate Chamber of the State Court of Bosnia and Herzegovina acquitted Momčilo Mandić on all charges for war crimes against civilians and crimes against humanity. Mandić was a justice minister in the government of the so-called Serbian Republic of Bosnia and Herzegovina during the Bosnian wars. Confirming the 2007 first-instance verdict, the court in Sarajevo acquitted Mandić of responsibility for the attack by Serbian forces on the Staff Training Center of the Ministry of Internal Affairs in Sarajevo and of responsibility for the functioning of the penal and correctional facilities in Sarajevo and Foča. The Appellate Chamber concluded that substantial proof was not provided that Mandić was responsible for the events that took place in the Foča, Butmir and Planjina kuća facilities in the period when he was justice minister.

A day later, the State Court convicted Predrag Bastah and Goran Višković of crimes against humanity, sentencing them to 22 and 18 years in prison respectively. According to the indictment, Bastah, who was a police reservist in a public security station in Vlasenica, and Višković, who was a member of the Republika Srpska army, were involved in the illegal imprisonment and murder of three civilians in Vlasenica, between April and September 1992. Višković was also found guilty of raping three women.

On 8 February 2010, the Appellate Chamber confirmed the first instance verdict sentencing Mladen Blagojević to seven years in prison for inhumane acts and acquitting Zdravko Božić, Zoran Živanović and Željko Zarić on war crimes charges. The court confirmed the first instance verdict which found Blagojević guilty of having shot at the Vuk Karadžić school building in Bratunac in July 1995 using an anti-aircraft gun. At the time, male residents of Srebrenica and the surrounding villages were being detained in the building. They had been charged in a JCE as members of the Military Police Squad with the Bratunac Light Infantry Brigade of the Republika Srpska Army (VRS), with having participated in persecution and murder and in guarding buildings in which Bosniaks (Bosnian Muslims) from Srebrenica were detained after the fall of the UN protected zone.

On 1 October 2009, the parliament of the BiH rejected a proposal to extend the involvement of the international personnel at the War Crimes Chamber, but on 14 December 2009, the High Representative for Bosnia and Herzegovina extended the mandate of international personnel working with war crimes sections of the Court of Bosnia and Herzegovina and its Prosecution, for three years.

Kosovo has a similar court as BiH, which was established on 10 June 1999 by the United Nations Mission in Kosovo (UNMIK) with jurisdiction for war crimes and genocide. There have been final judgments in five war crimes prosecutions of 28 individuals. Of these, 15 were convicted of various war crimes and 16 acquitted. At the time of writing, international prosecutors in Kosovo were prosecuting seven separate war crimes trials involving 11 defendants, and were directing 47 war crimes investigations involving 122 known suspects.[33] On 27 May 2008, an anti-war crimes unit of the international police arrested Dxelosh Krasniqi on

[33] For individual trials see Report 569 of the Institute for War and Peace reporting (IWPR) at http://www.iwpr.net/?p=tri&s=f&o=346778&apc_state=henitri200809; the 2007 Annual Report of the Humanitarian Law Center at http://www.hlc-rdc.org/Izvestaji/942.en.html and http://www.hlc-rdc.org/uploads/editor/Godisnji_izvestaj_engleski.pdf, pp. 48-58. For an assessment of the judicial system in Kosovo regarding war crimes prosecutions, see the Amnesty International report of 30 January 2008 at http://www.amnesty.org/en/news-and-updates/report/justice-failed-kosovo-20080130 and more in general the Human Rights Watch report of 28 March 2008 at http://hrw.org/reports/2008/kosovo0308/.

suspicion of the abduction and murder of a Kosovo citizen near Djakovica in March 1999.

On 3 February 2009, the newly deployed European Union justice mission in Kosovo opened its first war crimes trial since it took over from a UN mission. The trial of an ethnic Albanian started in the District Court of the capital Priština before a three-judge panel of whom two are from the European Union and one from Kosovo. Gani Gashi (58) is accused of killing an ethnic Albanian "by shooting him in the back" and wounding a second person trying to flee fighting between the ethnic Albanian separatist Kosovo Liberation Army and Serbian forces near Pristina in July 1998.

On 3 June 2009, the European Union announced it will investigate 1,119 Kosovo war crimes cases that remain unresolved a decade after the end of its conflict. Files on the cases were handed over to EULEX, an EU rule-of-law mission in Kosovo, from its U.N. predecessor UNMIK. EULEX was launched in December in place of the U.N. mission, which administered Kosovo since NATO bombing ousted Serbian forces waging a violent crackdown on ethnic Albanian separatists in 1999.

On 2 October 2009, three former Kosovo Liberation Army (KLA) fighters were sentenced to up to six years in prison for the beating and torture of civilians during the 1998-99 war. Latif Gashi, Nazif Mehmeti and Rrustem Mustafa were sentenced in 2003 to prison terms ranging from 13 to 17 years, but the Supreme Court ordered a retrial following appeals regarding the severity of the sentences. Gashi and Mehmeti were sentenced to six and three years in prison respectively. The court verdict said the three men ordered and participated in detention and torturing victims, mostly Kosovo Albanians, suspected of collaborating with the regime of Serbian leader Slobodan Milošević.

Another, albeit more weakened in that it only allows for international advisors, type of domestic hybrid tribunal is the Supreme Iraqi Special Tribunal which was established in *Iraq* without United Nations involvement on 10 December 2003 and which has jurisdiction for genocide, crimes against humanity and war crimes, the definitions of which are similar to the ones in the ICC Statute.[34] This court has indicted 20 persons of which 14 have been sentenced in four separate trials for

[34] See http://www.ictj.org/static/MENA/Iraq/iraq.cpaorder48.121003.eng.pdf.

genocide, war crimes and crimes against humanity[35], including Saddam Hussein, the former president,[36] Tariq Aziz, the former minister of foreign affairs and Ali Hassan al-Majid, known as "Chemical Ali", while three persons have been acquitted; Saddam Hussein and Al-Majid have been executed, the first on 30 December 2006, the latter on 25 January 2010; three others have been indicted.

As of 10 March 2010, the truly international or internationalized tribunals, namely the ICTY, ICTR, ICC, the SLSC and the ECCC have convicted 113 persons (out of 279 indictments) over the last 12 years[37] for genocide, crimes against humanity and war crimes in conflicts with millions of victims and thousands of perpetrators. It is unlikely that there will be a dramatic increase in the number of people being indicted and convicted by the above institutions given the fact that all of them, apart from the ICC, have a short temporal jurisdiction, which will not last beyond the year 2014[38] and since all of them will only investigate persons who have the greatest responsibility.[39]

---

35 See http://www.trial-ch.org/en/trial-watch/search/judgement-place/13.html.

36 See for commentaries on the institution and the trials: Michael P. Scharf and Gregory S. McNeal, *Saddam on Trial: Understanding and Debating the Iraqi High Tribunal*, Carolina Academic Press, 2006; Michael P. Scharf, "The Iraqi High Tribunal: A Viable Experiment in International Justice?", *JICJ*, 2007, vol. 5, no. 2, 258-263; Miranda Sissons and Ari S. Bassin, "Was the *Dujail* Trial Fair?", *JICJ*, 2007, vol. 5, no. 2, 272-286 and Nehal Bhuta, "Fatal Errors: The Trial and Appeal Judgments in the 'Dujail' Case", *JICJ*, 2008, vol. 6, no. 1, 39-65; see also the articles on the procedures before this tribunal in *YIHL*, 2006, vol. 9, 117-243 and an assessment by the ICTJ in October 2005 in a publication entitled "Creation and First Trials of the Supreme Iraqi Criminal Tribunal at http://www.ictj.org/images/content/ 1/2/123.pdf; see also http://www.trial-ch.org/en/trial-watch/search.html under "Iraqi Special Court" at "Judgment Places".

37 The first conviction was that of Duško Tadić by the Trial Chamber of the ICTY on 7 May 1997, http://www.un.org/icty/tadic/trialc2/judgement/index.htm.

38 As a result of the completion strategy for the ICTY (see http://www.un.org/icty/publications-e/index.htm) and the ICTR (see http://69.94.11.53/default.htm, "About the Tribunal", "ICTR Completion Strategy") imposed by the Security Council of the United Nations or as a result of the terms of the agreement between the United Nations and Sierra Leone and Cambodia. The international component of the internationalized domestic courts are also of temporary nature in that the East Timor courts have already become fully national and the same is expected in the next few years for the courts in Bosnia and Herzegovina and Kosovo.

39 Either as a matter of policy as for the ICTY and ICTR or as indicated in the establishing instruments, as is the case for the ICC, SLSC and the ECCC.

While there is no sufficient empirical evidence as to a causal effect between sentencing by international tribunals and possible general deterrence in terms of preventing genocide, crimes against humanity and war crimes in the future[40], it stands to reason that if many more perpetrators could be captured, tried, convicted and sentenced to very serious penalties commensurate with the commission of these crimes, this causal link would be strengthened.[41] Any increase of remedies to deal with perpetrators of atrocities will have to come at the domestic rather than the international level. This is specifically recognized in the statute of the ICC, which is only entitled to take jurisdiction if a state party is unwilling or unable to take action itself against perpetrators[42] and as such can be seen as a default jurisdiction in relation to domestic actions in this regard.

2.3. Domestic War Crimes Legislation

While it had always been possible in the domestic context to initiate criminal prosecutions for genocide and war crimes as a result of ratifying the 1948 Genocide Convention[43] and the 1949 Geneva Conventions[44], the coming into force of the Rome Statute provided an important impetus for a large number of countries to not only examine their domestic legislation dealing with the regulation of war crimes, crimes against humanity and genocide, but also to introduce changes to their laws to ensure that they were in compliance with international obligations and the tenets of the Rome Statute.

Four major trends can be identified in the manner in which individual countries have decided to prosecute persons suspected of the commis-

40 See Mark A. Drumbl, *Atrocity, Punishment and International Law*, Cambridge, 2007, 169-173; see also Mark B. Harmon and Fergal Gaynor, "Ordinary Sentences for Extraordinary Crimes", *JICJ*, 2007, vol. 5, no. 3, 683-712 and Ralph J. Henham, "Developing Contextualized Rationales for Sentencing in International Criminal Trials: A Plea for Empirical Research", 2007, *JICJ*, vol. 5, no. 3, 757-778.

41 Drumbl, *Atrocity, Punishment and International Law* see *supra* note 40, 207-208.

42 Article 17 of the Statute.

43 The Convention has 103 parties; see http://www.unhchr.ch/html/menu3/b/p_genoci.htm.

44 The Conventions have been acceded to by 194 parties; see http://www.icrc.org/Web/Eng/siteeng0.nsf/html/genevaconventions.

sion of atrocities.[45] Some countries, such as Denmark and Norway, use or used a combination of broad extraterritorial jurisdiction, regular criminal law provisions for substantive offences, such as murder or torture, and a harsher sentencing regime to take into account the unique and international nature of the domestic offences. This approach has as an advantage that the crimes under consideration are well known to domestic prosecutors and judges while at the same time there is no need to adduce evidence or legal arguments regarding the international elements of war crimes, crimes against humanity or genocide. The disadvantage is that although a harsher sentencing regime can reflect to some extent the seriousness of the crimes under consideration, the stigma attached to a longer sentence for murder committed during an armed conflict or in a systematic or widespread manner (the hallmarks of war crimes and crimes against humanity) is not the same as a similar or even shorter sentence for an international crime in a similar circumstances. As well, unlike domestic offences, international offences are not subject to statutes of limitations.[46]

This latter point was brought home by the ICTR in the Bagaragaza case where Norway has requested to have this case transferred to its jurisdiction from the ICTR as part of the ICTR completion strategy. Norway, the defendant and the ICTR prosecutor made arguments in support for such a transfer, but both the ICTR Trial[47] and Appeal Chambers[48] refused to do so since Norway did not have legislation criminalizing international offences and since a harsher sentencing regime was deemed not sufficient to overcome the lack of appropriate legislation. The case had been transferred to the Netherlands[49] and Norway amended its legislation on 7 March 2008[50].

---

45 For an overview of some of these regimes, see Stéphane J. Hankins, "Overview of Ways to Import Core International Crimes into National Criminal Law" in Morten Bergsmo, Mads Harlem and Nobuo Hayashi (eds.), *Importing Core International Crimes into National Criminal Law*, Second Edition, Torkel Opsahl Academic EPublisher, Oslo, 2010.

46 See the 1968 Convention on the Non-Applicability of Statutory Limitations to War Crimes and Crimes Against Humanity, http://www.ohchr.org/english/law/warcrimes.htm, which is now considered part of customary international law.

47 ICTR-2005-86-R11bis, 19 May 2006.

48 ICTR-05-86-AR11bis, 30 August 2006.

49 ICTR-2005-86-R11bis, 13 April 2007; because of adverse jurisprudence in 2007 in the Netherlands regarding the crime of genocide and universal jurisdiction (see below at footnotes 132-133), he was ordered transferred back to the ICTR on 17 March 2008

The other three trends involve different models for the implementation of international criminal law into domestic law. One trend is what has been called static implementation[51] where the national law dealing with international crimes repeats the definitions of genocide, crimes against humanity and war crimes as set out in articles 6, 7 and 8 of the Rome Statute. Within this trend one can distinguish three variations. The first one repeats the exact wording of these articles of the Rome Statute. This has for instance been done in the United Kingdom[52], Malta and in the draft legislation of Jordan[53]. Other countries using the static model do not reproduce the text of these three articles of the Rome Statute but only make reference to them. This can be seen for instance in the legislation of New Zealand, South Africa[54], Uganda and Kenya. The last variation on this model can be found in Australia where not only the text of the three articles of the Rome Statute are produced but also the full details set out in the ICC Elements of Crime document.[55] The advantage of this model in all three variations is that the domestic legislation provides by direct reference to the Rome Statute clear guidance to the essential elements of the

and was handed over on 23 May 2008 where a pled guilty to complicity to commit genocide on 17 September 2009 and was convicted on 5 November 2009.

50 See Mads Harlem, "Importing War Crimes into Norwegian Legislation", in Morten Bergsmo, Mads Harlem and Nobuo Hayashi (eds.), *Importing Core International Crimes into National Criminal Law*, Second Edition, Torkel Opsahl Academic EPublisher, Oslo, 2010.; see also http://www.iccnow.org/?mod= newsdetail&news=2704.

51 See Stéphane J. Hankins, "Overview of Ways to Import Core International Crimes into National Criminal Law" in Morten Bergsmo, Mads Harlem and Nobuo Hayashi (eds.), *Importing Core International Crimes into National Criminal Law*, Second Edition, Torkel Opsahl Academic EPublisher, Oslo, 2010.

52 See Robert Cryer and Olympia Bekou, "International Crimes and ICC Cooperation in England and Wales", 2007, *JICJ*, vol. 5, no. 2, 441-459.

53 The source for the domestic legislations is the Coalition for the International Criminal Court (CICC), a global network of over 2,000 non-governmental organizations (NGOs) advocating for a fair, effective and independent International Criminal Court (ICC) and can be found on its website (http://www.iccnow.org/) under "Regional and Country Info"; see also the National Prosecution of International Crimes Project by the Max Planck Institute in Germany, http://www.mpicc.de/ww/en/pub/forschung/forschungsarbeit/strafrecht/nationale_strafverfolgung.htm; other sources are separately mentioned where appropriate.

54 See Max du Plessis, "South Africa's Implementation of the ICC Statute", *JICJ*, 2007, vol. 5, no. 2, 460-479.

55 See http://www.un.org/law/icc/statute/romefra.htm.

international crimes both by using the text and the *travaux preparatoires* of the Statute as well as the jurisprudence of the ICTY and ICTR until 17 July 1998 when the Statute was agreed upon. The downside of this approach is that it cannot take into account new developments in international criminal law without amending the original legislation. Such new developments have already occurred to the extent that since the coming into force of the Rome Statute new crimes have found their way into the realm of international criminal law, namely the war crimes of slavery, forced labour[56], terrorism[57] and collective punishments[58] and the crime against humanity of forced marriage[59].

The third model, the dynamic model, is the mechanism whereby the conduct criminalized in the Rome Statute is redrafted in the domestic legislation either to provide a better connection to existing criminal offences in the domestic legislation or clarify some of the Rome Statute concepts especially where the crimes in the Statute are vague or imprecise as a result of the incorporation of existing customary international law notions such as the crimes against humanity of inhumane acts or persecution or as a result of lack of agreement during the negotiations of the Statute as was the case with the crime against humanity of imprisonment which uses the qualifier "in violation of fundamental rules of international law".

---

56 See ICTY TC in Krnojelac, paragraphs 350-360 and Naletilić, paragraphs 250-261.

57 See most recently at the ICTY the Appeals Chamber decision in Galić, IT-98-29A, 30 November 2006, pages 31-54, followed by the ICTY Trial Chamber decision in Milošević, IT-98-29/1-T, 12 December 2007, pages 287-293 and by two Trial and Appeals Chamber decisions of the Sierra Leone Special Court in the AFRC case (SLSC-04-16-T, 30 June 2007, pages 201-206, approved by the Appeals Chamber, SLSC-04-16-A, 22 February 2008, page 55) and the CDF case (SLSC-04-14-T, 2 August 2007, pages 50-53, approved by Appeals Chamber, SLSC-04-14-A, 28 May 2008, pages 114-117).

58 Sierra Leone Special Court in the AFRC case (SLSC-04-16-T, 30 June 2007, pages 206-209, approved by the Appeals Chamber, SLSC-04-16-A, 22 February 2008, page 55) and the CDF case (SLSC-04-14-T, 2 August 2007, pages 53-55).

59 Sierra Leone Special Court in the AFRC case in the Appeals Chamber, SLSC-04-16-A, 22 February 2008, pages 56-66 and the RUF case by the Trial Chamber, SLSC-04-15-T, 2 March 2009, pages 353-354.

Examples of this model are the legislation of Germany[60]; the Netherlands; Uruguay (where the targeted groups of genocide include national, ethnic, racial, religious, political, union or a group with its identity based in reasons of gender, sexual orientation, culture, social, age, disability or health while also adding the crime of instigating genocide); Argentina[61] (where the age in the war crime of forcible recruitment has been increased from 15 to18 years and where forced hunger as a grave violation of international law has been introduced); Ecuador (where the draft legislation adds to the groups of genocide the victims of gender, sexual orientation, age, health and conscience while ordering, planning or instigating genocide is also made an offence, even if genocide is not committed); the Republic of Congo (where the draft legislation adds to the definition of genocide, in addition the ones in the Rome Statute, any group that is defined by an arbitrary characteristic while under crimes against humanity "crimes de discrimination: tribale, ethnique ou religieuse" has replaced the crime of apartheid); and the Democratic Republic of the Congo (where the draft legislation increases the age in the war crime of forcible recruitment from 15 to 18 years).

The advantages and disadvantages of this model is similar to the previous one although since most legislation based on this model has been adopted more recently than when agreement regarding the Rome Statute text was reached, the disadvantage noted there is less obvious in this model.

The last model, the hybrid model, which has been used for instance in Canada[62], Costa Rica and Finland combines aspects of the both the static and dynamic models in that some crimes are specifically defined while others are made subject to a reference to international law. As with the other approaches variations have occurred both in terms of which crimes to define and in terms to which body of international law reference should be made. The Costa Rican legislation when employing the refer-

[60] See Claus Kreß, "The German Model" in Morten Bergsmo, Mads Harlem and Nobuo Hayashi (eds.), *Importing Core International Crimes into National Criminal Law*, Second Edition, Torkel Opsahl Academic EPublisher, Oslo, 2010.

[61] Alejandro E. Alvarez, "The Implementation of the ICC Statute in Argentina", *JICJ*, 2007, vol. 5, no. 2, 480-492.

[62] Joseph Rikhof, "The Canadian Model", in Morten Bergsmo, Mads Harlem and Nobuo Hayashi (eds.), *Importing Core International Crimes into National Criminal Law*, Second Edition, Torkel Opsahl Academic EPublisher, Oslo, 2010.

ence aspect of the legislation only mentions international treaty law (which means according to its legislation for war crimes international humanitarian law treaties and for crimes against humanity human rights conventions and the Rome Statute) while the Finnish statute refers to both treaty and customary international law but only for war crimes (prohibition of any acts which "otherwise violate the provisions of an international agreement on warfare binding upon Finland or the generally acknowledged and established rules and customs of war under public international law")[63]. The Canadian model goes the furthest in the reference portion by defining the three core international crimes by immediate reference to conventional international law, customary international law and general principles of law while at the same ensuring that the Rome Statute is considered a benchmark for customary international law as of 17 July 1998, but that further development in this area can continue independently.[64]

These latter approaches have both advantages and disadvantages. An advantage is that, by tying the regulation of core crimes very closely to international law, it will be assured that these countries will never be out of step with new developments in the international sphere. By virtue of this link, these new developments automatically become part of their domestic law without the need of legislative amendments. The disadvantage is that this linkage requires all actors in criminal prosecutions to be continually up to date with changes in the international jurisprudence.

2.4. War Crimes Proceedings Based on Territorial/Nationality Jurisdiction

At the time of writing, there have been processes involving international crimes based on territorial or active nationality jurisdiction in 26 countries (including the three internationalized domestic courts in Bosnia and Herzegovina, Kosovo and East Timor), namely seven in Europe, nine in Latin

[63] Stéphane J. Hankins, "Overviews of Ways to Import Core International Crimes into National Criminal Law" in Morten Bergsmo, Mads Harlem and Nobuo Hayashi (eds.), *Importing Core International Crimes into National Criminal Law*, Second Edition, Torkel Opsahl Academic EPublisher, Oslo, 2010.

[64] Joseph Rikhof, "The Canadian Model", in Morten Bergsmo, Mads Harlem and Nobuo Hayashi (eds.), *Importing Core International Crimes into National Criminal Law*, Second Edition, Torkel Opsahl Academic EPublisher, Oslo, 2010.

America, three in Asia and seven in Africa, resulting in over 10,000 convictions.

2.4.1. Europe

In *Europe*, apart from the national courts in Bosnia and Herzegovina and Kosovo, both of which were discussed above because of their international aspects, there have been a number of other war crimes prosecutions in the former Yugoslavia, namely in Serbia,[65] Croatia, Montenegro and Macedonia.

In *Serbia* 113 persons have been indicted in 24 separate indictments for international crimes since 2005, of whom 25 have been convicted at first instance by the War Crimes Chamber of the Belgrade District Court in eight judgments (plus two judgments in courts of general jurisdiction involving three persons) and 12 persons in seven final judgments for a total of 40 persons convicted. Eleven persons have been acquitted at the trial level. Nine cases involving 43 persons are at the trial stage.[66]

Of the 40 convictions, five were the result of one trial involving members of the paramilitary group the Scorpions, which had been active in Bosnia during the 1992-95 war and in Kosovo in the late 1990s. Its members were believed to have taken part in the capture of Srebrenica and the killing of up to 8,000 Muslim men and boys in July 1995. Aleksandar Medić (five years), Branislav Medić (20 years), Slobodan Medić (20 years) and Pero Petrašević (13 years) were convicted on 10 April 2007 while Saša Cvjetan (20 years) had already been convicted on 20 December 1995 by the Appeals Chamber of the Supreme Court of Serbia, which overturned the verdict against Aleksandar Medić. One other person belonging to this group was acquitted, namely Aleksandar Vukov. Four more persons belonging to this group were arrested on 19 October 2007,

[65] For more information, see the website of the Office of the War Crimes Prosecutor in Serbia (http://www.tuzilastvorz.org.rs/html_trz/index_eng.htm) and the regular war crimes monitoring updates of the War Crimes Unit of the Rule of Law and Human Rights Department of the OSCE (http://www.osce.org/serbia/ 13161.html). For an assessment of the war crimes prosecutions in Serbia, see the 11 February 2008 report by the International Center for Transitional Justice at http://www.ictj.org/images/content/7/8/780.pdf.

[66] See for a general assessment a report by the NGO Open Society Justice Initiative of 20 May 2008 at http://www.justiceinitiative.org/db/resource2/fs/?file_id=19803.

as was Aleksandar Medić, and indicted on 21 April 2008. On 17 June 2009, the court convicted three members, Željko Djukić, Dragan Medić, Dragan Borojević, to maximum sentences of 20 years imprisonment, and another one, Miodrag Šolaja to 15 years, because he was a minor at the time when the crime was committed.

In addition, Anton Lekaj, a member of the military police forces within the Kosovo Liberation Army, received a sentence of 13 years on 18 September 2006.

Saša Radak was convicted to 20 years on 6 September 2006 for his participation of in the events at the Ovčara Farm, which took place on the night of 20 November 1991, close to Vukovar, and during which 192 Croatian prisoners of war were executed. This latter conviction was overturned by the Serb Supreme Court in April 2007. Milan Bulić was also convicted for crimes at the same location on 2 March 2007. The same event at Ovčara Farm also resulted in a trial in 2005 in which 16 persons had been charged for war crimes, of whom 14 were convicted for a total of 231 years imprisonment. That result has also been overturned by the Serb Supreme Court in December 2006. A new trial for all original 16 persons began on 13 March 2007. On 10 April 2008 Milorad Pejić, a British citizen, was arrested in Belgrade and added as a suspect in this case.[67] On 12 March 2009, 13 were convicted in connection with these 1991 events; the 13 found guilty were sentenced to prison terms ranging from five to 20 years.

On 27 May 2009, a special Belgrade war crimes court sentenced a Croatian Serb, Bora Trbojević, to ten years in jail for imprisoning, torturing and killing Croatian civilians during the country's war of secession from the former Yugoslavia in 1991. Trbojević was a member of a rebel Serb unit and was charged with crimes and killing civilians in two villages near Grubišno Polje in eastern Croatia.

Two cases begun in 2007 are those of Sinan Morina (part of the Orahovac group case) who was indicted on 18 July 2007 for crimes committed in Kosovo and of Vladimir Kovačević who had been referred to Serbia by the ICTY in 2006[68] and who was indicted on 30 July 2007 for

67 Trial Watch, http://www.trial-ch.org/en/trial-watch/profile/db/facts/milorad_pejic_758.html.

68 Trial Watch, http://www.trial-ch.org/en/trial-watch/profile/db/facts/vladimir_kovacevic_184.html.

war crimes committed in Dubrovnik, Croatia. In the latter case charges were dropped in December 2007 because the accused was not mentally fit to stand trial while the former was acquitted on 20 December 2007.

Two trials involving personnel of the Serbian Ministry of Internal Affairs (MUP) started in late 2006. The first one involves Sreten Popović and Miloš Stojanović, in the so-called Bytyqi case, which started on 13 November 2006 and was completed on 22 September 2009 with their acquittal. The second, the Suva Reka trial, involving eight accused, began five weeks earlier and resulted in four convictions and three acquittals.

Another Orahovac case, involving Boban Petković for the murder of three Albanians which started in December 2007 resulted in an acquittal, while in June 2008 three of the four accused in the Zvornik 1 case were sentenced to 30 years imprisonment. On 5 August 2008, Branko Grujić and Branko Popović were charged with the killing of Muslims civilians near the town of Zvornik on the border with Bosnia.

On 12 March 2009, 13 Serbs were convicted in connection with the 1991 killings of over 200 Croatian POWs at a pig farm outside the Croatian town of Vukovar. Eighteen Serbs were originally charged over the incident. Charges against two were later dropped. Fourteen of the men were found guilty of war crimes in late 2005, but in 2006 Serbia's Supreme Court vacated that verdict and ordered a retrial. The 13 found guilty were sentenced to prison terms ranging from five to 20 years.

On 23 April 2009, Serbia's war crimes court sentenced four former police officers to prison terms ranging from 13 to 20 years for killing 50 Kosovo Albanians found buried with hundreds of others in a mass grave near Belgrade. Radojko Repanović and Sladjan Cukarić were sentenced to 20 years each in prison, while Miroslav Petković and Milorad Nišavić were sentenced to 15 and 13 years respectively for killing civilians. On 29 September 2009, Ilija Jurišić was sentenced to 12 years in jail for the attack on a convoy in Tuzla, having found Jurišić guilty of illicit means of warfare during the attack on the convoy, which consisted of members of the 92nd Motorised Brigade of the Yugoslav National Army, JNA, on 15 May 1992. On 7 December 2009, Nenad Malić was sentenced to 13 years in prison for the murder of two Muslim civilians in Bosnia.

At the time of writing, the on-going cases include the Zvornik 2 case (with the accused Grujić and Popović), the Zvornik 3 case (with the accused Savić and Ćilerdžić), the Medak case (with the accused Lazić and three others), the Banski Kovačevac case (with the accused Bulat and Vranešević), the Lovas case (with accused Devetak and 12 others), the Stara Gradiška case (with Španović), the Gnjilane group case (with Fazlija and 16 others) and the Orahovac group case (with Sinan Morina).

In *Croatia* 1,428 persons had been accused of crimes involving violations of international humanitarian law of whom 611 had been convicted between 1991 and 2006, a large number in absentia.[69] General Branimir Glavaš and six other defendants were indicted on 16 April 2007 for the commission of war crimes in Osijek in 1991 while a second indictment was issued on 9 May 2007. The trial started on 15 October 2007 and was adjourned until the end of September 2008.[70] The ICTY has transferred two persons to Croatia, namely generals Ademi and Norac[71] whose trial started in 2007; Norac was sentenced to seven years imprisonment on 30 May 2008, while Ademi was acquitted of all charges the same day. Croatia has also charged one person who had been acquitted by the ICTY, Miroslav Radić, in November 2007. Fifteen more persons were charged in January[72] and June 2008 while on 9 June 2008, a former Serb police commander, Mitar Arambašić, was sentenced to 20 years imprisonment for atrocities committed during Croatia's war of independence. On 5 September Ibrahim Jusić (43) and Zlatko Jusić (59), two Muslims who hold dual Bosnian and Croatian citizenship, were charged with having set up concentration camps and taken part in torturing and raping detainees in the Autonomous Province of Western Bosnia from 1993 to 1995.

On 3 October 2008, the Rijeka County Court sentenced Željko Šuput and Milan Panić of Korenica to four and 3.5 years of imprisonment for war crimes. The two men were charged with war crimes committed in 1991 against two police officers and a member of the Civil Defence in the then occupied town of Korenica. On 12 October, charges were laid

69 See the website of the Centre for Peace, Nonviolence and Human Rights, Osijek, at http://original.centar-za-mir.hr/sudenjeeng.html, specifically its 2006 Report, page 6, which can be found at (http://original.centar-za-mir.hr/pdf/ Summary Annual report 2006.pdf), as well as the International Justice Tribune (*IJT*), Issue 76, 22 October, pages 3-4 and the OCSE website at http://www.osce.org/zagreb/29857.html.

70 See http://www.trial-ch.org/en/trial-watch/profile/db/facts/branimir_glavas_572.html.

71 See http://www.un.org/icty/ademi/trialc/decision-e/050914.htm.

72 See the 2007 Annual Report of the Humanitarian Law Centre at http://www.hlc-rdc.org/uploads/editor/Godisnji_izvestaj_engleski.pdf, pages 44-48.

against Božidar Vučurović for expulsions of Croats, annexation of Croatian territory, and of planning, encouraging, ordering and in other ways helping the implementation of the so-called Greater Serbia idea. On 18 October, Ivan Husnjak (57) and retired Goran Sokol (40) were charged with war crimes against civilians for having failed to prevent illegal activities which occurred on 1 February 1992, during an armed conflict between Croatia's armed forces and police on one side and rebel Serb military and paramilitary units and the former Yugoslav People's Army (JNA) on the other.

On 17 December the Sisak County Court War Crimes Council sentenced Rade Miljević, to 12 years of imprisonment for war crimes against civilians in Glina in September 1991, when Croatian soldiers and civilians Milan and Borislav Litrić, Janko Kaurić and Ante Žužić were killed. The court had earlier sentenced Miljević for the same crime to 14 years imprisonment, but the Supreme Court quashed the sentence and demanded a retrial.

On 8 January 2009, five former military policemen were charged for the wartime murder and torture of ethnic Serb prisoners in the notorious Lora military prison in Split between March and August 1992. Two of the suspects, Tomislav Duić and Emilio Bungur, are at large. The five are among eight men already convicted by a Split court in 2006 for jail terms of up to eight years for the wartime murder and torture of Serb civilians also in the Lora prison. On 5 February 2009, the Vukovar County Court found 12 defendants guilty of war crimes against civilians and acquitted another two defendants of atrocities committed in the eastern Croatian village of Mikluševci in 1991 and 1992. According to the indictment, from October 1991 to 18 May 1992, after the Yugoslav People's Army (JNA) and Serb paramilitaries occupied the village, the occupation authorities tried to ethnically cleanse the village of non-Serbs. For that purpose, the authorities, including the defendants, intimidated non-Serb, threw bombs into their houses, tortured and killed them, and on 18 May 1992 they forced 92 non-Serbs to leave the village. The court sentenced two defendants to 15 years in jail, six defendants to six years, two defendants to four years and six months, and another two to four years each.

On 5 May 2009, Croatia's Supreme Court found former special forces policeman Mihajlo Hrastov guilty of killing and wounding unarmed prisoners of war in the early months of Croatia's war of independence and sentenced him to eight years imprisonment. On 8 May a court in Zagreb found that Branimir Glavaš had given orders to a paramilitary unit under his command to murder six Serbs in the eastern city of Osijek in 1991 and convicted him to ten years imprisonment.

In *Macedonia* four investigations into crimes committed by ethnic Albanian guerrillas during the 2001 armed conflict in that country were reopened on 4 March 2008. The four cases were originally brought before the ICTY but were returned to the Macedonian judiciary in mid-February after the ICTY prosecutor decided not to proceed with the cases.[73]

In *Montenegro* war crimes charges were filed on 1 August 2008 against eight former soldiers for their role in killing 23 ethnic Albanian refugees during the 1998-99 conflict in Kosovo. The group of former Yugoslav army soldiers was accused of the murder of the ethnic Albanians in the village of Kaludjerski Laz near the Montenegrin town of Rožaje on 16 April 1999. On 15 August 2008, seven more persons were indicted for the torture of 169 Croatian prisoners of war and civilians at the Morinj camp near the coastal town of Kotor, Montenegro, during the 1990s war in Croatia. Four has been arrested while two are in Belgrade. On 16 January 2009, nine former policemen were charged with deporting 79 Muslims who fled Bosnia's 1992-95 war only to be sent back to Bosnian Serb custody where most were killed.

2.4.2. Central and South America

In Central and South America, a number of countries have started prosecutions against persons involved in crimes against humanity and genocide carried out under previous regimes, namely Chile, Peru, Colombia, Argentina, Uruguay, Bolivia, and Mexico while Paraguay and Brazil have used the extradition approach for similar crimes.

In Chile, although Augusto Pinochet, the 91-year old former president, died on 10 December 2006, twenty some members of his military junta are now behind bars in Chile, and approximately 400 more are being prosecuted. The most high profile case is that of Manuel Contreras, a retired army general who led Chile's secret police, DINA, during the time of the Pinochet regime. He and eight other top DINA members were charged on 15 May 2003 for the 1974 kidnapping of a Spanish priest who

[73] See http://www.balkaninsight.com/en/main/news/8343/.

was tortured and then disappeared. On 18 April 2008, Contreras was sentenced to 15 years imprisonment for this crime. He had already been sentenced a month earlier to 15 years in prison for the kidnapping and disappearance of a young left-wing activist in 1975 and on 11 January 2008 to 10 years for the kidnapping of seven other people while he is also already serving time for plotting the 1976 car bomb murder in Washington of a Chilean diplomat. On 25 January 2009, an appeal court confirmed two consecutive life sentences for Contreras and lesser sentences for the other eight DINA members.

Another high profile case is that of Miguel Krassnoff Marchenko, an army brigadier general, member of the DINA and chief of the Villa Grimaldi torture centre. In 2003 he was sentenced to 15 years for the commission of a number of forced disappearances while receiving additional sentences of 10 years in June 2006 and four years in December 2006 for similar crimes. The latter sentence was also pronounced against six others including Marcelo Moren Brito, a colonel and head of one of the DINA brigades. France had already asked for the extradition of Krassnoff and Brito in 1998. As well, on 29 August 2007, the Chilean Supreme Court upheld a sentence of life imprisonment against general Hugo Salas Wenzel, the head of the intelligence service under Pinochet for the murder of 12 opponents of the regime.

On 18 April 2008, retired admirals Sergio Barros, Guillermo Aldoney and Adolfo Walbaum and retired navy captains Sergio Barra and Ricardo Riesgo were indicted for the abduction, torture and killing a British-Chilean priest, Michael Woodward, and other dissidents in the days following Chile's 1973 military coup. Also charged was Carlos Costa, a navy doctor. On 26 May 2008, another indictment against almost 100 former soldiers and secret service agents, including Manuel Contreras, was issued involving Operation Colombo, a 1975 attempt by Chilean security services to blame the dissidents' deaths on infighting among radical leftists during the Pinochet regime. On 15 October, Chile's Supreme Court sentenced Sergio Arellano Stark (88) to six years in prison for murdering four men who opposed dictator Augusto Pinochet soon after the 1973 coup that brought him to power. He had been convicted of killing the opposition members at the military prison of Linares, southern Chile.

On 25 May 2009, the Criminal Chamber of the Supreme Court of Chile delivered its decision on the merits in the Lejderman case. While overruling a previous decision by an appeals court, the Supreme Court found three former members of the armed forces (Fernando Polanco Gallardo, Héctor Vallejos Birtiola and Luis Fernández Monjes) guilty of killing Bernardo Lejderman and his wife María del Rosario Avalos in 1973, imposing on them a sentence of imprisonment of five years. Another accused was found not guilty, since his alleged criminal responsibility was not proved beyond reasonable doubt. The decision, adopted by three votes to two, contains interesting statements on a number of international criminal law issues, such as:

- a non-international armed conflict took place in Chile in 1973 in the terms of common Article 3 of the Geneva;
- article 146 of Geneva Convention IV provides that Chile was under the obligation to search for persons alleged to have committed grave breaches, and to bring such persons before its own judiciary – the Court seems to apply this provision to a non-international armed conflict;
- the amnesty law does not apply to grave breaches of the Geneva Conventions, which included a non-international armed conflict too;
- statutory limitations do not apply to crimes under international law;
- the killings by armed forces members also amount to crimes against humanity, since their killings were part of a "massive" and systematic practise against a civilian population;
- the prohibition of amnesty and statute of limitations regarding crimes against humanity is a peremptory norm of international law – *jus cogens*; and
- although Chile is not a State party to the 1968 Convention on the non applicability of statutory limitations to war crimes and crimes against humanity, the rule contained in article 1, which provides for the non applicability of the rule "irrespective of the date of their commission", was customary international law at the time killings were committed.

In Argentina, Miguel Etchecolatz, the former deputy with the Buenos Aires police during the 1976-83 "dirty war", was sentenced to life in prison on 19 September 2006. This has been considered a first since the court found the defendant guilty of crimes against humanity in direct application of international law, but especially since the crimes were committed "in the context of a genocide that took place in Argentina between 1976 and 1983". This was the second major ruling to be handed down since the amnesty laws for crimes against humanity were lifted in 2005.

On 13 February 2007, the Argentine government indicted and issued an extradition request to Spain for Isabel Perón, a former president, while the former chief of staff to Perón and subsequent president, Jorge Videla, has also been indicted. Videla and 20 other persons were also indicted on 24 November 2008 for crimes committed in police facilities and the San Martín prison in Córdoba, an area southwest of Buenos Aires in the foothills of the Andes. On 28 April 2008, a court in Spain denied the extradition request in the Perón case since the alleged crimes did not amount to crimes against humanity, a prerequisite for acceding to such a request.

After the opening of the trial of former chaplain Christian von Wernich on 5 July 2007, who was convicted to life imprisonment on 9 October 2007, another trial of ten military officers started a week later on 10 July 2007 in Buenos Aires. Notable among the accused are General Cristino Nicolaides, a member of the last junta in power in the early 1980s, who escaped prosecution thanks to a secret agreement with the democratic government in 1983. Nicolaides was the head of intelligence battalion 601 in the late 1970s. He and seven others were convicted on 18 December 2007 and ordered to serve prison terms of between 20 years and 25 years for kidnapping and killing several members of a leftist guerrilla group, Montoneros.

On 13 July 2007, the Supreme Court also overturned the presidential pardon granted to General Omar Riveros, accused of human rights violations in the 1970s.

On 1 February 2008, two retired military officers were arrested in connection with the massacre of 16 leftist guerrillas in 1972 on a military base in the Patagonian city of Trelew. They are Ruben Paccagnini (81) who captained a ship and headed the military base Almirante Zar Trelew, and Emilio Del Real (73), a frigate captain who allegedly was at the 22 August 1972 shooting of the guerrillas. On 25 April 2008, former police chief and mayor Luis Abelardo Patti was arrested for his involvement during the "dirty war", while on 27 May 2008 the trial of Luciano Menendez, who was the commander of the regional Third Army Corps at the time, and seven others began for activities during that same time period which resulted in a conviction for all of them on 25 July 2008. Another trial involving Menendez and Antonio Bussi, an 82-year-old former general who led military operations in Tucuman province, began on 6 August 2008 based on charges related to a 1976 kidnapping and disappearance of an Argentine senator. They were convicted on 4 September 2008.

On 6 August 2008, a court in the north-eastern Argentine province of Corrientes handed down sentences ranging from 18 years to life in prison to four former soldiers for torturing and killing political prisoners. Receiving a life sentence was Julio Barreiro, while Carlos de Marchi and Horacio Losito were each sentenced to 25 years in prison. The court sentenced to 18 years in prison Raul Raynoso and acquitted Carlos Piriz.

On 13 August 2009, Santiago Omar Riveros, a former general who commanded the notorious detention centre Campo de Mayo military barracks on the outskirts of Buenos Aires during Argentina's military rule, was sentenced to life in prison for human rights abuses. He was found guilty of involvement in the 1976 murder of 15-year-old communist youth member, Floreal Avellaneda, who was tortured to death. Riveros's former intelligence chief, Fernando Verplaetsen, was also jailed for 25 years in connection with the boy's killing while four other officers were given jail terms of between eight and 18 years.

On 23 October 2009, retired general Jorge Olivera Rovere and retired colonel Jose Menendez were sentenced to life imprisonment for crimes committed during the Argentine military dictatorship. Rovere, who had authority over several detention centres during the dictatorship, was found guilty of four murders and responsible for 116 abductions and disappearances. Menendez served as second chief of the Air Defense Artillery 101 between 1976 and 1979. Three others were acquitted during the proceedings.

On 2 November 2009, a trial began for Argentina's last dictator, Reynaldo Bignone, a retired general, as well as for five former generals and two others who are accused of kidnappings and murders that prosecutors say took place in the Campo de Mayo military base. General Bignone is accused of holding ultimate responsibility for myriad cases of torture, illegal break-ins and deprivations of human rights from 1976 to 1978, before he was appointed president by the military junta in the waning years of the dictatorship. As president from 1982 to 1983, General Bignone protected the military as Argentina returned to democracy while he granted amnesty to human rights violators.

On 11 December 2009, the ESMA (Escuela Mecánica de la Armada) trial started involving 19 former military officials accused of torture, forced disappearance, murder and theft. On 22 December 2009, former judge Victor Brusa to was sentenced to 21 years in prison for crimes against humanity as a judicial officer during the dictatorship. The court also sentenced five former police officers to between 19 and 23 years in prison for their roles kidnapping and torture.

On 17 December 2009, investigating judge Octavio Aráoz de Lamadrid issued, after four years of investigation, warrants of arrest against Jiang Zemin, the former head of state of China, and Luo Gan, the Communist Party Political Commissioner for Falun Gong, on charges of torture, but on 11 January 2010, investigating judge Rodolfo Canicoba Corral decided, on the very same day he replaced Justice Aráoz de Lamadrid, to withdraw the arrest warrants, based on their "premature" character.

In Colombia the government brought 59 paramilitary leaders to court on 14-15 December 2006. The trial of Salvatore Mancuso, the top paramilitary leader to stand trial before the Colombian courts, resumed on 15 January 2007 in Medellin. When the trial resumed, Mancuso admitted to at least 55 assassinations and six massacres. As well, on 27 May 2008, Ivan Ramirez, a retired army general, was arrested on the charge of the forced disappearance of 11 people during a violent episode from Colombia's civil war in 1985.

On 26 November 2009, Colombian officials said they may reclassify some crimes committed by the cartel led by late drug kingpin Pablo Escobar as crimes against humanity, allowing them to continue to prosecute the offenses. Escobar may have been guilty of crimes against humanity as the mastermind during the 1980s and early 1990s of countless kidnappings, bombings, and even the downing of a passenger jet. Designating the alleged offenses as crimes against humanity for which there is no statute of limitations will allow prosecutors to avoid the 20-year time limit for pursuing some of crimes allegedly committed by the Escobar and other members of his Medellin drug cartel.

In Peru the former president Alberto Fujimori has been accused of human rights violations and corruption. He was arrested in Chile as a result of an extradition request and while this request was denied on 12 July 2007 by a lower court, the Supreme Court agreed to his surrender on 21 September 2007. He was extradited a day later and put on trial in Peru. He was convicted and sentenced to 25 years in prison on 7 April 2009. On 30 December 2009, the Supreme Court of Peru rendered its judgement. The ruling confirmed all conclusions reached by the Supreme Court Special Criminal Chamber (as first instance court) on 9 April 2009 and the punishment then imposed. All Supreme Court conclusions were reached unanimously, save one – regarding some aggravating circumstances in the kidnapping of Samuel Dyer and Gustavo Gorriti – where there was a partially dissenting opinion. Since most complaints made by lawyers for Fujimori before the appeal's court were on procedural issues – that is to say, basically, on Peruvian law – the ruling is mainly a piece of interpretation of domestic law. However, there are a number of conclusions where the Supreme Court explains its view on international criminal law:

- the Supreme Court confirms that Alberto Fujimori had effective control over Peru's Armed Forces and Police;
- crimes against humanity are not subject to statute of limitations and must be investigated and prosecuted;
- while Fujimori was found guilty of three ordinary crimes (murder, kidnapping and serious bodily harm), as defined in the Penal Code enforced at the time the crimes were committed (1991 and 1992), the first instance court was right to conclude that these crimes amount to crimes against humanity, since they were committed as part of a widespread or systematic attack against a civilian population;
- although the Fujimori case is based on territoriality, the Supreme Court states that crimes under international law and crimes of international concern are subject to universal jurisdiction; and
- universal jurisdiction is the *raison d'être* of international criminal law.

On 14 December 2007, the Special Criminal Chamber of the Supreme Court of Peru confirmed the judgment against Abimael Guzman and other leaders of the Maoist Movement Shining Path who had received life imprisonment and other lengthy terms of imprisonment for violations of international humanitarian and human rights law. The individual responsibility of these persons was based on the notion of perpetration by means since none of the accused had personally committed any of the atrocities. This type of liability is based on the doctrine of functional power over an act by way of a hierarchical organizational structure as part of the Roxin theory, which has in general been rejected by the ICTY, but more recently revived by the ICC.

On 8 April 2008, the Higher Justice Court of Lima convicted members of the Army Intelligence Service (SIE) and the Army Intelligence Directorate (DINTE) for the detention, murdering and secretly burying in mass graves of nine students and one professor of the National University in 1992 in the so-called La Cantuta case. The court addressed a number of important legal issues. With respect to criminal liability it followed the Guzman case by applying the perpetration by means approach while it also found that in the overlap between the charges of kidnapping and enforced disappearance the latter should prevail as it the more serious if the two charges. Lastly, it rejected the defence of superior orders primarily based on the development of the parameters of this defence in international criminal law.

On 30 June 2008, the Supreme Court of Peru upheld the sentence of 16 years against Juan Carlos Mejia León for the forced disappearance of the university student Ernesto Castillo Páez in 1990. The main importance of this decision is that it fleshed out the elements of the crime of forced disappearance, namely the illegal deprivation of the victim's freedom as well as the continuing nature of the crime in that this element is present until the fate of the victim is known or his whereabouts established. This latter element also allowed the court to deal with the issue of retroactivity since Peruvian law only included this offence in its criminal code in 1991.

In Uruguay three persons were arrested on 17 December 2007 for crimes against humanity during the "dirty war" between 1976 and 1983, including former military dictator Gregorio Alvarez who was sentenced to 25 years imprisonment on 22 October 2009. As well, on 25 October 2009, Uruguayan voters rejected an initiative to end the country's Expiry Law which grants amnesty to military officials accused of human rights violations during the country's 1973-1985 dictatorship, although a week earlier the Supreme Court of Uruguay had found this law to be unconstitutional.

In Bolivia, the former president, Gonzalo Sánchez de Lozada and 16 ministers of his administration were indicted for genocide in February 2005 as a result of the killing of more than 80 people and the wounding of another 400 during mass demonstrations in September and October 2003, especially in La Paz and El Alto following the signing of an agreement by the government with US oil companies for the selling and exporting of natural gas. The trial began on 18 May 2009, but only eight of the accused were actually in court since de Lozada and several others were living abroad. Bolivian law does not allow a trial to proceed if the accused are not there, so Bolivia has requested the extradition of Lozada from the United States. On 16 September 2008, President Evo Morales announced the arrest of a provincial governor and political opponent on genocide charges in connection with the deaths of several Morales supporters during demonstrations a week earlier.

Former Mexican president Luis Echeverria Alvarez was accused of having ordered the Mexican army to fire on a demonstration in Mexico City on 2 October 1968 while he was Minister of the Interior. A federal tribunal ruled on 12 July 2007 that the massacre, which left between 200 and 300 people dead, constituted genocide, aimed at exterminating a national student group, but in the same ruling the charges against the president were dismissed since there was no evidence linking him to the massacres.

In Paraguay, a judge ordered the extradition on 5 August 2009 of an Argentine doctor, Norberto Atilio Bianco, on charges of child trafficking and forced disappearances of children born in a military hospital during his country's dictatorship.

A former Uruguayan military officer suspected of participating in Argentina's "Dirty War" was extradited from Brazil to Argentina to face charges on 23 January 2010. Major Juan Cordeiro Piacentini is accused of participating in Operation Condor, a plan to oppress opposition during Argentina's dictatorship in the 1970s, a period known as the "Dirty War". Specifically, Piacentini was charged with kidnapping related to the snatching of a 10 year old boy in 1976.

2.4.3. Asia

In *Asia*, *Indonesia* established in 2000 the Ad Hoc Tribunal for East Timor to deal with the same events as the special courts in East Timor. Of the twelve indictments with charges of crimes against humanity involving

18 defendants, six military and police officers have been convicted while the remainder were acquitted.[74]

There has been a conviction for war crimes in *Afghanistan*. Assadullah Sarwary, the former head of the Afghan intelligence services KhAD under the pro-Communist Najibullah regime that fell in 1992, was imprisoned in Kabul for 14 years. On 25 February 2006, the national security court sentenced him to death. Sarwary is the first person to be tried for war crimes in an Afghan court.[75]

While there have been no prosecutions yet, there have been growing calls in *Bangladesh* for a war crimes tribunal to look into atrocities that occurred during the country's 1971 war of independence. Bangladesh, then known as East Pakistan, accuses Pakistan of unleashing a brutal crackdown during its independence struggle that left up to three million people dead in a span of nine months. The Bangladeshi War Crimes Facts Finding Committee (WCFFC), a research organisation, unveiled on 3 April 2008 a list of 1,597 war criminals responsible for the mass killings, rapes and other atrocities during the Liberation War. Of those on the list, 369 are members of Pakistan military, and 1,150 are their local collaborators including members of Razakar and Al Badr (forces formed to aid the occupation army).[76] On 31 January 2009, the government in Bangladesh directed the security forces to prevent all war criminals, who allegedly collaborated with the Pakistani military during the 1971 liberation war, from leaving the country.

2.4.4. Africa

In *Africa*, prosecutions involving war crimes, crimes against humanity and genocide have begun in the Republic of the Congo, the Democratic Republic of the Congo, Ethiopia, Rwanda, Sudan and Burundi, to be followed by Uganda.

On 17 August 2005, after a three-week trial, a Brazzaville criminal court in the *Republic of the Congo* acquitted 15 officers in the so-called Beach case (related to the forced disappearance of 350 returning refugees

---

74 See http://socrates.berkeley.edu/~warcrime/East_Timor_and_Indonesia/Adhoc_jakarta.html and http://www.jsmp.minihub.org/Indonesia/indonesia.htm.

75 *IJT*, Issue, 42, 13 March 2006, page 4.

76 The Daily Star (Bangladesh), 23 April 2008.

at the Beach port in Brazzaville in 1999), finding them not guilty of the crimes of genocide, war crimes and crimes against humanity that were attributed to them.[77]

In the *Democratic Republic of the Congo (DRC)*, the military court in Bunia, Ituri, in the beginning of 2006, sentenced a captain in the Rwandan army, Blaise Bongi, to life in prison for war crimes. On 17 March 2006, the military court in Bukavu sentenced Jean-Pierre Biyoyo, ex-commander of the armed group Mudundu to five years in prison for the illegal detention of children. The military court in Mbandaka sentenced seven soldiers to life in prison on 12 April 2006 for crimes against humanity and for rapes committed in December 2003 in Songo Mboyo and Bongandanga, upheld by an appeals court on 18 February 2008.[78]

On 2 August 2006, the former Minister of Defense under Thomas Luganga, Yves Kahwa Panga Mandro, who founded the Party for Unity and the Protection of Congo's Integrity (PUSIC) in October/November 2002 (a "movement that has been working to date to destabilize Ituri", according to the court ruling) was sentenced to 20 years in prison by the military tribunal in Bunia for crimes against humanity and war crimes, in particular for massacres committed in October 2002 in Zumbe village 25 km from Bunia.[79] However, an appeals court acquitted him on 15 February 2008.

On 19 February 2007, the same military tribunal of Bunia handed down life sentences to four militiamen while two others were sentenced to 10 and 20 years in prison, and a seventh was acquitted, all of whom belonged to the first integrated brigade of the Armed Forces of the Democratic Republic of Congo (FARDC), a unit composed of former militiamen that was trained with Belgian military cooperation in 2004. They were prosecuted for war crimes following the discovery in November 2006 of a mass grave containing the bodies of 31 civilians in Bavi, a village 40 km south of Bunia.[80]

On 28 June 2007, the Military Court in Katanga acquitted all 12 defendants, both military and civilian, in the Kilwa trial. In 2004, members of the FARDC regained control of the town of Kilwa from a rebel group,

77 *IJT*, Issue 32, 26 September 2005, page 3.
78 See *YIHL*, 2008, vol. 11, page 468.
79 *IJT*, Issue 53, 25 September 2006, page 3.
80 *IJT*, Issue 64, 19 March 2007, page 3.

which had briefly occupied it. In investigating the events, human rights officers of the United Nations Mission in the DCR (MONUC) documented incidents of summary executions, torture, illegal detention and looting by the FARDC forces and concluded that little and sporadic fighting took place. Also charged for providing assistance to the armed forces had been three civilian employees of the mining company Anvil, namely one Canadian and two South Africans.[81] On 21 December 2007, the Military Court of Appeal in Lubumbashi refused to allow an appeal of the acquittals.[82]

On 5 March 2009, a former Congolese militia leader was sentenced to death by a military court in Kipushi for war crimes, crimes against humanity, insurrection and terrorism. Kyungu Mutanga, alias "Commander Gedeon", headed a so-called Mai-Mai militia group blamed for numerous attacks on civilians in parts of Katanga province between 2003 and 2006, when the country was wracked by civil war. He surrendered to United Nations peacekeepers in May 2006 at Mitwaba and was transferred to Lubumbashi, the capital of Katanga, pending trial. The court handed down the death penalty for war crimes; his wife was sentenced to seven years in prison and another defendant to ten years, but five others were acquitted for lack of proof.

In *Ethiopia*, former Ethiopian dictator Mengistu Haile Mariam, who is in exile in Zimbabwe, was convicted for genocide on 12 December 2006 by a court in Addis-Ababa and sentenced to life in prison on 11 January 2007.[83] The sentence was increased on 26 May 2008 to a death sentence. Another 54 accused were convicted for genocide as well and of these 54 accused, 35 were core members of the Derg, the ruling party in Ethiopia between 1977 and 1991 and a Marxist style revolutionary junta, while the remainder were ordinary members of the Derg and officials in urban dwellers associations (Kebeles).[84] Another 19 persons were convicted on 5 April 2008 including five who received the death penalty.

[81] See the detailed report by the NGO Global Witness of 17 July 2007 (http://www.globalwitness.org/media_library_detail.php/560/en/kilwa_trial_a_denial_of_justice).

[82] See http://www.raid-uk.org/docs/Kilwa_Trial/kilwa_appeal-21dec07-pdf.pdf.

[83] *IJT*, Issue 60, 22 January 2007, page 3.

[84] Firew K. Tiba, "The Mengistu Trial in Ethiopia", *JICJ*, 2007, vol. 5, no. 2, 513-528; see also http://www.trial-ch.org/en/trial-watch/profile/db/facts/mengistu_haile-mariam_262.html.

Over 5,000 persons have been tried for involvement in the Red Terror campaign by the Derg government of Mengistu as a result of investigations by the Office of the Special Prosecutor since 1994.[85]

In *Rwanda*, the 2,100 major perpetrators of the 1994 genocide will be tried in regular criminal court while the remainder will be the subject of specialized gacaca proceedings.[86] About 60,000 have been tried in those proceedings since 2005 while another 800,000 suspects are still awaiting a hearing. Rwanda will also receive 30 files involving major perpetrators from the ICTR in the context of its completion strategy.[87]

The numbers of suspected perpetrators in the genocide to be dealt with judicially in Rwanda are staggering: 818,564 people are suspected of genocide, of which 77,269 in the first category (punishable by life in prison), 432,557 in the second category (punishable by one to 30 years in prison and community service in the case of accepted confessions), and 308,738 in the "third category" or crimes against property (amicable settlement or sentenced to pay compensation).

The 1,545 gacaca district courts and 1,545 appeals courts are trying the crimes in the first and second categories, while 9,008 gacaca cell courts are trying crimes against property. Approximately 60,000 decisions have been rendered by the gacaca courts of which some 50% of the sentences are for punishments of 15 to 30 years in prison, 3% for community service, and 20-40% are acquittals depending on the regions. With respect to persons in detention, there were 120,000 prisoners at the end of 2002 which had been reduced to 92,000 in February 2007, including 30,000 from the gacaca courts while around 60,000 conditional releases took place between 2003 and 2007.[88] Conventional courts were still trying so-

85 Regarding the Office of the Special Prosecutor see *Emory International Law Review*, Fall Issue 1995.

86 See official website of the Republic of Rwanda, http://www.gov.rw/ under "Genocide".

87 See ICTR website, http://69.94.11.53/default.htm under "About the Tribunal", "ICTR Completion Strategy", "S2007/323", paragraph 7.

88 Primary source: National Service of Gacaca Jurisdiction, December 2006, quoted in *IJT*, Issue 64, 19 March 2007, p. 1, and Drumbl, *Atrocity, Punishment and International Law*, see *supra* note 40, 85-99 and *IJT*, Issue 87, 21 April 2008, page 1; see also Lars Waldorf ,"Mass Justice for Mass Atrocity: Rethinking Local Justice as Transitional Justice", *Temple Law Review*, 2006, vol. 79, no. 1; Karan Lahiri, "Rwanda's 'Gacaca' Courts A Possible model for local Justice in International

called "Category I" genocide cases (those in which the defendant exercised a leadership role or engaged in particularly egregious conduct) but in 2008 the government shifted thousands of the most serious genocide cases from conventional courts to community-based *gacaca* courts. Statistical information made available by the Rwandan government indicates that as of September 2008, 1,127,706 genocide cases had passed through *gacaca* courts and among those only 4,679 remained untried.

In *Sudan*. one of the most notorious figures in Darfur's conflict was arrested on 13 October 2008; Ali Kushayb, a tribal leader and a former commander of the Janjaweed militia, is the subject of an International Criminal Court arrest warrant on 51 counts of alleged war crimes and crimes against humanity.

In *Burundi,* a military court sentenced on 23 October 2008 colonel Vital Bangirinama to death in absentia and gave life imprisonment to three other officers on Thursday for the killing of 30 civilians during operations against rebels,

Uganda has set up a special war crimes court in May 2008 to deal with cases of human rights violations committed during the 20-year insurgency in the north. The court, a special division of the Uganda High Court, will be dealing with members of the Lord Resistance Army.[89]

2.5. War Crimes Proceedings Based on Universal Jurisdiction

2.5.1. Europe

In Europe[90] 13 countries have initiated criminal investigations and prosecutions for international crimes[91] committed elsewhere between 1994 and

Crime?", in *International Criminal Law Review*, 2009, vol. 9, no. 2, pp. 321-332, "Law and Reality, Progress in Judicial Reform in Rwanda"; Human Rights Watch, July 2008 at http://hrw.org/reports/2008/rwanda 0708/; Jones, *The Courts of Genocide, Politics and the Rule of Law in Rwanda and Arusha*; http://online.wsj.com/article/SB126162187619003811.html?mod=WSJ_hpp_sections_world; and the reports by Penal Reform International (PRI) at http://www.penalreform.org/reports-4.html.

89 BBC News, 26 May 2008.

90 In addition to these investigative and prosecutorial efforts by individual countries, there have also been attempts at co-ordinating these activities by improving exchange of information pertaining to investigations and by establishing best practices. Interpol has convened four International Expert Meetings on Genocide, War Crimes, and Crimes Against Humanity since 2005; see http://www.interpol.int/Public/Crimes

10 March 2010, resulting in over 50 indictments and arrest warrants (of which over 85% since 2000 alone) with 30 persons convicted (in 20 cases in 11 countries) and five acquittals (including one after an appeal).

The Netherlands has become the main centre of international criminal justice, both internationally and domestically. Internationally, both the ICC and the ICTY are located in The Hague[92] while the SLSC conducts its most high profile case, that of Charles Taylor, in that city as well.[93] As well, the Netherlands almost became the first country to have a case transferred from the ICTR as part of its completion strategy.[94]

On the domestic side, the activities of the Dutch government have been equally impressive in that six persons have been convicted for international crimes since 2001, although this effort has stalled somewhat most recently as a result of two acquittals in 2007 (although one of these was

AgainstHumanity/default.asp, while three years earlier the European Union decided to establish an European network of contact points in respect of persons responsible for genocide, crimes against humanity and war crimes, which meets on a regular basis, see the *Official Journal of the European Communities* L167/1 of 26/6/2002 and L118/2 of 14/5/2003 (http://eur-lex.europa.eu/JOIndex.do). As well, the ICC has started to convene meetings with some of the specialized war crimes units in order to develop an efficient co-operation model between national states and the ICC based on the complementarity principle enshrined in article 17 of its Statute. On the non-governmental side, the International Association of Prosecutors (IAP) established in 2009 a Specialist War Crimes Forum (http://www.iap-association.org/ressources/14AC_Conference_Outcome.pdf) while the International Bar Association had formed a War Crimes Committee a year earlier (http://www.ibanet.org/PPID/Constituent/War_Crimes_Committee/Default.aspx).

91 In most cases the international crimes considered in this section are war crimes and genocide although in some instances crimes against humanity were charged as well as torture, as defined by the 1984 Torture Convention.

92 In addition, the Special Tribunal for Lebanon has also been established in the Netherlands as of 1 March 2009, see http://www.un.org/apps/news/infocus/lebanon/tribunal/; see, regarding this tribunal, various contributors in *JICJ*, 2007, vol. 5, 1061-1174 and *Leiden Journal of International Law* (*LJIL*), 2008, vol. 21, no. 2, as well as the Handbook on the Special Tribunal for Lebanon by the International Centre for Transitional Justice (ICTJ), http://www.ictj.org/images/cont ent/9/1/914.pdf.

93 See http://www.sc-sl.org/Taylor.html.

94 ICTR-2005-86-R11bis, 13 April 2007; however, this person was never transferred from to the ICTR as a result of the judgments in the Mpambara case (see below as well as the Report on the Completion Strategy of the International Criminal Tribunal for Rwanda, 21 November 2007, paragraph 16).

later convicted on different charges) and the overturning of one conviction a year later.

Former Zairian army officer Sebastien Nzapali was convicted of torture in 2004 for his participation in leading death squads in the DRC in 1990 and 1995 and received 10 years imprisonment.[95] Heshamuddin Hesham and Habibullah Jalalzoy were convicted in 2005 for war crimes and torture due to their involvement in the KhAD in Kabul in Afghanistan between 1979 and 1989 and received a nine and twelve year prison sentence respectively,[96] a sentence upheld by an appeals court on 29 January 2007[97] and again by the Supreme Court of the Netherlands on 8 July 2008.[98]

Frans van Anraat, a Dutch national, was convicted at the trial level of complicity in war crimes on 23 December 2005 and sentenced to 15 years imprisonment as a result of having provided chemicals used in attacks against Kurds within in Iraq in 1988 and against the Iranian army during the Iraq-Iran war in 1980-1988 by the Saddam Hussein regime in Iraq. He was acquitted of complicity in genocide, as it was not established that he had actual knowledge of the genocidal intent of the Hussein government.[99] During the appeal of this case the court increased his sentence to 17 years imprisonment on 9 May 2007[100], even though the appeal court was of the view that there had been no evidence of genocide during the

95 See Menno T. Kamminga, "Netherlands Judicial Decisions involving Questions of International Law: First Conviction under the Universal Jurisdiction Provisions of the UN Convention against Torture", *Netherlands Int'l Law Review*, 2004, vol. 51, no. 3, 439-449.

96 See Guénaël Mettraux, "Dutch Courts' Universal Jurisdiction over Violations of Common Article 3 *qua* War Crimes", *JICJ*, 2006, vol. 4, no. 2, 362-371 (and further discussion as a result of this article in *JICJ*, 2006, vol. 4, 878-889.

97 Case numbers LJN AZ7147 and LJN AZ9365, which can be found at http://zoeken.rechtspraak.nl/.

98 Case number LJN BC7418, which can be found at http://zoeken.rechtspraak.nl/.

99 Case number LJN AX6406 which can be found at http://zoeken.rechtspraak.nl/.

100 See Harmen Van der Wilt, "Genocide, Complicity in Genocide and International v. Domestic Jurisdiction: Reflections on the *van Anraat* case", *JICJ*, 2006, vol. 4, no. 2, 239-257 and "Genocide *v*. War Crimes in the *Van Anraat* Appeal", *JICJ*, 2008, vol. 6, no. 3, 557-657.

Anfal campaign.[101] The verdict was confirmed by the Supreme Court on 30 June 2009.[102]

On 6 June 2006, another Dutch national, Guus van Kouwenhoven, was convicted for violating a United Nations arms embargo in Liberia and sentenced to eight years imprisonment. There was insufficient evidence of his knowledge or direct involvement to convict him of war crimes,[103] The verdict was overturned by an appeals court on 10 March 2008.[104] Later that month prosecutors announced their intention to seek an appeal to the Supreme Court of the Netherlands.[105]

In another case, an officer of the Afghan Military Intelligence Service in Afghanistan during the Najibullah regime was acquitted for charges of war crimes and torture on 25 June 2007[106] which was confirmed on appeal on 16 July 2009.[107] A Rwandan national, Joseph Mpambara, was arrested in August 2006 on charges of involvement in the genocide in Rwanda; jurisdiction was denied on 24 July 2007 by the court of first instance on the basis that neither the perpetrator nor a victim has Dutch nationality.[108] This judgment was confirmed on appeal on 18 December 2007[109] and again by the Dutch Supreme Court on 21 October 2008.[110] A trial with different charges against him, namely torture and war

101 Case number LJN BA6734, which can be found at http://zoeken.rechtspraak.nl/.

102 Case number LJN BG4822, which can be found at http://zoeken.rechtspraak.nl/.

103 Case number LJN AY5160, which can be found at http://zoeken.rechtspraak.nl/.

104 Case number LJN BC7373 which can be found at http://zoeken.rechtspraak.nl/.

105 See http://www.trial-ch.org/en/trial-watch/profile/db/legal-procedures/guus_van-kouwenhoven_289.html.

106 Case number LJN BA9575, which can be found at http://zoeken.rechtspraak.nl/.

107 Case number LJN BJ2796, which can be found at http://zoeken.rechtspraak.nl/.

108 Case number LJN BB0494, which can be found at http://zoeken.rechtspraak.nl/; see also *IJT*, Issue 78, 19 November 2007, page 2; see also Elies Van Sliedregt, "International Crimes before Dutch Courts: Recent Developments", *LJIL*, 2007, vol. 20, no. 4, 895–908.

109 Case number LJN BC1757, which can be found at http://zoeken.rechtspraak.nl/.

110 On 14 October 2009, the Dutch Minister of Justice introduced a law to address this problem and to make it possible to prosecute international crimes as far back as 1966.

crimes, began on 13 October 2008; he was convicted to 20 years for the torture charges only on 23 March 2009.[111]

On 6 November 2008, a Bosnian citizen suspected of having committed war crimes was arrested in the Netherlands.

All these cases have been investigated by a special police war crimes unit.

In *Belgium* there have been four cases since 2001 which have led to convictions for eight persons, all related to the Rwandan genocide. On 8 January 2001, the first universal jurisdiction case in Belgium resulted in the conviction of the "Butare Four" for war crimes and resulting in sentences of between 12 and 20 years for Julienne Mukabuera,[112] Consolata Mukangango,[113] Vincent Ntezimana[114] and Alphonse Higaniro.[115]

On 29 June 2005, the half-brothers Etienne Nzabonimana[116] and Samuel Ndashykirwa[117] were sentenced to 12 and 10 years respectively for murders of Tutsis in Kirwa.

The trial of Bernard Ntuyahaga[118] began in April 2007. He was found guilty of the murder of six Belgian peacekeepers in Rwanda and was sentenced to 20 years in prison on 4 July 2007 although he was acquitted of the murder of former prime minister of Rwanda, Agathe

[111] Case number LJN BI2444, which can be found at http://zoeken.rechtspraak.nl/; see also Larissa van den Herik, "A Quest for Jurisdiction and an Appropriate Definition of Crime: Mpambara before the Dutch Courts", *JICJ*, 2009, vol. 7, no. 5, 1117-1131.

[112] See http://www.trial-ch.org/en/trial-watch/profile/db/facts/julienne_mukabutera_186.html.

[113] See http://www.trial-ch.org/en/trial-watch/profile/db/facts/consolata_mukangango_185.html.

[114] See http://www.trial-ch.org/en/trial-watch/profile/db/facts/vincent_ntezimana_162.html.

[115] See http://www.trial-ch.org/en/trial-watch/profile/db/legal-procedures/alphonse_higaniro_163.html.

[116] See http://www.trial-ch.org/en/trial-watch/profile/db/facts/etienne_nzabonimana_327.html.

[117] See http://www.trial-ch.org/en/trial-watch/profile/db/facts/samuel_ndashyikirwa_328.html.

[118] See http://www.trial-ch.org/en/trial-watch/profile/db/facts/bernard_ntuyahaga_477.html.

Uwilingiyimana, and of involvement in other massacres.[119] His appeal was rejected on 12 December 2007.

On 9 December 2009, Ephrem Nkezabera was convicted to 30 years in prison on charges of violating international criminal law and war crimes. He is said to have played a key role within the Interahamwe (an extremist Hutu militia which was heavily involved in the genocide), of which National Committee he was a member. As a banker, he was said to have been in charge of financing the militia and furnishing arms to the militiamen.[120]

In addition to these convictions, Rwanda issued an international arrest warrant against Emmanuel Bagambiki who came to Belgium on 27 July 2007 based on accusations of rape and incitement to rape.

On 25 June 2002, Hervé Madeo and Thierry Desmarest, French citizens, were charged with complicity in crimes against humanity, perpetrated in Myanmar by military battalions who were in charge of the security of the pipeline project of which the company they worked for, TotalFinalElf, was aware. This case against TotalFinalElf was reopened in 2007[121] but dismissed on 5 March 2008[122]. They have also been charged for the same crimes in France.

In *Germany*[123] four individuals have been prosecuted and convicted, all for involvement in crimes committed in the former Yugoslavia.[124] Novislav Djajić, Maksim Sokolović, Djuradj Kušljić and Nikola Jorgić were all found guilty in first instance between 1997 and 1999. Djajić, a former member of the Bosnian Serb forces, was convicted in May 1997 to five years imprisonment for aiding and abetting manslaughter only although

[119] *IJT*, Issue 71, 9 July 2007, page 4.

[120] See http://www.trial-ch.org/en/trial-watch/profile/db/facts/ephrem_nkezabera_627.html and *IJT*, Issue 84, 3 March 2008, page 3.

[121] See http://www.trial-ch.org/en/trial-watch/profile/db/facts/thierry_desmarest_371.html.

[122] *IJT*, Issue 95, 17 March 2008, page 4.

[123] In general see the Amnesty International report of 16 October 2008, http://www.amnesty.org/en/library/info/EUR23/003/2008/en.

[124] See also Ruth Rissing van Saan, "The German Federal Supreme Court and the Prosecution of International Crimes Committed in the Former Yugoslavia", *JICJ*, 2005, vol. 3, no. 2, 381-399 and Salvatore Zappalà, "The German Federal Prosecutor's Decision not the Prosecute a Former Uzbek Minister, Missed Opportunity or Prosecutorial Wisdom?", *JICJ*, 2006, vol. 4, no. 3, 602-622.

he had been charged with genocide.[125] Sokolović was convicted to nine years imprisonment in November 1999 for aiding and abetting genocide and grave breaches of the Geneva Conventions (i.e., war crimes), which was upheld on appeal in February 2001.[126] Kušljić was convicted of genocide in December 1999 and received a life sentence, which was upheld on appeal in February 2001, but on the basis of grave breaches rather than genocide.[127] Jorgić was convicted of genocide and murder and received a life sentence in 1997, which was upheld by an appeal court in April 1999 and later by the European Court of Human Rights on 12 July 2007.[128]

More recently, German authorities arrested Augustin Ngirabatware on 17 September 2007 pursuant to an international arrest warrant issued by the ICTR while Onesphore Rwabukombe was arrested on 25 April 2008 and indicted for crimes against humanity and genocide on 3 June 2008. On 8 July 2008, Callixte Mbarushimana was arrested for charges involving the Rwandan genocide; he is wanted both in France and Rwanda.[129] Ngirabatware was transferred to the ICTR on 8 October 2008 while the other two whose extradition had been requested by Rwanda, were freed on 4 November 2008 for issues related to receiving a fair trial in Rwanda.

On 16 November 2009, police in Germany have arrested two Rwandan militia leaders on suspicion of crimes committed in the east of the Democratic Republic of Congo. Ignace Murwanashyaka, the leader of the FDLR rebel group, and his aide Straton Musoni were held on suspicion of crimes against humanity and war crimes. FDLR leaders fled to DRC after the Rwanda genocide in which some 800,000 people (mostly

125 See http://www.trial-ch.org/en/trial-watch/profile/db/legal-procedures/novislav_djajic_135.html.

126 See http://www.trial-ch.org/en/trial-watch/profile/db/facts/maksim_sokolovic_139.html.

127 See http://www.trial-ch.org/en/trial-watch/profile/db/facts/djuradj_kusljic_140.html.

128 See http://www.trial-ch.org/en/trial-watch/profile/db/legal-procedures/nikola_jorgic_283.html; see also the Judgment of the ECHR in the "Case of Jorgic v. Germany", Application no. 74613/01.

129 Generally for efforts in Europe in extraditing dealing with Rwandan suspects see REDRESS and African Rights, "Extraditing Genocide Suspects From Europe to Rwanda; Issues and Challenges" at http://www.redress.org/documents/Extradition_Report_Final_Version_4_Sept_08.pdf

ethnic Tutsis) died. The FDLR's presence in DRC has been at the heart of years of unrest.

On 20 January 2010, an arrest warrant was issued against Jorge Videla, the former president of Argentina for the murder of a German citizen during the dirty war period in that country.

On 20 April 2009, Germany's Ministry of Justice announced that it has created three dedicated positions in the General Prosecutor's Office to investigate cases of genocide, crimes against humanity and war crimes that fall under Germany's universal jurisdiction law. In addition, the Federal Criminal Police was to establish a specialised war crimes unit with seven investigators working on international crimes.

In *Denmark*, the Danish International Crime Investigation Section (SICO)[130] which is a specialized unit consisting of prosecutors and police investigators, has been instrumental in laying charges in two cases involving international crimes since 2003.[131] One was a former general in the Saddam Hussein government, Nizar al-Khazraji, who escaped prior to his arrest and is believe to have passed away. The second person is Rwandan national Sylvaire Ahorugeze (the former Chairman of the Civil Aviation Authority) who has been was arrested on genocide charges in September 2006, but was released on 10 August 2007,[132] then arrested in Sweden.

Before the establishment of SICO another person had been charged in Denmark. In 1994 Refik Šarić was convicted for torturing detainees in 1993 at a prison in Bosnia and convicted to eight years imprisonment for grave breaches, which was upheld on appeal in 1995.[133]

In *Spain*[134] there has been one conviction for international crimes and a number of indictments combined with arrest warrants for people

130 See http://www.sico.ankl.dk/page34.aspx.

131 There have also been two charges for other, domestic, crimes for which Denmark has extraterritorial jurisdictions. A Ugandan national was convicted in 2004 for armed robbery and abduction while another person was acquitted of charges of murder in Pakistan; see http://www.sico.ankl.dk/page34.aspx.

132 See http://www.trial-ch.org/en/trial-watch/profile/db/facts/sylvere_ahorugeze_476.html.

133 See http://www.trial-ch.org/en/trial-watch/profile/db/legal-procedures/refik_saric_517.html.

134 See in general the report of Amnesty International of 16 October 2008 at http://www.amnesty.org/es/library/info/EUR41/017/2008/es, as well as *YIHL*, 2006, vol. 9, 555-567.

who are not present in Spain although some of those were based on the passive nationality principle in that the victims were of Spanish nationality.

On 19 April 2005, Adolfo Scilingo was convicted and sentenced to 640 years imprisonment for attempted genocide and other crimes committed in Argentina's dirty war.[135] Scilingo had voluntarily appeared before the court. Another case involving the dirty war in Argentina pertained to ex-military officer Ricardo Miguel Cavallo who was extradited from Mexico to Spain and accused of 228 disappearances and 128 kidnappings. The Spanish Supreme Court decided on 17 July 2007 that he could be tried for genocide and terrorism[136] and on 31 March 2008 the Spanish government extradited him to Argentina.[137]

In December 2006, Rodolfo Eduardo Almiron Sena, former police commissioner in Argentina, was arrested on charges of murder and belonging to criminal organization. He allegedly participated in a death squad in Argentina during the dirty war that was responsible for killing 600 people. On 15 February 2008, a Spanish court agreed to extradite him to Argentina[138] where he arrived on 31 March 2008.

Several Guatemalan military officials, including former president Efrain Rios Montt, were investigated for genocide as a result of a scorched earth policy and widespread suppression, characterized by massacres against the Indian population and the obliteration of 440 Indian villages between March 1982 and August 1983.[139] Although initially the lower courts declined to issue arrest warrants, the Constitutional Tribunal found that Spain had jurisdiction over the case.[140] Since then, Spain has

---

135 See Christian Tomuschat, "Issues of Universal Jurisdiction in the *Scilingo* Case", *JICJ*, 2005, vol. 3, no. 5, 1074-1081; Alicia Gil Gil, "The Flaws of the *Scilingo* Judgment", *JICJ*, 2005, vol. 3, no. 5, 1082-1091; Giulia Pinzauti, "An Instance of Reasonable Universality: The *Scilingo* Case", *JICJ*, 2005, vol. 3, no. 5, 1092-1105.

136 http://www.trial-ch.org/en/trial-watch/profile/db/facts/ricardo-miguel_cavallo_48.html.

137 See *YIHL*, 2007, vol. 10, 428-442 and *YIHL*, 2008, vol. 11, 561-562.

138 *IJT*, Issue 86, 7 April 2008, page 1.

139 See http://www.trial-ch.org/en/trial-watch/profile/db/facts/efrain_rios-montt_260.html.

140 See Naomi Roht-Arriaza, "Guatemala Genocide Case, Spanish Constitutional Tribunal decision on universal jurisdiction over genocide claims", *American Journal of Int'l Law*, 2006, vol. 100, no. 1, 207-213; Hervé Ascensio, "The Spanish Constitu-

charged several suspects with genocide, and requested their extradition. In November 2006, at least two of the eight defendants were arrested in Guatemala, but on 17 December 2007 the Constitutional Court of Guatemala refused to acknowledge that a Spanish court has jurisdiction to put them on trial.[141]

On 22 February 2008, the Spanish Cabinet approved the second extradition of Ricardo Taddei to Argentina. Taddei had originally been handed over to the Argentine authorities on 26 April 2007, but as a result of this new decision he can now also be put on trial for the additional crimes of illegal arrest and torture committed in Argentina during its dirty war period.[142]

On 23 September 2009, the Spanish police arrested an Argentine-born commercial pilot, Julio Alberto Poch, wanted in connection with the deaths of 1,000 people during his South American country's "Dirty War" period between1976 and 1983. He was ordered extradited to Argentina by the High Court on 20 January 2010.

On 2 March 2010, Spanish police have arrested an alleged Serbian war criminal known as the "Monster of Grbavica" and wanted for the murders of more than 100 people during the Bosnian war. Veselin Vlahović was detained on Monday near his home in the eastern town of Altea as part of an investigation into a gang which was carrying out burglaries in Spain.

Thirteen other investigations have also been opened in the last couple of years, a number of them dealing with Chinese and American officials.

One of the investigations in respect to China was opened in 2006 involves the commission of genocide during the occupation in Tibet in

tional Tribunal's Decision in *Guatemalan Generals*: Unconditional Universality is Back", *JICJ*, 2006, vol. 4, no. 3, 586-594; Paul Scott, "The Guatemala Genocide Cases: Universal Jurisdiction and Its Limits" , *Journal of Int'l and Comp. Law*, 2009, vol. 9. This wide interpretation of universal jurisdiction was curtailed by the Spanish legislator on 15 October 2009 by limiting jurisdiction to those offenses committed by or against Spaniards, or where the perpetrators are in Spain but only for prospective investigations.

141 "Guatemalan officials dodge genocide extraditions", Reuters, 17 December 2007.

142 *YIHL*, 2008, vol. 11, 562.

1950.[143] A second one, launched in 2007, is against the Chinese government for actions against Falun Gong practitioners, while on 5 August 2008, a third investigation began against China for its actions in Tibet in March that same year. On 13 November 2009, a judge accepted charges of genocide and torture in the Falun Gong case.

With respect to the US four investigations have been opened. One case was against three American soldiers for murder and crimes against the international community in Iraq in 2007[144] (which was dismissed on 14 July 2009). Secondly, on 28 March 2008, the first steps were taken toward opening a criminal investigation into allegations that six former high-level Bush administration officials violated international law by providing the legal framework to justify the torture of prisoners at Guantánamo Bay, including John Yoo, the former Justice Department lawyer who wrote secret legal opinions saying the president had the authority to circumvent the Geneva Conventions, and Douglas Feith, the former under secretary of defence for policy. Thirdly, on 29 April 2009, an investigative magistrate opened an investigation into the Bush administration over alleged torture of terror suspects at Guantanamo Bay because documents declassified by the new U.S. government suggested the practice was systematic. Fourthly, on 30 January 2010, it was announced that Spain's top investigating judge, Baltasar Garzon, was to probe suspected torture and ill-treatment of inmates at the US prison of Guantanamo Bay. The judge will be acting on complaints lodged by a number of associations, focusing on one prisoner, Ahmed Abderraman Hamed, who has Spanish nationality.

Other investigations deal with the possible commission of genocide in the West Sahara by Morocco (in 2007); mass murder and crimes against humanity in the aftermath of the 1994 Rwanda genocide[145] against 40 Rwandan army officers (in February 2008[146]); the killing of six Jesuit

143 See http://www.trial-ch.org/en/trial-watch/profile/db/facts/jiang_zemin_468.html; see also Christine A.E. Bakker, "Universal Jurisdiction of Spanish Courts over Genocide in Tibet: Can it Work", *JICJ*, 2006, vol. 4, no. 3, 595-601.

144 See http://www.trial-ch.org/en/trial-watch/profile/db/facts/philip_decamp_411.html, http://www.trial-ch.org/en/trial-watch/profile/db/facts/shawn_gibson_409.html and http://www.trial-ch.org/en/trial-watch/profile/db/facts/philip_wolford_410.html.; see also *YIHL*, 2008, vol. 11, 559-561.

145 *IJT*, Issue 83, 18 February 2008, page 4.

146 See *YIHL*, 2008, vol. 11, 558-559.

priests and two other people in 1989 during that country's civil war against 14 ex-Salvadoran military officials (13 January 2009); the killing of a Hamas militant and 14 others, including nine children in 2002 in the Palestine Occupied Territories against Israeli IDF members (26 January 2009, although that case was dismissed by the National Criminal Court of Appeals on 17 July 2009 because the crimes in question were already the subject of a legal procedure in Israel which fully satisfied the requirements of an independent and impartial system of justice); and the torture and murder in 1976 of Mr. Carmelo Soria, a UN diplomat, against three former Chilean ministers, five generals and several officers[147] (20 November 2009).

The wide application of this notion of universal jurisdiction *in absentia* is beginning to be curtailed, both by the judiciary where in two instances the investigations have been quashed in 2009, and by the legislator which introduced on 3 November 2009 amendments to the Organic Law of the Judiciary to limit the scope of universal jurisdiction in Spain by requiring among other things a more substantial connection of the perpetrator to Spain.

In *France* two persons have been convicted of international crimes. In July 2006, Ely Ould Dah, a Mauritanian army captain was sentenced *in absentia* to ten years imprisonment for torture in Mauritania in 1990 and 1991. Ould Dah had been in France when the investigation was opened, but managed to flee to Mauritania during a conditional release.[148] His complaint against this conviction to the European Court of Human Rights was declared inadmissible on 30 March 2009. The second person convicted was Alfredo Astiz, an Argentine captain, convicted *in absentia* to life imprisonment in 1990 of the torture and disappearance of two French nuns based on the passive personality principle (the nationality of the victims) rather than universal jurisdiction.[149]

---

147 Hermán Brady (Defense Minister), Raul Benavides (Interior Minister), Juan Manuel Contreras, Pedro Espinoza Bravo, Jaime Lepe, Raul Eduardo Iturriaga Neuman; the undersecretary of the Interior, Captain Enrique Montero Marx; and officers Jorge Rios San Martin, Guillermo Salinas Torres, Pablo Belmar Labbé, Rene Patricio Quilhot Palma, Rolf Wenderoth Well and Ricardo Lawrence.

148 See http://www.trial-ch.org/en/trial-watch/profile/db/facts/ely_ould-dah_266.html.

149 See http://www.trial-ch.org/en/trial-watch/profile/db/facts/alfredo_astiz_311.html.

There have a number of proceedings involving Rwandans who took part in the 1994 genocide. Laurent Bucyibaruta was indicted for involvement in the Rwandan genocide, arrested in June 2007[150] and was supposed to be transferred to the ICTR. An investigation into Rwandan priest Wencelas Munyeshaka's involvement in genocide and crimes against humanity was opened in 1995 in France. After he was convicted *in absentia* by a Rwandan military court in November 2006, the ICTR made public an arrest warrant on 21 June 2007 as a result of which he was arrested in France on 20 July 2007, but released ten days later because of problems with the warrants. Ultimately, the ICTR decided to transfer these two cases to France courts on 20 November 2007[151] which was accepted by the French courts on 20 February 2008[152].

Dominique Ntawukuriryayo, a former deputy governor, was arrested in October 2007 pursuant to an ICTR warrant, which was held valid on 7 May 2008. On 19 May of the same year, the European Court of Human Rights rejected an urgent motion filed by Ntawukuriryayo. He was transferred to the ICTR on 9 June 2008.

As well, Isaac Kamali was arrested on 22 June 2007 in the US as a result of an arrest warrant issued by Rwanda and then transferred to France where he is a citizen three days later, but was released on 10 December 2008 by the Court of Appeal in Paris. On 8 January 2008, Marcel Bivugabagabo, a member of the FAR during the genocide was arrested, also pursuant to a arrest warrant by Rwanda,[153] as was Claver Kamana on 29 February 2008.[154] The former was released by the Toulouse Court of Appeal on 23 October 2008; the latter was ordered extradited on 2 April 2008, but this was overturned by the Court de Cassation on 9 July 2008 and he was released by the Lyon Court of Appeal on 9 January 2009. These three released persons were sought pursuant Rwandan extradition requests where the courts held that they would not get a fair trial in Rwanda upon return because of defence witness protection issues.

150 *IJT*, Issue 72, 23 July 2007, page 2.

151 See http://www.trial-ch.org/en/trial-watch/profile/db/facts/wenceslas_munyeshyaka_112.html.

152 *IJT*, Issue 84, 3 March 2008, page 3.

153 *IJT*, Issue 81, 21 January 2008, page 3.

154 *IJT*, Issue 86, 7 April 2008, page 3.

French prosecutors have also commenced investigations in March 2008 against Agathe Habyarimana (the widow of President Juvenal Habyarimana), Callixte Mbarushimana and Eugène Rwamucyo.[155] While on 14 November 2008, a French court ruled against the extradition of Pascal Simbikangwa. He was transferred on 20 November 2009 from the island of La Réunion to Paris at the request of an investigative judge. Also in November, Rose Kabuye, the director of state protocol in the present Rwandan government, was arrested in Germany and extradited to France for her involvement in the assassination of ethnic Hutu President Juvenal Habyarimana. On 21 January 2010, Sosthene Munyemana (45), who had been working in a hospital in Bordeaux for eight years, was arrested for involvement in the genocide, while on 2 March 2010, Agathe Habyarimana (67) was taken into custody as a result of a request of the Rwandan government over its allegations that she helped plan the 1994 genocide, in which 800,000 people were killed.

Five persons from the Republic of Congo are under investigation in the so-called Brazzavile Beach Case. They were alleged to have been involved in the forced disappearance of 350 returning refugees at the Beach port in Brazzaville in 1999. On 10 January 2007, the Criminal Chamber of the French Supreme Court decided that France had jurisdiction to investigate the case.[156] The charges against one of them, General Jean-Francois Ndengue, were dropped later in 2007 because of his diplomatic immunity which was confirmed by an appeal court on 9 April 2008.

Two Algerians have also been indicted for crimes against humanity, namely Abdelkader Mohamed and Hocine Mohamed, for the commission of crimes as members of a self-defense group in the Relizane province.[157]

On 26 January 2010, the Court of Appeal in Paris issued a decision allowing prosecution based on universal jurisdiction of the crimes of tor-

[155] See http://www.trial-ch.org/en/trial-watch/profile/db/facts/agathe_habyarimana_759.html.

[156] See http://www.trial-ch.org/en/trial-watch/profile/db/legal-procedures/pierre_oba_351.html, http://www.trial-ch.org/en/trial-watch/profile/db/legal-procedures/blaise_adoua_352.html, http://www.trial-ch.org/en/trial-watch/profile/db/facts/denis_sassou-nguesso_350.html and http://www.trial-ch.org/en/trial-watch/profile/db/facts/jean-fran%E7ois_ndengue_349.html.

[157] See http://www.trial-ch.org/en/trial-watch/profile/db/facts/abdelkader_mohamed_567.html and http://www.trial-ch.org/en/trial-watch/profile/db/facts/hocine_mohamed_568.html.

ture, imprisonment and forced disappearance in Cambodia between 1975 and 1979.

In the *United Kingdom*[158] the first successful prosecution using universal jurisdiction was against Afghan militia leader Faryadi Zardad. In 2005, a jury convicted him of torture and hostage taking committed in Afghanistan in the 1990s and convicted him to 20 years imprisonment.[159] Zardad had been in charge of a checkpoint between Kabul and Pakistan where his subordinates committed torture, murder and other atrocities for which he was found to be responsible. In 1999 charges against Sudanese doctor Mohammed Ahmed Maghoub of torturing detainees were dropped as a result of lack of evidence. The United Kingdom has a special war crimes unit within the New Scotland Yard.

As well, on 11 November 2008, Damir Travica, accused of war crimes, was extradited to Croatia. Extradition proceedings against four Rwandans (Célestin Ugirashebuja, Vincent Bajinya, Emmanuel Nteziryayo and Charles Munyaneza) for involvement in the 1994 genocide were commenced in 2006 on behalf of Rwanda.[160] On 6 June 2008, the court decided that there were no barriers to removing the four to Rwanda, this decision was overturned on appeal on 8 April 2009 by the High Court of Justice in London for the same reasons related to the defence witness protection as decided earlier in two German and three French cases as well as concerns regarding the independence and impartiality of the Rwandan judiciary.

On 20 August 2009, the UK extradited Serb Milan Španović to Croatia. Španović was sentenced by a Croatian court to 20 years for war crimes. The London Supreme Court accepted Croatia's arguments that Španović will be allowed a fair retrial and that he would not be discriminated against because of his nationality, nor would his human rights be violated in Croatia. Španović was sentenced *in absentia* in 1993 to 20

158 In general, see "Suspected War Criminals and Génocidaires in the UK, Proposals to Strengthen our Laws", by Aegis Trust, June 2009 (at http://www.aegistrust.org/images/PDFs/Suspected War Criminals and Genocidaires in the UK.pdf), as well as "Closing the Impunity Gap: UK law on genocide and related crimes" by the Human Rights Joint Committee of the UK Parliament, 11 August 2009 (at http://news.parliament.uk/2009/08/report-looks-at-uk-law-relating-to-war-criminals/).

159 See http://www.trial-ch.org/en/trial-watch/profile/db/facts/faryadi-sarwar_zardad_329.html.

160 See http://www.trial-ch.org/en/trial-watch/search/judgement-place/34.html.

years in jail for war crimes committed in Croatian villages of Maja and Svračica in 1991, including opening fire on unarmed citizens, torture, looting and arson.

On 1 March 2010, former Bosnian president Ejup Ganić was arrested in London on a Serbian extradition warrant for alleged war crimes committed at the start of the 1992-95 Bosnian war.

On 26 October 2009, the British government announced it will change the law on genocide, war crimes and crimes against humanity by retrospectively applying jurisdiction for most such crimes back to 1991.

Italy is requesting the extradition of more than 100 former South American leaders and their underlings over the disappearance, torture and death of Italians who were caught up in a crackdown on dissent in the 1970s and 1980s. In 2008, authorities made requests for 139 people involved in the military dictatorships of Chile, Uruguay, Argentina, Brazil, Bolivia and Paraguay and accused in the kidnapping and murder of 25 Italian dissidents as part of operation Condor. The suspects include Argentina's former junta leader Jorge Videla and Uruguay's former dictator Juan Bordaberry.[161] One person, Uruguayan former naval intelligence officer Nestor Jorge Fernandez Troccoli, had already been arrested in Italy but the extradition request was denied by a court in Rome.[162]

On 11 July 2009, Italian authorities arrested a Kosovo Albanian wanted by Serbia on war crimes charges; Muharem Gashi was a member of the so-called Kosovo Liberation Army, KLA, and is believed to have killed two Serb civilians during the 1999 conflict in the province. As well, on 20 October 2009, Italy arrested Emmanuel Uwayezu, a Catholic priest for his alleged role in the 1994 genocide, pursuant to an arrest warrant from Rwanda.

In *Switzerland* two cases went to trial in the late 1990s resulting in one conviction. Goran Grabež was charged with having committed war crimes against prisoners of the Omarska and Keraterm camps between May and August 1992, but was acquitted on 18 April 1997 for lack of evidence.[163] In July 1998, Fulgence Niyonteze was charged with war crimes, crimes against humanity and genocide for his involvement in

[161] Associated Press, 10 January 2008.

[162] See *YIHL*, 2008, vol. 11, 500-502.

[163] See http://www.trial-ch.org/en/trial-watch/profile/db/facts/goran_grabez_134.html.

Rwandan genocide. He was convicted on 30 April 1999 of war crimes only since Swiss law had not included the other two categories of crimes in its legislation at that time. He was sentenced to life imprisonment. On 26 May 2000, an appeals court reduced the sentence to 14 years.[164]

On 30 June 2009, the Swiss government refused to extradite a suspected genocidaire to Rwanda citing human rights concerns.

In *Austria* Duško Cvjetković, a Bosnian Serb, who had been charged with murder and genocide, was acquitted by a jury of all charges in 1994. In another case, an investigation was instituted but not concluded against a Croatian citizen living in Austria. In 1993, a Croatian court convicted him *in absentia* for war crimes under the Croatian Penal Code and handed down a ten-year prison sentence. The suspect moved from Austria to Hungary and was in September 2001 extradited to Croatia where he is currently serving his prison sentence. The Austrian case has been suspended.

Norway, which like Denmark, has a specialized war crimes unit with prosecutors and police investigators, arrested two persons from Bosnia, Sakib Dautović and Mirsad Repak, in May 2007. Dautović is suspected of having committed crimes in detention camps on the territory of Velika Kladuša.[165] Repak is linked to crimes committed against 18 Bosnian Serb civilians detained in camp Dretelj near Čapljina, which was controlled by Croatian forces (HOS) during 1992. On 10 July 2008, charges of rape, torture, illegal internment of civilians and crimes against humanity were laid against Repak, a 41-year old Norwegian citizen who came from Bosnia-Herzegovina as an asylum seeker in 1993. His trial started on 27 August 2008 and he was convicted and sentenced to five years imprisonment on 2 December 2008, although the recently amended war crimes law was held to be partially unconstitutional for retroactivity. On 8 March 2010, an appellate court found Repak guilty of 13 counts of the war crimes committed against, but he was acquitted on one count. The judgement was appealed by both parties.

A Croat, Damir Sireta, was arrested on 20 November 2006 as a result of a Serbian arrest warrant for war crimes committed around

164 See http://www.trial-ch.org/en/trial-watch/profile/db/facts/fulgence_niyonteze_115.html.

165 See http://www.bim.ba/en/62/10/2845/.

Vukovar.[166] He was extradited to Serbia on 16 May 2008. On 10 March 2009, a Serb accused of committing war crimes in Kosovo in 1999 during the Balkans conflict was arrested.

In *Finland* the National Bureau of Investigation (NBI) arrested a Rwandan citizen, François Bazaramba, on 14 April 2007 and remanded him in custody on suspicion of genocide.[167] On 20 February 2009, it was decided not to extradite him to Rwanda and on 1 June 2009 he was charged with genocide and murder. His trial commenced in September 2009.

In *Sweden*[168] a suspect in the Rwandan genocide, Sylvere Ahorugeze, was arrested on 16 July 2008[169] (after having left Denmark) and ordered extradited by the Supreme Court on 26 May 2009. On 9 July 2009, the Swedish government decided to extradite Ahorugeze to Rwanda. Ahorugeze appealed this decision before the European Court on Human Rights on 13 July 2009 claiming that he would not receive a fair trial before the ICTR. On 16 July 2009, the Swedish government indicated that it would abide by an ECHR order not to deport Ahorugeze until the European Court had examined the case.

On 12 January 2010, a 43-year old man from Bosnia-Herzegovina, Ahmet Makitan, was apprehended on suspicion of having committed graves breaches of the Geneva Conventions in Bosnia-Herzegovina in 1992. The man, who is now a Swedish citizen, is said to have been a camp guard at a detention facility where he allegedly illegally detained, tortured and murdered civilian Bosnian Serbs. A special war crimes unit was created in the fall of 2007.[170]

2.5.2. Africa

In *Senegal* a law was passed in February 2007 which permitted it to prosecute cases of genocide, crimes against humanity, war crimes and

[166] See http://www.b92.net/eng/news/society-article.php?yyyy=2006&mm=11&dd=21 &nav_category=113&nav_id=38115.

[167] See http://www.rwandagateway.org/article.php3?id_article=5039.

[168] In general, see the report of Amnesty International of 1 January 2009 at http://www.amnesty.org/en/library/info/EUR42/001/2009/en.

[169] See http://www.thelocal.se/13090/20080716/.

[170] See http://www.thelocal.se/8454/20070911.

torture, even when they are committed outside of Senegal. On 23 July 2008, a constitutional amendment was adopted confirming that Senegalese courts can prosecute crimes against humanity which were committed before the 2007 law[171], which would allow Senegal to try exiled former president of Chad, Hissène Habré, for international crimes committed between 1982 and 1990, after Senegal was asked to do so in 2006 by the African Union as result of a 2005 extradition request by Belgium[172]. On 16 September 2008, fourteen abuse victims, backed by a coalition of African and international rights groups, filed complaints with a Senegalese prosecutor accusing Habré of crimes against humanity and torture. On 19 February 2009, Belgium filed a memorandum with the International Court of Justice to force Senegal to exercise its obligation to prosecute or extradite in this case; on 28 May the provisional measures requested by Belgium to ensure that Habré would not abscond were refused by the ICJ because of assurances given by Senegal in this regard.

2.5.3. North America

In *Canada* Désiré Munyaneza was charged on 19 October 2005 with genocide, war crimes and crimes against humanity for his involvement in Butare during the Rwandan genocide. The trial began in May 2007. He was convicted on all counts on 22 May 2009[173] and sentenced to life imprisonment on 29 October 2009[174]. On 6 November 2009, a second Rwandan genocidaire was arrested, Jacques Mungwarere. Canada has specialized war crimes units both with the federal police and the Department of Justice.

---

171 See Mandiaye Niang, "The Senegalese Legal Framework for the Prosecution of International Crimes", *JICJ*, 2009, vol. 7, no. 5, 1047-1062.

172 For an assessment see 16 May 2008 report by Human Rights Watch at http://hrw.org/english/docs/2008/05/14/senegal8826.htm

173 See Canada's Program on Crimes Against Humanity and War Crimes, Tenth Annual Report 2006-2007, http://www.cbsa-asfc.gc.ca/security-securite/wc-cg/wc-cg2007-eng.html, under "Criminal Investigation and Prosecution".

174 See for a comment, Fannie Lafontaine, "Canada's Crimes against Humanity and War Crimes Act on Trial: An Analysis of the *Munyaneza* Case", *JICJ*, 2010, vol. 8, no. 1, 269-288.

In the *United States*[175] Charles "Chuckie" Taylor, the son of Liberia's ex-president Charles Taylor was charged with torture on 6 December 2006. He was the leader of the elite Anti-Terrorist Unit (ATU) from approximately 1997 through at least 2002 when that unit committed torture,[176] including various violent assaults, rape, beating people to death and burning civilians alive.[177] He was convicted on 30 October 2008 and sentenced to 97 years incarceration on 9 January 2009.[178]

2.5.4. Australia

An Australian court ordered the extradition of Dragan Vasiljković to Croatia on 12 April 2007. He was born in Belgrade in 1954, but moved to

175 The US has already arrested 26 Serbs, one person from Bosnia, one Argentine, one person from El Salvador and a Peruvian for involvement in atrocities in their homeland, but these prosecutions are launched under its immigration legislation for immigration fraud, three of which have been deported; see testimony of Eli Rosenbaum, Director, Office of Special Investigations, Department of Justice, before the Subcommittee on Crime, Terrorism, and Homeland Security of the US House of Representatives Committee on the Judiciary, re Genocide and the Rule of Law, 23 October 2007 (http://judiciary.house.gov/committeestructure.aspx?committee=6) . On 23 April 2009, Lazare Kobagaya was arrested based on an indictment for unlawfully obtaining American citizenship in 2006 and fraud and misuse of an alien registration card as he had participated in the 1994 Rwandan genocide.

176 He was charged with this crime because he was a US national although US law (http://www.gpoaccess.gov/USCODE/index.html) does provide universal jurisdiction for *torture* (US Code, Title 18, Chapter 113C, section 2340A(b)) as it does as of 21 December 2007 for *genocide* (Chapter 50A, section 1091, as amended by Genocide Accountability Act of 2007), but not for *war crimes* (Chapter 118, section 2441(b), except for the war crime of child recruitment (by virtue of the Child Soldiers Accountability Act of 2008 which came into force on 3 October 2008 and adds section 2442 to Title 18, Chapter 118) and for trials by Military Commissions of unlawful enemy combatants, see Military Commissions Act of 17 October 2006, sections 948d(a) and 950v, amending Title 10, Chapter 47; war crimes trials under the latter provision against inmates at Guantanamo Bay started on 21 July 2008); there is no provision for *crimes against humanity*.

177 See http://hrw.org/english/docs/2006/12/06/usint14777.htm.

178 On 5 February 2010, a US federal court ordered a final judgment of 22 million dollars against him to be paid to five torture victims. The order issued by the judge outlined the multiple forms of torture, cruel, inhuman, or degrading punishment or treatment, arbitrary arrest and prolonged detention to which the plaintiffs were subjected, and recognizes the past, present and future physical and mental suffering those abuses inflicted.

Australia in 1969 and became an Australian citizen. In 1991, as the Serbian-controlled army sought to quench the Croatian bid for independence, he returned to Serbia to take part in the fighting. Dragan Vasiljković, or "Kapetan Dragan", as he was called, was in charge of a training camp for paramilitaries near Knin, and he also founded a paramilitary group called the "Kninjas" or the "Red Berets", which allegedly took part in war crimes. He is accused of having tortured and killed captured members of the Croatian army and police in the region of Knin and Benkovac in June and July 1991.[179] The extradition was confirmed on 4 February 2009 by the Federal Court of Australia and is now before the High Court.

As well, there is an investigation underway by the Australian Federal Police into the possible role of mining company Anvil Mining Limited in facilitating a military offensive in the town of Kilwa in the Democratic Republic of the Congo.[180]

2.6. Trends and Legal Issues

2.6.1. Trends

A number of important trends can be found in the application of international criminal justice in the last fifteen years.

The first one, which applies to both international and domestic practice, is the fact that 15 erstwhile[181] and one sitting[182] heads of state have been indicted or prosecuted and sentenced for international

[179] See http://www.trial-ch.org/en/trial-watch/profile/db/facts/dragan_vasiljkovic_478.html.

[180] See Joanna Kyriakakis, "Australian Prosecution of Corporations for International Crimes, the Potential of the Commonwealth Criminal Code", *JICJ*, 2007, vol. 5, no. 4, 809-826; see also footnotes 104-105.

[181] The case of Radovan Karadžić, who was the war-time president of the Republika Srpska in Bosnia and Herzegovina in the early nineties and who was indicted by the ICTY in 1995 and arrested on 21 July 2008, is not included in this number, nor is Khieu Samphan, the former president of Democratic Kampuchea, who is being investigated by the ECCC in Cambodia but has not been made the subject of an indictment yet.

[182] The ICC Pre-Trial Chamber issued a warrant for arrest for Omar al-Bashir, the president of Sudan on 4 March 2009.

crimes.[183] On the international level, the ICTR sentenced the prime minister of Rwanda during the 1994 genocide, Jean Kambanda, to life imprisonment in 1998.[184] President Slobodan Milošević of the former Yugoslavia was indicted by the ICTY in 1999 and 2001 and put on trial in 2002, which would have been completed if he had not died while in custody during the proceedings in 2006.[185] The Sierra Leone Special Court indicted the former president of Liberia, Charles Taylor in 2006 and his trial has started in early 2008[186] in The Hague while another hybrid tribunal, the Special Court of Iraq, completed proceedings against Saddam Hussein in 2006 resulting in his execution the same year[187].

In addition, there have eleven attempts at the domestic level to take action against former heads of state since 1992.[188]

In South and Central America, Argentina has indicted three former presidents, namely Isabel Perón, Jorge Videla (who is also the subject of arrest warrants from Italy and Germany) and Reynaldo Bignone, while Chile did the same with Augusto Pinochet, Peru with Alberto Fujimori, Uruguay with Gregorio Alvarez and Bolivia with Gonzalo Sánchez de Lozada. In Mexico, former president Luis Echeverria was tried for the commission of genocide, albeit while at the time in his capacity as Minis-

183 While two others have been tried (Pol Pot in Cambodia) or indicted (Bordaberry in Uruguay) for regular crimes by domestic courts; for more background see Héctor Olásolo, *Criminal Responsibility of Senior Political and Military Leaders for Genocide, Crimes against Humanity and War Crimes: with Special Reference to the Rome Statute and the Statute and Case Law of the Ad Hoc Tribunals*, Hart, 2008; Héctor Olásolo, *The Criminal Responsibility of Senior Political and Military Leaders as Principals to International Crimes*, Hart, 2009; Ellen L. Lutz (ed.), *Prosecuting Heads of State*, Cambridge, 2009 and Héctor Olásolo, *The Criminal Responsibility of Senior Political and Military Leaders as Principals to International Crimes*, Hart, 2010.

184 ICTR 97-23-S, 4 September 1998, upheld by the Appeals Chamber on 19 October 2000, ICTR 97-23-A.

185 See http://www.un.org/icty/cases-e/cis/smilosevic/cis-slobodanmilosevic.pdf.

186 See http://www.sc-sl.org/taylor-timeline.pdf.

187 See http://www.trial-ch.org/en/trial-watch/profile/db/facts/saddam_hussein-al-majid-al-tikriti_125.html.

188 While international institutions can bring sitting heads of state to justice, national states can only do so against former heads of state according to the International Court of Justice in the Democratic Republic of the Congo versus Belgium case, decided 14 February 2003 (http://www.icj-cij.org/docket/index.php?p1=3&p2=3&k=36&case=121&code=cobe&p3=4).

ter of the Interior, but he was acquitted in 2007. As well, the former president of Guatemala, Efrain Rios Montt, has been indicted by Spain and the former president of Uruguay, Juan Bordaberry, by Italy.

In Africa, Mengistu Haile Mariam of Ethiopia was sentenced to death in May 2008, but he remains at large in Zimbabwe. Senegal, after proceedings had already begun in Belgium, has put legislation in place to indict the former president of Chad, Hissène Habré.

Of the action taken against the 16 former state leaders, nine have been put on trial. Of these nine, five (Kambanda, Saddam Hussein, Mengistu, Fujimori and Alvarez) were convicted while two proceedings (Taylor and Bignone) are ongoing, one person died during his trial (Milošević) and another was acquitted (Echeverria). The trials of the other seven persons have not been commenced yet; of these proceedings, one has been permanently suspended because of the death of the suspect (Pinochet), two have been temporarily suspended as a result of non-compliance of extradition requests by other countries (Peron by Spain and Montt by Guatemala) even though they were indicted, in one case an indictment has not been issued even though urged to do so by an international institution (in Senegal for the Habré case) while in the remaining three cases indictments have been issued (Videla, Bordaberry and Lozada).

In addition, there is some anecdotal evidence that other heads of state might be adjusting their behaviour albeit after the fact as was the case when president of Suharto of Indonesia decided not to travel to Switzerland for medical treatment during the Pinochet extradition proceedings in the United Kingdom out of fear that he might be indicted as well while in Europe.

A second encouraging trend is the fact that there have been some proceedings against corporate players, albeit most have not been successful in the end. While the prosecution of corporate executives is not a new phenomenon as there had already been prosecutions of this kind after the Second World War against German corporate officials, including by the International Military Tribunal in Nuremberg[189], the international and hybrid tribunals have not ventured into this area so far.

[189] Gustav Krupp von Bohlen und Halbach was indicted but did not stand trial during the IMT proceedings due to mental illness. Other trials carried out against industrialists included the Krupp (Law Reports of Trials of War Criminals, Volume X, 69), Flick

On the domestic front there have been two convictions in the Netherlands for corporate executives for providing weapons to the Charles Taylor regime in Liberia (the van Kouwenhoven case) and for selling precursors for chemical weapons to the Saddam Hussein regime in Iraq (the van Anraat case). Both were convicted and received substantial prison sentences of 12 and 17 years respectively in 2005 and 2007, although the former was acquitted by an appeal court in 2008. In the DRC during the Kilwa trial both Congolese soldiers and three executives of the mining company Anvil were charged for war crimes but eventually acquitted in 2007[190]; this same incident is being investigated in Australia. As well, two executives of the French oil company TotalFinaElf, Hervé Madeo and Thierry Desmarest, have been indicted in both France and Belgium in 2002 for involvement for crimes against humanity in Burma in recent years; the proceedings in Belgium came to an end in 2008.

Although it might be difficult for international institutions to hold corporations themselves responsible for breaches of international criminal law (it is for instance explicitly forbidden in the Rome Statute[191]), it is clear that the human actors representing such corporations are not immune from the reaches of this area of the law.[192] As well, the fact that

(Law Reports of Trials of War Criminals, Volume IX, 1), I.G. Farben (Law Reports of Trials of War Criminals, Volume X, 1), Zyklon B (Law Reports of Trials of War Criminals, Volume I, 93) and the Roechling (Law Reports of Trials of War Criminals, Volume X, 56-57) trials.

190 The trial has been severely and widely criticized. Two of the more poignant commentaries are that of the United Nations High Commissioner of Human Rights of 4 July 2007 (http://www.unhchr.ch/huricane/huricane.nsf/0/9828B052BBC32B08C125730E004019C4?opendocument) and the detailed report by the NGO Global Witness of 17 July 2007 (http://www.globalwitness.org/media_library_detail.php/560/en/kilwa _trial_a_denial_of_justice).

191 Article 25.1.

192 See on this issue A. Reggio, "Aiding and betting In International Law: The Responsibility of Corporate Agents and Businessmen for 'Trading With The Enemy of Mankind'", *International Criminal Law Review*, 2005, vol. 5, 623-696; Jonathan Clough, "Punishing the Parent: Corporate Criminal Complicity in Human Rights Abuses" *Brooklyn Journal of International Law*, 2008, vol. 33, 899; Daniel Leader "Business and Human Rights - Time to Hold Companies to Account", in *International Criminal Law Review*, 2008, vol. 9, no. 2, pp. 447-462; Ronald Slye, "Corporations, Veils, and International Criminal Liability", *Brooklyn Journal of International Law*, 2008, vol. 33, 955; W. Cory Wanless, "Corporate Liability for International Crimes under Canada's Crimes Against Humanity and War Crimes Act", *JICJ*, 2009, vol. 7, no. 1, 201; Andrew Clapham, "Extending International Criminal Law beyond the Individual to

criminal liability can be extended to these players is becoming part of the recent mantra that corporations are urged to ascribe to, namely the notion of corporate social responsibility or CSR. A number of international standards are being developed to implement the general rules of corporate behaviour, especially in less developed areas of the world.[193]

The combination of taking action against both the leadership, including heads of state or leaders of non-governmental militia (as was done by the ICC in the cases of the LRA leadership in Uganda[194] and the four indictments for the situation in the DRC[195]), and the purveyors of the means to carry out international crimes sends out a powerful message that the international community understands the complex forces involved in carrying out these crimes and it is willing to take action against both direct and indirect participants.

2.6.2. Legal Issues

There are a number of legal issues arising out of the domestic efforts to bring perpetrators of serious human rights violations to justice, which require some further exploration.

2.6.2.1. Universal Jurisdiction

The first one is the issue of *universal jurisdiction*. While this type of jurisdiction has been available for domestic criminal investigations for international crimes since the early 1950s as a result of the Eichmann case in Israel[196], most countries, even after implementing the Rome Statute,

Corporations and Armed Opposition Groups", *JICJ*, 2008, vol. 6, no. 5, 899-926; and Jennifer A. Zerk, *Multinationals and Corporate Social Responsibility: Limitations and Opportunities in International Law*, Cambridge, 2006, as well as the International Commission of Jurists (ICJ) Expert Panel on Corporate Complicity in International Crimes, http://www.icj.org/IMG/June_06_Update.pdf and http://www .business-humanrights.org/Updates/Archive/ICJPaneloncomplicity, as well as the website "Business and International Crimes" at http://www.fafo.no/liabilities /index.htm.

193 See for instance http://www.cebcglobal.org/index.php?/knowledge/corporate-social-responsibility/, http://www.voluntaryprinciples.org/, http://eitransparency.org/, and http://www.international.gc.ca/trade-agreements-accords-commerciaux/ds/csr-strategy-rse-stategie.aspx.

194 See http://www.icc-cpi.int/library/cases/ICC-02-04-01-05-53_English.pdf.

195 See http://www.icc-cpi.int/cases/RDC.html.

196 *International Law Reports*, vol. 36, no. 1.

have opted for a limited type of jurisdiction whereby the presence of a perpetrator in the country carrying out the criminal investigation is required[197]. While presence is usually not defined in such statutes, some countries have declined to take action where such presence is of a short duration such as a temporary visit and insist on a more permanent type of presence. This decision is usually made based on general prosecutorial discretion rather than addressing the type of presence.[198]

However, the notion of universal jurisdiction where no link at all is required between the state initiating investigations or prosecutions and the perpetrator of international crimes – called universal jurisdiction in absentia – has gained some currency in Europe in the last 15 years.

In 1993 Belgium enacted a law to deal with the punishment of grave breaches of the Geneva Conventions under which civil petitioners could bring cases where no territorial link existed between the crimes and Belgium. This law did result in prosecutions of some Rwandans involved in the genocide, but also included complaints against Fidel Castro of Cuba, Ariel Sharon of Israel, Yasser Arafat of the PLO and Tommy Franks, Commander in Chief of the American-British Coalition forces in the war in Iraq in 2003. In 2003, the original law was amended to require a territorial link between Belgium and the perpetrator while also limiting the ability of private persons to initiate cases and providing the public prosecutor discretion over the handling of a case.[199]

[197] See Judgment of the ECHR in the "Case of Jorgic v. Germany", Application no. 74613/01, 12 July 2007, paragraph 53 for European examples. A notable exception is New Zealand where the legislation does not contain this restriction; see article 8 of its International Crimes and International Criminal Court Act 2000.

[198] For instance for Germany, see Ruth Rissing-van Saan, "The German Federal Supreme Court and the Prosecution of International Crimes Committed in the Former Yugoslavia", *JICJ*, 2005, vol. 3, no. 2, 381-399 and Salvatore Zappalà, "The German Federal Prosecutor's Decision not the Prosecute a Former Uzbek Minister, Missed Opportunity or Prosecutorial Wisdom?", *op. cit.*, 602-622 while for Canada, see the Kunlan Zhang case, http://decisions.fct-cf.gc.ca/en/2006/2006fc276/2006fc276.html, paragraph 6 at the trial level and http://decisions.fca-caf.gc.ca/en/2007/2007fca201/2007fca201.html at the appeal level. In the Netherlands jurisdiction was even denied in a situation involving genocide where neither the victim nor the perpetrator had Dutch nationality, namely in the Mpambara case.

[199] See Damien Vandermeersch, "Prosecuting International Crimes in Belgium", *JICJ*, 2005, vol. 3, no. 2, 400-421.

The choice of country for universal jurisdiction *in absentia* since the changes in Belgium in 2003 has become Spain. Traditionally, the courts in Spain had required one of the traditional links between Spain and the perpetrator of international crimes, which was found mostly in the passive nationality principle where the victims of the crimes had included Spanish nationals.[200] But this changed in 2005 when the Spanish Constitutional Tribunal overturned lower courts decisions in the Guatemala case and allowed universal jurisdiction *in absentia* by interpreting Spanish jurisdiction broadly for legal provisions aimed at combating international impunity.[201] As a result, in addition to the indictments issued with respect to Guatemala, investigations have now been opened in 13 other cases involving situations in China, the US, Iraq, Rwanda, Occupied Palestine Territories, Western Sahara and Chile. This wide interpretation of universal jurisdiction was curtailed in 2009 both by the higher courts in two instances and by the legislator which amended the Organic Law of the Judiciary limiting jurisdiction to those offences committed by or against Spaniards, or where the perpetrators are in Spain, but this law only applies to prospective investigations.

2.6.2.2. Genocide

The second legal issue concerns the interpretation of the crime of *genocide*. The 1948 Genocide Convention limits the parameters of the victim groups to only four, namely belonging to a national, ethnical, racial or religious group. This characterization did not change for any of the international institutions such as the ICTY, ICTR, SLSC or ECCC and although during the ICC negotiations there were calls to open this part of the definition, article 6 of the Rome Statute remains faithful to the original definition.

Domestic legislators or judicial authorities have had no such compunctions. On the legislative side the following affected groups in the

200 See Christian Tomuschat, "Issues of Universal Jurisdiction in the *Scilingo* Case", see *supra* note 135; Alicia Gil Gil, "The Flaws of the *Scilingo* Judgment", see *supra* note 135; Giulia Pinzauti, "An Instance of Reasonable Universality: The *Scilingo* Case", see *supra* note 135.

201 See Roht-Arriaza, "Guatemala Genocide Case, Spanish Constitutional Tribunal decision on universal jurisdiction over genocide claims", see *supra* note 140, 207-213; Ascensio, "The Spanish Constitutional Tribunal's Decision in *Guatemalan Generals*: Unconditional Universality is Back", see *supra* note 140, 586-594.

domestic genocide definition have been added: "political, union or a group with its identity based in reasons of gender, sexual orientation, culture, social, age, disability or health" (Uruguay); "gender, sexual orientation, age, health and conscience" (Ecuador); "any group that is defined by an arbitrary characteristic" (Republic of the Congo); "political groups and population transfer or dispersion" (Ethiopia[202]) or even replaced the traditional definition of groups with "an identifiable group of persons", as was done in Canada[203].

Based on broad definitions of the term group, national courts have determined that the following situations amounted to genocide, in addition to the 1994 genocide in Rwanda and the Srebrenica massacre in the former Yugoslavia in July 1995[204]: the dirty war in Argentina between 1976 and 1983 (by Argentine courts); a 1968 massacre in Mexico City which left between 200 and 300 students dead (by a Mexican court); a 2003 killing of more than 80 people in Bolivia (by a Bolivian judicial authority); the crimes committed by the Derg in Ethiopia between 1977 and 1991 (by Ethiopian courts); the Anfal campaign against Iraqi Kurds in 1988 (by the Iraqi Special Court and by a Dutch trial court but the latter overruled by an appeal court); the human rights violations against indigenous people in Guatemala in 1982-83 (by Spanish courts); the occupation of Tibet by China since 1951 (by a Spanish court); and other events amounting to ethnic cleansing in the former Yugoslavia outside Srebrenica (by the war crimes chamber of the Court of Bosnia and Herzegovina and by German courts although in the latter two of the four cases overruled the finding on appeal).[205]

It would appear that the crime of genocide was initially used in a number of instances as a result of the fact that the police and prosecutors felt strongly that perpetrators of very serious crimes should be brought to

[202] See Firew K. Tiba, "The Mengistu Trial in Ethiopia", see *supra* note 84, 513-528.

[203] Crimes against Humanity and War Crimes Act, sections 4 and 6, http://laws.justice.gc.ca/en/showtdm/cs/C-45.9.

[204] These are the only genocides recognized by the international tribunals, namely the ICTR for Rwanda and the ICTY and the International Court of Justice (in the case of Application of the Convention on the Prevention and Punishment of the Crime of Genocide (Bosnia and Herzegovina *v.* Serbia and Montenegro) of 26 February 2007 (http://www.icj-cij.org/docket/index.php?p1=3&p2=3&code=ybh&case=122&k=8d) for Srebrenica.

[205] See also *IJT*, Issue 77, 5 November 2007, pages 1-2.

justice, but were limited by the restrictions of their national laws as they applied to crimes against humanity or war crimes. Since most situations under consideration involved at most a civil war but not an international armed conflict, it was not possible to rely on the national implementation provisions related to the Geneva Conventions which do not provide for personal liability for war crimes committed in non-international armed conflicts. Similarly, crimes against humanity provisions could not be used since the national legislations did in most cases not regulate these crimes until the implementation of the Rome Statute in the new millennium.[206] However, now that national legislation and courts have expanded the number of groups which can be victims of genocide, it is possible to speak of an emerging rule of customary international law since the conclusion of the Rome Statute in 1998 which may have an effect not only on how other countries intend to make use of this expansion, but conceivably also an institution such as the ICC.

While there has been an expansion with respect to the group element of the crime of genocide, it appears that the high level *mens rea* of genocide, namely the specific intention to destroy these groups as developed by the ICTY, ICTR and now by the ICC (indirectly when it indicted two persons related to the Darfur situation[207]) will remain intact at the domestic level as well. While not entirely clear since the allegations dealt with complicity in genocide rather than direct involvement, it would appear that the decision in Mexico to acquit former president Echeverria and

206 See for instance Tomuschat, "Issues of Universal Jurisdiction in the *Scilingo* Case", see *supra* note 135, 1074-1081; Gil Gil, "The Flaws of the *Scilingo* Judgment", see *supra* note 135, 1082-1091; Pinzauti, "An Instance of Reasonable Universality: The *Scilingo* Case", see *supra* note 135, 1092-1105. In addition to the examples mentioned above for countries relying on universal jurisdiction, this approach was also used by the Court of Appeal for East Timor in the Armando dos Santos case, Case Number 16/2001, 9 September 2002, pages 19/20.

207 The two people were only charged with war crimes and crimes against humanity although the situation in Darfur has been characterized by the international community frequently as a genocide, see the decision to indict of 27 April 2007, http://www.icc-cpi.int/library/cases/ICC-02-05-01-07-1_English.pdf. More recently, however, the charges laid against the third person, Omar al-Bashir, on 14 July 2008 concerning the Darfur situation do include counts of genocide (http://www.icc-cpi.int/library/cases/ICC-02-05-152-ENG.pdf). They were not approved by the Pre-Trial Chamber on 4 March 2009 (http://www.icc-cpi.int/iccdocs/doc/doc639078.pdf), but remitted by the Appeals Chamber for re-consideration of this crime on 3 February 2010 (http://www.icc-cpi.int/iccdocs/doc/doc817795.pdf).

the decision not to find the Dutch businessman Van Anraat guilty of genocide charges were related to the mental requirement of genocide.[208] On the other hand, this element was present in the convictions for the Derg leadership in Ethiopia[209] and for Yugoslav soldiers convicted in Germany for this crime although in the latter situation ethnic cleansing below the threshold of actual killing was also considered genocide, a finding upheld by the European Court of Human Rights.[210]

2.6.2.3. Crimes Against Humanity

Until recently, very few domestic cases have dealt with *crimes against humanity*. The reason is that – especially in Europe – the notion of legality or retroactivity is a very important concept with the result that it has been impossible to charge this crime in situations that occurred before national legislation made provision for it, normally when implementing the Rome Statute since 2000. While imaginative prosecutors have been trying to resolve this problem by laying charges based on genocide and war crimes, it is not clear how many more cases could have been investigated especially in an extra-territorial context if crimes against humanity had been available.

As well, there has been little or no debate with respect to the possible use of crimes against humanity by applying article 15 of the 1966 International Covenant on Civil and Political Rights,[211] which states:

> 1. No one shall be held guilty of any criminal offence on account of any act or omission which did not constitute a

[208] Van der Wilt, "Genocide, Complicity in Genocide and International v. Domestic Jurisdiction: Reflections on the *van Anraat* case", see *supra* note 100, 239-257; see also the decision of the appeal court of 9 May 2007, Case number LJN BA4676, which can be found at http://zoeken.rechtspraak.nl/.

[209] Tiba, "The Mengistu Trial in Ethiopia", see *supra* note 84, 513-528.

[210] Rissing-van Saan, "The German Federal Supreme Court and the Prosecution of International Crimes Committed in the Former Yugoslavia", see *supra* note 198, 381-399; see also Judgment of the ECHR in the "Case of Jorgić v. Germany", Application no. 74613/01, 17 July 2007, paragraphs 103-116.

[211] See http://www.ohchr.org/english/law/ccpr.htm. The 1948 Universal Declaration of Human Rights contains a similar provision in article 11 as does the 1950 European Convention on Human Rights in article 7; for background information concerning this article, see Kenneth Gallant, *The Principle of Legality in International and Comparative Criminal Law*, Cambridge, 2009, pages 156-174.

> criminal offence, under national or international law, at the time when it was committed. Nor shall a heavier penalty be imposed than the one that was applicable at the time when the criminal offence was committed. If, subsequent to the commission of the offence, provision is made by law for the imposition of the lighter penalty, the offender shall benefit thereby;
>
> 2. Nothing in this article shall prejudice the trial and punishment of any person for any act or omission which, at the time when it was committed, was criminal according to the general principles of law recognized by the community of nations

The *travaux preparatoires* of this Covenant indicate that the term "according to the general principles of law recognized by the community of nations" in article 15(2) has the same meaning as customary international law.[212] Given the fact that crimes against humanity have been known to international criminal law since the judgment of the International Military Tribunal in Nuremberg in 1948 and considering the fact that this Covenant has been ratified by 160 countries it is somewhat surprising that no argument has made along the lines that crimes against humanity are part of domestic law from the time that a country has ratified the Covenant.[213]

---

212 See Marc J. Bossuyt and John P. Humphrey, *Guide to the Travaux Preparatoires of the International Covenant on Civil and Political Rights*, Kluwer, 1987, pages 330-333.

213 The connection between crimes against humanity and customary international law was discussed by a Spanish court in the Scilingo case and was criticized for doing so by Tomuschat, "Issues of Universal Jurisdiction in the *Scilingo* Case", see *supra* note 135, 1074-1081 and Gil Gil, "The Flaws of the *Scilingo* Judgment", see *supra* note 135, 1082-1091 but supported by Pinzauti, "An Instance of Reasonable Universality: The *Scilingo* Case", see *supra* note 135, 1092-1105. It could be argued that the European Court of Human Rights opened the door to this type of reasoning in its Judgment in the "Case of Jorgić v. Germany", Application no. 74613/01, paragraphs 100 and 106-109. Norway has overcome this issue of legality in its new legislation by allowing the retroactivity of international crimes if the underlying crime was known in Norwegian law in the past and the international crime was known in international law beforehand as well; however, this law was found to be unconstitutional by a criminal court of first instance. See also Ward N. Ferdinandusse, *Direct Application of International Criminal Law in National Courts*, TMC Asser Press, 2006, pages 224-268 and Kenneth Gallant, *The Principle of Legality in International and Comparative Criminal Law*, see *supra* note 211, pages 175-200; 352-410 and 411-424.

Recent decisions by the highest courts in Chile and Peru have held that crimes against humanity are not subject to statutes of limitation. This, according to the courts, is a norm set out in customary international law.

2.6.2.4. War Crimes

Regarding *war crimes*, most prosecutions charging this international crime have based their indictments on the grave breaches regime in the Geneva Conventions[214] with one interesting exception, namely the decisions of the Dutch courts (at both the trial and appeal levels) in two parallel cases involving the activities of two high officials of the KhAD in Afghanistan between 1979 and 1989.[215]

Since neither genocide (due to the fact situation did not allow for such a charge) nor crimes against humanity (due to legality concerns) charges were possible, the indictment was based on war crimes. The courts came to the conclusion that the armed conflict in Afghanistan at that time amounted to a non-international armed conflict so that the grave breaches regime was not applicable, but that common article 3 of the Geneva Conventions (which in a very abbreviated manner regulates the conduct during non-international armed conflicts) could be used to ascribe criminal liability to the two perpetrators.

This conclusion appears to be at odds with the development of the concept of individual criminal responsibility in non-international armed conflicts in other realms of international law.[216] The Geneva Conventions do not contain a provision similar to the grave breaches to enforce common article 3 on an individual level. As a matter of fact, Additional Proto-

---

214 See for instance Ward Ferdinandusse, "The Prosecution of Grave Breaches in National Courts", *JICJ*, 2009, Volume 7, Issue 4, 723-741.

215 See Guénaël Mettraux, "Dutch Courts' Universal Jurisdiction over Violations of Common Article 3 *qua* War Crimes", see *supra* note 96, 362-371 (and further discussion as a result of this article in *JICJ*, 2006, vol. 4, 878-889 with respect to the trial decision; see the decisions of the appeal court of 29 January 2007, Case numbers LJN AZ7147 and LJN AZ9365, and the decision of the Supreme Court of the Netherlands of 8 July 2008, Case number LJN BC7418, all of which can be found at http://zoeken.rechtspraak.nl/).

216 A similar problematic conclusion with respect to the specific war crime of collective punishments can be found in the decisions of the SLSC Trial Chamber in the AFRC case (SLSC-04-16-T, 30 June 2007, pages 206-209) and the CDF case (SLSC-04-14-T, 2 August 2007, pages 53-55).

col II, which regulated in 1977 in further detail the conduct during non-international armed conflicts, still did not contain such a provision. The ICTY Appeals Chamber came to the conclusion in 1995 in the Tadic case[217] that individual liability for such conflicts had become part of international criminal law for the time period of its jurisdiction, namely as of 1991, but it did not pronounce itself about situation between 1977 and 1991. In the domestic context, a study of the International Committee of the Red Cross in 2005 concluded that there was no evidence in customary international law for such a proposition before 1990.[218]

The Dutch appeals courts in their decisions declined to examine international jurisprudence on this point (or for that matter on the issue whether the conflict in Afghanistan could be described as an international non-international armed conflict given the involvement of international players in that situation along the lines of ICTY reasoning in the same Tadić decision or that of the International Court of Justice in the Bosnia and Herzegovina v. Serbia and Montenegro case[219]), but limits its reasoning by observing that national law can go beyond the confines of international law which is not prescriptive but rather provides a minimum standard to be followed.[220] As such, according to the court, the Dutch legislator was within its powers to extend its legal reach for individual liability beyond that of the grave breaches regime of the Geneva Conventions.[221]

217 See http://www.un.org/icty/tadic/appeal/decision-e/51002.htm.

218 Henkaerts and Doswald-Becks (eds.), *Customary International Humanitarian Law, Volume 1: Rules*, Cambridge, 2005, pages 552-554.

219 See http://www.icj-cij.org/docket/index.php?p1=3&p2=3&code=ybh&case=122&k=8d.

220 The liability for war crimes in non-international armed conflicts was already recognized in Dutch legislation in 1952 (see Henkaerts and Doswald-Becks (eds.), *Customary International Humanitarian Law, Volume II, Practice*, Cambridge, 2005, Part 2, page 3641, paragraphs 163-164); the Supreme Court of the Netherlands refers in paragraph 5.4.3 of its decision to the fact that this inclusion at that time was already very usual.

221 This was the same reasoning used by the Ethiopian court in the Mengistu case when extending the protected groups of genocide beyond the four mentioned in the Genocide Convention even though it could have convicted for crimes against humanity under Ethiopian law, see Tiba, "The Mengistu Trial in Ethiopia", *supra* note 84, 513-528, as well the reasoning of German courts and the European Court of Human Rights when extending the crimes of genocide to situations of ethnic cleansing, see Judgment of the ECHR in the "Case of Jorgić v. Germany", Application no. 74613/01, 12 July

2.7. Conclusion

International criminal justice is only one aspect of transitional justice[222] and by itself cannot ensure that a society will be able to leave a traumatic past behind for a peaceful and just future. Similarly, international criminal justice by itself cannot prevent future conflicts from occurring, not even in the sense that there is convincing evidence that sentencing by international and domestic institutions has a retributive or deterrent impact.[223] However, a similar criticism can be made to some extent of domestic criminal and penal systems and these systems have had hundreds of years to flourish and mature. As a minimum the international legal system should be given an equal opportunity to prove its worth.

In order for the international criminal justice system to make a robust contribution to transitional justice it would appear that a number of requirements should be met.

The first requirement is that as a legal system it needs to be internally consistent and predictable. When the main actors in this arena are either an international or hybrid tribunal it has not been a difficult task to main such consistency since the ICTY and ICTR were the first in the field, had enormous political influence, and were populated with prosecutors and judges of the highest calibre. Other international institutions found it easy to follow suit. For instance, the judicial decisions by the East Timor Special Panels and the Special Court of Sierra Leone have followed very closely the principles and parameters set down by the ICTY

2007, paragraphs 100-102; see also Harmen Van der Wilt, "Equal Standards? On the Dialectics between National Jurisdictions and the International Criminal Court", *International Criminal Law Review*, Volume 8, 2008, 229 at 254-263 for international legal reasons why national jurisdictions could depart from international criminal law concepts by international institutions.

222 Generally concerning transitional justice see: M. Cherif Bassiouni (ed.), *Post-Conflict Justice*, Ardsley, 2002; Naomi Roht-Arriaza and Javier Mariezcurrena, *Transitional Justice in the Twenty-first Century: Beyond Truth versus Justice*, Cambridge, 2006; Daniel Philpott (ed.), *The Politics of Past Evil: Religion, Reconciliation, and the Dilemmas of Transitional Justice*, Notre Dame, 2006; and E. Hughes, W. Schabas and C. Thakur (eds.), *Atrocities and International Accountability: Beyond Transitional Justice*, UN University Press, 2007.

223 See Drumbl, *Atrocity, Punishment and International Law*, see *supra* note 40, 149-173.

and ICTR when discussing international criminal law, especially its shared Appeals Chamber.

The situation has changed. Now that a large number of domestic players have entered the international justice arena there is a risk of unbridled and uncontrolled diversity. In itself diversity at the local level is not problematic since international law can and should take into account local conditions and customs. In addition, given the fact that international law still finds a great deal of its sources in domestic practice[224] eventually these state practices will have an effect on international law and therefore international institutions, especially in international criminal law where little state practice is required to create a new custom.[225] But this strong relationship between individual state practice and international custom in international criminal law creates an equally strong responsibility for states, now that they are engaging in this area of law, to ensure that they adhere to the basic principles of international criminal law as developed by the international institutions while still retaining the ability to infuse such principles with local content.

The fact that a number of states are of the view that the number of groups contained in the Genocide Convention and the Rome Statute do not accord anymore with modern realities and consequently have expanded on this number of groups is perfectly legitimate as long as other aspects of the crime of genocide, such as the requirement of specific intention or the destruction of a group, are not diluted and sacrificed on the altar of legal expedience. Some of the situations described by the various national courts as genocide appear to belong more to the category of crimes against humanity. From an international legal perspective it would be more astute to address the issue of retroactivity for crimes against humanity and customary international law than dispense with the essential elements of the crime of genocide.[226]

---

224 This can be both in treaty law where a multilateral convention gains more strength if more countries ratify such treaties and in customary international law where states are still a very important direct source of law.

225 See J. Rikhof, "Crimes against Humanity, Customary International Law and the International Tribunals for Bosnia and Rwanda", *National Journal of Constitutional Law*, 1996, vol. 6, 233-268.

226 For possible solutions, see for instance a report by Aegis Trust, "Enforcement of International Criminal Law", 20 February 2009 at http://www.aegistrust.org/index.php?option=com_content&task=view&id=803&Itemid=88.

Apart from issues regarding the possible problematic divergence of international criminal law, the fact that 43 countries have become involved in the prosecutions of perpetrators of international crimes in the last 15 years is very encouraging, especially the efforts of the 26 countries where such crimes occurred in the past. More than 10,000 perpetrators have been brought to justice in such countries compared to 145 persons convicted by the five international institutions and the 17 countries relying on universal jurisdiction combined.

This reality suggests the second requirement of a maturing international legal system, namely a logical division of labour which is already taking place in an amorphous manner, but which could benefit from higher levels of international policy decision-making and further co-operation between the various states and international institutions. Such a division of labour would be based on a dual complementarity approach. At the first level states with an ability to carry out meaningful prosecutions for war crimes, crimes against humanity and genocide should be responsible for doing so for crimes committed on their territory or by their nationals. Persons, who have fled such countries should be returned there either by employing the means of extradition or immigration remedies such as deportation. If a prosecution in such a country is not possible and a perpetrator is present in another country, the latter should rely on either passive or universal jurisdiction to take action against that perpetrator. At the highest level, that is, when the other two avenues are not possible, the ICC (being most likely the only institution at the international level as of a few years from now) could step in.[227]

Impunity is still often the norm for perpetrators involved in international crimes, but given the slow pace and the incremental approach in international law generally, the advances made by international criminal law, both from a legal perspective and in terms of impact on perpetrators, in the last 15 years have been nothing short of amazing. And indeed, there are now fewer places to hide.

227 See for examples of possible co-operation between the ICC and domestic jurisdictions, William Burke-White, "Proactive Complementarity: The International Criminal Court and National Courts in the Rome System of International Justice", *Harv. Int'l L.J.*, 2008, vol. 49, no. 1, 53, at 86-96 and 101-105; Van der Wilt, "Equal Standards? On the Dialectics between National Jurisdictions and the International Criminal Court", see *supra* note 221, at 271-272; and Carsten Stahn, "Complementarity: A Tale of Two Notions", *Criminal Law Forum*, 2008, vol. 19, 87 at 100-113.

Endnote

This chapter is limited to criminal prosecutions, including processes leading up to prosecutions, such as extradition, although other remedies with respect to the commission of war crimes, crimes against humanity and genocide are also being employed in a number of countries. In the United States, the Center for Justice and Accountability (CJA) has sued 16 individuals from 10 countries in civil courts for damages under the Alien Tort Statute (ATS) and the Torture Victim Protection Act (TVPA) (for more information, see http://www.cja.org/) as has the Center for Constitutional Rights (CCR, see http://ccrjustice.org/international-law-and-accountability). In addition, a number of asylum and immigrant receiving countries have used the 1951 Refugee Convention and it domestic immigration legislation to refuse refugee status or deported perpetrators of international crimes; see for instance results in this area in Canada in the Ninth Annual Report of its War Crimes Program at http://www.cbsa-asfc.gc.ca/security-securite/wc-cg/wc-cg2006-eng.html#app3; some of these countries such as Australia, New Zealand, Canada, the United Kingdom and the Netherlands have established specialized war crimes units for this purpose. For the application of some of the substantive law in this regard see Rikhof, "Complicity in International Criminal Law and Canadian Refugee Law", *JICJ*, 2006, vol. 4, 702-722. Lastly, some civil law suits have been filed against foreign states for involvement in international crimes, against corporations or against the United Nations, none of which have been successful to date (see the lawsuits against corporations in Canada such as the case of Bil'in v. Green Park in 2009 and in the U.S. the cases of Caterpillar, http://ccrjustice.org/files/Ninth Circuit Opinion 07.7.06.pdf, Talisman http://www.nysd.uscourts.gov/courtweb/pdf/D02NYSC/06-03562.PDF and http://caselaw.lp.findlaw.com/data2/circs/2nd/070016.pdf, Unocal http://www.earthrights.org/legal/unocal/, the latter of which resulted in a settlement for these and other cases against corporations in the United States, see Malone, "Enforcing International Criminal Law Violation with Civil Remedies: The U.S. Alien Tort Claims Act", presented at the 22nd International Conference of the International Society for the Reform of Criminal Law (http://www.isrcl.org/); for suits against governments, see the cases of Jones in the UK against Saudi Arabia, http://www.publications.parliament.uk/pa/ld200506/ldjudgmt/jd060614/jones-1.htm, and Bouzari in Canada against Iran, http://www.ontariocourts.on.ca/decisions/2004/june/bouzariC38295.htm; for the latter see Rikhof, Correspondents Report, *Yearbook of International Humanitarian Law*, 2003, vol. 6, 478, while in general see the website of the Canadian Center for International Justice, http://www.ccij.ca/programs/cases/index.php; for a case filed against the United Nations for not protecting the safe haven of Srebrenica in 1995 in the Netherlands, see http://news.bbc.co.uk/2/hi/europe/7500456.stm and case number LJN BD6795, which can be found at http://zoeken.rechtspraak.nl/). For an overview of the various means of bringing war criminals to justice see: Yves Beigbeder, *Judging War Criminals*, Macmillan, 1999; Mark Freeman and Gibran van Ert, *International Human Rights Law*, Irwin Law, 2004; and Yves Beigbeder, *International Justice against Impunity*, Martinus Nijhoff, 2005.

3

Complementarity: Contest or Collaboration?

Rod Rastan[*]

3.1. Introduction

Complementarity under the Rome Statute can be understood in two ways: as an admissibility principle governing case allocation between competing jurisdictions, and as a burden sharing principle for the consensual distribution of caseloads. Complementarity as admissibility posits the relationship between the ICC and States as a contest, leading one forum to exercise jurisdiction to the exclusion of the other. This is because the framework is case-specific: two forums cannot try the same case at once.

Complementarity as burden-sharing embraces a broader system-wide approach that promotes the concurrent assumption of jurisdiction by different forums. This is complementarity set against the problem of mass criminality, where the fear is not that the same person will be tried twice, but that the many will not be tried at all. It seeks to address the impunity gap created as a consequence of insufficient judicial coverage.

If admissibility focuses internally on the cases before the ICC, burden-sharing looks outward towards effecting universal compliance. Thus, predictably, the answer to the question, much like Niels Bohr's description of quantum phenomena, is both things at once, depending on the perspective adopted.[1] Both dimensions are necessary: limiting com-

[*] **Rod Rastan** is Legal Advisor at the Office of the Prosecutor of the International Criminal Court. The views expressed herein are solely the author's and do not necessarily reflect those of the Office of the Prosecutor or the ICC.

[1] On Niels Bohr and the origin of the term 'complementarity' to describe the paradox of particle-wave duality in the field of quantum mechanics see Mohamed El Zeidy, *The Principle of Complementarity in International Criminal Law: Origin, Development and Practice*, Martinus Nijhoff, 2008, 1-5. On the twin aspects of complementarity see generally Carsten Stahn, "Complementarity: A Tale of Two Notions", *Crim.L.F.*, 2008, vol. 19, 87-113; El Zeidy, *op. cit.*, 298-306; William Burke-White, "Proactive Complementarity: The International Criminal Court and National Courts in the Rome System of International Justice", *Harv. Int'l L.J.*, 2008, vol. 49, 53-108.

plementarity to a contest paradigm will prevent the realisation of the statutory goal to put an end to impunity and thereby contribute to the prevention of crimes.

This chapter provides an overview of complementarity as informed by the Court's judicial pronouncements and prosecutorial policies, examining how models of contests and collaboration interact. This is intended to serve as an introduction to the examination by other contributors to this volume of the 'horizontal' application of complementarity to guide the relationship between national criminal jurisdictions.

3.2. Complementarity as Contest

As an admissibility principle, complementarity forms part of the statutory scheme foreseen in article 17 for determining whether a particular case should be heard before the Court.[2] For this purpose, complementarity assumes the existence of an interested State or States with a competing claim to jurisdiction with the Court.[3] The assessment of complementarity as admissibility is designed to answer the question of who should exercise jurisdiction where two or more forums are seized of a case. As Pre-Trial Chamber II has observed "admissibility is the criterion allowing the Court to identify which cases, among those in respect of which it has jurisdiction concurrently with one or more national judicial systems, it is appropriate for it to investigate and prosecute under the complementarity

[2] The ICC Appeals Chamber has characterized the Statute's admissibility as "referable in the first place to complementarity (article 17(1)(a) to (b)), in the second to *ne bis in idem* (articles 17(1)(c), 20) and thirdly to the gravity of the offence (article 17(1)(d))"; *Prosecutor v. Thomas Lubanga Dyilo,* Judgment on the Appeal of Mr. Thomas Lubanga Dyilo against the Decision on the Defence Challenge to the Jurisdiction of the Court pursuant to article 19(2)(a) of the Statute of 3 October 2006, ICC–01/04–01/06-772, 14 December 2006, para. 23. Strictly speaking, the first three limbs of article 17(1) collectively embrace complementarity, since all three scenarios are set against the Court's powers to determine the genuineness of national proceeding *vis-à-vis* the case brought before the ICC, namely: cases that are subject to ongoing investigations or prosecutions (sub-paragraph (a)); cases that have been investigated, but not a decision has been taken not to prosecute (sub-paragraph (b)); and cases where prosecution has been completed (sub-paragraph (c)). Although *ne bis in idem* is referenced in 17(1)(c), it is dealt with proper under article 20.

[3] Jeffrey Bleich, "Complementarity", *Nouvelles Études Pénales*, 1997, vol. 13, 231. A ruling on admissibility may be prompted by a State with jurisdiction, an accused person, the Prosecutor or the Court on its own initiative; Article 19, ICC Statute.

regime".[4] According to the Statute, the rule by which such conflicts of jurisdictions are to be resolved is that the Court should declare a case before itself inadmissible in deference to genuine domestic proceedings in relation to that same case.[5] Accordingly, a case before the ICC may proceed in one of two circumstances: (i) where there is an absence of relevant domestic proceedings, or (ii) where such domestic proceedings are vitiated by an inability or unwillingness to conduct them genuinely.[6] The preference for genuine domestic proceedings applies irrespective of how a situation is brought before the Court, whether by the Prosecutor acting *proprio motu*, by a State or by the Security Council.[7] It coincides with the preamble affirmation "*Recalling* that it is the duty of every State to exercise its criminal jurisdiction over those responsible for international crimes".[8] At the same time, it is the Court that is vested with exclusive

[4] *Prosecutor v. Joseph Kony et al.*, Decision on the admissibility of the case under article 19(1) of the Statute, ICC-02/04-01/05-377, 10 March 2009, para. 46.

[5] The term "genuine" was considered during negotiations of the Statute as the least subjective from a series of options including 'diligently', 'good faith', 'effectively' and 'sufficient grounds'; John Holmes, "The Principle of Complementarity", in Roy Lee (ed.), *The International Criminal Court, The Making of the Rome Statute: Issues, Negotiations, Results*, Springer, 1999, 49.

[6] As confirmed by the Appeals Chamber, "in considering whether a case is inadmissible under article 17(1)(a) and (b) of the Statute, the initial questions to ask are (1) whether there are ongoing investigations or prosecutions, or (2) whether there have been investigations in the past, and the State having jurisdiction has decided not to prosecute the person concerned. It is only when the answers to these questions are in the affirmative that one has to look to the second halves of sub-paragraphs (a) and (b) and to examine the question of unwillingness and inability. Accordingly, an absence of relevant domestic proceedings will render a case before the ICC admissible, subject to an assessment of gravity; *Prosecutor v. Germain Katanga and Mathieu Ngudjolo Chui,* Judgment on the Appeal of Mr. Germain Katanga against the Oral Decision of Trial Chamber II of 12 June 2009 on the Admissibility of the Case, ICC-01/04-01/07-1497, 25 September 2009, para. 78; Darryl Robinson, "The Mysterious Mysteriousness of Complementarity", *Criminal Law Forum*, 2010, vol. 21, 67-102.

[7] The referral of a situation by the Security Council does not alter the basic framework of the complementarity regime. The only exemption under is the non-applicability of article 18. Thus, the Security Council cannot circumvent the complementarity thresholds of article 17, *e.g.*, by declaring that a State is unwilling or unable to genuinely investigate or prosecute: such a finding would be merely indicative and could not bind the ICC.

[8] Preamble, para. 6, ICC Statute.

authority to rule on the question of forum allocation.[9] This assessment is ongoing: made on the basis of the underlying facts as they exist at the time,[10] and potentially subject to revision based on any change to those facts.[11]

As required by articles 15 and 53(1), complementarity must also be assessed at the stage before an investigation is launched in order to ensure the efficient allocation of judicial resources and to pre-emptively avoid future challenges.[12] Because at this stage a case will not yet have been formed in the sense of specific incidents, crimes and identified suspects, the assessment is predictive. Hence, the Office of the Prosecutor must at this stage consider the potential cases that would likely arise from an investigation into the situation, which can for example be construed in the light of its stated prosecutorial strategy of focusing on those who appear to bear the greatest responsibility for the most serious crimes.[13] PTC II in authorising the Prosecutor's *proprio motu* investigation into the Situation in the Republic of Kenya thus framed the parameters of such potential cases as: "(i) the groups of persons involved that are likely to be the focus of an investigation for the purpose of shaping the future case(s); and (ii) the crimes within the jurisdiction of the Court allegedly committed during the incidents that are likely to be the focus of an investigation for the purpose of shaping the future case(s)".[14] The same considerations apply for the assessment of gravity at this stage.[15]

---

9 *Prosecutor v. Joseph Kony et al.*, Decision on the admissibility of the case under article 19(1) of the Statute, ICC-02/04-01/05-377, 10 March 2009, paras. 45, 51.

10 *Prosecutor v. Germain Katanga and Mathieu Ngudjolo Chui,* Judgment on the Appeal of Mr. Germain Katanga against the Oral Decision of Trial Chamber II of 12 June 2009 on the Admissibility of the Case, ICC-01/04-01/07-1497, 25 September 2009, para. 56.

11 *Ibid*; *Prosecutor v. Kony et al.*, Judgment on Admissibility Appeal by Ad-Hoc Defence, ICC-02/04-01/05-408 OA3, 16 September 2009, para. 85. See also article 19(4)-(5) and 19(10), ICC Statute.

12 Articles 15 and 53(1), ICC Statute, Rule 48, ICC RPE. See also article 18.

13 *Prosecutorial Strategy 2009-2012* (ICC-OTP 2010).

14 *Situation in the Republic of Kenya*, Decision Pursuant to Article 15 of the Rome Statute on the Authorization of an Investigation into the Situation in the Republic of Kenya, Case No. ICC-01/09-19, 31 March 2010, paras. 50 and 183.

15 *Ibid*, para.188.

The ICC complementarity regime is often contrasted with that of the ICTY and ICTR with the assertion that the principle of primacy exemplified by the *ad hoc* Tribunals has been reversed.[16] However, this confuses the issue of admissibility with that of primacy. Under the Rome Statute, while States retain *primary responsibility* for the investigation and prosecution of core crimes, once a case has been found admissible before the Court it is the ICC that has primacy over any concurrent domestic proceedings with respect to the same case. Had the Rome Statute created the reverse of the *ad hoc* Tribunals domestic primacy would have resulted in national judges entering determinative decisions on forum allocation, with the power to overrule a contrary finding of the ICC. Instead, the Rome Statute establishes the competence of the ICC judges to review the *bone fides* of national proceedings and, moreover, empowers the Court to recall cases previously deferred where it deems this appropriate.[17] Thus, while complementarity reflects the *primary*

---

16 The ICC Appeals Chamber, *e.g.*, has referred to "the primacy of domestic proceedings vis-à-vis the International Criminal Court"; *Prosecutor v. Germain Katanga and Mathieu Ngudjolo Chui,* Judgment on the Appeal of Mr. Germain Katanga against the Oral Decision of Trial Chamber II of 12 June 2009 on the Admissibility of the Case, ICC-01/04-01/07-1497, 25 September 2009, para. 85. See also Mireille Delmas-Marty, "The ICC and the Interaction of International and National Legal Systems", in Antonio Cassese, Paola Gaeta, John R.W.D. Jones (eds.), *The Rome Statute of the International Criminal Court: A Commentary*, Oxford, 2002, 1916; Bartram Brown, "Primacy or Complementarity: Reconciling the Jurisdiction of National Courts and International Criminal Tribunals", *Yale Journal Int'l L*, 1998, vol. 23, 386; Mohamed El Zeidy, "The Principle of Complementarity: A New Machinery to Implement International Criminal Law", *Mich. J. Int'l L.*, 2002, vol. 23, 887-889; Stahn, see *supra* note 1, p. 91 and pp. 94-96. Compare Federica Gioia, "State Sovereignty, Jurisdiction, and 'Modern' International Law: The Principle of Complementarity in the International Criminal Court", *Leiden Journal of International Law* (*LJIL*), 2006, vol. 19; Frederic Megret, "Why Would States Want to Join the ICC? A Theoretical Exploration Based on the Legal Nature of Complementarity", in Jann Kleffner and Gerben Kor (eds.) *Complementarity Views on Complementarity*, Asser Press, 2006, 23; Héctor Olásolo, "The Lack of Attention to the Distinction between Situations and Cases in National Laws on Co-operation with the International Criminal Court with Particular Reference to the Spanish Case", *LJIL*, 2007, vol. 20, 193–205.

17 As Pre-Trial Chamber II has observed: "once the jurisdiction of the Court is triggered, it is for the latter and not for any national judicial authorities to interpret and apply the provisions governing the complementarity regime and to make a binding determination on the admissibility of a given case", a function which it recalls has been labelled "the 'fundamental strength' of the principle of complementarity"; ICC-02/04-01/05-377, 10 March 2009, para. 45.

responsibility of States, and the *preference* for genuine domestic proceedings, it does not enshrine their primacy.[18]

3.2.1. Unwilling or Unable

Where there is a concurrent exercise of jurisdiction over a case at the international and national level, the judges of the ICC will be required to enter an assessment as to the genuineness of the domestic proceeding in question. The criterion by which the Court is to enter this determination is set against two tests: unwillingness and inability.[19]

Although there is a wealth of commentary analysing the manner in which the Court should engage in its assessment of unwillingness and inability, the Court has only had limited resort to cases of contested juris-

---

18 The *dicta* of the ICTY Appeals Chamber on the pre-requisite of primacy for the effective functioning of the Tribunal should be understood in this light, since the ICC judges posses in equal measure the competence to determine forum allocation over the objection of a State, based on an assessment of genuineness: "Indeed, when an international tribunal such as the present one is created, it must be endowed with primacy over national courts. Otherwise, human nature being what it is, there would be a perennial danger of international crimes being characterised as "ordinary crimes" (Statute of the International Tribunal, art. 10, para. 2(a)), or proceedings being "designed to shield the accused", or cases not being diligently prosecuted (Statute of the International Tribunal, art. 10, para. 2(b)). If not effectively countered by the principle of primacy, any one of those stratagems might be used to defeat the very purpose of the creation of an international criminal jurisdiction, to the benefit of the very people whom it has been designed to prosecute", *Prosecutor v. Dusko Tadić*, IT-94-1-AR72, Decision on the Defence Motion for Interlocutory Appeal on Jurisdiction (2 October 1995), para. 58. Broadly speaking complementarity is a neutral notion referring to the existence of concurrent jurisdictions: primacy is not *in opposition* to complementarity, but merely describes one way by which conflicts between complementary forums are to be resolved; see Fausto Pocar, "Completion or Continuation Strategy? Appraising Problems and Possible Developments in Building the Legacy of the ICTY", *JICJ*, 2008, vol. 6, 655-665; Gioia, see *supra* note 16, 1115-7; Mohamed El Zeidy, "Admissibility in International Law", in *Handbook of International Criminal Law*, forthcoming, 2010.

19 The term 'genuineness' attaches to the phrases "to carry out the investigation or prosecution" (article 17(1)(a)) and "to prosecute" (article 17(1)(b)) to the extent that they result from a State's inability or unwillingness as described in sub-paragraphs 2 and 3. See *Informal Expert Paper* (2003), paras. 21-23; El Zeidy, 2008, see *supra* note 1, 165; Kleffner, 2008, 114-115.

diction.[20] Among judicial determinations to date is the above noted observation of the Appeals Chamber that a finding of unwillingness or inability is not a pre-requisite for the admissibility of a case under article 17(1)(a), meaning that if a State is inactive in relation to the case before the ICC, the question of assess unwillingness or inability does not arise and the case will be rendered admissible, subject to a ruling on gravity.[21] Turning to article 17(1)(b), the Appeals Chamber has held that the provision comprises two cumulative elements: the case must have been investigated and the relevant State must have made a decision not to prosecute.[22] Where a State has investigated a case, but proceeds not to prosecute due to the surrender of the person to the ICC, this is not a "decision not to prosecute" within the meaning of article 17(1)(b).[23] Finally, with respect to the linkage to *ne bis in idem* in article 17(1)(c), Trial Chamber III has indicated that this provision is only engaged where there has been a national decision on the merits of the case resulting in a final decision or acquittal of the accused.[24]

[20] To date, complementarity jurisprudence has been limited to a *proprio motu* examination triggered by the Pre-Trial Chamber pursuant to article 19(1) in *Prosecutor v. Joseph Kony et al.*, Pre-Trial Chamber II, Decision on the admissibility of the case under article 19(1) of the Statute, ICC-02/04-01/05-377 (10 March 2009), and the admissibility challenge brought by the defence in *Prosecutor v. Germain Katanga and Mathieu Ngudjolo Chui,* Judgment on the Appeal of Mr. Germain Katanga against the Oral Decision of Trial Chamber II of 12 June 2009 on the Admissibility of the Case, ICC-01/04-01/07-1497, 25 September 2009. As noted above, complementarity has also been considered in the context of *proprio motu* authorisation in *Situation in the Republic of Kenya*, Decision Pursuant to Article 15 of the Rome Statute on the Authorization of an Investigation into the Situation in the Republic of Kenya, Case No. ICC-01/09-19, 31 March 2010; *The Prosecutor v. Jean-Pierre Bemba Gombo*, Decision on the Admissibility and Abuse of Process Challenges, Case no. ICC-01/05-01/08-802, 24 June 2010.

[21] *Prosecutor v. Germain Katanga and Mathieu Ngudjolo Chui,* Judgment on the Appeal of Mr. Germain Katanga against the Oral Decision of Trial Chamber II of 12 June 2009 on the Admissibility of the Case, ICC-01/04-01/07-1497, 25 September 2009, para. 78.

[22] *Ibid.*, para. 82

[23] *Ibid.*, para. 83. A similar reasoning was followed by Trial Chamber III in its decision on admissibility in the *Bemba* case; see *The Prosecutor v. Jean-Pierre Bemba Gombo*, Decision on the Admissibility and Abuse of Process Challenges ('*Bemba Admissibility Decision*'), Case no. ICC-01/05-01/08-802, 24 June 2010, paras. 239-242.

[24] *Bemba Admissibility Decision*, para. 248. See below section 3.2.2.

The Court is yet to develop guiding jurisprudence on the contours of the terms 'unwillingness' and 'inability'. Nonetheless, in examining the meaning of unwillingness, Trial Chamber III has held that, pursuant to article 17(2), the Court must consider whether: (i) the relevant individual is being shielded from prosecution, (ii) there has been unjustified delay that is inconsistent with an intention to bring the accused to justice and (iii) the proceedings lack independence and impartiality. If the State is unwilling to proceed with a case domestically in view of the relinquishment of its jurisdiction to the Court, and if none of the considerations specified in article 17(2) apply, the Chamber ruled that this is not 'unwillingness' within the meaning of article 17(1)(b).[25] In view of inability, although the Chamber did not elaborate on the parameters of its inquiry, it considered several factual indicia that rendered the domestic authorities unable to proceed with the case.[26] Finally, Trial Chamber III pronounced on the question of whose assessment is relevant for the purpose of the Court's own determination. In view of the varying assessments before it, the Chamber observed that under Article 17(l)(a) and (b) of the Statute "as regards unwillingness or inability, it is not the national courts' determination as to whether or not they are unwilling or unable genuinely to carry out the investigation or prosecution, but the State's unwillingness or inability, that is relevant. Whilst the State can no doubt take into consideration relevant observations made by the judiciary, it is not bound by them"; going on to emphasize that, nonetheless, "the ultimate determination on these matters is made by the ICC".[27]

---

25 *Ibid.*, paras. 243-244.

26 The Chamber considered the cumulative effect of the submissions by the Central African Republic indicating that it did not have the capacity to conduct a trial of the kind before the ICC, given the human resources required, the number of cases pending before the national courts and the shortage of judges, as well as the budget of the Ministry of Justice. Other practical problems included the continued operations of the MLC militia and the consequent instability of the region; *Bemba Admissibility Decision*, paras. 245-246. See also discussion on unwillingness in the decision of Trial Chamber II in the *Katanga and Ngudjolo case*, although the requirement for the assessment was set aside on appeal; see *Prosecutor v. Germain Katanga and Mathieu Ngudjolo Chui*, Reasons for the Oral Decision on the Motion Challenging the Admissibility of the Case (Article 19 of the Statute), Case No. ICC-01/04-01/07-1213-tENG, 16 June 2009, paras. 74-95.

27 *Bemba Admissibility Decision*, para. 247.

As the ICC develops jurisprudence on the application of the article 17 it is likely that national authorities may increasingly turn for reference to legal principles derived from the Court's rulings on admissibility.[28] This may include, for example, elaboration on the interpretation of genuineness, respect for due process, intent to shield a person from justice, unjustified delay, independence and impartiality, the applicability of amnesty exceptions, pardons, or conditional immunities, and whether national jurisdictions can be deemed unable due to an incomplete rendering of international offences in domestic law or other lacunae in the domestic process.

3.2.2. *Ne Bis in Idem*

The *ne bis in idem* rule is closely inter-related with complementarity determinations before the Court.[29] In particular, article 17(1)(c) cross-references article 20(3) to govern cases where a person has already been tried at a national level, but that trial is vitiated by a lack of genuineness.

Comparing each of the sub-paragraphs of the provision, article 20(1) provides that the conviction or acquittal of a person by the ICC will preclude a subsequent trial for the same conduct by the Court. The '*idem*' relates to the same conduct being re-tried under a different categorisation, that is, murder as a war crime being subsequently re-tried as a crime against humanity or genocide.[30]

28 Jann Kleffner, "The Impact of Complementarity on National Implementation of Substantive International Criminal Law", *JICJ*, 2003, vol. 1, 86-113; Bruce Broomhall, *International Justice and the International Criminal Court: Between Sovereignty and the Rule of Law*, Oxford, 2004, 92, 102; Burke-White, 2005, 576.

29 See footnote 2 above.

30 The provision would be without prejudice to cumulative charging which, according to ICTY practice, has been permitted where the crimes charged protect different values or contain different elements; *Prosecutor v. Kupreskić et al., Decision on Defence Challenges to Form of the Indictment rendered in Kupreskić et al.* (15 May 1998). On cumulative charges at the penalty stages see *Prosecutor v. Tadić, Decision on Defence Motion on Form of the Indictment* (14 November 1995), 10. *Compare Prosecutor vs. Bemba*, Pre-Trial Chamber II, *Decision Pursuant to Article 61(7)(a) and (b) of the Rome Statute on the Charges of the Prosecutor Against Jean-Pierre Bemba Gombo*, ICC-01/05-01/08-424 (15 June 2009). The only exception to article 20(1) is for revision of a conviction or a sentence based upon newly discovered evidence, the discovered falsification of decisive evidence, or serious misconduct or serious breach of duty by one of the participating judges, in which case the Appeals Chamber may

Article 20(2) prevents the trial of an individual by another court for a crime that s/he has been already tried for by the ICC. In contrast to paragraph 1, the '*idem*' relates to the crime and not the conduct. Thus a person who has been tried by the ICC for rape as a war crime could be later tried for rape as a crime against humanity[31] or rape as an ordinary crime by another court. This corresponds to the right recognised in many national legal systems to prosecute an individual who has been tried abroad, and which is accompanied in most States with a deduction of sentence for previous time served abroad. The provision also reflects the fact that neither national nor international principles exist for the application of *ne bis in idem* across different jurisdictions.[32]

Corresponding to the rule that the Court must be final arbiter on the *bona fides* of national action when determining admissibility in any case before it, article 20(3) provides that the ICC may subject a person to a new trial for conduct for conduct also proscribed under article 6, 7 or 8 for which s/he has already been tried before another court, based on an assessment of genuineness.[33] Without such a provision, the exclusionary rule under article 20 could have enabled national authorities to avert the Court's jurisdiction by simply instituting sham domestic proceedings. As a result, any domestic proceedings must be genuine as exposed to the scrutiny of the ICC judges.

reconvene the original trial chamber, constitute a new one or itself rule on the matter; Article 84, ICC Statute.

31 Compare Christine Van Den Wyngaert and Tom Ongena, "*Ne bis in idem* Principle, Including the Issue of Amnesty", in Cassese, Gaeta and Jones, see *supra* note 16, 723 who suggest that the article 20(2) prevents another court from retrying any crime under article 5.

32 This has resulted in the complete non-recognition of foreign judgments by some States and limited recognition (deduction of sentence principle) by others; Wyngaert and Ongena, 2002, 708. See also Christine Van Den Wyngaert and Guy Stessens, "The International *Non Bis In Idem* Principle: Resolving Some of the Unanswered Questions", ICLQ, 1999, vol. 48, 779-804; see *infra* section 3.2.4.

33 The circumstances in which re-trial before the ICC would be permissible are where proceedings in the other court: "(a) Were for the purpose of shielding the person concerned from criminal responsibility for crimes within the jurisdiction of the Court; or (b) Otherwise were not conducted independently or impartially in accordance with the norms of due process recognized by international law and were conducted in a manner which, in the circumstances, was inconsistent with an intent to bring the person concerned to justice".

The '*idem*' that is protected under article 20(3) relates to "conduct also proscribed under articles 6, 7 or 8". This is because the Rome Statute is not a standard-setting instrument in the traditional sense of requiring domestication of the applicable crimes by way of implementing legislation. As such, the Statute does not set out to regulate how a State incorporates and represses the listed crimes.[34] As the preamble makes clear, the obligation of States in this area represents a pre-existing duty to exercise their criminal jurisdiction over those responsible for international crimes.[35] Therefore it is possible that the conduct may have been categorized differently from the Rome Statute.

This also means that oversight functions of the ICC in terms of *ne bis in idem*, and arguably in terms of complementarity, do not technically rely on the identical categorisation of crimes, but will apply instead to a case by case assessment of the adequacy of national repression of each of the proscribed conduct criminalised under the Rome Statute.[36] Nonetheless, as ICTR 11*bis* ruling in the *Bagaragaza* case illustrates, an ordinary crimes approach that does not adequately take into account the requisite mental and material elements to make out an international crime

34 The Statute formally requires States Parties to adopt implementing legislation in three areas: to ensure that procedures are available under national law for all forms of co-operation foreseen in Part 9; to extend their criminal laws to include offences against the administration of justice (article 70); and to enforce fines or forfeitures ordered by the Court (article 109).

35 According to the preamble, these are duties that are 'recalled' under the Rome Statute: they are not established by it *strictly speaking*; para. 6, Preamble, ICC Statute.

36 For a more detailed discussion see Kleffner, 2008, 118-125; Rastan, "Situation and Case: Defining the Parameters of Complementarity", in Stahn and El Zeidy, forthcoming 2010. It should also be noted that while the *ne bis in idem* provision in the ICC Statute not does explicitly require any application of the deduction of sentence principle in the re-trial of a person for the same conduct before the ICC, article 79(2) provides that the Court may deduct any time spent in detention in connection with the conduct underlying the crime. The deduction of sentence principle appeared in earlier ILC (Art. 42(3)) and PrepCom (Art 12(3)) drafts, but was omitted during the final drafting stages on the view that its placement in the provision on *ne bis in idem* was superfluous, and could better be addressed under sentencing. Immi Tallgren and Astrid Reisinger Coracini suggest the absence of an explicit provision may have been an unintended omission of the final drafting process; '*Ne bis in* idem', in Triffterer, 2008, 697.

may fall foul of an admissibility determination before the ICC.[37] Accordingly, the Court's will need to examine a range of factors, including: submissions by the State as to how its legislative scheme would apply in practice; an assessment of any discernable lacunae in the applicable domestic law, both in terms of the range of available offences as well as the satisfaction of the requisite mental and material elements; whether the sentencing framework adequately reflects the gravity of the offence;[38] and whether the domestic crime in question is subject to defences not available under international law, to statutes of limitation, or to domestic immunities and/or amnesties.[39]

3.2.3. Gravity

The last factor that may determine the admissibility of a case before the ICC is gravity.[40] For States considering the exercise of extra-territorial jurisdiction the gravity of the case, whether in terms of its nature, its qualification, its severity or its broader impact, may act as a relevant indicator for determining whether the State should assert jurisdiction. For the ICC, gravity serves a different function to complementarity. While the former arises from contested jurisdiction, gravity is applied independently regardless of any concurrent action. It essentially serves as an internal filtering mechanism to determine which cases are worthy of being heard

37 *Prosecutor v. Michel Bagaragaza*, Decision On Rule 11*bis* Appeal, Case No. ICTR-05-86-Ar11*bis* (30 August 2006). Compare *Prosecutor v. Rahim Ademi and Mirko Norac*, Case No. IT-04-78-PT, Referral Decision (14 September 2005).

38 The inclusion of a provision on sentencing discrepancies was expressly omitted during the drafting process due to the wide variations in national practice and the difficulty in arriving at an appropriate standard; see Draft article 19, *Report of the Preparatory Committee on the Establishment of an International Criminal Court, Draft Statute and Draft Final Act* (A/Conf.183/2/Add.1, 1998). Earlier formulations were also included in the 1995 Siracusa Draft Statute and 1996 and 1998 PrepCom proposals. The failure to secure the language during negotiation of the article 17, however, does not mean that the Court is excluded from ruling on the issue. Thus, the Court could arguably examine national decisions resulting in a significantly lower sentence disproportionate to the applicable international offence, which could be examined as an indicator of whether such proceedings were designed to shield the person from criminal responsibility or were conducted in a manner which, in the circumstances, is inconsistent with an intent to bring the person concerned to justice for that crime.

39 For example, non-applicability of statutes of limitation, article 29 ICC Statute; exclusion of defences of superior orders, article 33 ICC Statute.

40 Article 17(1)(d), ICC Statute.

before the Court.[41] Thus, a case that has satisfied the criteria under article 17(1)(a)-(c) may nonetheless be found to be inadmissible due to deficit gravity.

In the first decision that sought to define gravity, Pre-Trial Chamber (PTC) I, in finding the warrant application against Bosco Ntaganda inadmissible, developed a mandatory set of criteria for its determination of admissibility.[42] The PTC required that: (i) the alleged conduct was either systematic or large-scale, the due regard paid to the social alarm caused to the international community; (ii) the person fell within the category of most senior leaders of the situation under investigation; and (iii) the person fell within the category of most senior leaders suspected of being most responsible, considering their own role and the role played by group or entity to which they belong in the overall commission of crimes within the jurisdiction of the Court in the relevant situation.

On appeal, the Pre-Trial Chamber's findings were overturned. The Appeals Chamber found it inappropriate to narrow the type of cases that could come before the Court by imposing restrictions on the exercise of jurisdiction by the Court as a matter of law. As the Appeals Chamber observed, "[t]he predictable exclusion of many perpetrators on the grounds proposed by the Pre-Trial Chamber could severely hamper the preventive, or deterrent, role of the Court which is a cornerstone of the creation of the International Criminal Court, by announcing that any perpetrators other than those at the very top are automatically excluded from the exercise of the jurisdiction of the Court".[43] While the Chamber affirmed what gravity

---

41 As Batros states, "A declaration that a case is inadmissible on the basis that it is 'not of sufficient gravity to justify further action by the Court' is thus absolute, rather than relative"; Ben Batros, "The Evolution of the ICC Jurisprudence on Admissibility", in Stahn and El Zeidy, 2010, forthcoming.

42 *Prosecutor v. Lubanga Dyilo* (Pre-Trial Chamber I), Decision on the Prosecutor's Application for Warrant of Arrest, Article 58, ICC-01/04-01/06, 10 February 2006, para. 64.

43 *Situation in the Democratic Republic of the Congo*, Judgment on the Prosecutor's appeal against the decision of the Pre-Trial Chamber I entitled "Decision on the Prosecutor's Application for Warrants of Arrest, Article 58", ICC-01/04-169, under seal 13 July 2006; reclassified public 23 September 2008, paras. 69-79. As the Appeals Chamber observed, "[t]he particular role of a person or, for that matter, an organization, may vary considerably depending on the circumstances of the case and should not be exclusively assessed or predetermined on excessively formalistic grounds"; *ibid*., para. 76.

is not, it did not define what it is.[44] This is perhaps understandable in the light of the role of the appellate chamber to provide sufficient flexibility for future jurisprudence to develop on the basis of case by case assessments.[45]

In the absence of guiding jurisprudence, the task of determining what constitutes gravity and applying it to individual cases has been left to the Office of the Prosecutor through its case selection strategy.[46] The general factors relevant for assessing gravity have been set out in the Regulations of the Office of the Prosecutor as including the scale of the crimes, their nature, manner of commission, and their impact.[47] This assessment includes both quantitative and qualitative considerations.[48] The appropriateness of the application of these factors has more recently been upheld by Chambers of the Court.[49]

The Office of the Prosecutor has also adopted a policy of focussing on those bearing the greatest responsibility for the most serious crimes, meaning it will select for prosecution those situated at the highest echelons of responsibility, including those who ordered, financed, or otherwise organised the alleged crimes.[50] The category could include persons situated in *de jure* or *de facto* hierarchical control as well as others who play a

---

44 *Compare* Separate and Partly Dissenting Opinion of Judge Georghios M. Pikis, Judgment on Appeal Against Arrest Warrant Decision, Case No. ICC-01/04-186 para. 40.

45 Ben Batros, "The Judgment on the Katanga Admissibility Appeal: Judicial Restraint at the ICC", *LJIL*, 2010, vol. 23, 343-362.

46 In particular, the Prosecutor must consider gravity as part of the admissibility assessment under article 53(1)(b).

47 Regulation 29(2), Regulations of the Office of the Prosecutor.

48 See also Prosecution submissions in *Abu Garda*, *The Prosecutor v. Bahr Idriss Abu Garda*, Filing in the Record of Prosecution's Public Redacted Version of the Prosecutor's Application under Article 58, pursuant to the request contained in the Decision on the Prosecutor's Application under Article 58, dated 7 May 2009, ICC-02/05-02/09-16-Anx1, 20 May 2009, para. 173.

49 *Prosecutor v. Abu Garda* (Pre-Trial Chamber I), Decision on the Confirmation of Charges, ICC-02/05-02/09-243-Red, 8 February 2010, para. 31; *Situation in the Republic of Kenya*, Decision Pursuant to Article 15 of the Rome Statute on the Authorization of an Investigation into the Situation in the Republic of Kenya, Case No. ICC-01/09-19, 31 March 2010, para. 62.

50 *Paper on some policy issues before the Office of the Prosecutor* (ICC-OTP 2003); *Prosecutorial Strategy 2009-2012* (ICC-OTP 2010).

major causal role in the commission of crimes or exceptionally notorious perpetrators who may not occupy a hierarchical position. The Office of the Prosecutor has stated that this principle is applied as a general rule in recognition that in some cases the focus of an investigation may go wider if investigation of certain type of crimes or those officers lower down the chain of command is necessary for the whole case.[51]

As can be seen, the factors applied by the Prosecutor, though different in some respects, are not entirely alien to those applied in the overturned decision of PTCI in the overturned *Ntaganda* decision. At issue in the appeal, essentially, was not so much which factors are relevant for determining gravity, but rather the nature of this assessment. The PTC had interpreted gravity as a narrow legal threshold for ascertaining which cases should be admissible before the ICC. By contrast, the Prosecutor's Office had applied gravity to guide the exercise of prosecutorial discretion. It had applied gravity in the light of such discretion to identify Bosco Ntaganda, Deputy Chief of the General Staff of the *Forces Patriotiques pour la Libération du Congo*, as among those bearing the greatest responsibility pursuant to its stated prosecutorial policy. The PTC examined the same individual and rejected the case for not meeting statutory legal thresholds of gravity. The Appeals Chamber judgment appears to indicate that once base-line parameters of gravity have been met deference should be given to the Prosecutor's choice in identifying suspects warranting prosecution. This suggests that while gravity should not be construed narrowly as a legal threshold for the purpose of admissibility, it may have a broader function in guiding the exercise of discretionary powers in order to identify and prioritize the selection of cases.[52]

3.2.4. Forum Determination

Admissibility is framed primarily as a contest between the Court and a State with jurisdiction. Nonetheless, several questions that may arise in the future, and which may have analogies at the inter-State level, remained unanswered. For example, what if there are multiple contestations of jurisdiction: how should the Court determine forum allocation where

[51] *Ibid.*

[52] Apart from admissibility, considerations of gravity also apply for determining the gravity of the crime and the individual circumstances of the convicted person for the purpose of sentencing; article 78(1), ICC Statute, rule 145, ICC RPE.

there are two or more competing claims? The challenging States may have different bases of jurisdiction (active personality vs. passive personality) or overlapping claims (conduct spanning two territories). What should the Court do where various grounds of jurisdiction interweave? Should the ICC in principle prioritise certain claims over others? The Statute itself does not prioritise jurisdictional bases for the purpose of admissibility. Article 19 merely provides that a challenge to the jurisdiction of the Court or the admissibility of a case may be brought by "[a] State which has jurisdiction over a case", leaving for States to regulate how their courts may exercise their jurisdiction.[53]

At the inter-State level there is no general rule of international law establishing a hierarchy between the various bases of jurisdiction where different national authorities want to prosecute the same conduct.[54] This arises from the prerogatives of State sovereignty as well as considerations relating to variable access to evidence. Since the failure to prove an offence or the imposition of lesser penalties in one jurisdiction may have arisen from the absence of evidence that may be available in another jurisdiction, it has generally been deemed unreasonable for a national court to be definitively bound by decisions delivered in a foreign jurisdiction.[55] Accordingly, multilateral instruments dealing with extradition or the transfer of proceedings in criminal matters normally leave the requested State with discretion to evaluate the circumstances on

53 Article 19(2)(b), ICC Statute. See also article 18(1) and article 90 discussed *infra* at footnote 60.

54 A notable exception is the application of rule at the European level; article 9, *European Convention on Extradition*, ETS no. 024 (13 December 1957); articles 53-55, *European Convention on the International Validity of Criminal Judgments*, ETS No. 070; articles 35-37, *European Convention on the Transfer of Proceedings in Criminal Matters*, ETS No. 073. On whether the territorial principle enjoys priority under customary international law see Cedric Ryngaert, *Jurisdiction in International Law*, Oxford University Press, 2008, 27-31.

55 *Additional Protocol to the European Convention on Extradition - Explanatory Report*; [1975] COETSER 2 (15 October 1975), para. 19. As the Report notes, in the context of the European Convention on Extradition, "[t]he recognition of a foreign judgment clearly presupposes a certain degree of confidence in foreign justice"; *ibid.*, para. 22.

pragmatic grounds, without establishing any hierarchical order between concurrent jurisdictions.[56]

Territorial jurisdiction is widely held to be the strongest and primary basis for jurisdiction.[57] Legal doctrine normally grants preference to the place where the offence took place subject to genuine ability and willingness. Prosecution in the territorial State will normally have several advantages, including the convenience to the parties, cost-effectiveness and procedural efficiency.[58] The proximity of the courts to the events, moreover, may enable a better appreciation of the socio-political, historical, cultural context of the case, and may more readily contribute to restorative justice and to domestic legitimacy and acceptance. It may also better contribute to public debate and deliberation, and heighten pedagogical initiatives to deter the future recurrence of violence and to inculcate a culture of accountability. Other valid reasons, however, may militate against assigning priority to the State where the crime occurred. The State of nationality of the accused or of the victim may have equally compelling arguments for prosecuting the case. Granting primacy to the territorial State may risk creating priority claims to ownership, which could be linked to concepts of sovereignty and non-intervention in order to limit action by other States.[59] Practical factors, moreover, may dictate the choice, such as the presence of the victim and the accused, perhaps by way of asylum, in another country. Finally, as with admissibility proceedings before the ICC, there may be a determination that the territorial State is unwilling to genuinely prosecute or it may be unable to do so.

The silence of the Rome Statute on which domestic jurisdiction should be granted priority when there are competing admissibility challenges means that the issue is likely to be treated on a case by case

[56] See, *e.g.*, article 8, *European Convention on the Transfer of Proceedings in Criminal Matters*.

[57] Robert Jennings and Arthur Watts (eds.), *Oppenheim's International Law*, 9th Edition, Longman, 1992, 458.

[58] M. Cottier in H. Fischer, C. Kreß and S.R. Lüder (eds.), *International and National Prosecution of Crimes under International Law: Current Developments 2*, Verlag Arno Spitz, 2004, 851.

[59] Ward Ferdinandusse, "The Interaction of National and International Approaches in the Repression of International Crimes", *EJIL*, 2004, vol. 15, 1050.

basis.[60] The ICTY Appeals Chamber has similarly ruled against that the notion of any predetermined hierarchy between domestic jurisdictions for the transfer of cases under rule 11*bis* proceedings, holding that "[a] decision of the Referral Bench on the question as to which State a case should be referred (vertical level, *i.e.* between the International Tribunal and individual States) must be based on the facts and circumstances of each individual case in light of each of the prerequisites set out in Rule *11bis*(A) of the Rules".[61] As the Appeals Chamber went on to observe, "attempts among States to establish a hierarchy of criteria for determining the most appropriate jurisdiction for a criminal case, where there are concurrent jurisdictions on a horizontal level (*i.e.* among States), have failed thus far. Instead, States have agreed on various criteria and opted to give weight to certain criteria over others depending on the circumstances of a particular case".[62] Accordingly, the ICTY Appeals Chamber has

---

60 See M. Morris, "Complementarity and Its Discontents: States, Victims, and the International Criminal Court", in Dinah Shelton (ed.) *International Crimes, Peace, and Human Rights: The Role of the International Criminal Court*, Hotei, 2000, who points out that "the ICC Treaty articulates no principles or policies to govern … decision making on fundamental issues". Turning by analogy to article 90 which deals with competing cooperation requests for extradition and surrender does not provide much guidance as it relies in large part on traditional rules in extradition treaties: States Parties are to prioritise claims based *inter alia* on "The interests of the requesting State including, where relevant, whether the crime was committed in its territory and the nationality of the victims and of the person sought". Several criteria, moreover, would appear incompatible with admissibility proceedings, such as prioritising a claim based on the respective date of receipt or on the basis of whether the challenging forum is a State Party.

61 *Prosecutor v. Gojko Janković*, Referral Appeals Decision, IT-96-23/2-AR11bis.2, 15 November 2005, para. 33.

62 *Ibid*. para. 34. See also *Prosecutor v. Mejakić et al.*, Decision on Joint Defence Appeal Against Decision on Referral Under Rule 11bis, IT-02-65-*AR11bis*, 7 April 2006, paras. 43-44. The Referral Bench in *Mejakić* similarly noted, "it has not been shown that there is an established priority in international law in favour of the State in whose territory a crime was committed. International extradition treaties, whether multilateral or bilateral, offer some analogy, but these do not typically provide for primacy of any one ground of jurisdiction. In domestic jurisdictions, the question is often regulated by statute and there is no universal provision or practice"; *Prosecutor v. Mejakić et al., Decision on Prosecutor's Motion for Referral of Case Pursuant to Rule 11*bis (20 July 2005). See also inconclusive post-WWII discussions between the United Nations War Crimes Commission and its affiliated National Offices over which country should enjoy priority in situations of competing extradition requests for

affirmed that the determination of the Tribunal should be based on pragmatic considerations based on an assessment of which State has a "significantly greater nexus".[63]

The Princeton Principles on Universal Jurisdiction provide a non-exhaustive set of criteria based on an aggregate balance of multilateral or bilateral treaty obligations; the place of commission of the crime; the nationality connection of the alleged perpetrator to the requesting State; the nationality connection of the victim to the requesting State; any other connection between the requesting State and the alleged perpetrator, the crime, or the victim; the likelihood, good faith, and effectiveness of prosecution in the requesting State; the fairness and impartiality of the proceedings in the requesting State; convenience to the parties and witnesses, and the availability of evidence in the requesting State; and the interests of justice.[64]

At the same time, subsidiarity has been proposed as an effective vehicle of resolving competing jurisdictional claims. This would accord forum determination to a foreign State only where the State with a stronger nexus fails to adequately deal with a particular case. As applied in the area of international crimes to date Spanish and German courts have applied subsidiarity as a principle of judicial restraint to hold that their national courts are only able to exercise universal jurisdiction if the State that has a direct link (on the basis of territoriality or active personality) fails to do so, or does not do so genuinely.[65] The principle has been compared to the operation of complementarity between States.[66]

Eurojust, the European Union's judicial cooperation body, following consultations with practitioners and institutional representatives, has provided the most detailed guidance to date for deciding which jurisdiction should prosecute in those cross-border cases where

the prosecution of Axis war criminals; *History of the United Nations War Crimes Commission and the Development of the Laws of War*, 1948, 156.

63 *Janković* Referral Appeals Decision, para. 37.

64 Principle 8, *Princeton Principles on Universal Jurisdiction*, Princeton University Press, 2001.

65 Ryngaert, 2008, see *supra* note 54, 211-218; Ryngaert, Chapter 6 in this volume.

66 *Ibid*; Xavier Philippe, "The principles of universal jurisdiction and complementarity: how do the two principles intermesh?", International Review of the Red Cross No. 862, 2006, vol. 88.

there is a possibility of a prosecution being launched in two or more different jurisdictions.[67] The Guidelines have been designed to provide reminders to EU Member States and to define the issues that are important when such decisions are made; with emphasis being laid that the priority and weighting to be given to each factor in the below matrix will be different in each case, bearing in mind the facts and merits of each individual case.

Factors to be taken into consideration according to the Eurojust Guidelines include: the identification of each jurisdiction where a prosecution is not only possible but also where there is a realistic prospect of successfully securing a conviction; the preliminary presumption that, if possible, a prosecution should take place in the jurisdiction where the majority of the criminality occurred or where the majority of the loss was sustained; the possibility of a prosecution in the jurisdiction where the accused in located and whether extradition proceedings or transfer of proceedings are possible; the capacity of the competent authorities in one jurisdiction to extradite or surrender a defendant from another jurisdiction to face prosecution in their jurisdiction; in complex cross border cases where the criminality occurred in several jurisdictions, the possibility, practicability and efficiency for dealing with all the prosecutions in one jurisdiction;[68] the willingness of a witness to travel and give evidence in another jurisdiction, or the possibility of receiving their evidence in written form or by other means such remotely (by telephone or video-link); the possibility of one jurisdiction being able to offer a witness protection programme not available in another; the length of time which proceedings will take to be concluded in a jurisdiction, in view of avoiding delays (not a lead factor and to be considered where other factors are balanced); the interests of victims and whether they would be prejudiced if any prosecution were to take place in one jurisdiction rather than another, including the possibility of claiming compensation; given that evidence is collected in different ways and often in very different

67 *Eurojust Guidelines, Annual Report 2003, Making the Decision - "Which Jurisdiction Should Prosecute?"*; available at http://www.eurojust.europa.eu/press_annual_report_2003.htm

68 As the Eurojust guidelines note: "In such cases prosecutors should take into account the effect that prosecuting some defendants in one jurisdiction will have on any prosecution in a second or third jurisdiction. Every effort should be made to guard against one prosecution undermining another"; *ibid.*

forms in different jurisdictions, the availability of evidence in a form that would render it admissible and acceptable before the courts of the jurisdiction; and the possible effects of a decision to prosecute in one jurisdiction rather than another and the potential outcome of each case, including the liability of potential defendants and the availability appropriate offences and penalties.

Factors that the Eurojust Guidelines suggest should not be taken into consideration include prosecution in one jurisdiction rather than another simply to avoid complying with the legal obligations that apply in one jurisdiction but not in another. The relative sentencing powers of courts in the different potential prosecution jurisdictions, similarly, must not be a primary factor in deciding in which jurisdiction a case should be prosecuted, although it should be ensured that the potential penalties available reflect the seriousness of the criminal conduct. Prosecution should also not be undertaken in one jurisdiction rather than another only because it would result in the more effective recovery of the proceeds of crime, noting that reliance should instead be placed on the most effective use of international cooperation agreements in such matters. The cost of prosecuting a case, or its impact on the resources of a prosecution office, moreover, should only be a factor in deciding whether a case should be prosecuted in one jurisdiction rather than in another when all other factors are equally balanced, and that competent authorities should not refuse to accept a case for prosecution in their jurisdiction because the case does not interest them or is not a priority the senior prosecutors or the ministries of justice.

As the discussion above suggests, competing domestic jurisdictional claims before the ICC may be determined by comparative analysis of the nexus between the crime and each challenging State as well as pragmatic considerations. The process of indentifying the willingness and ability or the challenging State(s) may also serve to filter the most appropriate forum for a deferral based on such factors as the adequacy of witness protection, the safety and security of judges and lawyers, and the independence of the judicial process from political interference. As with all decisions related to forum allocation, such decisions may prove controversial, particularly in volatile conflict or post-conflict political settings where the States directly affected by the conflict bring competing claims.[69] Nonetheless, as described in section 3.3. below, the problem most often faced by international courts is not the competing activism of several national jurisdictions, but the prevalence of impunity as a result on domestic inactivity.[70]

3.2.5. Collaboration Within Contest

Although complementarity as admissibility posits a contest model, there remains significant scope for collaboration even within this paradigm. Such collaboration lies not in the realm of admissibility litigation, but of case selection. This seeks to avoid unnecessary litigation with States by reserving investigative and prosecutorial activities for where it appears clearly appropriate. Thus, the ICC Prosecutor's Office has stated, as a general rule, it will seek to investigate and prosecute cases only in "a clear case of failure to act by the State or States concerned". This has been expressed under a policy of "[c]lose co-operation between the Office of the Prosecutor and all parties concerned ... to determine which forum may be the most appropriate to take jurisdiction".[71] The approach calls for

---

69 See, *e.g.*, the case of the *Vukovar Three*, relating to one of the most notorious episodes of the Croatian war, where the ICTY Prosecutor's rule 11*bis* motion provoked competing claims for transfer from Croatia (the territorial State) and Serbia and Montenegro (the State of nationality of the accused), with approximately equivalent degrees of political willingness and domestic capacity to prosecute the accused. Several other practical factors were considered by the Referral Bench including the impact on the effected population and local reconciliation in Croatia v. the judicial efficiency of joining the case with ongoing related domestic proceedings against several co-perpetrators on trial in the *Ovčara* case in Belgrade. The Prosecutor ultimately decided to withdraw the motion after concluding that "any decision by the Chambers to transfer it would provoke deep resentment in one or the other country considered for the transfer" and "would not be in the interest of justice". The case was therefore retained by the Tribunal, an option that will likely not be open to the ICC Prosecutor in a contested admissibility proceeding. *Prosecutor v. Mejakić et al.*, *Decision on Prosecutor's Motion for Referral of Case Pursuant to Rule 11*bis (20 July 2005); *Address by ICTY Prosecutor to the Security Council* (13 June 2005) CDP/MOW/977-e.

70 See below section 3.3.1.

71 *Policy Paper* (ICC-OTP 2003), p. 2: "To the extent possible the Prosecutor will encourage States to initiate their own proceedings. As a general rule, the policy of the Office of the Prosecutor will be to undertake investigations only where there is a clear case of failure to act by the State or States concerned. / Close co-operation between the Office of the Prosecutor and all parties concerned will be needed to determine which forum may be the most appropriate to take jurisdiction in certain cases, in par-

partnership and dialogue, encouraging genuine national proceedings, while remaining vigilant should such efforts fail.[72] At the same time, the statutory regime itself foresees a system of early notice, interaction and dialogue with States to ascertain the existence of or possibility for relevant national proceedings.[73]

The early practice of the Court demonstrates that situations have been opened and cases brought forward primarily where domestic authorities have remained inactive in relation to persons bearing the greatest responsibility for the most serious crimes. Such inactivity has occurred: (i) where the State has determined itself unable to conduct proceedings and has either invited the Court to exercise jurisdiction (Democratic Republic of Congo, Uganda, Central African Republic) or expressed its readiness to cooperate (Kenya); or (ii) where the State authorities are allegedly complicit in the commission of crimes (Darfur, Sudan). This also explains why to date there have been no challenges to the jurisdiction of the Court or the admissibility of its cases by States: because they agree with the exercise of jurisdiction by the Court or, in respect of Darfur, they refuse to recognise the Court's jurisdiction by lodging a formal challenge before it.

Contests, of course, can never be ruled out. A State that initially welcomes the exercise of ICC jurisdiction may, possibly due to a change of circumstance, later bring a challenge with respect to a particular case. A recalcitrant State, similarly, may launch relevant domestic proceedings that will require judicial examination. In other, less clear-cut situations, such as in Colombia, there may be national proceedings, but aspects of their genuineness or the focus of their case selection strategy may require further preliminary examination or possibly a ruling from the Court.[74]

---

ticular where there are many States with concurrent jurisdiction, and where the Prosecutor is already investigating certain cases within a given situation".

72 *Informal expert paper: The principle of complementarity in practice* (ICC-OTP 2003), 3-4.

73 Article 18, ICC Statute; rules 44, 51-54, ICC RPE; *Prosecutorial Strategy 2009-2012*, paras. 38-39. See also Jann Kleffner, "Complementarity as a Catalyst for Compliance", in Jann Kleffner and Gerben Kor (eds.), *Complementarity Views on Complementarity*, Cambridge, 2006, 82; Federica Gioia, "Comments on Chapter 3 of Jann Kleffner", *ibid.* 108-110; Stahn, 2008, 106.

74 Annual Report of the International Criminal Court to the United Nations, A/64/356 (17 September 2009), para. 47.

In sum, while complementarity as admissibility rests on an assumption of contested jurisdiction, contests with States can be reduced through the effective exercise of prosecutorial discretion and cooperation. The next section takes this framework one step further to describe how the Court can collaborate with States not just in relation to its own cases, but also to promote cases at the national level. In line with the thematic focus on this volume, the emphasis is primarily on what measures States can take, individually or collectively, to combat impunity.

3.3. Complementarity as Collaboration

Complementarity as a collaborative principle is based on a burden-sharing perspective.[75] From this standpoint, the Rome Statute creates not only a court, but a system for the enforcement of core crime norms between national and international authorities.[76] The overarching goal of this system – to put an end to impunity and so contribute to the prevention of crimes – can only be achieved by collaboration between the ICC and national courts.[77]

This statement is informed by both conceptual and practical realisations. As a permanent body, it would be clearly undesirable for the Court to replace the routine functioning of national bodies: this would offend both the duty as well as the right of States. The preamble to the Rome Statute recalls that the primary duty to exercise criminal jurisdiction over international crimes rests with States, not international institutions. States have pre-existing duties "to exercise [their] criminal

---

75 See C. Stahn, "*Complementarity: A Tale of Two Notions*", *Crim.L.F.*, 2008, vol. 19, 87-113, who refers to a managerial approach; see similarly J. Kleffner, *Complementarity in the Rome Statute and National Criminal Jurisdictions*, Oxford, 2008, 326-331; W. Burke-White, "*Proactive Complementarity: The International Criminal Court and National Courts in the Rome System of International Justice*", *Harv. Int'l L.J.*, 2008, vol. 49, 53-108.

76 "The Rome Statute created a comprehensive and global criminal justice system", *Address by Luis Moreno-Ocampo, Prosecutor of the ICC, Building a Future on Peace and Justice* (Nuremberg, 26 June 2007). The UN Secretary-General has also described the ICC as "the centrepiece of our system of international criminal justice"; *Remarks at the General Debate of the Sixth Assembly of States Parties to the Rome Statute of the International Criminal Court* (3 December 2007); echoed by *EU Presidency Statement - United Nations General Debate, International Criminal Court: Sixth Session of the Assembly of States Parties* (3 December 2007).

77 Preamble, para. 4, ICC Statute.

jurisdiction over those responsible for international crimes".[78] This may derive from treaty and/or customary obligations derived, *inter alia*, from the Hague Conventions[79], the Charter of the IMT at Nuremberg[80], the Genocide Convention,[81] the Geneva Conventions and the Additional Protocols,[82] as well as specific treaty regimes prohibiting international crimes such as the slavery,[83] apartheid,[84] and torture.[85] The responsibility of States in this area is not dependent on what the ICC does: States have duties to exercise criminal jurisdiction irrespective of the situations before the ICC. As a matter of right, moreover, the exercise of criminal jurisdiction over a territory is reflective of one of the most traditional aspects of sovereignty.[86] A permanent international body with unlimited powers to deny States the exercise of their sovereign powers would offend basic principles of non-intervention. As a rule, thus, the exercise of an international jurisdiction should remain the exception, to be triggered where warranted by the circumstances: based on an assessment of the inaction of national courts or otherwise their unwillingness or inability to genuinely conduct proceedings for the most serious crimes of international concern.[87]

---

78 Preamble, para. 6, ICC Statute.

79 *Hague Convention (IV) Respecting the Laws and Customs of War on Land* and *Regulations* (1907).

80 *Agreement for the Prosecution and Punishment of the Major War Criminals of the European Axis, and Charter of the International Military Tribunal. London, 8 August 1945.*

81 *Convention on the Prevention and Punishment of the Crime of Genocide* (1948).

82 *Geneva Conventions*,(1949); *Additional Protocol I and II* (1979).

83 *Slavery Convention* (1926); and *Amending Protocol* (1953).

84 *International Convention on the Suppression and Punishment of the Crime of Apartheid* (1973).

85 *Convention Against Torture and Other Cruel, Inhuman or Degrading Treatment or Punishment* (1984).

86 As the Permanent Court of Arbitration recognised in 1928, "[s]overeignty in the relations between States signifies independence. Independence in regard to a portion of the globe is the right to exercise therein, to the exclusion of any other State, the functions of a State"; *Island of Palmas Case (Netherlands v. U.S.)*, PCA (1928), 2 UN Rep. Int'l Arbitral Awards, 829.

87 The exceptionality of international intervention is arguably justified also by the differential cost of holding trials at the international and national levels and the need to provide for an effective system for the delivery of justice; *Report of the Secretary-*

Practical considerations, moreover, dictate that even where an international court does act, the reality is that it cannot carry on the entire burden. The focus of international courts, whether as a matter of law or policy, will tend to rest on those bearing the greatest responsibility and on the most serious incidents of crimes.[88] Thus, even with an international process focussing on the top strata of criminal activity, most potential perpetrators will simply not be the subject of international proceedings. This assumes, however, that national legal systems have the capacity and political will to enforce their corresponding duty. Where domestic authorities cannot fulfil their complementary role a gap may persist in the enforcement of core international crimes at the national level. As Madeline Morris pointed out over a decade ago in relation to the ICTR:

> Clearly the rational for a regime of "stratified-concurrent jurisdiction," in which the international tribunal prosecutes (or strives to prosecute) the leaders, leaving to national governments the rest of the defendants, cannot rest on a view of international tribunals as supplements or substitutes for reluctant, ineffective, or incapacitated national courts. Having an international tribunal try a few top-level defendants while leaving the staggering bulk of the caseload to the national courts would not necessarily be a sensible strategy for an incapacitated or unwilling national judicial system.[89]

The Rome Statute will equally fall short of its goal to end impunity if it merely creates an instrument to replace failed national courts. This has profound implications. It means that the role of domestic jurisdictions can never be set aside in sole favour of international trials. The system will fail unless there is complementary national action. If the States

General: The rule of law and transitional justice in conflict and post-conflict societies, S/2004/616, para. 42.

88 *Paper on some policy issues before the Office of the Prosecutor* (ICC-OTP 2003); *Prosecutorial Strategy 2009-2012*; ICTY Rule 28; Art. 1, Statute of the Special Court for Sierra Leone; Art.1 Law on the Establishment of the Extraordinary Chambers, with inclusion of amendments as promulgated on 27 October 2004 (NS/RKM/1004/006). The availability of State or diplomatic immunity for certain incumbent State officials before national courts also supports the focus of international courts on leadership crimes.

89 Madeline Morris, "The Trials of Concurrent Jurisdiction: The Case of Rwanda", *Duke Jrn'l Comp. IL*, 1997, vol. 7, 367.

directly affected by the crimes are inactive or otherwise unwilling or unable to proceed genuinely with complementary trials, the responsibility will fall to the international community to foster the conditions necessary to enable proceedings to take place in those territories or by third States.[90]

The concept of burden sharing is of course not new. It served as the model after World War II by which the Allies divided caseloads between the leadership at the international level while leaving the bulk of cases to be processed through military or criminal tribunals established in the territory where the crime occurred.[91] It is estimated that apart from the principals who were tried at the International Military Tribunal (IMT) in Nuremberg, collectively the U.S. convicted 1,814 persons, the UK 1,085, France 2,107, and the Union of Soviet Socialist Republic ('USSR') an

90 On the notion of a collective responsibility to enforce core crimes norms see R. Rastan, "The Responsibility to Enforce: Connecting Justice with Unity" in Carsten Stahn and Göran Sluiter (eds.), *The Emerging Practice of the International Criminal Court*, Martinus Nijhoff, 2009, 163-182.

91 The 1945 London Agreement distinguished between the "case of major criminals whose offences have no particular geographical location and who will be punished by the joint decision of the Governments of the Allies" (*i.e.*, the IMT) and others who were to be prosecuted according to 1943 Moscow Declaration: "those German officers and men and members of the Nazi party who have been responsible for or have taken a consenting part in the above atrocities, massacres and executions will be sent back to the countries in which their abominable deeds were done in order that they may be judged and punished according to the laws of these liberated countries and of free governments which will be erected therein"; *Declaration Concerning Atrocities Made at the Moscow Conference* (30 October 1943); *Agreement for the Prosecution and Punishment of the Major War Criminal of the European Axis* (8 August 1945). This was meant to be given legislative effect in each of the Allies respective zones of occupation through Allied Control Council Law No. 10 (3 Official Gazette Control Council for Germany (1946), 50-55), although formally CCL No.10 derived its legal basis from the authority of the four occupying powers acting as the surrogate government of Germany, with jurisdiction asserted on the basis of territoriality. See generally United Nations War Crimes Commission, *History of the United Nations War Crimes Commission and the Development of the Laws of War*, 1948; Robert Woetzel, *The Nuremberg Trials in International Law*, Stevens, 1962; Otto Triffterer, "Preliminary Remarks: The permanent ICC - Ideal and Reality", in Triffterer (ed.), *Commentary on the Rome Statute of the International Criminal Court*, Beck, 2008, 34; Dominic McGoldrick, "Criminal Trials Before International Tribunals", in Dominic McGoldrick, Peter Rowe, and Eric Donnelly (eds.), *The Permanent International Criminal Court: Legal and Policy Issues*, Hart, 2004, 14-21; Darryl Mundis, "Completing the Mandates of the *Ad hoc* International Criminal Tribunals: Lessons from the Nuremberg Process?", *Fordham Int'l L J*, 2005, vol. 28, 591-615.

inestimable figure; with a number of adjacent trials held in other Allied countries such as Australia, Kuomintang China, Greece, the Netherlands and Poland,[92] with the vast majority of WWII war crimes trials being processed through the national courts of the Federal Republic of Germany.[93] A division of labour similarly occurred after the International Military Tribunal for the Far East in Tokyo, with estimates that between 1945-1951 Allied military tribunals passed the death penalty on 920 Japanese from some 3,000 sentenced.[94] We would no doubt find it difficult today to accept that responsibility of international community in response to the atrocities of WWII would have been discharged by charging only 24 persons in Nuremburg[95] and 28 persons in Tokyo[96] had there not been any complementary proceedings at the national level.[97]

Burden sharing is evident also in the former Yugoslavia and Rwanda, although this was less as a feature of original design and more a result of evolving contextual factors. The ICTY and ICTR were endowed with primacy in view of Security Council's assessment at the time over the unwillingness of the courts in the former Yugoslavia to hold impartial

92 Woetzel, *op. cit.*; See also United Nations War Crimes Commission, *op. cit.*

93 Adalbert Rückerl, *NS - Verbrechen vor Gericht. Versuch einer Vergangenheitsbewältigung*, Müller, 1984. See generally Erich Haberer, "History and Justice: Paradigms of the Prosecution of Nazi Crimes", *Holocaust and Genocide Studies*, 2005, vol. 19, 487-519.

94 P. Piccigallo, *The Japanese on Trial: Allied War Crimes Operations in the East, 1945-1951*, University of Texas Press, 1987, xi. In contrast to Germany, very few cases were prosecuted by domestic authorities in Japan.

95 Of the 24 persons charged, 22 were tried: 12 were sentenced to death by hanging (including Martin Bormann who was tried *in absentia*); three to life imprisonment; four received sentences of between ten and twenty years; three were acquitted; one committed suicide before trial; and one was declared medically unfit; see Morten Bergsmo, Catherine Cissé and Christopher Staker, "The Prosecutors of the International Tribunals: The Cases of the Nuremberg and Tokyo Tribunals, the ICTY and ICTR, and the ICC Compared", in Louise Arbour, Albin Eser, Kai Ambos and Andrew Sanders (eds.), *The Prosecutor of a Permanent International Criminal Court*, Freiburg im Breisgau, 2000, 123; McGoldrick, 2004, see *supra* note 91, 18.

96 Of the 28 charged, seven were sentenced to death by hanging; 16 to life imprisonment; two to lesser terms; two died; and one suffered a mental breakdown, was sent to a psychiatric ward and released in 1948; see Bergsmo *et al.*, 2000, *supra* note 95, 123; McGoldrick, 2004, see *supra* note 91, 21.

97 It would of course also be unacceptable today that only the members of the defeated Axis powers were put on trial.

trials and the sheer institutional inability of the Rwandan authorities following a devastating genocide. The Statutes of both Tribunals, however, formally recognised the concurrent jurisdiction of national courts.[98] During the first decade or so of the Tribunals' mandates there were some domestic proceedings at the national level. This included trials before Specialised Chambers and *gacaca* jurisdictions in Rwanda,[99] *in absentia* and other proceedings in Croatia and Serbia, proceedings resulting from returned domestic case files that were reviewed by the ICTY Prosecutor's Office under the *Rules of the Road*,[100] as well as a handful of cases in third States.[101] Burden sharing, however, was not implemented as a component of institutional design until the adoption by each Tribunal of a completion strategy.[102] While each strategy were undoubtedly driven by political fatigue and resource considerations within the Security Council, less attention is given to the diminishing justifications for retaining a strict primacy model in view of the evolving situation at the national level. Over the course of the several years since the establishment of the Tribunals the various territorial States, some with international assistance, and with mixed levels of success, had engaged in numerous rounds of reform aimed at transforming the domestic rule of law landscape. Such efforts were aimed, in part, at increasing the prospects for genuine core crimes proceedings. As these developments progressed, they provided further justification for an adjustment of initial

---

[98] Article 9, ICTY Statute; Article 8, ICTR Statute.

[99] *Organic Law on the Organization of Prosecutions for Offences Constituting the Crime of Genocide or Crimes Against Humanity Committed Since 1 October 1990*, Law No.8/96, (30 August 1996); *Organic Law on the Establishment of "Gacaca Jurisdictions" and the Organization of Prosecutions for Offences Constituting the Crime of Genocide or Crimes Against Humanity Committed between 1 October 1990 and 31 December 1994*, Law No 40/2000, Rwanda Official Gazette (26 January 2001).

[100] *The Rome Statement on Sarajevo, Reflecting the Work of the Joint Civilian Commission Sarajevo* (18 February 1996), article 5. See generally David Tolbert and Aleksandar Kontić, "The International Criminal Tribunal for the former Yugoslavia: Transitional Justice, the Transfer of Cases to National Courts, and Lessons for the ICC", in Carsten Stahn and Göran Sluiter (eds.), *The Emerging Practice of the International Criminal Court*, Martinus Nijhoff, 2009, 138-145.

[101] Human Rights Watch, *Universal Jurisdiction in Europe: The State of the Art*, Vol. 18, No. 5(D) (June 2006).

[102] Tolbert and Kontić, 2009, 136-137.

assumptions in response to prevailing domestic circumstances. As a result of these several processes, the mandates of the Tribunals were adjusted, resulting in a division of labour similar to the post-WWII period with the Tribunals focussing on the most senior leaders responsible for the most serious crimes while national courts dealt with intermediate and lower ranked accused persons.[103] The task of forum determination, moreover, assumed judicial form to be entered by each Tribunal. Today, it is recognised that the vast majority of accused persons will need to be processed through national accountability mechanisms.[104]

Looking at the problem of mass criminality, thus, a managerial approach recognises that the response of the international community will need to be multifaceted and complementary. It acknowledges the concurrent responsibilities of both national and international actors: the latter asserting jurisdiction only where appropriate and with the primary burden residing at the domestic level. Drawing on these lessons learned, the ICC Prosecutor's Office stated early on that it would adopt a policy to encourage and assist national investigations and prosecutions.[105] The stated objective was not to compete for case allocation with national courts, but to ensure that the most serious crimes did not go unpunished through adoption of a policy of coordinated action between the ICC and national authorities.[106] This approach, labelled 'positive complementar-

[103] According to ICTY rule 11*bis*, this assessment required consideration of "the gravity of the crimes charged and the level of responsibility of the accused" in the light of Security Council resolution 1534 (2004), which refers, *inter alia*, to concentration on "the most senior leaders suspected of being most responsible for crimes within the jurisdiction of the relevant Tribunal" and "the transfer of cases involving intermediate and lower rank accused to competent national jurisdictions".

[104] In Bosnia and Herzegovina alone, the National War Crimes Strategy (adopted by the BiH Council of Ministers) estimates that as of end 2008, there were a total of 4,990 cases involving 9,879 suspects/accused in BiH; see Morten Bergsmo, Kjetil Helvig, Ilia Utmelidze and Gorana Žagovec, *The Backlog of Core International Crimes Case Files in Bosnia and Herzegovina*, Second Edition, Torkel Opsahl Academic EPublisher, 2010.

[105] *Policy Paper* (ICC-OTP 2003), pp. 2-3, 5.

[106] Luis Moreno-Ocampo, *Statement made at the ceremony for the solemn undertaking of the Chief Prosecutor of the ICC* (16 June 2003); Office of the Prosecutor, *Report on the activities performed during the first three years (June 2003 – June 2006)*, para. 2, 12; *Informal Expert Paper on Complementarity*, 2003, paras. 2-3, 61. See also *Report of the African Union High-Level Panel on Darfur (AUPD): The Quest for Peace, Justice and Reconciliation*, PSC/AHG/2(CCVII (29 October 2009) ('Mbeki Report'):

ity', has been described by the Prosecutor's Office as meaning that it "encourages genuine national proceedings where possible; relies on national and international networks; and participates in a system of international cooperation". At the same time it has recalled that "according to the Statute national states have the primary responsibility for preventing and punishing atrocities" and that

> [a] Court based on the principle of complementarity ensures the international rule of law by creating an interdependent, mutually reinforcing system of justice.[107]

The approach resonates with the a number of principles found in the preamble to the Rome Statute which emphasise that the "effective prosecution [of the most serious crimes of concern to the international community] must be ensured by taking measures at the national level and by enhancing international cooperation" and that the Court shall be "complementary to national criminal jurisdictions".[108]

Although the next section focuses on the role of State-to-State collaboration, arguably the ICC itself could play a significant role in promoting such an approach.[109] In particular, article 93(10) of the Statute provides that the Court may cooperate with and provide assistance to a State conducting an investigation into or trial in respect of conduct which constitutes a crime within the jurisdiction of the Court or which constitutes a serious crime under the national law of the requesting State. Such reverse cooperation[110] may include, *inter alia*, the transmission of statements, documents or other types of evidence obtained in the course of an investigation or trial; and the questioning of any person detained by order of the Court. Such assistance is framed under the Statute in discretionary rather than reciprocal terms, and therefore cannot be

"For the Panel, however, what matters, above all else, is that justice must be dispensed for Darfur in a credible, comprehensive, coherent and timely manner. The needs in this regard are immense, and it is equally clear that the entire burden of justice cannot be placed on any single institution or model, be it the ICC, special courts, traditional courts, other tribunals or a hybrid court"; para. 255.

107 *Report on Prosecutorial Strategy* (14 September 2006), p. 5. See also *Policy Paper* (ICC-OTP 2003), p. 3.

108 Preamble ICC Statute, paras. 4 and 10.

109 See *Prosecutorial Strategy 2009-2012*.

110 Gioia (2006), 1117-1119; Federica Gioia "Complementarity and Reverse Cooperation", in Stahn and El Zeidy, 2010.

imposed as a prerequisite by a State for the observance of its obligations to cooperate with the Court.[111] Nor can it be invoked in the context of admissibility litigation to suggest that organs of the Court carry a statutory burden to assist national authorities to investigate and prosecute any case before it.[112] Where the item in question has been collected with the assistance of a State, moreover, the provision is subject to the principle of originator consent. Any transmission of a statement or other evidence is also subject to the Court's obligations with respect to the protection of victims and witnesses, which cannot be put at peril as a result of such cooperation. Where the request originates from a national system in or emerging from a situation of conflict, it is possible that the Prosecutor and/or the Chambers may decide to consider the satisfaction of additional benchmarks before granting cooperation. This might include the existence of a credible local system for the protection of judicial personnel and witnesses. It may also extend to guarantees that any judicial assistance or evidence provided to a State will not lead to a violation of fundamental human rights standards, such as the prohibition against torture and inhumane treatment, the subjecting of persons to arbitrary arrest or detention, or the denial of the right to an effective remedy.[113] In other cases, limits could be placed on the categories of information that the

[111] The obligation to cooperate with the Court may derive from the Rome Statute for a State Party or a State accepting the jurisdiction of the Court on an *ad hoc* basis pursuant to article 12(3), from a bilateral agreement or arrangement, or otherwise from a Chapter VII Security Council resolution imposing cooperation obligations on a State.

[112] Thus in its admissibility challenge, while acknowledging the Statute does not impose such a burden, Defence for Katanga suggested that "there is a strong procedural duty incumbent upon the Prosecutor [to do so], as a relevant precondition for the substantive admissibility test"; *Prosecutor v. Germain Katanga and Mathieu Ngudjolo Chui, Motion Challenging the Admissibility of the Case by the Defence of Germain Katanga, pursuant to Article 19(2)(a) of the Statute*, ICC-01/04-01/07-949 (11 March 2009), para. 48. *Compare* Prosecution response observing "Compliance with a request [under article 93(10)] is discretionary and dependent of the fulfilment of the factors listed therein"; *Prosecutor v. Germain Katanga and Mathieu Ngudjolo Chui, Prosecution Response to Motion Challenging the Admissibility of the Case by the Defence of Germain Katanga, pursuant to Article 19(2)(a)*, para. 101.

[113] See Christopher Hall, "Positive Complementarity in Action", in Stahn and El Zeidy 2010, who locates the imposition of additional preconditions for the provision of assistance by the Court to national authorities in article 21(3) of the Statute. *Compare* ICTY/R Rule 11*bis*, which requires as a precondition satisfaction of the fair trials guarantees and the non-imposition of the death penalty.

Prosecutor or the Court is prepared to provide, for example by excluding certain evidentiary items such as witness statements or the identity of sources, and concentrating instead on non-confidential information, crime patterns, leads and background information.[114] Particular care, moreover, will need to be given in cases involving particularly vulnerable victims or witnesses, including victims of sexual violence and violence against children.[115] Clearly, any information or assistance provided by the Court should not lead to harm.

As part of its approach to positive complementarity, the Office of the Prosecutor has also stated that it recognises the role of justice processes other than those performed by criminal trials. In line with the goal of developing comprehensive strategies to combat impunity, it has taken a position that it "fully endorses the complementary role that can be played by domestic prosecutions, truth seeking, reparations programs, institutional reform and traditional justice mechanisms in the pursuit of a broader justice".[116] Such complementarity between punitive and reparative processes is notably located in the Statute itself since, in addition to determining criminal responsibility, the Court may issue orders against a convicted person specifying appropriate reparations to, or in respect of, victims, including restitution, compensation and rehabilitation.[117] The Statute also provides for the establishment of a Trust Fund for Victims, which may implement awards for reparation ordered by the Court against a convicted person or directly use its resources for the benefit of victims.[118] Similarly, the UN Secretary-General's *Report on the*

114 See *Prosecutorial Strategy 2009-2012*, para. 17.

115 A related policy issue is whether the Prosecutor or the Court should cooperate with national proceedings related to the prosecution of persons under 18; see also *United Nations Standard Minimum Rules for the Administration of Juvenile Justice* ('The Beijing Rules'); A/RES/40/33 (29 November 1985).

116 *Policy Paper on the Interests of Justice* (OTP-ICC 2007), p. 8.

117 Article 75, ICC Statute.

118 Article 79, ICC Statute; Rule 98, ICC RPE. To date, the Fund has supported a large number projects in the eastern DRC and northern Uganda, including initiatives in physical rehabilitation, psychological rehabilitation and material support, reaching a projected 75,200 beneficiaries (directly and indirectly) in Uganda and 150,400 beneficiaries (directly and indirectly) in the DRC by the end of 2009; *Report to the Assembly of States Parties on the activities and projects of the Board of Directors of the Trust Fund for Victims for the period 1 July 2008 to 30 June 2009*, ICC-ASP/8/18 (18 September 2009).

rule of law and transitional justice in conflict and post-conflict societies emphasizes the need to embrace an integrative and complementarity approach between different transitional justice tools. This may include a variety of goals including ending impunity, truth-seeking, reparations, institutional reform, vetting, dismissal and the transparent re-selection of qualified public servants, as well as the reform of law enforcement agencies and prison services, victim protection, legal education and crime prevention, as supported by transparent and accountable government.[119] Effectively combining different responses to situations of mass atrocity will enable complexity. Complementary approaches can be described as complex to the extent that they distribute benefits of different distinct types to a larger universe of persons than isolated activities.[120] Given the diversity of actors and institutional mandates involved, there will also be a need to promote internal and external coherence between different justice mechanisms.[121] Anti-impunity strategies that are complex and integrative are more likely to be comprehensive and therefore better able to contribute to maximizing the impact of accountability processes.

[119] *Rule of Law Report*, S/2004/616, para. 25.

[120] This framework of complexity is borrowed from *Rule-of-Law Tools for Post-Conflict States: Reparations Programmes* (OHCHR 2008), p. 22.

[121] See *ibid.*, pp. 33-34. Compare the interoperability between concurrent criminal and truth and reconciliations processes in East Timor where, despite the challenges encountered in practice, the work of the Commission for Reception, Truth and Reconciliation was built into the serious crimes prosecution framework (UNTAET/REG/2001/10, 13 July 2001); and the experience of Sierra Leone where the Truth and Reconciliation Commission had already been established on paper by the 1999 Lomé Peace Accord several years before the creation of the Special Court for Sierra Leone and faced an uncoordinated relationship. A twin track mechanism with a national truth commission and a special criminal chamber, both internationalised, was similarly recommended for Burundi, but never implemented; *Report of the assessment mission on the establishment of an international judicial commission of inquiry for Burundi, transmitted to the Security Council on 11 March 2005* (S/2005/158). See generally Elizabeth Evenson, "Truth and Justice in Sierra Leone: Coordination Between Commission and Court" *Colum. L Rev*, 2004, vol. 104, no. 3, 730; William Schabas, "The Relationship Between Truth Commissions and International Courts: The Case of Sierra Leone", *HRQ*, 2003, vol. 25, 1035-1066; Marieke Wierda, Priscilla Hayner and Paul van Zyl, *Exploring the Relationship Between the Special Court and the Truth and Reconciliation Commission of Sierra Leone*, ICTJ, 24 June 2002. Compare Nicole Fritz and Alison Smith, "Current Apathy for Coming Anarchy: Building the Special Court for Sierra Leone", *Fordham Int'l LJ*, 2001, vol. 25.

In line with the focus of this volume on the exercise of national jurisdiction, the section below examines three avenues for complementary national action to support domestic criminal accountability: (i) proceedings in the States directly affected by the crimes; (ii) proceedings in third States, including on the basis of universal jurisdiction; (iii) proceedings in third States, based on the accomplice liability of their own nationals.

3.3.1. Proceedings in the States Directly Affected by the Crimes

The focus of national prosecutions will normally reside in the States directly affected by the crimes, whether the State on whose territory the crimes occurred, whose nationals are the victims, or whose nationals are the alleged perpetrators. In some situations this may constitute a single territory; in others it may traverse the jurisdiction of several States. Experience shows, however, that the States directly affected by the crimes may often be the least equipped to undertake the type of large scale, politically sensitive and resource intensive investigations and prosecutions required. Even in peacetime, well functioning national jurisdictions find it difficult to undertake similar complex organised crime cases. Challenges include the need for specialised units with dedicated expertise; the risk of political interference in high-profile inquiries; security and protection for insiders, victims and witnesses; the obtaining of classified information, possibly including national security intelligence; the uncovering of linkage evidence tying the planners and organisers with those who execute the crime; the selection for prosecution and arrest of suspects who may be protected by the State apparatus or armed groups; the possible immunity of state officials; the need for inter-State judicial assistance; as well as the more general task of communicating the criminal process within the public discourse, which may be informed by highly contested and mutually exclusive historical narratives. Such challenges may be exacerbated several fold in the midst of the immediate conflict or post-conflict environment. The prevailing context may evince a rule of law vacuum, resulting in parts of the territory possibly being beyond effective government control. Where basic services exist chronic problems may persist, including a lack of the requisite human, financial and material infrastructure to support accountability processes. The legislative framework itself may show "the accumulated signs of neglect and political distortion" or contain discriminatory elements that fall short of international human rights and criminal law standards.[122] Particular risks associated with volatile areas may also result in deficient security and protection for persons and premises and for the collection of evidence. State officials whose cooperation is required to undertake accountability processes may be complicit in the crimes or fear retribution. In other situations, former combatants may have been demobilized and integrated into the very same security structures that are now responsible for the safety of high-risk witnesses. More generally, there may be due process concerns over the dispensation of fair and impartial justice. Faced with uncertain political backing and weak institutional support, where investigations have been pursued in such circumstances, pragmatic risk calculations have typically resulted in domestic prosecutors focusing on low-mid level suspects rather than on senior members of the state security apparatus and armed opposition or of the political and business elite. The reality is that these conditions represent the type of situations that the ICC will most frequently confront.[123]

As daunting as the prospect is, for States in or recently emerging from conflict, ignoring massive crimes in lieu of blanket amnesties may simply not be a viable option.[124] The need to devise strategies to preserve

---

[122] *Rule of Law Report*, S/2004/616, para. 27. As the Report comments with regard to post-conflict settings: "National judicial, police and corrections systems … often lack legitimacy, having been transformed by conflict and abuse into instruments of repression. Such situations are invariably marked by an abundance of arms, rampant gender and sexually based violence, the exploitation of children, the persecution of minorities and vulnerable groups, organized crime, smuggling, trafficking in human beings and other criminal activities. In such situations, organized criminal groups are often better resourced than local government and better armed than local law enforcement. Restoring the capacity and legitimacy of national institutions is a long-term undertaking"; *ibid.*

[123] As Louise Arbour has commented, "No one should expect that States emerging from armed conflict marked by the commission of massive human rights violations, will revert to well-functioning and co-operative democracies as soon as hostilities cease", "The Need for an Independent and Effective Prosecutor in the Permanent International Criminal Court", *Windsor Yearbook of Access to Justice*, 1999, vol. 17, 207-220. See also Géraldine Mattioli and Anneke van Woudenberg, "Global Catalyst for National Prosecutions? The ICC in the Democratic Republic of Congo", in Nicholas Waddell and Phil Clark (eds.), *Courting Conflict? Justice, Peace and the ICC in Africa*, Royal African Society, 2008.

[124] As observed by the OHCHR: "[E]xperience has shown that amnesties that foreclose prosecution or civil remedies for atrocious crimes are unlikely to be sustainable, even when adopted in the hope of advancing national reconciliation rather than with the

hard-won peace processes and to build democratic foundations will often necessitate an examination of accountability processes to combat the prevalence of a culture of impunity, and to prevent a relapse to the patterns of violence and discriminatory practices that precipitated past bloodshed.[125] That which is challenging in the best of times is what is asked of States in the worst, in the wake of conflict. One approach, therefore, could be to assess to what extent the political will and capacity of such States can be buttressed and supported by the international community. This may involve financial or technical support or the provision of judicial assistance.[126] Where the problem is one of unwillingness, it may be possible to resort to external inducement or coercion by instituting the adoption of issue-linkage strategies by the international community.[127]

The most recent example of a viable domestic model is the internationalised War Crimes Chamber within the State Court of Bosnia

---

cynical aim of shielding depredations behind a fortress of impunity … Amnesties that exempt from criminal sanction those responsible for human rights crimes have often failed to achieve their goals and instead seem to have emboldened beneficiaries to commit further crimes"; *Rule of Law tools for post conflict states - Amnesties*, HR/PUB/09/1, p. 1-3. See generally Darryl Robinson, "Serving the interests of justice: amnesties, truth commissions and the International Criminal Court", *European Journal of International Law*, 2003, vol. 14, 481.

125 E.g. as the *Report of the United Nations Independent Special Commission of Inquiry for Timor-Leste* points out in relation to recurrence of violence in 2006, reportedly viewed by many Timorese as a continuum encompassing the violence and factionalism from the years of Indonesian occupation and the violence that accompanied the referendum of 1999: "the crisis which occurred in Timor-Leste can be explained largely by the frailty of State institutions and the weakness of the rule of law … It is vital to Timor-Leste that justice be done and seen to be done. A culture of impunity will threaten the foundations of the State. The Commission is of the view that justice, peace and democracy are mutually reinforcing imperatives. If peace and democracy are to be advanced, justice must be effective and visible", S/2006/822, pp. 3, 12. As Joseph Rikhof points out in Chapter 2 to this volume, resort to judicial proceedings of some form or another is actually more frequent than commonly assumed.

126 See, e.g., Review Conference of the Rome Statute, Focal points' compilation of examples of projects aimed at strengthening domestic jurisdictions to deal with Rome Statute Crimes, RC/ST/CM/INF.2 (30 May 2010).

127 See Rod Rastan, "The Responsibility to Enforce: Connecting Justice with Unity" in Carsten Stahn and Göran Sluiter (eds.), *The Emerging Practice of the International Criminal Court*, Martinus Nijhoff, 2009, 163-182.

and Herzegovina.[128] The creation of the War Crimes Chamber in Sarajevo was viewed as an essential component of the ICTY Completion Strategy, enabling a stable downward distribution of case loads from the Tribunal to the domestic level.[129] The model of the War Crimes Chamber is not entirely typical due to the high level of institutional support and infrastructure that enabled its establishment, including the existing international presence *in situ* at the time which had already spent several years engaged with domestic reform efforts in BiH.[130] With ICTY backing, neighbouring States, representing former adversaries, were also brought into a regional programme to support international cooperation and judicial assistance.[131] The establishment of the necessary legal framework also relied in part on the ability of the Office of the High

[128] Established in 2005, almost decade after the end of conflict, the WCC is a hybrid court consisting of a mixed bench and staff of international and national personnel, to be phased over time into a fully national body. The Chamber is dealing primarily with four categories of cases: those cases transferred by the ICTY in accordance with rule 11*bis*; cases arising from other files, dossiers and investigative materials that did not led to indictments and which were transferred directly by the ICTY Prosecutor to the State Prosecutor's Office (so called 'Category 2 cases'); those approved Rules of the Road cases which, due to their sensitivity, the State Prosecutor's Office decided to pursue before the WCC; and cases arising from investigations begun after March 2003 under the State level BiH Criminal Code. See generally International Criminal Law Services, *Final report of the International Criminal Law Services (ICLS) experts on the sustainable transition of the Registry and international donor support to the Court of Bosnia and Herzegovina and the Prosecutor's Office of Bosnia and Herzegovina in 2009* (15 December 2008).

[129] All but two ICTY rule 11*bis* cases have been transferred to the WCC (comprising 6 cases against 10 accused), as well as other 'Category 2 cases'; see generally Tolbert and Kontić, 2009, 157-159.

[130] This included variously the Office of the High Representative (OHR), the Organisation for Security and Cooperation in Europe (OSCE), the Council for Europe, the NATO-led SFOR, the Office of the High Commissioner for Human Rights (OHCHR), the UN Mission in BiH (UNMIBH) and later EU Police Mission (EUPM). Arrangements were also concluded with the OSCE to monitor the rule 11*bis* cases on behalf of the ICTY Prosecutor's Office and to report to it on the genuineness of the proceedings in view of the Tribunal's power to recall cases previously transferred; *Co-operation between the Organization for Security and Co-operation in Europe and the International Criminal Tribunal for the Former Yugoslavia*, OSCE Permanent Council Decision no. 673 (PC.DEC/673), 19 May 2005.

[131] See, *e.g.*, "The Palić Process" involving regional cooperation between relevant judicial and state administration actors from BiH, Croatia and Serbia and Montenegro; ICTY *Press Release* OK/PR1310e (30 March 2009) http://www.icty.org/sid/10092.

Representative to rely on its Bonn powers to impose laws where necessary, where parliament failed to do so.[132] This included the passage of a complex set of laws to provide for the transfer of accused persons and evidence from the international to the national level; to ensure that the charges contained in Tribunal indictments could not be withdrawn, although new charges could be added; and that evidence previously introduced in ICTY proceeding could be used before the State Court.[133] Other places may struggle to find such an integrated level of political and financial investment, and may face far greater capacity issues.[134] Nonetheless, the experience of the War Crimes Chamber illustrates the possibilities for external assistance to States directly affected by the crimes in the implementation of an effective model for complementary national and international action.[135]

There are obvious benefits from building the capacity of the States directly affected by the crimes rather than relying on the exercise of jurisdiction by international courts or third States. In some situations much of this assistance may not be possible early on, when the temporal proximity to the crimes may mean that the recovery, restructuring and

[132] The 'Bonn powers' as derived from Annex XI para. 2 of the Conclusions of the Peace Implementation Council (charged with implementing the Dayton Peace Agreement) in Bonn, 10 December 1997.

[133] This required the adoption, *inter alia*, of the Law on the Court of BiH; imposed by the decision of the High Representative on 12 November 2000, adopted by Parliamentary Assembly of BiH on 25 June 2002 and 3 July 2002; *Official Gazette of BiH*, no. 29/00, 16/02, 24/02, 3/03, 37/03, 42/03, 4/04, 9/04, 35/04, 61/04 and 32/07; the Law on the Prosecutor's Office of BiH, *Official Gazette of BiH*, no. 24/02, 3/03, 37/03, 42/03, 9/04, 35/04, and 61/04; amendments to the BiH Criminal Code, *Official Gazette of BiH*, no. 37/03, 54/04, 61/04, 30/05, 53/06, 55/06, and 32/07; the BiH Criminal Procedure Code, *Official Gazette of BiH*, no. 03/03, 26/04; and the Law on the Transfer of Cases, *Official Gazette of BiH*, no. 61/04, 46/06, 53/06, 76/06; http://www.sudbih.gov.ba/. As Tolbert and Kontić have described, "a series of steps were required to establish the legal mechanism whereby the ICTY, as an UN body, could, in accordance with international standards, turn over its cases to local courts. In order to ensure that these standards were protected, the ICTY needed internal legislation to establish its own procedures but also required some assurances as to the procedures and processes that would be followed in the countries to which the cases would be transferred"; Tolbert and Kontić, 2009, 146-8.

[134] For a similar view see *ibid.* 161.

[135] The WCC also demonstrates the potential catalyst effect of international proceedings on the domestic rule of law.

reform processes required to put such an effort in place may not have sufficiently matured. In other situations, the international community might be able to consider from the start how national and other possible international processes could potentially complement each other. In the context of the situations before the ICC, this task may fall to the Assembly of States Parties, the UN Security Council where it makes a referral, or to other regional bodies such as the African Union, the Arab League, the OAS, the OSCE or the EU.[136] A coherent pattern for collaborative action between the international community and national authorities could provide opportunities for synergies, including through the exchange of best practices and lessons learned; the cross-fertilisation of jurisprudence; operational assistance and collaboration in the investigation of and prosecution of crimes; the temporary secondment of legal professionals and specialised trainings; the transfer of knowledge management, legal tools and evidence storage techniques; the promotion of international co-operation and judicial assistance; as well as the promotion of the rule of law and transitional justice efforts more generally.[137]

3.3.2. Proceedings in Third States, Including on the Basis of Universal Jurisdiction

Where the State directly affected simply cannot assume the primary burden to prosecute crimes, either due to sheer incapacity or lack of political will, the role of other States in the international system may be invoked. As observed in the Report of the Secretary-General on the rule of law and transitional justice in conflict and post-conflict societies, "Of course, domestic justice systems should be the first resort in pursuit of accountability. But where domestic authorities are unwilling or unable to prosecute violators at home, the role of the international community becomes crucial".[138]

---

[136] See, *e.g.*, S/RES/1593, para. 5; Report of the African Union High-Level Panel on Darfur (AUPD), *supra* n. 98.

[137] Tolbert and Kontić, 2009, 159-162. In practice the opportunities for such synergies have typically been underutilised, see Cesare Romano, Andre Nollkaemper and Jann Kleffner (eds.), *Internationalized Criminal Courts Sierra Leone, East Timor, Kosovo, and Cambodia*, Oxford, 2004.

[138] As the *Rule of Law Report* notes, "Of course, domestic justice systems should be the first resort in pursuit of accountability. But where domestic authorities are unwilling

One possible base for the exercise of jurisdiction is that of universality. Jurisdiction is asserted not on the basis of any nexus with the forum State, but by virtue of common interests which threaten the international community as a whole and in which all states have a interest in their repression. Although an act may have been committed by a foreigner against a foreign target outside the territory of the State, jurisdiction is asserted as a matter of international public policy.[139] The offender "is treated as an outlaw, as the enemy of all mankind - *hostis humanis generis* - whom any nation may in the interests of all capture and punish".[140] This echoes the well-known dictum in the *Barcelona Traction* case regarding the observance of obligations *erga omnes*.[141] A limited number of crimes attract universal jurisdiction. The crime of piracy is the classical instance,[142] but the modern day classification can be said to include slave trading,[143] genocide,[144] apartheid,[145] and certain categories

or unable to prosecute violators at home, the role of the international community becomes crucial"; S/2004/616, para. 40.

139 Ian Brownlie, *Principles of Public International Law*, Oxford University Press, 2003, 304.

140 *France v. Turkey* (*Lotus case*), PCIJ, Series A. No.10 (1927), Dissenting Opinion of Judge Moore, 70; *Eichmann case*, District Court of Jerusalem, *ILR*, 1961, vol. 36, no. 5.

141 The ICJ distinguished between obligations owed to particular States and those owed "towards the international community as a whole" which "[i]n view of the importance of the rights involved, all States can be held to have a legal interest in their protection; they are obligations *erga omnes*"; *Barcelona Traction case*, para. 33. The statement finds expression in draft article 48(1)(b) of the ILC *Draft Articles on the Responsibility of States for Internationally Wrongful Acts* (2001), which provides that "[a]ny State other than an injured State is entitled to invoke the responsibility of another State ... if ... the obligation breached is owed to the international community as a whole"; A/56/10 (2001). This is subject to draft articles 43 (notice of claim), 44 (admissibility of claims) and 45 (loss of the right to invoke responsibility).

142 While there may be uncertainty as to the customary law definition of piracy (Jennings and Watts, *op. cit.*, §.272), its customary status is beyond doubt. For a treaty definition *see* article 15, *Convention on the High Seas* (1958).

143 Jennings and Watts, *op. cit.* §429.

144 *Advisory Opinion on Reservations to the Convention on the Prevention and Punishment of the Crime of Genocide*, ICJ Rep. 1951, 15; *Barcelona Traction, Light and Power Company, Limited, Second Phase*, ICJ Rep. 1970; *Report of the Secretary General*, S/25704, para. 35; *Restatement of the Law: Third Restatement of US Foreign Relations Law*, vol. 2 (1987), §702, 3.

of war crimes, notably as reflected in grave breaches of the 1949 Geneva Conventions.[146] Thus, as the United Nations War Crimes Commission declared "the right to punish war crimes ... is possessed by any independent State whatsoever".[147]

There has been an increased tendency for third States to exercise their concurrent jurisdiction through a range of extra-territorial jurisdictional bases, including active personality, passive personality and universality.[148] The relatively recent upswing of national activity over offences committed abroad has in part been based on a reinvigorated legislative framework for the prosecution of serious human rights and humanitarian law violations that has been introduced in many States under the rubric of legislation implementing for the Rome Statute. Action has also been forthcoming through intergovernmental organisations. In the context of EU, for example, Members States have established a *European Network of contact points in respect of persons responsible for genocide, crimes against humanity and war crimes* to enable direct communication and facilitated exchange of information between centralised, specialised contact points.[149] The EU has also encouraged the exchange of core crimes information between national law enforcement and immigration authorities within and between EU Member States, the establishment of dedicated war crimes units and regular coordination meetings together with representatives of the *ad hoc* Tribunals and the

[145] *Advisory Opinion on Legal Consequences for States of the Continued Presence of South Africa in Namibia,* ICJ Rep. 1971, 57.

[146] *Report of the Secretary General*, S/25704.

[147] *War Crimes Reports*, 1949, vol. 15, no. 26. The British Manual of Military Law reads: "[w]ar crimes are crimes *ex jure gentium*" granting jurisdiction over persons of any nationality to the courts of all States; *British Manual of Military War*, 1958, 637. Similarly, the Supreme Military Tribunal of Italy in the *Wagener* trial held: "[t]hese norms [laws and customs of war], due to their highly ethical and moral content, have a universal character, not a territorial one ... They are .... crimes of *lese-humanite* ... and are to be opposed and punished, in the same way as the crime of piracy, trade in women and minors, and enslavement are to be opposed and punished, wherever they may have been committed"; 13 March 1950, *Rivista Penale* 753, 757 (unofficial translation).

[148] For an overview *see* Rikhof, Chapter 2 above.

[149] EU Council Decision 2002/494/JHA(13 June 2002). The Decision notably recalls the affirmation in Rome Statute preamble that the effective prosecution of the core crimes "must be ensured by taking measures at national level and by enhancing international cooperation".

ICC.[150] Interpol has also established a world-wide national focal points system to provide coordination and support for law enforcement agencies and international organisations responsible for the investigations of genocide, war crimes and crimes against humanity.[151]

Such heightened interaction between and within competent national authorities augments the scope for complementary support for the ICC's own investigative efforts. International cooperation between different jurisdictions may also increase the efficiency and viability of launching criminal proceedings on the basis of universal jurisdiction. This may involve the sharing of information and evidence, the transfer of criminal proceedings or the recognition of foreign judgments, the temporary transfer of a person in custody for purposes of identification or for obtaining testimony or other assistance, or the extradition of suspects. The expectation, however, that national authorities will be able routinely engage significant resources into costly trials for crimes committed abroad, and which may have little connection to the forum State, appears misplaced. At present, investigations leading to domestic prosecutions for crimes committed abroad remain exceptional.[152] Instead, the majority of investigations lead to exclusion from refugee and immigration procedures and to deportations.[153] As important as is the guarantee of not providing a safe haven for persons suspected of committing international crimes, a global system for the enforcement of international criminal law norms cannot rest on the exercise of universal jurisdiction alone.

The experience of universal jurisdiction demonstrates that it may give rise to complex legal, political and diplomatic questions.[154]

---

150 EU Council Decision 2003/335/JHA(8 May 2003). *See also* FIDH and REDRESS, *Fostering a European Approach to Accountability for genocide, crimes against humanity, war crimes and torture: Extraterritorial Jurisdiction and the European Union* (April 2007).

151 Source: http://www.interpol.int/public/CrimesAgainstHumanity/default.asp.

152 For an overview *see AU-EU Expert Report on the Principle of Universal Jurisdiction*, 8672/1/09 REV1 (16 April 2009); Rikhof, Chapter 2 above.

153 This is pursuant, *inter alia*, to article 1(f), *Convention Relating to the Status of Refugees* (1951). *See* Joseph Rikhof, "War Criminals Not Welcome; How Common Law Countries Approach the Phenomenon of International Crimes in the Immigration and Refugee Context", *International Journal of Refugee Law*, 2009, vol. 21, no. 3, 453-507.

154 *Rule of Law Report*, S/2004/616, para. 48.

Nonetheless, where there is no prospect for criminal trials being undertaken in the State(s) directly affected by the crimes, or in situations falling outside of the jurisdiction of the ICC, the exercise of universal jurisdiction may offer the only prospect for holding perpetrators accountable. The assertion of criminal jurisdiction by a foreign court, moreover, may catalyse public debate and a re-examination of domestic amnesties or immunities in the territorial State.[155] Universal jurisdiction will therefore continue to form a significant component of an overall global strategy to combat impunity. Enhancing the domestic extraterritorial jurisdiction will help close gaps in the global compliance regime, as will extending the number and range of treaties governing extradition and mutual legal assistance in criminal matters.

3.3.3. Proceedings in Third States, Based on the Accomplice Liability of their Nationals

Another way in which third States can exercise jurisdiction in response to situations of mass atrocity is to examine the liability of their own nationals. This may stem from their participation as a principal to crimes committed abroad. It may also take the form of accomplice liability. Complicity may arise from activities related to supporting fugitives or the channelling of material or other assistance to armed groups suspected of committing crimes. Another form of complicity, explored below, relates to corporate wrongdoing.

It is well known that conflict in unstable governance zones is often driven by financial gain. This may accrue from the exploitation of natural resources, the control of transportation and supply routes, or the corrupt influencing of government oversight mechanisms to protect vested business interests. As documented by numerous Security Council mandated Exert Panels, a significant number of allegations involve companies complicit in abuses committed by armed forces or groups.[156] In a survey of the allegations of the worst cases of corporate-related human rights harm, the Special Representative of the Secretary-General on

[155] *See*, *e.g.*, domestic debates triggered by proceedings in third States against, *inter alia*, Augusto Pinochet, Hissène Habré and Ricardo Miguel Cavallo.

[156] See *Report of the Secretary-General on the implementation of Security Council resolution 1625 (2005) on conflict prevention, particularly in Africa*, S/2008/18 (14 January 2008).

human rights and transnational corporations and other business enterprises, has noted that they

> … occurred, predictably, where governance challenges were greatest: disproportionately in low income countries; in countries that often had just emerged from or still were in conflict; and in countries where the rule of law was weak and levels of corruption high … The human rights regime cannot function as intended in the unique circumstances of sporadic or sustained violence, governance breakdown, and absence of the rule of law.[157]

The response of the international community has included targeted sanctions against individuals and corporate entities, such as asset freezes and travel bans, deemed to have contributed to conflicts.[158] The number of domestic jurisdictions in which charges for international crimes can be brought against corporations and their executives has also increased, as has the possibility for companies to incur non-criminal liability for complicity in human rights abuses.[159]

The criminal liability of corporate agents under international law may from stem a number of available modes of complicity. Under the Rome Statute, for example, this may arise by soliciting or inducing the commission of such a crime which in fact occurs or is attempted; or for the purpose of facilitating the commission of such a crime, aiding, abetting or otherwise assisting in its commission or its attempted commission, including providing the means for its commission; or in any

157 *Protect, Respect and Remedy: a Framework for Business and Human Rights*, Report of the Special Representative of the Secretary-General on the issue of human rights and transnational corporations and other business enterprises, John Ruggie, A/HRC/8/5 (7 April 2008), para. 16.

158 "It is … imperative that we also broaden our responses and adopt a more comprehensive approach that includes the development of appropriate norms and frameworks aimed at ensuring that the activities of the business sector do not exacerbate or fuel conflicts … The Security Council has played a role in advancing that agenda, but more needs to be done to strengthen the international regulatory framework and encourage States to forcefully and constructively promote conflict-sensitive practices in their business sectors"; S/2008/18, paras. 19-20.

159 A/HRC/8/5 (2008), para. 74. See also Andrea Reggio, "Aiding and betting In International Law The Responsibility of Corporate Agents and Businessman for Trading With The Enemy of Mankind", *ICLR*, 2005, vol. 5, 623-696; International Commission of Jurists (ICJ) Expert Panel on Corporate Complicity in International Crimes, http://www.icj.org/IMG/June_06_Update.pdf.

other way contributing to the commission or attempted commission of a crime by a group of persons acting with a common purpose. In the case of the latter, such contribution must be intentional and must either be made with the aim of furthering the criminal activity or criminal purpose of the group, where such activity or purpose involves the commission of a crime within the jurisdiction of the Court; or be made in the knowledge of the intention of the group to commit the crime.[160] The responsibility of a civilian superior, moreover, may be invoked where crimes are committed by subordinates under his or her effective authority and control, as a result of his or her failure to exercise control properly over such subordinates.[161]

Criminal prosecutions have precedents in the prosecutions of industrialists after WWII[162] and are reflected in a number of domestic test cases.[163] Despite the range of permissible jurisdictional bases, however,

[160] Article 25(3), ICC Statute. See also *Prosecutor v. Furundžija*, Judgment, No IT-95-17/1 (ICTY Trial Chamber, 10 December 1998) and *Prosecutor v. Akayesu*, Judgment, No ICTR-96-4-T (ICTR Trial Chamber 2 September 1998).

[161] Article 28(b), ICC Statute. Liability arises where: (i) the superior either knew, or consciously disregarded information which clearly indicated, that the subordinates were committing or about to commit such crimes; (ii) the crimes concerned activities that were within the effective responsibility and control of the superior; and (iii) the superior failed to take all necessary and reasonable measures within his or her power to prevent or repress their commission or to submit the matter to the competent authorities for investigation and prosecution.

[162] See cases against *Krupp* (Law Reports of Trials of War Criminals, Volume X, 69), *Flick* (Law Reports of Trials of War Criminals, Volume IX, 1), *I.G. Farben* (Law Reports of Trials of War Criminals, Volume X, 1), *Zyklon B* (Law Reports of Trials of War Criminals, Volume I, 93) and Roechling (Law Reports of Trials of War Criminals, Volume X, 56–57). See *History of the United Nations War Crimes Commission and the Development of the Laws of War* (1948).

[163] See prosecutions brought in The Netherlands against van Anraat (LJN: AX6406 Rechtbank's-Gravenhage, 09/751003-04 English translation; LJN: BA6734, Gerechtshof's-Gravenhage, 2200050906-2) and van Kouwenhoven (LJN: AY5160, Rechtbank's-Gravenhage, 09/750001-05 English translation; LJN: BC7 373, Gerechtshof's-Gravenhage, 22-004337-06V); prosecutions brought in France and Belgium against two executives of TotalFinaElf (CITE); and the Kilwa case involving three executives of Anvil (High Commissioner for Human Rights Concerned at Kilwa Military Trial in the Democratic Republic of the Congo; Press Release; Geneva, 4 July 2007). *See also* the more than forty civil class action suits brought in the US under the ATCA dealing with corporate liability for international crimes, such as: *Roe and Doe v. Unocal*, Case No. 00-56603; 00-56628 (9th Cir. 2002); *Wiwa v. Royal Dutch Petroleum Co. et al.*, Case No.96 CIV 8386 (KMW) (S.D.N.Y. 2002); *The Presbyterian Church of Sudan et al. v. Talisman Energy, Inc.*, Case No. 01CV9882 (S.D.N.Y. 2001); *Villeda et al. v.*

domestic criminal proceedings involving transnational corporate actors have to date rarely proved successful. Variations in national law for attributing liability within transnational corporate structures mean that a parent company often cannot be held responsible for the acts of its subsidiaries.[164] In particular, under the doctrine of separate corporate personality, each member of a corporate group will typically be treated as a distinct legal entity.[165] In criminal actions against individual agents, moreover, the substantiation of the mental element may prove a further challenge for domestic prosecutions.

Collaboration between international and national actors could facilitate linkages and create synergies for pursuing criminal proceedings. In the DRC, for example, the Security Council mandated Group of Experts has highlighted the connections between various armed groups and the ongoing exploitation of natural resources in the troubled Kivu regions, notably gold and cassiterite reserves, which the Group of Experts calculates continues to deliver millions of dollars in direct financing into the coffers of one group alone (*Forces démocratiques de libération du Rwanda*, FDLR) through trading networks comprising a variety of corporations operating in Africa, Asia, the Middle-East and Europe.[166]

Upon taking office, the ICC Prosecutor stated that according to information received, crimes reportedly committed in the DRC appeared to be directly linked to the control of resource extraction sites: "Those who direct mining operations, sell diamonds or gold extracted in these

---

Fresh Del Monte Produce Inc. et al., Case No. 01-CIV-3399 (S.D. Fla.2001); *Bowoto et al. v. Chevron et al.*, Case No. C99-2506 (N.D. Cal. 2000); *Estate of Rodriguez et al. v. Drummond Company, Inc. et al.*, Case No. CV-02-0665-W (N.D. Ala. 2002). For an overview see *Business and International Crimes: Assessing the Liability of Business Entities for Grave Violations of International Law*, International Peace Academy and Fafo, available at http://www.fafo.no/ liabilities; International Peace Information Service (a research institute focused on arms trade, exploitation of natural resources and corporate social responsibility in Sub-Saharan Africa): http://www.ipisresearch.be/?&lang=en.

164 *Business and Human Rights: Mapping International Standards of Responsibility and Accountability for Corporate Acts*, Report of the Special Representative of the Secretary-General (SRSG) on the issue of human rights and transnational corporations and other business enterprises, A/HRC/4/035 (9 February 2007), para. 29.

165 *Ibid.*

166 *Final report of the Group of Experts on the DRC submitted in accordance with paragraph 8 of Security Council resolution 1857 (2008)*, S/2009/603 (23 November 2009).

conditions, launder the dirty money or provide weapons could also be authors of the crimes, even if they are based in other countries".[167] More recently, the Office of the Prosecutor has announced that is developing a law enforcement network project for this purpose with a number of interested States.[168] Through such a collaborative approach, international investigators and prosecutors who have crime base information could potentially cooperate with third State counterparts to facilitate the building of complicity cases back home.[169] It has also entered into discussions with the Organisation for Economic Cooperation and Development to cooperation with its efforts to promote responsible behaviour of multinational enterprises in the mining sector in areas of conflict or fragility where the ICC is investigating.[170]

As the experience of the DRC shows, repression of accomplice liability is not marginal to the commission of crimes: the economic benefits derived from the commission of crimes may be instrumental to exacerbating or fueling conflict. Efforts to curb the sources of funding to the parties of an armed conflict or to prevent illegal exploitation of natural resources may thus be intimately intertwined with efforts to disrupt the cycle of violence. States could take active steps to counter the permissive environment for corporate wrongdoing in conflict zones. Such action could

167 *Second Assembly of States Parties to the Rome Statute of the International Criminal Court Report of the Prosecutor of the ICC,* Mr. Luis Moreno-Ocampo on 8 September 2003. "The investigation of financial transactions, for example for the purchase of arms, may well provide evidence proving the commission of atrocities. Here again the interaction between State authorities and the Office of the Prosecutor will be crucial: national investigative authorities may pass to the Office evidence of financial transactions which will be essential to the Court's investigations of crimes within the Court's jurisdiction; for its part, the Office may have evidence of the commission of financial crimes which can be passed to national authorities for domestic prosecutions. Such prosecutions will be a key deterrent to the commission of future crimes, if they can curb the source of funding"; *ibid.*

168 *See Prosecutorial Strategy, 2009-2012* (ICC-OTP). *See also* R. Gallmetzer, "Prosecuting Persons doing Business with Armed Groups in Conflict Areas – the Strategy of the OTP and the OTP's Law Enforcement Network", *JICJ* 2010, Special Issue.

169 Examples include the *van Anraat case* where Dutch prosecutors collaborated with the Prosecutor's Office at the Special Court for Sierra Leone, which was concurrently investigating Charles Taylor, to build a case against a Dutch industrialist accused of complicity in the crimes; *supra* n. 155.

170 *OTP Weekly Briefing 26 January-1 February (Issue #22)*; available at http://www.icc-cpi.int.

form an important part of a global system for the repression of international crimes.

3.4. Conclusion

The complementarity regime of the ICC is the cornerstone of the Rome Statute.[171] While confirming the notion of concurrent jurisdiction, it emphasises a preference for the exercise of domestic jurisdiction over international crimes. In doing so, the ICC is often described as the weaker sibling of *ad hoc* Tribunals because it lacks primacy. Arguably, however, the institutional relationship created between the ICC and national authorities is far more coherent than that of previous international courts and tribunals.[172] This is because the complementarity framework and the accompanying admissibility provisions grant the Court strong supervisory powers over national proceedings and create powerful incentives to promote domestic compliance. Indeed, compared to the oft unfulfilled obligations created by previous treaty regimes, the Statute establishes a far more profound set of interactions between international norms and domestic practice, resulting in heightened prospects for actual enforcement.

In this sense, the entry into force of the Rome Statute is about more than the establishment of a new court: it creates a global compliance system for the enforcement of international criminal law.[173] This is done by locating the ICC within the existing framework of customary and treaty obligations binding States. Within this system, the ICC operates as

---

[171] *Prosecutor v. Joseph Kony et al.*, Pre-Trial Chamber II, Decision on the admissibility of the case under article 19(1) of the Statute, ICC-02/04-01/05-377 (10 March 2009), para. 34.

[172] As discussed above, this has been tempered, in part, by the adoption and practice of rule 11*bis* transfers and the Tribunal's completion strategies.

[173] Yuval Shany, *The Competing Jurisdictions of International Courts and Tribunals*, Oxford, 2004, 86-127, in reference to the community of international courts and tribunals, suggests "the combined effect of more organized jurisdictional inter-fora relations and a higher degree of jurisprudential consistency could transform international courts and tribunals into a judicial system, enjoying meaningful levels of inner-coherence, and thus result in the strengthening of the unity of international law" – an observation that could equally apply to the relationship between States Parties and the ICC within the framework of the Rome Statute. See also William Burke-White, "A Community of Courts: Toward a System of International Criminal Law Enforcement", *Mich. J. Int'l L.* 2003, vol. 24, no. 1.

the exception and not the norm, since the primary responsibility for the repression of international crimes resides with domestic institutions. The Court can stir States to take action by contestual competition over forum allocation, but it can also encourage collaboration and synergies across multiple fora. The success of this global justice system will therefore rely on the balance struck between international and national action; between incentives and coercion; between contest and collaboration.

The Court has started to prosecute its first cases. At the same time, the international community appears to be increasingly concerned with emphasising the responsibility of national authorities to combat impunity. For some States this may mask a reactive posture to protect vested interests under the cloak of national sovereignty. But for an increasing number of States it appears to arise out of concern for the viability of a sustainable rule of law system.[174]

As described above, there are numerous ways in which complementarity national approaches can be implemented. While the primary locus of domestic action will tend to reside in the States most directly affected by the crimes, in many situations it may be premature or unrealistic to expect countries in the midst of or recently emerging from massive violence to resort to the investigations and prosecutions of atrocity crimes. In these situations, the role of third States may become invoked within the international system. This may take the form of institutional assistance to those States directly affected by the crimes; the exercise of universal jurisdiction; and the investigation of individual or corporate accomplice liability stemming from the territory of a third State.

[174] Notably the issue of complementarity, in view of what more States can do to combat impunity, formed one of the four thematic strands of the stocktaking exercise undertaken by ICC States Parties at the 2010 Review Conference. *See* Assembly of States Parties, *Report of the Bureau on stocktaking: Complementarity*, ICC-ASP/8/51 (18 March 2010); Resolution RC/Res.1, *Complementarity*, adopted at the 9th plenary meeting of the Review Conference (8 June 2010).

4

The Relationship between the Principle of Complementarity and the Exercise of Universal Jurisdiction for Core International Crimes

Jo Stigen*

4.1. Introduction

The International Criminal Court (ICC) and the concept of universal jurisdiction have striking conceptual similarities: Both mechanisms shall prevent impunity for core international crimes by letting an alternative judiciary step in when the states that should normally have prosecuted fail. In this light, they should be seen as fallback mechanisms that intended to complement and not supplant the states with the closest links to the crimes. Prosecuting core international crimes remains the primary responsibility of the territorial state and the perpetrator's home state.

Prosecutions in these two states, and in particular the territorial state, are usually preferable. This is where the likelihood of a successful prosecution is greatest, and the process can strengthen a fragile democracy and reinstate the rule of law by signalling the condemnation of a former violent regime.[1] From a sovereignty perspective, a state's right to exercise criminal jurisdiction over acts committed in its territory and elsewhere by its citizens is, although not amounting to a prerogative, an undisputed part of its sovereignty, and the exercise of jurisdiction in a bystander state can be seen as undue interference and create dangerous

* **Jo Stigen** is Associate Professor at the University of Oslo. He holds a doctorate on complementarity from the same University. He has previously worked for the Solicitor General and Ministry of Justice of Norway.

[1] Neil J. Kritz, "Coming to terms with atrocities: A review of accountability mechanisms for mass violations of human rights", *Law and Contemporary Problems*, 1996, vol. 59, 127, at 133, noting that "domestic courts can be more sensitive to the nuances of local culture". He also suggests that the local effects will be greater, at p. 131. For a discussion on the interrelation between resolution, reconstruction and reconciliation and their implications for peacebuilding, see Johan Galtung's editorial in *The Challenge of peace: An interactive Newsletter of the War-Torn Societies Project*, vol. 2, United Nations Research Institute for Social Development (UNRISD), October 1995.

friction. Domestic prosecutions are also in line with liberal international law theories which argue that the primary function of public international law is to influence and improve the functioning of domestic institutions.[2]

Despite these advantages, a clear rule of priority to domestic proceedings is only established for the ICC, not for universal jurisdiction. Under the principle of complementarity, a case is inadmissible before the ICC if it is being or has been genuinely investigated or prosecuted by a state with jurisdiction (note that priority is enjoyed not only by the directly affected states, but any state with jurisdiction).[3] This rule is arguably the single most important factor as to why more than 110 states have accepted the ICC's jurisdiction.[4] It therefore seems reasonable to suggest that a rule of priority for the states directly affected by the crime would contribute to making universal jurisdiction more acceptable.

States have among them so far failed to establish *any* comprehensive regime for allocating cases between states with competing jurisdiction. Besides, it should be noted that the right of states to exercise universal jurisdiction remains controversial.[5] Yet this chapter will show that a subsidiarity principle for universal jurisdiction, requiring the forum state to first offer the case to the territorial state and the suspect's home state, is in the process of being developed. After a brief survey of relevant international law instruments and national jurisprudence, the chapter will discuss how the ICC's complementarity principle might contribute to the development and refinement of a subsidiarity principle.

---

2 William Burke-White, "A Community of Courts", *Michigan Journal of International Law*, 2002, vol. 24, p. 1, at 90, referring to Anne-Marie Slaughter, "A Liberal Theory of International Law", *American Society of International Law Proceedings*, 2000, vol. 94, p. 240, at 246.

3 Rome Statute of the International Criminal Court article 17.

4 Number of states parties to the Rome Statute as of 31 January 2010, see http://www.icc-cpi.int/Menus/ASP/states+parties/The+States+Parties+to+the+Rome+Statute.htm.

5 This author is of the opinion that international law currently allows the exercise of universal jurisdiction between the parties to the Geneva Conventions, the First Additional Protocol and the Convention against Torture. A customary rule allowing universal jurisdiction for these and perhaps other core international crimes, including for genocide and crimes against humanity, seems to be under development, see Jo Stigen, "The Right or Non-Right of States to Prosecute Core International Crimes under the Title of 'Universal Jurisdiction'", *Baltic Yearbook of International Law* (forthcoming summer 2010).

4.2. Subsidiarity and International Instruments and Jurisprudence

It is doubtful whether the Geneva Conventions, their First Additional Protocol or the Convention against Torture establishes a subsidiarity criterion. The respective wordings speak against it. The Geneva Conventions and the first Additional Protocol obligate the forum state to bring the suspect before its courts or, "if it prefers", extradite to another affected state party "in accordance with the provisions of its own legislation".[6] The Convention against Torture instructs the forum state to bring the suspect before its competent authorities for criminal prosecution "if it does not extradite him". It thus seems that the forum state has a free choice, to either prosecute or extradite, under these conventions.[7]

The ICJ has not pronounced on the existence of a subsidiarity criterion (indeed, it has yet to pronounce on the legality of universal jurisdiction as a basis for states to prosecute). In the *Arrest Warrant* case, judges Higgins, Kooijmans and Buergenthal opined in their separate opinion that a state seeking to exercise universal jurisdiction "must … ensure that certain safeguards are in place [that] are absolutely essential to prevent abuse and to ensure that the rejection of impunity does not

6 Articles 49, 50, 129 and 146 of the Geneva Conventions I-IV respectively.

7 Burgers and Danelius seem to find that the Torture Convention establishes subsidiarity in the sense that an extradition request from the state concerned enjoys priority: "During the *travaux préparatoires* it was suggested that jurisdiction should exist after a certain time had elapsed without extradition having been requested, but no such time-limit appears in the text of the Convention. Each State is therefore free to determine, within reasonable limits, at what stage it is justified to *conclude that no extradition request will be made*", see Herman J. Burgers and Hans Danelius, *The United Nations Convention against Torture: A Handbook on the Convention against Torture and other Cruel, Inhuman, or Degrading Treatment or Punishment*, Dordrecht, 1988, pp. 132-133 (my emphasis). Bantekas suggests that the convention does not establish subsidiarity, see Ilias Bantekas and Susan Nash, *International Criminal Law*, Oxon, 2007, p. 88. Higgins *et al.* believe that the Geneva Conventions give the *forum state* primary jurisdiction, see *Democratic Republic of the Congo v. Belgium*, *ICJ Reports* 2002, p. 3 (*Arrest Warrant* case), p. 71, para. 30. The latter is supported by the ICRC's pronunciation that "[e]xtradition is restricted by the municipal law of the country which detains the accused person", see Jean Pictet (ed.), *Commentary on the Geneva Conventions of 12 August 1949*, Vol. IV, Geneva ICRC, 1958, p. 593.

jeopardize stable relations between States".[8] More specifically, the three judges remarked:

> A State contemplating bringing criminal charges based on universal jurisdiction must first offer to the national State of the prospective accused person the opportunity itself to act upon the charges concerned.[9]

As for international instruments of an advisory character, the International Law Institute's *Krakow Resolution* proposes that the forum state shall "carefully consider" extradition to another state with territorial or personal connection to the crime, the perpetrator or the victim.[10] Likewise, the *Princeton Principles* on universal jurisdiction proposes that the forum state shall, when it receives a request for extradition to another state, take into account, *inter alia*, "the place of commission of the crime" and "the nationality connection of the victim to the requesting state",[11] proposing priority for the victim's home state but not for the suspect's home state.

A rule of priority for the state most affected by the crime *vis-à-vis* other states with jurisdiction is not supported by wording of the Rome Statute. The principle of complementarity instructs the ICC to yield to genuine proceedings in any "State which has jurisdiction", including proceedings based on universal jurisdiction.[12]

---

8 *Arrest Warrant* case, *supra* note 7, p. 80, para. 59. The remark concerned universal jurisdiction *in absentia*, but seems relevant also with regard to universal jurisdiction more generally.

9 *Ibid.*

10 Institute of International Law, *Universal criminal jurisdiction with regard to the crime of genocide, crimes against humanity and war crimes* (2005), see http://www.idi-iil.org/idiE/resolutionsE/2005_kra_03_en.pdf, provision 3(d).

11 The Princeton Principles on Universal Jurisdiction Principle, principle 8(b) and (d), available at http://www1.umn.edu/humanrts/instree/princeton.html.

12 Rome Statute article 17. The priority of states without any link to the crime stands in contrast to the initial concern expressed by the International Law Commission in its discussion on the establishment of the ICC that "the principle of universal jurisdiction has major drawbacks. States are often placed under extreme duress, or even become victims of blackmail or violent crimes perpetrated by groups of terrorists or other criminals bent on blocking either the trial of an offender by the State concerned or extradition", see *Yearbook of the International Law Commission*, 1992, vol. II, A/CN.4/SER.A/1992/Add.1, p. 52, para 7.

One can hope that the ICJ in the near future will pronounce not only on the lawfulness and scope of universal jurisdiction, but also on the existence or non-existence of a subsidiarity criterion. It might happen in *Certain Criminal Proceedings in France* concerning the exercise of universal jurisdiction over crimes against humanity and torture, where Congo has invoked a subsidiarity principle "which it contends is applicable to criminal proceedings having an international element".[13]

4.3. Subsidiarity and Customary International Law?

In Spain, legislation does not establish subsidiarity, but in 2003, the Supreme Court found, in the *Guatemalan Genocide* case, that Spanish courts could apply universal jurisdiction only if there were legal impediments or prolonged judicial activity in the territorial state or the home state of the perpetrator. The application of such subsidiarity was, however, very deferential as the court noted that to base the decision whether to intervene on real or apparent inactivity in the territorial state "implies judgment by one sovereign State on the judicial capacity of similar judicial bodies in another sovereign State".[14] The Supreme Court refrained from making such inquiry noting that,

> the present case is one of a sovereign State with which Spain maintains normal diplomatic relations. A declaration of this nature, which has the potential of extraordinary importance in terms of international relations, does not belong to the judicial bodies of a State. Article 97 of the Spanish Constitution provides that the Government directs foreign affairs, and one should not ignore the potential repercussions of such a declaration by the judiciary in this area.[15]

---

13 *Republic of the Congo v. France*, Request for the indication of a provisional measure, Order 17 June 2003, *ICJ Reports*, 2003, p. 102, para. 25.

14 *Tribunal Supremo*, 25 February 2003, Case No. 327-2003, section II, sixth paragraph. For Spanish text and English translation (see separate link), see http://www.derechos.org/nizkor/guatemala/doc/gtmsent.html. The case concerned the prosecution of five Guatemalan generals for genocide and other crimes against the Maya Indians in Guatemala in the 1970s and 1980s. No direct connection to Spain existed.

15 It should be noted that some national legislations require political authorization of any exercise of universal jurisdiction. In Norway, that used to be the case (Penal Code 1902, section 13(1)), but a recently adopted penal code leaves the decision with the Norwegian Chief Prosecutor (Penal Code 2005, section 65).

The Supreme Court's minority noted, however, that such severe limits on the application of universal jurisdiction for genocide were "incompatible with treatment of this grave crime against humanity in accordance with our domestic law and in accordance with international law".[16] It noted that any limits had to come from a flexible, prudential rule of reason aimed at practical concerns like the potential effectiveness of an investigation and extradition request or a potential high burden on the Spanish courts. In the minority's opinion it should be sufficient for Spanish courts to exercise jurisdiction that

> in the present case, from the documentation presented by the complaint and validated by the investigating judge, it is manifestly clear that many years have passed since the occurrence of these acts, and for some reason or another, the courts in Guatemala have not been able to effectively exercise jurisdiction with regard to genocide of the Mayan population.[17]

In 2005, after Zapatero had become Prime Minister, the Constitutional Court found only one legal criterion, namely *ne bis in idem*. The Court noted that a subsidiarity test as applied by the Supreme Court amounted to a *probation diabolica* which would jeopardize the right of victims to seek an effective remedy as guaranteed by article 24(1) of the Spanish Constitution.[18]

In the *Al-Daraj* case, regarding alleged war crimes in Gaza in 2002, the *Audiencia Nacional* in May 2009 authorized an investigation into the matter on the basis of universal jurisdiction, noting that "the judicial authorities of Israel have not initiated any criminal proceedings with the objective of determining if the events denounced could entail some

[16] *Ibid.*, dissenting opinion, first paragraph.

[17] *Ibid.*, fourth paragraph.

[18] *Tribunal Constitucional*, 26 September 2005, Case No. STC 237/2005. The judgment is commented on in Naomi Roht-Arriaza, "International Decisions", *American Journal of International Law*, 2006, vol. 100, no. 1, 207. In 2006, a Spanish judge issued an international arrest warrant for Montt and his co-suspects, see Arrest warrant for Ríos Montt, Óscar Humberto Mejía Victores and Romeo Lucas Garc, issued by Spanish judge Santiago Pedraz on 7 July 2006. In 2007, the *Guatemalan* Constitutional Court refused the extradition noting that that Spain lacked jurisdiction (Decision of Guatemala's Constitutional Court of 18 December 2007).

criminal liability".[19] Neither an internal military probe nor a commission of inquiry appointed by the prime minister could be seen as independent and impartial. As a response to this, however, Israel informed Spanish authorities that the case was subject to proceedings in Israel. Shortly thereafter, the prosecutor requested the court not to proceed with the case. In July 2009 the Appeals Court reversed the decision to prosecute by a 14-4 vote, referring to the Israeli investigation. This prompted widespread criticism that the Spanish judiciary had yielded to political pressure from the Spanish Ministry for Foreign Affairs and Israel. Be that as it may, the decision still suggests that Spanish courts will defer only if the case is being adequately dealt with by the territorial state.

A similar principle was applied by the Spanish Supreme Court in the *Peruvian Genocide* case, only here it was referred to as a "principle of necessity of jurisdictional intervention".[20]

In Belgium, the federal prosecutor may refuse to initiate proceedings if the

> specific circumstances of the case show that, in the interest of the proper administration of justice and in order to honor Belgium's international obligations, said case should be brought either before the international courts, or before the court of the place in which the acts were committed, or before the court of the State of which the perpetrator is a national, or the court of the place in which he can be found, and to the extent that said court is independent, impartial, and fair, as may be determined from the international commitments binding on Belgium and that State.[21]

This formulation is somewhat problematic as it can be interpreted so as to give relevance to the mere fact that Belgium and the state concerned are parties to a treaty instructing states to proceed independently and impartially. Thus, the provision may make it possible to base a deferral on the state's general obligation instead of its compliance with this obligation *in casu*.

---

19 Audiencia Nacional, Preliminary Proceedings No. 157/2008, 4 May 2009, English translation available at www.pchgaza.org/files/PressR/English/2009/04-05-2009-2.html.

20 Tribunal Supremo, Judgment No. 712/2003, 20 May 2003, Spanish text available at www.derechos.org/nizkor/peru/doc/tsperu.html.

21 *Code de procédure pénale*, article 12*bis*, para. 4.

In Germany, the legislation on universal jurisdiction is clearly inspired by the complementarity principle. The federal prosecutor may hand over a case to an international or foreign national court when this is "zulässig und beabsichtigt".[22] The legislator has explained that the

> jurisdiction of third-party states must in any case be understood as a subsidiary jurisdiction which should prevent impunity, but not otherwise inappropriately interfere with the primary responsible jurisdictions.[23]

This wording leaves crucial questions open: what is meant by "prevent impunity" and "inappropriately interfere"?

In 2004, the German Federal Prosecutor decided not to initiate criminal proceedings against the United States' Secretary of Defence, Donald Rumsfeld, for alleged abuses in the Abu Ghraib prison. The Federal Prosecutor referred to sovereignty and pragmatic considerations and found that the jurisdictional priority of the suspect's home state was contingent upon that state's willingness and ability to prosecute. The prosecutor based his deferral on a finding that there were "no indications that the authorities and courts of the United States of America are refraining, or would refrain, from penal measures as regards the violations described in the complaint".[24] The fact that the possibility of American authorities investigating Rumsfeld was utterly remote was not problematized.[25] In a 2007 decision not to prosecute Rumsfeld the federal prosecutor lowered the belief in an American criminal proceeding, as expressed in the 2004 decision. Instead, the deferral was now based on a finding that a German investigation would be futile:

---

22 *Strafprozessordnung* (BGBl. I, S. 1074, 1319) para. 153f(2), English translation available in *International Legal Material*, 2003, vol. 42, p. 1258, at 1267.

23 *Referentenentwurf: Entwurf eines Gesetzeszur Einführung des Völkerstrafgesetzbuches*, 22 June 2001, p. 85 (my translation); for German text, see http://www.lrz-muenchen.de/~satzger/unterlagen/V3D.pdf.

24 Decision 3 ARP 207/04-2, 10 February 2005, English translation available at http://www.brusselstribunal.org/pdf/RumsfeldGermany.pdf. The federal prosecutor found that German courts had universal jurisdiction over the acts, but the territorial state and the suspect's home state had priority according to *Strafprozessordnung*, para. 153f (2).

25 The decision is criticized in Andreas Fischer-Lescano, "Torture in Abu Ghraib: The complaint against Donald Rumsfeld under the German code of crimes against international law", *German Law Journal*, 2005, vol. 6, p. 689.

> [I]t is necessary to counteract the danger that complainants will … force investigative authorities into complicated, but ultimately unsuccessful investigations … The view of the complainant that the Federal Republic of Germany must act as a representative of the 'international community' and therefore at least take up investigations is thus mistaken … [An investigation would only be justified] if significant success in resolving the situation could be achieved by investigations by German prosecution authorities, in order to prepare for future prosecutions (either in Germany or abroad). But this is not the case.[26]

This brief survey has demonstrated that a subsidiarity principle for universal jurisdiction can be convenient both for states genuinely seeking to combat international crimes and for states reluctant to interfere in other states' affairs. The principle can justify the exercise of universal jurisdiction by highlighting that neither the territorial state nor the perpetrator's home state deals genuinely the case. But it can also justify non-interference by referring to it as an unqualified rule of priority for the affected states. The major difference is that states with a deferential approach assume *a priori* that the states concerned will deal adequately with the case and base this on a general evaluation of the domestic judiciary without questioning whether the concrete case in question will be genuinely dealt with.

Currently, there is too little state practice to conclude that international law attaches a subsidiarity principle to universal jurisdiction.[27] Universal jurisdiction is still relatively rarely exercised, and when it is, some states apply a subsidiarity principle and some do not. It seems, however, fair to suggest that a subsidiarity criterion is in the process of being developed. Colangelo notes that,

[26] Decision 3 ARP 156/06-2, 5 April 2007; English translation available at http://ccrjustice.org/files/ProsecutorsDecision.pdf.

[27] It may be noted that the UN Darfur Report suggests that "customary rules in question … arguably make the exercise of universal jurisdiction subject to two major conditions. … Second, before initiating criminal proceedings [the forum state] should request the territorial state … or the State of active nationality … whether it is willing to institute proceedings against that person and, hence, prepared to request extradition", see Report on the International Commission of Inquiry on Darfur to the UN Secretary-General of 25 January 2005, § 614.

> it is probably premature to conclude that state practice and *opinio juris* already have combined to definitively establish that a State with territorial or national jurisdiction has adjudicative priority over States with only universal jurisdiction. Nonetheless, a legal trend appears to be developing in this direction.[28]

4.4. How Can the ICC's Principle of Complementarity Contribute to the Development and Refinement of a Subsidiarity Criterion for Universal Jurisdiction?

With the ICC's principle of complementarity widely recognized as a sensible way of allocating cases between the ICC and national jurisdictions, applying such a deferential understanding of universal jurisdiction as in the 2004 German decision, has become increasingly difficult. As will be noted below, this is especially the case for States Parties to the Rome Statute.

In this section it will be shown that the material and procedural rules governing the ICC's principle of complementarity can serve as a useful model for how a subsidiarity criterion for universal jurisdiction should be defined and applied.[29]

4.4.1. Criminal Proceedings in the State Affected

Once universality is established as a valid jurisdictional basis, neither the territorial state nor the suspect's home state can object to the exercise of jurisdiction as such. If the right to exercise universal jurisdiction is to have any meaning, a subsidiarity principle should not require the forum state to defer unless a criminal proceeding has been, is being or will be conducted in one of the two said state. If neither offers an alternative venue for bringing the suspect to justice, deferring will mean impunity, and the purpose of universal jurisdiction will be undermined.

---

[28] Anthony J. Colangelo, "Universal Jurisdiction as an International 'False Conflict' of Laws", *Michigan Journal of International Law*, 2009, vol. 30, p. 881, at 900.

[29] Tomuschat notes that universal jurisdiction is to be understood as default jurisdiction and that "it would seem reasonable to address this issue by analogy to the jurisprudence under Article 17 of the Rome Statute", see Christian Tomuschat, "Issues of universal jurisdiction in the Scilingo case", *Journal of International Criminal Justice*, 2005, vol. 3, p. 174, at 1081.

Under the complementarity principle, only existing criminal proceedings will pre-empt the ICC's exercise of jurisdiction. Article 17(1)(a)-(c) make a case inadmissible before the ICC only if it has been subject to criminal proceedings in a state with jurisdiction. It is suggested that a similar rule should apply *mutatis mutandis* when a third state considers exercising universal jurisdiction.

One can of course, as a matter of policy, debate whether alternative accountability mechanisms – such as a truth and reconciliation commission (TRC) – should also pre-empt the exercise of universal jurisdiction. A TRC may serve some of key purposes that a trial is supposed to serve.[30] The choice made in the Rome Statute should, however, be viewed as a policy choice and an expression that only criminal justice is an adequate reaction to international crimes. With more than 110 states now having ratified the Statute, it is difficult to imagine that states would require less than criminal proceedings as a subsidiarity criterion. Reference is nevertheless made to the discussion below on prosecutorial discretion, whereby a state may discretionally decide not to exercise universal jurisdiction when the case has been subjected to an alternative accountability mechanism.

4.4.2. Proceedings With Regard to the Same Case or the Entire Situation as Such

It may be questioned whether the home state or the territorial state should be allowed to invoke that it is dealing with the whole situation as such, that is, the genocide or the armed conflict in which the crime in question was committed, but not with that particular crime. In the *Rumsfeld* case, the German federal prosecutor deferred after having noted that the United States were dealing with the entire situation (crimes allegedly committed in an Iraqi prison), referring to the "Gesamtcomplex", although there clearly were no prospect of proceedings against Rumsfeld. The complementarity principle, on its part, only makes a case inadmissible

30 Jo Stigen, *The Relationship between the International Criminal Court and National Jurisdictions. The Principle of Complementarity*, Martinus Nijhoff, 2008, pp. 417 *et seq*.

when the same case has been or is being dealt with by a state with jurisdiction.[31] Ryngaert notes that,

> if a situation is only *generally* being dealt with by the home State, and some individual offenders are not punished for their transgressions, deference … under the subsidiarity principle may not be warranted, unless the home State could advance very good reasons for granting impunity.[32]

If the state concerned advances convincing reasons for not having dealt with the case in question, this might motivate the forum state to discretionally decide not to proceed with the case, but this cannot amount to a duty. Thus, if the forum state decides to defer, this will not be a consequence of a subsidiarity principle but of a discretional decision when proceeding would not be in the interests of justice (see below).

4.4.3. The Standard of the Domestic Proceedings

The complementarity principle does not focus on the proceedings' outcome but on the adequacy of the proceedings as such. The point is not whether the suspect eventually is found guilty or not, but whether the investigation or trial is genuine. According to article 17(1) of the Rome Statute the domestic proceedings must not reflect the state's "unwillingness" or "inability" to proceed genuinely. The case is admissible, despite the existence of domestic proceedings, if the proceedings' purpose has been to shield the perpetrator or if they otherwise are inconsistent with an intent to bring the person to justice.[33] The case is also admissible if the domestic judiciary, due to a total or partial collapse, is unable to carry out the proceedings.[34]

Given the underlying rationale of universal jurisdiction, it is difficult to argue that less than genuine proceedings should pre-empt the exercise of universal jurisdiction. If the forum state were required to defer

---

31 It can be noted that article 17 refers to the inadmissibility of "a case", and there is no link between this provision and article 14 allowing an entire "situation" to be referred to the ICC Prosecutor.

32 Cedric Ryngaert, "Applying the Rome Statute's Complementarity Principle: Drawing Lessons from the Prosecution of Core Crimes by States Acting under the Universality Principle", *Institute for International Law, Working Paper*, 2008, 98, p. 14.

33 Article 17(2).

34 Article 17(3).

to any criminal proceeding, regardless of its adequacy, the risk of impunity would be evident. If the forum state is among the 110 States Parties to the Rome Statute, the expressed responsibility to combat impunity referred to in the preamble also makes it difficult to apply a higher threshold than that outlined by the complementarity principle.[35]

States seem increasingly to realise this. As shown above, there has been a development in Spain from a very deferential application of subsidiarity toward a more meaningful subsidiarity requiring genuine proceedings in the state concerned. As noted, in the *Al Daraj* case, the *Audiencia Nacional* based its decision on a finding the proceedings in Israel did not have the objective of determining if the alleged events could entail criminal liability.[36] This formulation reflects the "unwillingness" standard in the Rome Statute.

In the Rome Statute, "unwillingness" refers to proceedings that are undertaken "for the purpose of shielding the person concerned from criminal responsibility" or otherwise are "inconsistent with an intent to bring the perpetrator to justice". Relevant factors are whether there is "an unjustified delay in the proceedings" and whether the proceedings are not "conducted independently or impartially".[37] With regard to a general subsidiarity criterion, deferring to such non-genuine domestic proceedings would clearly undermine the purpose of universal jurisdiction will be undermined.

As regards the "inability" criterion, the factor mentioned in the Rome Statute is whether the state "due to a total or substantial collapse or unavailability of its national judicial system" is "unable to obtain the accused or the necessary evidence and testimony or otherwise unable to carry out its proceedings".[38] This is a high threshold for deferral, arguably too high to be applied to universal jurisdiction. If the state concerned is unable to carry out its proceedings, the forum state should not be required to defer, regardless of the reason for the domestic inability. The somewhat exaggerated sovereignty concerns which dictated the high threshold in the

35 Preambular paragraph 5 expresses the States Parties' determination "to put an end to impunity for the perpetrators of these crimes and thus to contribute to the prevention of such crimes".

36 See *supra* note 19.

37 Article 17(2). See Stigen 2008, *supra* note 30, pp. 251 ff.

38 Article 17(3). See Stigen 2008, *supra* note 30, pp. 313 ff.

Rome Statute at this point should not be the standard to follow. Instead, states should rely on existing safeguards for the exercise of national jurisdiction, such as immunity for the most prominent state representatives and other representatives carrying out official acts.

The Geneva Conventions and the first Additional Protocol allow the forum state to extradite to another State Party which "has made out a prima facie case".[39] This could be construed as to require that the latter state is both willing and able to proceed genuinely as required by the complementarity principle. Yet the ICRC's authoritative comments merely suggest that a "prima facie case" means "a case which … would involve prosecution before the courts", without any further qualification.[40] As for the Convention against Torture, adopted 35 years later, it has no similar requirement as it only instructs the forum state to submit the suspect to its prosecutorial authorities "if it does not extradite him".[41]

In *Belgium*, deferral to a foreign court is only allowed if that court meets the requirements imposed by international law on Belgium and that state.[42] This is a vague threshold. It can be construed so as to only require that the courts more generally adhere to international law, as opposed to requiring that the case in question be handled genuinely. In *Germany*, exercising universal jurisdiction is only allowed when this is necessary in order to prevent impunity and does not "inappropriately interfere with the primary responsible jurisdictions".[43] This too is vague. What is meant by preventing impunity and to "inappropriately interfere"? As demonstrated by the German *Rumsfeld* case of 2004, the provision has not always been applied in a manner consistent with its spirit.

---

39 Articles 49, 50, 129 and 146 of the Geneva Conventions I-IV and Article 85(1) of the First Additional Protocol.

40 Pictet 1958, *supra* note 7, p. 593.

41 Convention against Torture and Other Cruel, Inhuman or Degrading Treatment or Punishment (1984) article 7 (1).

42 *Code de procédure pénale*, article 12*bis* para. 4.

43 *Referentenentwurf: Entwurf eines Gesetzeszur Einführung des Völkerstrafgesetzbuches*, 22 June 2001, p. 85 (my translation); for German text, see http://www.lrz-muenchen.de /~satzger/unterlagen/V3D.pdf.

4.4.4. Subsidiarity – a Duty or Discretion?

In some states subsidiarity is considered not a criterion as such, but a basis for prosecutorial discretion. In *Belgium*, for example, the federal prosecutor *may* decide, taking into consideration the interests of justice and Belgium's international obligations, to transfer a case to an international tribunal or to a court in the territorial state, the suspect's home state or the custodial state.[44] If the crime falls within the ICC's jurisdiction, the ICC shall be informed of a deferral.[45]

In *Germany* too, subsidiarity is formulated as a matter of prosecutorial discretion where one factor is whether there is an investigation by a state with closer connection.[46] This regulation should be seen in connection with the *Legalitätsprinzip* according to which the German federal prosecutor is, at the outset, under a duty to prosecute any crime under German jurisdiction, arguably also including crimes covered by universal jurisdiction.

Discretion may also be appropriate in another sense. Even if there is jurisdiction and the case is not genuinely dealt with by any state, it might not be in the interest of justice to pursue the matter. Under the Rome Statute, the ICC prosecutor can thus decide not to proceed when proceeding will not serve the "interests of justice".[47] This term is delightfully complex, leaving room for a plethora of considerations. The ICC Prosecutor has noted:

> The issue of the interests of justice, as it appears in Article 53 of the Rome Statute, represents one of the most complex aspects of the Treaty. It is the point where many of the philosophical and operational challenges in the pursuit of international criminal justice coincide (albeit implicitly), but there is no clear guidance on what the content of the idea is.[48]

This provision *allows* the ICC Prosecutor to defer when he or she finds that justice so requires, but one might question whether a sub-

[44] *Code de procédure pénale*, article 12*bis* para. 4.

[45] *Ibid.*

[46] *Code of Criminal Procedure*, section 153f.

[47] Rome Statute article 53(1)(c) and (2)(c).

[48] Policy Paper on the Interests of Justice, Office of the Prosecutor, September 2007, p. 1, available at http://www.icc-cpi.int/otp/otp_docs.html.

sidiarity criterion should be construed so as to *require* that the forum state defer when proceeding will not be in the interest of justice. It is easy to argue that the forum state should not proceed when that is the case, but there seems to be no foundation for requiring that. Because the very decision as to what is in the interest of justice is so typically discretional, a discussion as to whether the forum state should be required or only advised not to proceed seems highly theoretical. And as long as the forum state has jurisdiction and there is no genuine criminal proceeding in the affected state, the sovereignty of the latter can hardly be said to be violated should the former proceed. That the proceedings might interfere with genuine efforts in the affected state to respond to the crime by other means than criminal proceedings, does not mean that the exercise of universal jurisdiction amounts to an undue interference in that state's internal affairs.

A wish not to generate dangerous friction might be a very real and under the circumstances also legitimate reason for deferring. The forum state should not, however, defer just because it is politically convenient.

4.4.5. Which States Can Invoke Subsidiarity?

One important difference between the complementarity principle and a subsidiarity criterion for universal jurisdiction, as usually understood, is that while the former gives priority to any state with jurisdiction,[49] the latter only give priority to the states affected by the crime, typically the territorial state and the suspect's home state. This is natural, as the ICC is supposed to be complementary to national judiciaries in general, while a third state seeking to exercise universal jurisdiction has as much reason to proceed as any other state, and it should only have to yield to a state with a closer link to the crime.

One might, however, argue that subsidiarity should cover also the victim's home state. It should be noted, however, that among the jurisdictional principles recognised by international law, the jurisdiction of the territorial state and the home state of the perpetrator enjoys a particularly strong recognition. It is *vis-à-vis* these two states that an exercise of universal jurisdiction can be considered as a sovereignty

[49] Articles 17(1) and 19(2)(b).

violation. No other link between the crime and a given state seems sufficiently strong to justify jurisdictional priority.

It should be noted that judges Higgins, Kooijmans and Buergenthal in the *Arrest Warrant* case only suggest a priority for the "national State of the prospective accused".[50] The Krakow Resolution, on its part, refers to "another state with territorial or personal connection to the crime, the perpetrator or the victim".[51] The *Princeton Principles* propose that the forum state must take into account "the place of commission of the crime" and "the nationality connection of the victim to the requesting state", without referring to the suspect's home state.[52]

A particular argument is that the danger that the suspect's human rights will be violated arguably is greater in the victim's home state than in the suspect's home state or the territorial state when this is not the victim's home state.

It may be noted that in his *Policy Paper*, the ICC Prosecutor envisages an informal and pragmatic consultation process between the Prosecutor and interested states:

> The exercise of the Prosecutor's functions under article 18 of notifying States of future investigations will alert States with jurisdiction to the possibility of taking action themselves. In a case where multiple States have jurisdiction over the crime in question the Prosecutor *should consult with* those States best able to exercise jurisdiction ... with a view to ensuring that jurisdiction is taken by the State best able to do so.[53]

4.4.6. Safeguarding the Suspect's Human Rights

So far the focus has been on the danger that the domestic proceeding will seek to shield the suspect. There is also, however, a danger that the suspect's right to a fair trial will not be respected: that he or she is treated

[50] *Arrest Warrant* case, *supra* note 7, p. 80, para. 59.

[51] Institute of International Law, *Universal Criminal Jurisdiction with Regard to the Crime of Genocide, Crimes against Humanity and War Crimes*, 2005, available at http://www.idi-iil.org/idiE/resolutionsE/2005_kra_03_en.pdf, provision 3(d).

[52] The Princeton Principles on Universal Jurisdiction Principle, available at http://www1.umn.edu/humanrts/instree/princeton.html, principle 8(b) and (d).

[53] *Paper on some policy issues before the Office of the Prosecutor*, Office of the Prosecutor, September 2003, p. 5, available at http://www.icc-cpi.int/otp/otp_policy.html.

too strictly. The danger is evident when there has been a political transition and a new government seeks to prosecute a violent former regime. As just noted this might be an additional argument why the victim's home state should not have the right to invoke subsidiarity.

The question remains whether a third state seeking to exercise universal jurisdiction should also observe this concern, that is, whether it should be allowed to proceed if the domestic proceeding will violate the suspect's right to a fair trial. It is generally accepted that under the complementarity principle the ICC cannot interfere on the grounds that the rights of the suspect will be violated. The ICC is no "human rights court", and its purpose is only to prevent impunity. (Whether the ICC nevertheless can refuse to surrender a person who is already in its custody if the state seeking surrender cannot present a *prima facie* case and is likely to violate the person's rights or if the person risks capital punishment, will not be discussed here.)

For a state, the situation seems more open. It is difficult to see why the forum state should not be allowed to refuse to extradite a suspect if that would jeopardize the suspect's human rights. Indeed, the state might be in violation of international law if it extradites to a state where the person risks capital punishment or torture.[54]

To the extent that the forum state can refuse to extradite the person to the territorial state or his or her home state on human rights grounds, this is not a consequence of the subsidiarity principle which (just as the complementarity principle) is intended to prevent impunity. It will be the result of a duty of the forum state to ensure the suspect's human rights.[55] If the forum state does not extradite on this ground, there might be a duty for the state to actually investigate and eventually prosecute if a *prima facie* case can be established.

---

54 See, *e.g.*, European Convention on Human Rights article 3, as concluded in *Soering v. United Kingdom*, European Court of Human Rights, 7 July 1989, 11 EHRR 439 (Ser. A).

55 Nevertheless, the AU-EU Expert Report on the Principle of Universal Jurisdiction notes that the forum should only extradite the suspect to an affected state "on the condition that the latter state is willing and able to conduct a fair trial consistent with international human rights standard …", see § R9, available at http://www.africa-eu-partnership.org/pdf/rapport_expert_ua_ue_competence_ universelle_en.pdf.

4.4.7. A Duty for the Forum State to Inform the Affected States

Under the complementarity principle the ICC Prosecutor shall, when he or she intends to initiate an investigation, "notify all States Parties and those States which … would normally exercise jurisdiction".[56] A pertinent question is whether the forum state, under the subsidiarity principle, should have a similar duty to notify the states that enjoy jurisdictional priority. From the perspective of the territorial state and the suspect's home state, their right to invoke subsidiarity will be little worth if they are not informed that he forum state considers exercising universal jurisdiction.

In their separate opinion in the *Arrest Warrant* case judges Higgins *et al.* note that a "State contemplating bringing criminal charges based on universal jurisdiction must first *offer* to the national State of the prospective accused person the opportunity itself to act upon the charges concerned".[57] These judges thus seem to suggest that the forum state must actively inform the states concerned. Indeed, it is difficult to see how a subsidiarity principle could work without such a duty. One cannot expect states to stay informed of any investigation abroad concerning crimes committed on their territory or elsewhere by their citizens.

During the negotiations on the ICC's Rules of Procedure and Evidence, adopted in 2000, the United States argued that the states concerned should be informed of the suspect's identity in order to determine whether relevant national proceedings existed. Several states noted, however, that the ICC Prosecutor under the circumstances might need to "limit the scope of the information provided to States" in order not to unduly impede the ICC proceedings.[58] The rules therefore provide that the notification shall "contain information about the acts that may constitute crimes [under the ICC's jurisdiction], relevant for [invoking complementarity]", but "[s]ubject to the limitations provided for in article 18, paragraph 1 [which allows the Prosecutor to limit the information]".[59] It thus suffices to identify the respective incidents that might constitute

56 Rome Statute article 18(1).

57 *Arrest Warrant* case, *supra* note 7, p. 80, para. 59 (emphasis added).

58 John Holmes, "Jurisdiction and Admissibility", in Roy S. Lee (ed.), *The International Criminal Court: Elements of Crimes and Rules of Procedure and Evidence,* Transnational Publishers, 2001, p. 339.

59 Rule 52(1).

crimes, and to the extent possible their time and place, such as a massacre of civilians in a certain place on a certain day. This will enable the state concerned to determine whether it is conducting or has conducted competing proceedings.

The same should, it is submitted, apply when a state considers exercising universal jurisdiction. Before an investigation has been conducted, the forum state will scarcely have sufficient basis for identifying the names of suspects, and to reveal a list of suspects at such premature stage would appear irresponsible. There is a risk that the suspect, if he or she is not yet in the form state's custody, will try to escape, or remove or destroy evidence or intimidate witnesses once he or she becomes aware of the forum state's intention to investigate. In order to prevent such obstruction of justice, the forum state should be allowed to notify the states concerned on a limited basis.[60]

Under the complementarity principle a state may, if it deems the notification from the ICC Prosecutor inadequate for the purpose of determining whether competing national proceedings exist, "request additional information from the Prosecutor".[61] Such an option should also remain for a state affected under the subsidiarity principle.

It will be in the interest of the forum state to establish good communication and provide the state concerned with sufficient information so that any subsidiarity issue can be resolved at the earliest stage, instead of being raised at a later stage after much effort and expense.

4.4.8. Information from the Forum State to the Affected State

An important question is whether a forum state which has conducted an investigation before it gives the case to the territorial state or the suspect's home state should also hand over any gathered information regarding the case. As a matter of policy this might seem reasonable and it would usually promote the interests of justice.[62] It is, however, difficult to construe this as a duty under international law. When the information is gathered by the forum state, this state will have a sense of "ownership" to

[60] Rome Statute article 18(1).

[61] Rules of procedure and Evidence rule 52(2).

[62] AU-EU report, *supra* note 55, § R9.

the information, and it can hardly be under a duty to hand it over to another state.

4.4.9. When Should Subsidiarity be Applied?

Another crucial question is when the subsidiarity principle should be applied. Should it be once an investigations starts, after the investigation or before a trial starts? It can be argued that if the forum state has come a long way with its proceedings, it may make little sense to hand the case over to the territorial state or the home state of the victim, even if that state now will proceed in a genuine manner.[63] If it turns out that the state concerned has already carried out relevant proceedings, deferring would, however, still make sense, again provided that proceedings have been genuine.

It is also a point that the state concerned should be given a real opportunity to invoke subsidiarity. Thus, it might still be reasonable to require the forum state to defer if that state has failed to inform the state concerned of it proceedings, and the latter state invokes subsidiarity within reasonable time after it has become aware of the forum state's proceeding.

Operating with a time limit earlier than the start of a trial in the forum state would be in contrast to the ICC's complementarity principle according to which a state may challenge the admissibility of a case "prior to or at the commencement of the [ICC] trial" and in exceptional circumstances even later.[64] Yet it makes sense that the time limit in the Rome Statute is more generous as the negotiating states were particularly anxious to safeguard their sovereignty. Besides, the fact that the ICC will have very limited capacity might also make it desirable to let the state concerned take over even at a very late stage.

In *Rumsfeld et al.* the German Federal Prosecutor applied the subsidiarity principle before the opening of an investigation. While this under the circumstances might be appropriate and prudent, the forum state should hardly have to apply subsidiarity that early. It would make more

63 Roht-Arriaza argues that "considerations of judicial economy and 'sunk costs' counsel continuing a prosecution where it has begun", see Naomi Roht-Arriaza, "International Decisions: Guatemala Genocide Case", see *supra* note 18, at 212-213.

64 Rome Statute article 19(4). Note that the right to make a challenge might be precluded if the state does not make the challenge "at the earliest opportunity", see article 19(5).

sense to first let the forum state conclude its investigation. This is supported by the joint separate opinion of Higgins, Kooijmans and Buergenthal[65] and by the Krakow Resolution's paragraphs 3(c) and (d).

4.4.10. The Right of the Person Concerned to Challenge the Admissibility

Both the complementarity principle and the subsidiarity principle reflect the primary right of the *states* affected to investigate and prosecute. The principles do not reflect a right of the suspect to be investigated and prosecuted by his or her domestic judiciary.[66] Nevertheless, the complementarity principle gives the suspect the right to challenge the admissibility of his or her case.[67] Here, the Statute probably reflects the current view in international law. The view has changed from one seeing the state, and only the state, as entitled to invoke inadmissibility and lack of jurisdiction. Some 50 years ago, in *Israel v. Eichmann*, the District Court of Jerusalem noted that "[t]he right to plead violation of the sovereignty of a State is the exclusive right of that State. Only a sovereign State may raise the plea or waive it, and the accused has no right to take over the rights of that State".[68] In *Prosecutor v. Tadić*, however, the Appeals Chamber noted with regard to both jurisdiction and admissibility that the accused could not

> be deprived of a plea so intimately connected with, and grounded in, international law as a defence based on violation of state sovereignty. To bar an accused from raising such a plea is tantamount to deciding that, in this day and age, an international court could not, in a criminal matter where the liberty of an accused is at stake, examine a plea

[65] Arrest *Warrant* case, *supra* note 7, p. 80, para. 59, noting that "commencing an investigation on the basis of which an arrest warrant may later be issued does not of itself violate those principles [for the exercise of universal jurisdiction]".

[66] Because the forum state acts as a trustee of the international community, one might argue that human rights standards must be rigorously applied, including a *ne bis in idem* principle across legal systems, but the subsidiarity principle as such does not reflect an individual right of the perpetrator.

[67] Rome Statute article 19(2)(a).

[68] *Attorney General of Israel v. Eichmann*, Judgement of the Supreme Court of Israel of 29 May 1962, 36 *International Law Reports*, 1968, vol. 36, p. 277 *et seq.*, para. 44. See also United *States v. Noriega* (1990), 746 F. Supp. (1506), S. D. Fla., para. 1533.

> raising the issue of violation of State sovereignty. Such a startling conclusion would imply a contradiction in terms which the Chamber feels it is its duty to refute and lay to rest.[69]

The right of the individual under the Rome Statute is in line with this statement. Similarly, the suspect should arguably have the right to invoke subsidiarity, at least when the argument is that the suspect has already been tried domestically. The suspect should not, however, be allowed to invoke that he *should be* prosecuted by the home state or the territorial state, and certainly not if the failure of these states to invoke subsidiarity can be interpreted as a tacit approval of the forum state's proceeding with the case.

4.4.11. The Burden of Proof

Under the complementarity principle, the state invoking it bears the burden of proof as to the existence of jurisdiction and the existence of domestic proceedings. This follows from the fact that these requirements are not contained in the phrase commencing with the word "unless", but are formulated as a criterion for inadmissibility in the first place.[70]

As for the domestic proceeding's genuineness, the threshold enshrined in article 17 is probability, and the burden of proof rests with the ICC Prosecutor who must demonstrate on a preponderance of the evidence that the admissibility criteria in article 17 are met.[71] It is submitted that the opposite should be the case when a state seeks to exercise universal jurisdiction. When a state invokes subsidiarity and chooses to invoke its prior right to proceed, it would be proper to require

69 *Prosecutor v. Tadić*, IT-95-16-T, Decision of the Appeals Chamber on the Defence motion on interlocutory appeal, 2 October 1995, para. 55.

70 Markus Benzing, "The Complementarity Regime of the International Criminal Court: International Criminal Justice between State Sovereignty and the Fight against Impunity", in von Bogdandy and Wolfrum (eds.), *Max Planck Yearbook of United Nations Law*, 2003, vol. 7, p. 629.

71 This follows from the fact that a domestic proceeding makes the case inadmissible "unless" the state is or was unwilling or unable to proceed genuinely, See Jo Stigen 2008, *supra* note 30, pp. 128-129. For a different view, see Christopher K. Hall, *Suggestions concerning International Criminal Court: Prosecutorial* Policy *and Strategy and External Relations*, 28 March 2003, p. 29, available at http://www.icc-cpi.int/library/organs/otp/hall.pdf.

that that state demonstrate that its proceedings are genuine and that its intent is not merely to deprive the forum state of jurisdiction.[72] Moreover, as a matter of respect to the very same state, it will be more appropriate to deny a State jurisdiction on the basis of a failure to satisfy the burden of proof as opposed to an affirmative conclusion by the forum state that the proceeding is inadequate.

Having said that, if the burden of proof should nevertheless be placed on the forum state, this would probably not impose a prohibitively onerous burden. In lack of sufficient information from the state concerned regarding the proceeding's genuineness, it should be possible to presume that the proceeding is non-genuine. In *Velásquez Rodríguez v. Honduras*, the Inter-American Commission noted with regard to the state's failure to address the complainant's submission that the local remedies were ineffective:

> The Commission's requests for information were ignored to the point that the Commission had to presume … that the allegations were true.[73]

4.4.12. Who Should Have the Final Say Regarding the Adequacy of the Domestic Proceedings?

Regardless of the burden of proof: who is to decide whether the proceedings in the territorial state or the perpetrator's home state are adequate? In the ICC regime, the final word lies with the ICC.[74] This is perhaps the single most important procedural rule of the complementarity principle,

[72] Jeffrey L. Bleich, "Complementarity", in M. Cherif Bassiouni (ed.), *The International Criminal Court: Observations and Issues before the 1997-98 Preparatory Committee; and Administrative and Financial Implications*, *Novelles Études Pénales*, 1997, vol. 13, p. 242, arguing along these lines that states should have the burden of proof *vis-à-vis* the ICC.

[73] *Velásquez Rodríguez v. Honduras*, Judgment of 29 July 1988, Ser. C, No. 4, para. 180.

[74] Rome Statute article 119(1) on settlement of disputes leaves the final authority to settle "any dispute concerning the judicial functions of the Court" with the Court (this provision covers issues of admissibility and prosecutorial discretion). Alain Pellet notes that article 119(1) applies, noting that "[a]rticles 17 to 19 clearly entrust the ICC with deciding on the admissibility of a case […]", see Pellet, "Settlements of Disputes", in Antonio Cassese, Paola Gaeta, and John R.W.D. Jones (eds.), *The Rome Statute of the International Criminal Court: A Commentary. Volume II*, Oxford University Press, 2002, p. 1843.

and it could hardly have been different. A state which is unwilling or unable to conduct genuine proceedings could not be entrusted with the authority to determine its own proceeding's genuineness.

It seems equally obvious that the state seeking to invoke the subsidiarity principle cannot make the final determination either. A problem is, however, that while the ICC by most states will be perceived as an independent and impartial arbiter, the forum state might not be viewed as that. One may also ask whether the forum state will have the required expertise and resources to conduct a complex in-depth evaluation of another state's proceedings. Besides, having one state assessing the genuineness of the proceedings of another state might more easily create friction than when such assessment is made by an international arbiter.

Claus Kreß argues that an international judicial organ should be entrusted with the power to decide on the genuineness of the domestic proceeding where such a decision is necessary to apply the subsidiarity principle, noting that this function could be assumed by the ICC.[75] Alternatively, presupposing that clear rules on subsidiarity are established, the state contesting the exercise of jurisdiction could always turn to the ICJ, arguing that the forum state has violated the principle.

If states cannot agree on an international arbiter, giving the forum state the final say *vis-à-vis* the territorial state or the suspect's home state appears to be the only viable alternative.

4.5. Some Tentative Conclusions

Attaching a sensibly formulated subsidiarity criterion to the exercise of universal jurisdiction will promote the purposes underlying such jurisdiction (provided of course that the *forum state* proceeds genuinely with the case, an issue which is not discussed in this chapter[76]). This

[75] On the potential of the ICC with respect to national proceedings, albeit not within the universal jurisdiction context, see Jenia Iontcheva Turner, "Nationalizing International Criminal Law", *Stanford Journal of International Law*, 2005, vol. 41, at 29 *et seq*.

[76] Claus Kreß notes that an international system of accreditation could be established allowing for a preventive screening of any state willing to exercise universal jurisdiction, see Claus Kreß, "Universal Jurisdiction over International Crimes and the *Institut de Droit International*", *Journal of International Criminal Justice*, 2006, vol. 4, p. 561, at 584, referring to Susanne Walther, "Terra Incognita: Wird staatliche internationale Strafgewalt den Menschen gerecht?", in Jörg Arnold *et al.* (eds.), *Men-*

chapter has shown that on many points subsidiarity should be modeled after the ICC's principle of complementarity. This will ensure the best balance between avoiding impunity and safeguarding the sovereignty of the states affected.

A jurisdictional priority for the territorial state and the suspect's home state conditioned on the existence of genuine criminal proceedings can serve as an incentive for these states to bring the perpetrator to justice, with the advantages of domestic proceedings outlined above. With a duty for the forum state to inform the two states and offer them the case, the principle will pave the way for a "proactive subsidiarity", where the affected states are encouraged to respond as they should to core international crimes.[77] Burke-White notes that for the state concerned, considering the alternative, "having some control over the proceedings and locating the trial in their own courts might well be a preferred outcome".[78]

A subsidiarity criterion would limit the interference in state sovereignty, and the main rationale behind universal jurisdiction will be better reflected. It will give the forum state a subsidiary right to prosecute when necessary to prevent impunity, not an unconditional right to prosecute on the grounds of the seriousness of the crime.

There is, however, an inherent paradox with the application of such a subsidiarity criterion. Absent an international scrutiny mechanism, it presupposes a horizontal scrutiny between states of the adequacy of their respective proceedings. This is quite different from the vertical scrutiny exercised by the ICC. Thus, while initially aiming at reducing the risk of interstate friction, subsidiarity can also make the application of universal jurisdiction more intrusive.[79] This makes it all the more important that the most essential aspects of the complementarity principle aimed at safeguarding the integrity of states *vis-à-vis* the ICC are applied *mutatis mutandis* to the exercise of universal jurisdiction.

---

schengerechtes Strafrecht. Festschrift für Albin Eser zum 70. Geburtstag, Verlag C.H. Beck, 2005, p. 953.

77 See Julia Geneuss, "Fostering a Better Understanding of Universal Jurisdiction", *Journal of International Criminal Justice*, 2009, vol. 7, p. 945, at 958.

78 William Burke-White, see *supra* note 2, p. 92.

79 Jo Stigen, "What's in the ICC for states?", in Marius Emberland and Christoffer C. Eriksen (eds.), *New International Law*, Brill, forthcoming 2010.

One noteworthy advantage with establishing a subsidiarity principle along the lines of the ICC's complementarity principle is that the affected states could look to the criteria outlined in the Rome Statute and developed further by the ICC as to what will constitute genuine criminal proceedings.

In order to facilitate the development of a sensible subsidiarity principle, states considering exercising universal jurisdiction should as a matter of policy offer the case to the territorial state or the suspect's home state when that state is willing and able to carry out genuine proceedings.[80] While currently not amounting to a duty under international law, this is certainly a right of the forum state.

[80] The AU-EU report on universal jurisdiction, *supra* note 55, § 9, recommend: "In prosecuting serious crimes of international concern, states should, as a matter of policy, accord priority to territoriality as a basis of jurisdiction, since such crimes … primarily injure the community where they have been perpetrated and violate not only the rights of the victims but also the general demand for order and security in that community…".

5

Between Territoriality and Universality: Reflections by a Core International Crimes Prosecutor*

Pål Lønseth**

Let me start by reminding us all that the reason for discussing this important topic, is that the main objective of criminal prosecutions of international crimes – whether in the *ad hoc* tribunals, the International Criminal Court (ICC) or in national jurisdictions – is to bring perpetrators to justice and by doing so trying to avoid or at least reduce the possibility of future atrocities.

The topic of this seminar – if you reduce it to a practical level – is basically a question of how to be more efficient. How does the international community as a whole use its police and prosecution resources in the best way in order to bring perpetrators to justice?

I think we all can agree that investigations and prosecutions in the field of core international crimes are quite inefficient. The problem of impunity is very much alive. Although there has been tremendous progress in the field of international criminal and humanitarian law in the past 65 years, starting with the Nuremberg process, the international community – and I would say states worldwide – has not done enough to implement this development into national legislation, investigations and prosecutions. All states have been more or less evasive, for a number of reasons including:

- the fact that atrocities have often taken place far away from the immediate interests of the state concerned;

* The following chapter is based on an intervention made at the FICHL Seminar "The Principle of complementarity and the exercise of universal jurisdiction for core international crimes" held in Oslo on 4 September 2009.

** **Pål Lønseth** is State Secretary of the Norwegian Ministry of Justice. He was formerly Senior Public Prosecutor at the Norwegian National Authority for Prosecution of Organised and Other Serious Crimes. Views expressed in this chapter do not necessarily reflect those of the Norwegian Government.

- the preferance of states to use their police and prosecution resources on domestic crimes; and
- the evasiveness caused by political convenience.

So how can we be more efficient – how do we prevent impunity? The answer to this question is of course more resources, better domestic legislation, and so on. But what about the legal principles on where to prosecute, exactly the theme of this volume, a very important question in the struggle against impunity.

Should there be a central principle on where to prosecute that overrides other principles? As I see it, the three main principles debated in this book need to function side by side.

First of all, as the concept note on the FICHL seminar on 4 September 2009 suggested, one should – at least in an ideal world – prefer the principle of territoriality. In my former prosecutor's office we always searched for an option to extradite a suspect before considering prosecution by us. In 2008-2009, we extradited a person to Serbia to stand trial there for a massacre committed in November 1991, and to Bosnia and Herzegovina suspected of war crimes in 1994. Both suspects resided in Norway. It would have been possible to prosecute them in Norway under the principle of universal jurisdiction, but we preferred extradition.

The reason for this preference is that most witnesses reside in the territorial state, the crime scene is obviously in the territorial state – you might say that the territorial state is closest to the evidence and the closest to evaluating the evidence and to fully understand the context of the crime.

So the principle of territoriality should have preference.

But we are not living in an ideal world. Many prosecutors often encounter obstacles that prevent extradition to the territorial state. It can be several reasons:

a) The suspect has become a national of the *forum deprehensionis*, in the timeframe between the alleged crime and the time when the suspicion did occur. Most countries do not extradite their own nationals and many have quite rigorous regulations for the withdrawal of that status. This is the main reason why we prosecuted a Norwegian national of Bosnian origin in Oslo in 2008-2009 for war crimes and crimes against humanity committed against Serb civilians in Bosnia and Herzegovina in 1992.

b) Another aspect that often prevents extradition is the possibility of human rights violations in the territorial state, typically lack of a fair trial. Human rights instruments frequently prevent a state from extraditing when human rights violations are likely to occur. Several recent court decisions around Europe rejecting extradition requests from Rwanda can be illustrative. The Supreme Court in Sweden decided to extradite a suspect to Rwanda to stand trial there, but that decision was appealed as I understand to the European Court of Human Rights and Sweden has announced that it will follow the recommendations of the Court. If it denies extradition, justice can only be done if Swedish authorities conduct criminal proceedings on the basis of universal jurisdiction – like the Finns are did in their Rwanda case.

This is why I am pleased with the development of universal jurisdiction. I think all friends of international law should be happy about it, because without it the world would be a safer place for war criminals. This is also why I am sceptical of principles that might do irreparable damage to the struggle against impunity.

However, I do recognize that the principle of universality needs to be balanced, as in its absolute form it is open to misuse, and it could actually work against us. It is a waste of police and prosecution recourses if several states go after the same incident. There should be coordination. It is even more problematic when the witnesses get exhausted, having to testify in more than one jurisdiction. So how do we balance it?

Having in mind what I just said about the preference of territoriality, the principle of complementarity could be a valid way to balance the principle of universality.

If the territorial state is not able or willing to investigate and prosecute, other jurisdictions need to step up, preferably the *forum deprehensionis*, because exercising universal jurisdiction, in its absolute form, is not a very recommendable solution as it will frequently lead to trials *in absentia* which easily entails breaches of human rights.

If the principle of complementarity is set to balance the principle of universality, maybe with the Rome Statute as a model, the "able and willing" criterion needs to comprise a demand for fair trial and principles that allow foreign jurisdictions to disregard mock trials, only set up to avoid interference from foreign jurisdictions.

Although this debate about the different jurisdictional principles is very important, and very interesting, let me conclude by reminding that that these principles can only give some guidance in cases of a positive conflict between jurisdictions – where at least two jurisdictions want to investigate and prosecute. A deeper problem still remains: What about the numerous atrocities that no jurisdiction will ever touch? That no jurisdiction steps up, is the number one problem in the fight against impunity for core international crimes.

6

Complementarity in Universality Cases: Legal-Systemic and Legal Policy Considerations

Cedric Ryngaert*

6.1. Introduction

As becomes clear from other contributions to this volume, the complementarity principle, as designed by the drafters of the Rome Statute, was meant to apply *vertically*. Vertical complementarity means that a *supranational* institution, the International Criminal Court (ICC), would supervise the investigative and prosecutorial work of States (Parties to the Rome Statute), and, applying Article 17 of the Statute, assume its responsibilities (that is, declare a case admissible) if that work proved to be below acceptable standards.

So far, however, scant attention has been paid to the *horizontal* dimension of complementarity. This is why this volume is such a welcome addition to the existing literature. Horizontal complementarity, the term used in this contribution, refers to the complementary prosecutorial role played by 'bystander' states, these are states that do not have a strong nexus with an international crime situation and that are exercising universal jurisdiction, *vis-à-vis* states that are directly concerned with such a situation, for example, because the situation occurred on their territory or because the crimes were perpetrated by their nationals (hereinafter denoted as 'the territorial/national state', or generically, as 'the home state').

When the ICC and bystander states, acting under the universality principle, investigate and prosecute international crimes, they may be

* **Cedric Ryngaert** is Assistant Professor of international law, Leuven University and Utrecht University; research grant-holder VENI NWO. This contribution is largely based on the author's contribution to C. Stahn and M. El-Zeidy (eds.), *The International Criminal Court and Complementarity: From Theory to Practice*, Cambridge University Press, 2010, under the title "Horizontal Complementarity".

considered as acting as agents of the international community.[1] Because they both vindicate international interests, it appears logical that they apply the same principles, not only at the level of substantive law (many States Parties to the Rome Statute have indeed incorporated the Statute's incriminations upon ratification), but also at a procedural level. One of the central procedural principles in the Rome Statute is precisely the principle of complementarity.[2] In the past, I have argued that "there is no compelling reason for international and national courts to use a different standard for subsidiarity/complementarity, certainly not for states that have ratified the Rome Statute and have thus subscribed to the vision of justice underlying the complementarity principle".[3] At the time, however, I did not theoretically flesh out that claim to the fullest extent, as I was mainly concerned with identifying relevant tendencies in state practice and emerging rules of customary international law. In this contribution, I revisit my doctrinal position by listing the arguments for and against horizontal complementarity (sections 6.2.-6.6.). I will subsequently link the insights of this theoretical discussion to the most recent state practice, especially in Spain (sections 6.7.-6.8.). Because most universality cases are currently brought in Spain (which boasts probably the world's most liberal universality statute), Spain provides a fertile breeding ground for the application, or non-application for that matter, of a horizontal complementarity principle. Not surprisingly, it will become clear that I am in favour of the application of a horizontal complementarity principle. Carrying out a horizontal complementarity analysis is normatively desirable for a number of reasons, not least the imperative of respecting and encouraging

---

1 Compare the Rome Statute of the ICC, fourth preambular paragraph ("*Affirming* that the most serious crimes of concern to the international community as a whole must not go unpunished and that their effective prosecution must be ensured by taking measures at the national level and by enhancing international cooperation").

2 Compare M. Chadwick, "Modern Developments in Universal Jurisdiction: Addressing Impunity in Tibet and Beyond", *International Criminal Law Review*, 2009, vol. 9, 359, 390 (arguing, in respect of the complementarity principle as enshrined in Article 17 of the Rome Statute that "[f]urther harmonisation will occur at the procedural level as ICC provides guidance on the question of at what point following an international offence it is legitimate to intervene in domestic affairs").

3 C. Ryngaert, "Applying the Rome Statute's Complementarity Principle: Drawing Lessons from the Prosecution of Core Crimes by States Acting under the Universality Principle", *Crim.L.F.*, 2008, vol. 19, 153, at 178.

genuine proceedings in the home state, and forestalling diplomatic tension arising from overly broad jurisdictional assertions.

6.2. The Sovereignty Dimension

In the ICC system, complementarity implies that the primary jurisdiction over violations of international criminal law lies with the state. The jurisdiction of the ICC is merely a complementary (or subsidiary) one: the ICC only steps in when the state proves unable or unwilling to genuinely investigate and prosecute a case. As is well known, in this respect the ICC system differs considerably from the *ad hoc* tribunals, which have primacy of jurisdiction *vis-à-vis* national courts.[4] If the ICC's vertical complementarity system is now turned into a horizontal one, this would imply that the jurisdiction of the bystander state – which may, as indicated, and just like the ICC, be seen as representing the interests of the international community – is only complementary to the jurisdiction of the territorial or national state. This implication is somewhat problematic from a sovereignty perspective.

It is recalled that the classic international law of jurisdiction is perceived as leaving a wide measure of jurisdictional discretion to states.[5] Even if international law were seen as authorizing jurisdiction only on the basis of permissive principles, there is no evidence that there is a hierarchy among these principles.[6] Accordingly, assuming that the (majority of the) international crimes over which the ICC has jurisdiction are also amenable to jurisdiction under the universality principle, which is one of the permissive jurisdictional principles, the (bystander) state exercising such jurisdiction is not supposed to back down in the face of a purportedly superior claim by a state with a stronger nexus, such as the territorial or national state. Put differently, in classic international law, the jurisdiction of the bystander state is concurrent with, and not complementary to, the jurisdiction of the territorial or national state.[7] This idea is rooted in the

4 ICTY Statute, Art. 9 and ICTR Statute, Art. 8.

5 *SS Lotus (France v. Turkey),* Permanent Court of International Justice ('P.C.I.J.') Reports, Series A, No. 10, pp. 18-19 (1927).

6 C. Ryngaert, *Jurisdiction in International Law*, Oxford University Press, 2008, 128-129.

7 See also Juzgado Central de Instrucción No Cuatro, Audiencia Nacional Madrid, No. 157/2.008, 4 May 2009, p. 13 ("... dichos Convenios [the Geneva Conventions], suscritos por España, establecen de forma expresa un régimen de jurisdicción univer-

principle of sovereign equality, pursuant to which the legal claims of one state do not and cannot prevail over the claims of another state. All states are equal, and restrictions on the power of states to prescribe laws and apply them to a given situation should not be presumed.[8] This holds all the more true if those laws govern violations of obligations arising under a peremptory norm of general international law.[9] These are obligations in which every state has an interest,[10] which it could (although not necessarily *should*) vindicate by conferring on its prosecutors and courts the power to investigate and prosecute violations of those obligations.

Admittedly, the jurisdiction of the ICC and the States Parties to the Rome Statute is *also* concurrent. After all, the complementarity principle only comes into play at the level of admissibility.[11] Yet the international law of prescriptive state jurisdiction has not made the distinction between jurisdiction and admissibility.[12] If a state has jurisdiction under international law, it is also allowed to *exercise* that jurisdiction. Restrictions have been imposed on the exercise of jurisdiction, but these find their legal basis in domestic law rather than international law. In classic international law, therefore, there are no indications that some sort of 'horizontal' complementarity principle – by virtue of which the bystander state's courts are only courts of last resort which ordinarily defer to an 'able and willing' territorial/national state – would be mandatory.

---

sal concurrente, claramente alternativa respecto de otras jurisdicciones y en ningún caso estrictamente subsidiaria").

8 *SS Lotus*, *supra* note 5, at 18-19.

9 Cf., International Law Commission (ILC), *Articles on Responsibility of States for Internationally Wrongful Acts*, 2001, Art. 40.

10 *Ibid.*, at Art. 41.

11 The complementarity principle is enshrined in Art. 17 of the Rome Statute, which bears the heading "Issues of admissibility". Systemically, Art. 17 comes after the provisions on jurisdiction (Arts. 5-14).

12 It is noted that there *is* such a distinction at the level of international tribunals other than the ICC, *e.g.*, at the International Court of Justice (ICJ). While the Statute of the ICJ only addresses issues of competence/jurisdiction (Arts. 34-38 of the Statute), issues of admissibility may also arise before the Court, *e.g.*, in relation to State claims for diplomatic protection for their nationals. Cf., ILC, *supra* note 9, at Art. 44. ("Admissibility of claims"), stating that "the responsibility of a State may not be invoked if: (a) The claim is not brought in accordance with any applicable rule relating to the nationality of claims; (b) The claim is one to which the rule of exhaustion of local remedies applies and any available and effective local remedy has not been exhausted".

Despite these misgivings, however, complementarity has implicitly been referred to in the separate opinion of Judges Higgins, Kooijmans and Buergenthal in the International Court of Justice's (ICJ) *Arrest Warrant* judgment (2002). The opinion states that "a State contemplating bringing criminal charges based on universal jurisdiction must first offer to the national State of the prospective accused person the opportunity itself to act upon the charges concerned".[13] This statement, which was not further elaborated upon, might be taken as requiring deference on the part of the bystander state if the state of nationality (often also the territorial state) proves willing, and presumably also able, to prosecute. In the *Arrest Warrant* case itself, the bystander state (Belgium) had allegedly offered to the territorial/national state (the DRC) that it would investigate and prosecute, and only when this offer was turned down (either explicitly or implicitly) did Belgium take its own initiative.[14] As is known, the ICJ eventually went on to only address issues of immunity, and not the criteria for a lawful exercise of universal jurisdiction (such as an alleged principle of horizontal complementarity).

Litigants before the ICJ have not put the issue of horizontal complementarity to rest, however. In an application a year after the ICJ's judgment in the *Arrest Warrant* case, the DRC asserted that the jurisdiction of states exercising universal jurisdiction on the basis of Article 5.2 of the UN Torture Convention[15] "is subsidiary [or, in the terminology mainly used in this article, 'complementary'] to that of the States mentioned in paragraph 1 [these are the states exercising jurisdiction on the basis of nationality or territoriality] and, above all, to that of the State which has territorial sovereignty". The DRC went on to state:

> it follows that, if one of those States has commenced proceedings in respect of the alleged offences, the State pro-

[13] *Case concerning the Arrest Warrant of 11 April 2000 (Democratic Republic of the Congo v. Belgium),* ICJ, Separate Opinion of Judge Higgins *et al.*, Judgment of 14 February 2002, para. 59.

[14] *Ibid.*, at para. 16 of the majority opinion.

[15] This article provides: "Each State Party shall likewise take such measures as may be necessary to establish its jurisdiction over such offences [acts of torture within the meaning of Article 1] in cases where the alleged offender is present in any territory under its jurisdiction and it does not extradite him pursuant to article 8 to any of the States mentioned in paragraph 1 of this article [that is to say, the state in which the offence was allegedly committed and that of which the alleged offender or the victim is a national]".

> vided for in paragraph 2 [of Article 5 of the UN Torture Convention] will lack jurisdiction, even if the alleged offender is present on its territory and it has not received a request for his extradition.[16]

Apparently, the claimant believes that this interpretation flows from the very text of the Convention. However, apart from the fact that the principle of the *aut dedere aut judicare*-based universal jurisdiction as set out in Article 5.2 of the Convention is to be found, in the system of the said article, *after* the other jurisdictional grounds as set out in Article 5.1 of the Convention, there is not much evidence that the drafters intended to establish a jurisdictional hierarchy between the different paragraphs of Article 5 of the Convention. Possibly, the DRC may rely on (or has already relied on) a more general ICC-style principle of complementarity which is applicable, across the board, to all investigations and prosecutions of international crimes. If it does so, it will have to adduce evidence of state practice and *opinio juris* with a view to establishing the existence of the principle under customary international law. The case is still pending, but a judgment by the ICJ was expected at the time of writing this contribution.[17] Needless to say, this judgment might well be groundbreaking for the clarification of the claimed principle of horizontal complementarity. As pointed out in this section, however, classic international law does not augur well for a limitation of the sovereign right of states to exercise the jurisdiction which the law allots to them.

6.3. The Absence of a Transnational *Ne Bis In Idem* Principle

Somewhat related to the argument of sovereignty and jurisdictional entitlement is the argument based on the absence of a transnational *ne bis in idem* principle. This argument, which similarly undermines the claim that there is such as horizontal complementarity, primarily comes into play in relation to the initiation of proceedings by the 'bystander' state acting under the universality principle, in case the territorial state or the state of nationality had already started investigations which resulted in the convic-

[16] *Certain Criminal Proceedings in France (Republic of the Congo v. France),* Judgment of 11 April 2003, at p. 9 (arguing that the Republic of the Congo is not a party to the UN Torture Convention, and that, accordingly, its provision on universal jurisdiction cannot be opposed to it).

[17] The deadline for the filing of a rejoinder by France was 11 August 2008. See *Press Release 2006/2*, 12 January 2006 (Certain Criminal Proceedings in France).

tion or acquittal of the defendant. If a transnational *ne bis in idem* principle does indeed not exist, it cannot act as a bar to the initiation of prosecutions by a bystander state. It is then immaterial whether or not the defendant has been convicted or acquitted in another state: the bystander state's jurisdiction is not complementary but primary and original.

It is noted that, in a domestic context, courts are not allowed to prosecute the defendant again when he has already been convicted or acquitted. This is denoted as the principle of *ne bis in idem* or the prohibition of double jeopardy, a principle which is codified in international and regional human rights instruments.[18] It is widely accepted, however, that the principle is not applicable at the transnational level, as has been pointed out amongst others by the Human Rights Committee, and as implied by Protocol no. 7 to the European Convention on Human Rights.[19] For our purposes, this implies that, before the courts of bystander states, there is no *res judicata* effect of judgments relating to the prosecution of international crimes delivered in the territorial state or the state of nationality of the offender. Seen from the angle of international human rights law, it would be perfectly legitimate for a bystander state to open an investigation into crimes for which the presumed offender has already been acquitted or convicted (and for which he has possibly served his sentence) in another state.[20] International human rights law does not condition reprosecution on the quality of the prior proceedings. This implies that even if the conviction or acquittal by a court of the territorial state or the state

18 See International Covenant for Civil and Political Rights (ICCPR), Art. 14(7) ("No one shall be liable to be tried or punished again for an offence for which he has already been finally convicted or acquitted in accordance with the law and penal procedure of each country"); Protocol No. 7 (1984) to the European Convention on Human Rights (ECHR), Art. 4.

19 *A.P. v. Italy*, Communication No. 204/1986, UN Doc. CCPR/C/OP/2 at 67 (1990), para. 7.3, Report of the Human Rights Committee, 43rd Sess., Supp. No. 40, UN Doc. A/43/40 (1998) (stating that "article 14, paragraph 7 of the Covenant does not guarantee *ne bis in idem* with regard to the national jurisdiction of two or more states … This provision prohibits double jeopardy only with regard to an offence adjudicated in a given state"). Article 4 of Protocol No. 7 (1984) to the ECHR (referring to the applicability of the principle within the "jurisdiction of the same State").

20 Obviously, this angle is not necessarily the same as the angle from which general international law looks at the matter, the latter being primarily concerned with the interests of states and the delimitation of their respective spheres of competence, and the former being concerned with the rights and interests of the individual (human rights).

of nationality was the result of a genuine ability and willingness to bring a person to justice, a bystander state can still consider the case as admissible. The jurisdiction of the bystander state is accordingly not complementary in the sense set out in the Rome Statute, pursuant to which the ICC can only exercise its jurisdiction (declare a case admissible) if the state has not been able and willing to genuinely investigate and prosecute. On the contrary, any state has, in principle, a full right to reprosecute and retry a presumed offender, irrespective of the result of any prior proceedings in another state.[21]

6.4. The Absence of a Credible Threat Posed by the Bystander State

Carsten Stahn has observed that "[c]omplementarity enhances observance through threat".[22] If a situation risks being investigated, and a case being declared admissible by the ICC, states are well advised, and even encouraged, to conduct their own investigations and prosecutions if they do not want to lose face. The threat potential of the ICC crucially depends on its effectiveness in monitoring compliance. If the Court is not backed by an international community that wants to throw its weight behind the enforcement of arrest warrants and other requests for cooperation, the Court will be viewed as a toothless institution. When it is indeed seen as harmless and lacking deterrence, states will feel more at ease not to take their

[21] This principle may evidently be derogated from in specific treaties. This has happened in the European Union: cf., Art. 54 of the Convention implementing the Schengen Agreement, *O.J.* L239/19 (2000) ("A person whose trial has been finally disposed of in one Contracting Party may not be prosecuted in another Contracting Party for the same acts provided that, if a penalty has been imposed, it has been enforced, is actually in the process of being enforced or can no longer be enforced under the laws of the sentencing Contracting Party"). There is no such convention at the global level. Some states have also derogated from it in their legislation. See, *e.g.*, Canada, Art. 12.2 of the Crimes Against Humanity and War Crimes Act (c. 24) (stating, however, along the lines of Article 20 of the Rome Statute, that "a person may not plead *autrefois acquit, autrefois convict* or a pardon in respect of an offence under any of sections 4 to 7 if the person was tried in a court of a foreign state or territory and the proceedings in that court (*a*) were for the purpose of shielding the person from criminal responsibility; or (*b*) were not otherwise conducted independently or impartially in accordance with the norms of due process recognized by international law, and were conducted in a manner that, in the circumstances, was inconsistent with an intent to bring the person to justice").

[22] C. Stahn, "Complementarity: A Tale of Two Notions", *Crim.L.F.*, 2008, vol. 19, at 97-98.

primary responsibility to investigate and prosecute international crimes seriously. Because of the legitimacy with which the ICC is imbued (widespread ratification of the Statute, an independent prosecutor, highly qualified staff), it is quite likely that the international community will bring pressure to bear on states in order for them to live up to their duty to cooperate with the Court (either for state parties, on the basis of the Statute,[23] or for states which are not Parties, on the basis of a Security Council resolution), and to genuinely investigate and prosecute crimes. Put differently, compliance, backed up by the principle of vertical complementarity, is increased on the ground that the ICC can rely on multilateral bargaining power.

In contrast, the *national* threat of prosecution by bystander states is not nearly as much of a deterrent as the *international* threat of prosecution. Irrespective of the strength of their case, bystander states cannot possibly harness the level of international support that the ICC can count on. It is therefore uncertain whether bystander states' efforts to have a person arrested outside the jurisdiction could bear fruit. The bilateral bargaining power which the state of which the indicted person is a national could use against the state that has received the bystander state's request for cooperation may impel it not to honour the request, whereas the outcome could well be very different if the request were made by the ICC backed up by multilateral bargaining power. Compliance will of course even be less likely if the indicted individual is still present in and protected by his home state. Thus, states will ordinarily not be very impressed by bystander states' threat of prosecution, and are unlikely to set about investigating and prosecuting the crimes in the territory proper. As a result, the complementarity principle may be considered not to serve its purpose of inducing compliance with the duty to prosecute international crimes.

Nevertheless, it should not be overlooked that the mere initiation of an investigation, apart from 'immobilizing' the targets of the investigation in their safe haven, could set in motion a flurry of investigative and prosecutorial activity in the territorial state. The bystander state's investigation may indeed bring to light a past that was not particularly bright, and strengthen the hand of progressive domestic powers that want to bring the presumed offenders (often belonging to a former regime) to justice in the

[23] Rome Statute, Art. 86.

territorial state. At the end of the day, that state also wants to maintain its reputation on the international scene. In the literature, this has been called the "Pinochet effect".[24] It is a term that is derived from the increased willingness of Chilean investigators to dig up the crimes committed in Chile between 1973 and 1990; more generally, it denotes the investigative efforts that have been undertaken throughout the whole of Latin America in the wake of criminal proceedings in Europe (in particular in Spain) in the 1990s and 2000s. The Pinochet effect shows that bystander states' prosecutions can enhance compliance through a combination of a wake-up call and embarrassment.

What has been said about the lack of a credible threat that could be posed by bystander states' prosecutions may appear to apply mainly to a situation of an individual being indicted, and possibly a warrant for his arrest issued, *in his absence* (jurisdiction *in absentia*). After all, if the individual is present in the bystander state's territory, a warrant for his arrest could easily be enforced. It is noted that most states only allow the exercise of universal jurisdiction in case the suspect is present in the territory. Nonetheless, this is not what is exactly meant by the compliance-enhancing power of complementarity through deterrence. At most, the threat of arrest will prevent sought individuals from voluntarily stepping onto the territory of the bystander state seeking his arrest. The deterrent effect of prosecutions initiated in the bystander state is, from that perspective, limited to deterring individuals from leaving safe havens. This is obviously not the deterrence that complementarity is hoped and supposed to deliver.

Genuine complementarity is geared towards effecting *systemic change* in the way states address international crimes through threatening international or extraterritorial prosecution. The indictment, arrest, and eventual trial of a single individual who has taken the risk of entering the territory of a bystander state willing to bring a prosecution is unlikely to effect lasting change in the territorial state as far as the implementation of the rule of law is concerned. It should also be realized in this respect that the typical individual that enters the territory of a bystander state of his or her own volition is an individual who no longer feels safe in his home state. Individuals against whom prosecution has successfully been brought

[24] Cf., N. Roht-Arriaza, *The Pinochet Effect: Transnational Justice in the Age of Human Rights*, University of Pennsylvania Press, 2005.

are often refugees or asylum seekers who are later unmasked as international criminals. These individuals have already been sidelined in their home state (for example, because a new regime has seized power), which would possibly even bring criminal prosecutions if it had the chance or capacity to do so. The home state will normally welcome the prosecution by the bystander state (it can also do so by acquiescence, that is, by not protesting against the exercise of jurisdiction), so that the antagonism which accompanies the threat-based compliance enhancement of the complementarity principle will often not be present.

6.5. Positive Complementarity

The absence of antagonism between the bystander state and the territorial state now brings us to the *positive* side of the complementarity principle. This side has been emphasized by both the ICC Office of the Prosecutor and the recent doctrine on complementarity.[25] Basically, positive complementarity means that the Court and the state *cooperate* with a view to bringing international criminals to justice. To that effect, the Court encourages domestic prosecution in a positive manner. Also, the Court and the state may decide to divide tasks.

Positive complementarity will only work effectively if the state shows some willingness to work together with the Court in acting against suspects of international crimes, and, importantly, does not view the Court as an opponent. As far as bystander states are now concerned, it is common, as shown above, that the territorial state does not view the bystander state as an opponent, given the typical outcast status in the territorial state of the suspects that are voluntarily present in the territory of the bystander state. This augurs well for the implementation of a system of positive complementarity.

However, is this translated into an effective system of positive complementarity? There are some instances of territorial states cooperating rather well with the bystander states that have brought the prosecution (under the universality principle). In prosecuting Rwandan *génocidaires*,

[25] Cf., ICC Office of the Prosecutor, *Paper on Some Policy Issues before the Office of the Prosecutor*, September 2003, p. 4, available at http://www.icc-cpi.int/library/organs/otp/030905_Policy_Paper.pdf; W.W. Burke-White, "Implementing a Policy of Positive Complementarity in the Rome System of Justice", *Crim.L.F.*, 2008, vol. 19, p. 59, at 61; Stahn, *supra* note 22.

for instance, bystander states, such as Belgium, have greatly benefited from the assistance of Rwanda. There is, however, no evidence that positive complementarity is approached *in a systematic fashion* by states. Bystander states' public prosecutors have so far not directly incited territorial states to investigate and prosecute. Making demands for information about investigations and prosecutions – which bystander states have done – is one thing,[26] but it is quite another to actively encourage the territorial state to initiate prosecutions. To be honest, a "Pinochet effect" may sometimes be discernable. Yet this is merely a side-effect of bystander states' prosecutorial efforts; it is not the result of an active, systemic and overarching vision of international criminal justice.

Bystander states should not be chided for not developing such a vision, however. After all, national prosecutors have many more things on their minds than international prosecutors. International prosecutors can focus exclusively on a limited number of international crimes, they can develop specific expertise in the field, and they have access to resources and a sizable international network. It is not surprising, then, that they are able to lay out a thorough positive complementarity vision (although they do not always implement this vision).[27] For national prosecutors, it will always be an uphill struggle to mobilize resources for prosecutions that do not directly reduce *domestic* criminality. Often, only to the extent that the territorial presence of international criminals disturbs the peace of the country will prosecutors intervene. The intervention will typically limit itself to either the prosecution or the extradition of the presumed offender (*aut dedere aut judicare*). When opting for extradition, the prosecutor will normally not undertake efforts to facilitate the trial of the individual in his home state. It should nonetheless be conceded that human rights exceptions in extradition laws (which lay down a ground for refusing to extradite when there is a lack of due process or other human rights guarantees

[26] For instance, in 2009, Spain asked Israel to inform it about any investigations carried out by Israel in relation to a number of senior Israeli military officers against whom a Spanish human rights group had filed a case (the 'Shehadeh case'). Investigating Judge Andreu later determined that the documents forwarded by the Israeli embassy in Madrid made it clear that Israel was not willing to prosecute the officers, see *infra* section 6.9.

[27] Cf., C. Ryngaert, "The Principle of Complementarity: a Means of Ensuring Effective International Criminal Justice", in C. Ryngaert (ed.), *The Effectiveness of International Criminal Justice*, Intersentia, 2009, 145-172.

in the requesting state) may bring some pressure to bear on the requesting home/territorial state to ensure that the individual receives a fair trial, and thus effect some local change.

6.6. The Direct Effect of Article 17 of the Rome Statute in the Domestic Legal Order

In some jurisdictions, notably in those with a strong monist tradition of giving effect to international law, the courts appear to believe that they can directly apply the provisions of the Rome Statute if the domestic legislation implementing the Rome Statute is not satisfactory and leaves impunity gaps. This opens up some possibilities of applying the elaborate complementarity regime as laid down in the Rome Statute in domestic legal orders. If the Rome Statute could be directly applied at the national level, the ICC's vertical complementarity regime would be automatically transformed into a horizontal complementarity regime that is based on the same procedural and substantive criteria.

It should be realized that there are no systems that are fully monist in that they automatically give effect to treaties in domestic law. Typically, only to the extent that treaty provisions are self-executing will they be given effect. It is submitted here that the Rome Statute is non-self-executing and does not lend itself to direct application in domestic courts. There is no evidence that the drafters ever wanted the Statute to be self-executing at the domestic level.[28] Moreover, many provisions of the Statute simply do not lend themselves to direct application in domestic courts because they are procedural in nature, and set out the division of competences within the International Criminal Court proper. As far as the complementarity principle is concerned, admittedly, its substantive core could be applied in domestic courts (such courts deferring to another state's jurisdiction if the latter state is genuinely able and willing to investigate and prosecute the case).[29] Yet the direct application of the procedural aspects of the principle is problematic. The principle needs to be imple-

---

28 Cf., *Restatement (Third) of Foreign Relations Law of the United States*, Section 111(4)(a) (1987) (stating that a treaty is non-self-executing "if the agreement manifests an intention that it shall not become effective as domestic law without the enactment of implementing legislation").

29 Along the same lines, the substantive criminalization in Arts. 6-8 of the Rome Statute could be given direct application.

mented, transposed and adapted for it to be useful at the domestic level. The operationalization of the principle at the ICC indeed involves Court-specific organs such as the Prosecutor, the Pre-Trial Chamber and the Appeals Chamber,[30] which may not readily have an equivalent at the national level. In addition, it reserves a prominent procedural position for the state challenging the jurisdiction of the Court;[31] such a position does not ordinarily exist at the domestic level. Moreover, the jurisdiction of bystander states over international crimes is typically based on the (anticipated) presence of the presumed offender on their territory. This is very unlike the jurisdiction of the ICC, which is not dependent on the territorial presence of the offender.[32]

The argument that the complementarity principle could be applied in domestic courts on the ground that it is enshrined in a treaty which the state has ratified is therefore misguided. This is of course not to say that the complementarity principle is not good law for domestic courts. It could certainly be so, yet not on the basis of a treaty but, *de lege lata,* on the basis of another source of international law, or *de lege ferenda* on the basis of policy arguments. The most useful other international law sources from which the principle could spring are customary international law and general principles of law. Evidence should therefore be adduced that the principle of complementarity indeed borrows its normative validity from the fulfilment of those two sources' constitutive criteria, state practice and, as far as custom is concerned, *opinio juris* (see section 6.7.).

Two instances of courts directly applying the Rome Statute in a criminal case have so far been reported. The first one is a case reported

30 Rome Statute, Arts. 17-19.

31 Rome Statute, Art. 19.

32 See also T. Singelnstein and P. Stolle, "Völkerstrafrecht und Legalitätsprinzip – Klageerzwingungsverfahren bei Opportunitätseinstellungen und Auslegung des §153f StPO", *Zeitschrift für Internationale Strafrechtsdogmatik*, 2006, 118 at 121 (arguing that the effect given to the Rome Statute's complementarity principle in the German legal order is "unabhängig von der Frage, in welchem Masse das gegenüber einer Bezugnahme auf das deutsche Recht nachrangige Statut für eine Auslegung des § 153f StPO tatsächlich herangezogen werden kann – nicht zutreffend, da die Subsidiaritätsregeln für den IStGH [ICC] anders strukturiert sind als die des deutschen Völkerstrafrechts", and citing the "Inlandsbezug" as a central criterion for national prosecution in footnote 32).

from the DRC, *Military Prosecutor v. Bongi Massaba* (2006).[33] The DRC is a party to the Rome Statute (and has on that basis also referred a situation to the ICC) and has, like its former colonial power Belgium, a monist system of giving effect to international law in domestic courts. In the *Massaba* case, the DRC Military Tribunal of Ituri – an area where many atrocities have occurred – convicted the accused for war crimes as provided for in Article 8 of the Rome Statute. Finding that the Congolese military penal code did not provide for a penalty for the said crimes, it directly applied Article 77 of the Rome Statute, that is, the article listing the penalties that the ICC can impose.[34] A commentator has observed that the Military Tribunal, in doing what it did, actually failed to appreciate the true meaning of complementarity, which is of course also part of the Rome Statute. As Article 26 of the Congolese military penal code listed in general terms the penalties that military courts can impose, without specifically referring to the penalties that are applicable to war crimes, there was in fact no gap that ought to be filled by Article 77 of the Rome Statute.[35] Under the complementarity principle, if the domestic level can adequately deal with a case, there is no need for the ICC, or ICC law for that matter, to step in. If anything, the *Massaba* case illustrates how far we have come since the inclusion of the complementarity principle in the Rome Statute. Whereas the complementarity principle as embodied in Article 17 of the Statute was primarily designed to protect the sovereign interests of states against undue encroachment by the Court, we now see that states are more than ready to resort to the ICC or the Rome Statute, not only by referring situations on their own territory to the Court, but also by giving effect to ICC law over domestic law in their own legal orders.

For our purposes – a study of the horizontal complementarity principle along the lines of Article 17 of the Rome Statute – the more impor-

33 Criminal trial judgment and accompanying civil action for damages, RP No 018/2006; RMP No 242/PEN/06, ILDC 387 (CD 2006).

34 It is noted that in an earlier case, the Military Tribunal of Mbandaka (DRC) had given effect to the Rome Statute's regime governing crimes against humanity (RP No. 086/05, RMP No. 279/GMZ/WAB/2005, 12 January 2006). The decision in the *Massaba* case is based on the *Mbandaka* case. The text of the *Mbandaka* decision is not available. Reference to the case was made, however, in the comment by Dunia P Zongwe, ILDC 387 (CD 2006), A8.

35 *Ibid.*, A7.

tant case is the second one, which was reported from Germany. Germany is a state that boasts one of the world's most liberal universality laws. The Code of Crimes against International Law (*Völkerstrafgesetzbuch*) in conjunction with the relevant provisions of the Code of Criminal Procedure (*Strafprozessordnung*, *StPO*) even provides for universal jurisdiction *in absentia*, provided that the presence of the suspect can be anticipated.[36] Given the broad sweep of the law, it was not surprising that the legislature also provided for *subsidiary* universal jurisdiction, in accordance with Article 17 of the Rome Statute: the *StPO* provides that the federal prosecutor (*Generalbundesanwalt*) can renounce the prosecution of an act under the *Völkerstrafgesetzbuch* if that act is prosecuted by a state on whose territory the offence was committed (the territoriality principle), whose national is suspected of having committed it (the nationality principle), or whose national was harmed by it (the passive personality principle).[37] In so doing, Germany appeared to implement the Rome Statute's complementarity principle in the German legal order, and thus to give it horizontal effect. It is noted that, precisely because of the implementation, the German complementarity principle is only *indirectly* based on Article 17 of the Rome Statute; there is no evidence that Germany, upon ratification, wanted to give Article 17, including any ICC case law in respect of the application of the article, direct effect in Germany.[38] Giving direct effect to the Rome Statute was, however, exactly what the German federal prosecutor did in the *Abu Ghraib* case (2005), a case against a number of U.S. officials and members of the armed forces relating to the incidents in the infamous Iraqi prison.[39] Applying Article 14 of the Rome Statute in the mistaken belief that it clarified the complementarity principle, he observed that the Abu Ghraib 'situation' (that is, the term that figures in

[36] Cf., in particular Section 153(f) of the *Strafprozessordnung*. See generally on universal jurisdiction in Germany: C. Ryngaert, "Universal Jurisdiction over Violations of International Humanitarian Law in Germany", *The Military Law and the Law of War Review*, 2008, vol. 47, 377.

[37] Section 153(f)(2)(4) StPO.

[38] Governmental statements upon ratification may play a role in determining the self-executive character of treaties. Compare Restatement (Third) of Foreign Relations Law of the United States, Section 111(4)(b) (1987) ("if the Senate in giving consent to a treaty, or Congress by resolution, requires implementing legislation").

[39] *Juristenzeitung*, 2005, p. 311. The federal prosecutor actually held that the Rome Statute was "Richtschnur für die Auslegung und Anwendung des Section 153f *StPO*".

Article 14) had been dealt with by the United States, and decided, accordingly, that there was no reason for Germany to bring its own laws to bear.

While the German prosecutor incorrectly applied the complementarity principle, if anything the *Abu Ghraib* case bears witness to a willingness on the part of states to apply Article 17 of the Rome Statute in the domestic legal order. Normatively, there are powerful arguments against this method, but what is at this juncture relevant for our purposes is that some states believe that the complementarity principle has a role to play at a horizontal level. If a critical number of states share the same belief and practice, it may crystallize as a norm of customary international law, irrespective of the normative desirability of such as a norm.

6.7. Customary International Law: Ascertaining State Practice with Respect to Horizontal Complementarity

The effect given to the Rome Statute by the German federal prosecutor in the *Abu Ghraib* case has seamlessly brought us to the role that states, in their legislative, prosecutorial and judicial practice, reserve for the horizontal complementarity principle. The leading question here is whether states generally apply the principle and consider themselves to be bound by it as a matter of law (*opinio juris*), or, put differently, whether customary international law mandates the application of a horizontal complementarity principle. There is little practice of states conducting a complementarity analysis. Yet it would not be the first time that limited positive practice translates into a norm of customary international law.[40] But then, it should be established that the limited practice which is put forward is indeed unambiguous for it to form the basis for a claimed customary norm. It is argued that on the basis of the state practice available – German and Spanish practice in particular – it cannot reasonably be stated that the states concerned consider a complementarity analysis to be mandated by law.

Let us first further discuss the federal prosecutor's reasoning in the *Abu Ghraib* case. This reasoning has been heavily criticized in the doc-

[40] See, *e.g.*, the limited practice cited by the International Court of Justice with respect to the absolute immunity of incumbent Ministers of Foreign Affairs in *Case concerning the Arrest Warrant of 11 April 2000 (Dem. Rep. Congo v. Belg.)*, Judgment of 14 February 2002, para. 52.

trine, including by myself.[41] Article 14 of the Rome Statute, which was cited by the German prosecutor, can indeed hardly be considered as applicable to the case, as the article addresses the referral of a situation by a State Party (the article cannot even applied by analogy, as the U.S., of course, did not refer the *Abu Ghraib* situation to the German federal prosecutor). More importantly, even if, *arguendo*, the Rome Statute could have direct effect in the domestic legal order, the reference to 'situation' in the Rome Statute does not mean that the ICC or a bystander state can satisfy itself with the fact that 'something' is done to investigate and prosecute crimes committed in respect of a situation under review, even if the individuals who are targeted in the complaint in fact remain unpunished. This is precisely what the German federal prosecutor decided: since, at the time of deciding, a number of persons presumed to be responsible for the transgressions had been prosecuted in the United States, the U.S. should have been regarded as adequately and genuinely dealing with the situation. Accordingly, in the prosecutor's view, there was no need for German complementary jurisdiction over any individuals allegedly involved in the situation.[42]

Regardless of the merits of the prosecutor's application of the complementarity principle in the German legal order, it is unclear from the decision whether the prosecutor believed that he was *bound* to apply the principle under international law. Seen from one perspective horizontal complementarity, as interpreted idiosyncratically by the prosecutor, may appear to be a welcome tool for the prosecutor to dispose of a politically sensitive case. Taking the purportedly objective character and application of the principle seriously, however, it is useful to take a closer look at the structure of the procedural provisions of the German stop in order to ascertain the normative character of the horizontal complementarity princi-

41 K. Ambos, "Völkerrechtliche Verbrechen, Weltrechtsprinzip und § 153f StPO", *Neue Zeitschrift für Strafrecht*, 2006, 434, at 436; M.E. Kurth, "Zum Verfolgungsermessen des Generalbundesanwaltes nach §153f StPO", *Zeitschrift für Internationale Strafrechtsdogmatik*, 2006, 81, at 85; Ryngaert, above note 2, at 171-172; C. Ryngaert "Universal Jurisdiction in an ICC Era: A Role to Play for EU Member States with the Support of the European Union", *Eur. J. Crime, Crim. L. and Crim. Justice*, 2006, 43, at 63.

42 It is noted that the *Oberlandesgericht* of Stuttgart refused to judicially review the federal prosecutor's decision on the ground that such a decision is a discretionary one that is not subject to review. *Neue Zeitschrift für Strafrecht,* Decision of 13 September 2005, 2006, p. 117.

ple in Germany. When doing so, doubts emerge as to whether German law actually *allows* the complementarity principle to play a strong normative role in the first place.[43] The relevant article in the StPO provides that the federal prosecutor may renounce the prosecution, in relation to an act committed abroad, of a foreigner present in Germany, in case surrender to an international tribunal or extradition to a prosecuting state is admissible (*zulässig*) and intended (*beabsichtigt*).[44] Accordingly, to the extent that a complaint targets an individual present in Germany the federal prosecutor will normally only be able, under German law, to defer to a foreign state if that state is bringing a prosecution *and* the individual could be extradited to that state. If he cannot be extradited – for instance because there has been no extradition request, because there is no extradition treaty between Germany and the other state, or because there is a risk that his substantive or procedural human rights will be violated in the other state – the German federal prosecutor is under an obligation to prosecute; there will be no room for deferring on the basis of the complementarity principle. There is more room for deference in the event that the complaint targets individuals who are not yet present on German soil, but even then, renouncing prosecution is not mandatory on the basis of the text of the law.[45] Therefore, Germany arguably does not consider the principle of horizontal complementarity to be a norm that binds prosecutors and courts.

In Germany, the complementarity principle appears to provide only a non-binding guideline for prosecutors and courts. The same holds true in Belgium, whose Preliminary Title of the Code of Criminal Procedure provides that the federal prosecutor may refuse to initiate proceedings if "the specific circumstances of the case show that, in the interest of the proper administration of justice and in order to honor Belgium's international obligations, said case should be brought either before the international courts, or before the court of the place in which the acts were committed, or before the court of the state of which the perpetrator is a national, or the court of the place in which he can be found, and to the extent that said court is independent, impartial, and fair, as may be determined

[43] Singelnstein and Stolle, *supra* note 32, at 121.

[44] Section 153 (f)(2) *in fine* StPO.

[45] Section 153 (f)(2) StPO ("Die Staatsanwaltschaft *kann insbesondere* von der Verfolgung einer Tat, die nach den §§ 6 bis 14 des Völkerstrafgesetzbuches strafbar ist, in den Fällen des § 153c Abs. 1 Nr. 1 und 2 absehen ...") (emphasis added).

from the international commitments binding on Belgium and that state".[46] No application of this provision has so far been reported.

Other states have not laid down the principle of horizontal complementarity in their criminal codes. The absence of statutory codification of a horizontal complementarity principle does not mean, however, that the principle cannot impose limits on the exercise of universal jurisdiction. It surely can, if prosecutors and courts derive it directly from international law, comity, or general principles underlying the legal system. A good example of this category of states is offered by Spain, whose prosecutors have initiated many investigations on the basis of the universality principle. As will be demonstrated, however, Spain does not seem to believe that international law *requires* the application of a binding horizontal complementarity principle to prosecute international crimes.

The principle of subsidiarity/horizontal complementarity in relation to international crimes has quite a history in Spain. Its application went largely unchallenged until 2003, when a conservative Spanish Supreme Court rejected it in its *Guatemala Genocide* judgment. This was not because the principle *limited* Spain's exercise of jurisdiction to an unacceptable degree, but, on the contrary, because the principle unjustifiably *expanded* Spain's jurisdiction in that it allowed Spain – on the basis of an 'able and willing' test – to pass judgment on another state's judicial acts, thereby possibly impeding the political branches' conduct of foreign relations.[47] On closer inspection, these combined act of state and political question doctrines in fact militated not so much against horizontal complementarity, but rather against the very application of the universality principle, given the political sensitivity of many cases arising under that principle. It should be realized in this context that complementarity only comes into play at the admissibility stage, *after* a court has upheld juris-

46 See Art. 10, 1*bis*, and Art. 12*bis* of the Preliminary Title of the Belgian Code of Criminal Procedure. English translation available in *I.L.M.*, 2003, vol. 42, 1258, 1267.

47 The Court noted that basing this test "on the real or apparent inactivity of local courts implies a judgment of one state's courts about the ability to administer justice of the similarly situated organs of another sovereign state (Section II[6]), while such an 'unable or unwilling' inquiry might be appropriate for the International Criminal Court, national courts should not be making these kinds of judgments, which could have an important effect on foreign relations and should be left to the political branches". Cf., N. Roht-Arriaza, "International Decisions", *American Journal of International Law*, 2006, vol. 100, no. 1, 208-209.

diction. This is indeed the regime in the Rome Statute, where the jurisdictional articles (5-16) logically precede those on admissibility (17-19). If a court does not have jurisdiction over a case, there is no need to conduct an admissibility analysis. Accordingly, in Spain, complementarity could only have an autonomous meaning provided that the universality of jurisdiction over international crimes was no longer contested.

The lawfulness of universal jurisdiction was eventually reaffirmed, however, in relation to the same *Guatemala Genocide case*, by a progressive Spanish Constitutional Court in 2005, which consequently quashed the Supreme Court's judgment. Logically, the Court subsequently addressed the admissibility question, that is, the question of whether a horizontal complementarity/subsidiarity principle, which was in fact also applied by the courts *after* the Supreme Court's 2003 judgment,[48] would impose hard and fast *legal* limits, under international law, on Spain's exercise of universal jurisdiction. This was in fact the first, and so far the only time that a domestic court has inquired into the *international legal basis* of horizontal complementarity.[49] Shortly after the Constitutional Court's judgment, in early 2006, the *Audiencia Nacional* applied horizontal complementarity in a decision on a complaint brought by victims of China's alleged genocide in Tibet, and established its jurisdiction in light of the unlikelihood of a judicial remedy for the victims in Chinese courts after so much time had passed since the acts complained of occurred.[50]

48 *E.g.*, in the *Scilingo* case, decided by the Spanish High Court a few months before the Constitutional Court handed down its judgment in *Guatemala Genocide*. *Public Prosecutor's Office v. Scilingo Manzorro*, Final appeal judgment, No. 16/2005, 19 April 2005, available in Oxford Reports on International Law in Domestic Courts, ILDC 136 (ES 2005), para. B.5 of the judgment.

49 Horizontal complementarity has been codified in a number of national codes of criminal procedure (*e.g.*, Section 153(f) of the German StPO and Article 12*bis* of the Preliminary Title of the Belgian Code of Criminal Procedure). If domestic courts apply the complementarity principle, they do so in the first place as a matter of *national* law, rather than of *international* law.

50 Audiencia Nacional, no. 196/05, 10 January 2006. See on the Tibet case also C. Bakker, "Universal Jurisdiction of Spanish Courts over Genocide in Tibet: Can it Work?", *Journal of International Criminal Justice*, 2006, vol. 4, 595, and Chadwick, *supra* note 2, 384 (believing that the main condition for application of the complementarity principle – that the territorial/national state should be given the opportunity to act first – were met in the case).

It was not wholly surprising that the Constitutional Court ruled that international law did *not* oblige states to conduct a complementarity analysis along the lines of Article 17 of the Rome Statute. As noted above, international law does not seem to prioritize the grounds of jurisdiction;[51] there is no evidence that the universality principle is a subsidiary principle which can only be relied on in case the exercise of jurisdiction based on 'stronger' principles, such as territoriality or nationality, proves to be ineffective. Horizontal complementarity/subsidiarity may exist as a principle, of course, but not one endowed with legal normativity. Instead, it may merely constitute a principle of politico-criminal policy. Prosecutors may thus invoke it to justify their unwillingness to commence proceedings in the face of evidence of proceedings occurring, or having occurred, in the territorial state or the state of nationality, *in the exercise of their prosecutorial discretion* (possibly guided by national prosecutorial guidelines), and not because international law contains a binding obligation to that effect.

It is reiterated here that the relevant German 'complementarity' provision (Section 153f of the *Strafprozessordnung*), discussed in the previous section, has no binding character either, as a matter of international law or as a matter of domestic law. While, admittedly, that provision has carved out an exception to the German principle of mandatory prosecution in cases of crimes against international law, it clearly does not *require* that German prosecutors forego their exercise of jurisdiction. The article may urge them to dismiss a case if the criteria for the exercise of complementary jurisdiction by German authorities are not met. Yet in essence, German prosecutors remain entitled to exercise jurisdiction, even in spite of rather strong evidence that a state with a stronger nexus is able and willing to genuinely investigate and prosecute a case.

Hostility towards, or uneasiness with the principle of complementarity – at least as applied by the ICC – may also be gleaned from Spain's 2006 progress report on the implications for Council of Europe member states of the Ratification of the Rome Statute. In this report, Spain stated that,

> Article 7.3 of the Organic Act on Cooperation with the ICC expressly states that if the ICC Prosecutor does not initiate an investigation related to the facts that have been reported,

[51] Cf., above section 6.2.

> *or the ICC determines the inadmissibility of the matter*, the report, complaint or request may be resubmitted to the competent Spanish authorities, which thus recover their full jurisdiction and competence.[52]

Accordingly, Spain does not consider itself to be bound by an inadmissibility finding of the ICC made on the basis of the vertical complementarity principle. In all likelihood, Spain is indeed not bound by the Rome Statute or ICC decisions on the basis of the Statute, as the ICC does not directly apply in the domestic legal order (see above). Yet it is telling that the Spanish authorities are not even willing to defer to ICC admissibility findings as a matter of *prosecutorial policy*: these authorities may thus second-guess authoritative ICC determinations (even though Spain is a party to the Rome Statute), and conduct either a horizontal complementarity analysis of a different order (possibly using a lower threshold of admissibility), or no complementarity analysis at all. As discussed above, the Spanish courts may of course apply some sort of horizontal complementarity analysis as a matter of non-binding *criminal policy*. But this analysis is very different from the one conducted by the ICC, which separates the legal requirements relating to admissibility/complementarity from the exercise of prosecutorial discretion.[53]

6.8. In Support of Domestic Courts Applying a Horizontal Complementarity Principle

So far, six elements that have a bearing on the answer to the question whether there is, or should be, a principle of horizontal complementarity have been discussed. None of these elements yields a convincingly positive answer to the question. As set out in section 6.3., the principle of sovereignty may fail to circumscribe the jurisdiction which states are entitled to: as soon as states can invoke a jurisdictional ground, no further limiting principles, such as a principle of horizontal complementarity, may apply under the classic international law of jurisdiction. Along similar lines, in

---

52 CE Doc. 4th Consult/ICC (2006), Strasbourg, 14 September 2006 (emphasis added), quoted in Jo Stigen, *The Relationship between the International Criminal Court and National Jurisdictions. The Principle of Complementarity*, Martinus Nijhoff, 2008, 192-193.

53 Admissibility/complementarity is discussed in Arts. 17-19 of the Rome Statute, whereas the 'interests of justice' criterion, which forms the basis for the Prosecutor's policy, is discussed in Art. 53.

section 6.3., it was noted that there is no principle of transnational *ne bis in idem*. The absence of this principle allows bystander states to cast aside judgments pronounced by courts in other states, resulting in the conviction or acquittal of the accused, even if the latter states have genuinely investigated and prosecuted the crime. Then in section 6.4. it was shown that one of the main systemic rationales of the complementarity principle is enhancing compliance through threat. Because the ICC can make good its threat to exercise jurisdiction and declare cases admissible by enlisting the support of the international community, the complementary nature of its jurisdiction may, at least in theory, guarantee the success of its mission. In contrast, states *ut singuli*, when exercising universal jurisdiction, cannot carry that big a stick, as enlisting international support to coax the territorial or national state into compliance will ordinarily prove much more difficult to garner. Moreover, as argued in section 6.5., states may lack the wherewithal to effectively develop and implement a complementarity strategy aimed at enhancing compliance with territorial or national states' duties to prosecute ('positive complementarity'). section 6.6. turned its gaze to techniques for giving effect to international law in domestic courts, but also on that front, the argument does not particularly weigh in favour of horizontal complementarity. Indeed, there is no evidence that Article 17 of the Rome Statute was meant to have direct effect in domestic courts hearing international criminal cases. In its section 6.7., eventually, it was shown that states exercising universal jurisdiction do not consider a horizontal complementarity principle to be binding on their prosecutors and courts.

All this presents a rather gloomy picture of horizontal complementarity under international law. However, none of the elements discussed allows us to reject horizontal complementarity outright. Indeed, there are indications that horizontal complementarity has its rightful place in the structure of international law and relations. After all, sovereignty, as discussed in section 6.2., also has a *negative* connotation. When bystander states bring their laws to bear, they are not allowed to violate the principle of non-intervention. Precisely by casting aside investigations and prosecutions brought in other states, bystander states may encroach on the latter's legitimate interests, thus causing international friction and protest. Furthermore, while there may be no hard and fast principle of transnational *ne bis in idem* (section 6.3.), it remains no less true that some states respect the *res judicata* effect of foreign judgments in relation to international crimes.[54] And from a policy perspective, there is some evidence that the threat of prosecution by bystander states has contributed to the initiation of local prosecutions (cf. section 6.4.). As a related matter, it is not excluded that bystander states with some experience in prosecuting international crimes cases might beef up their investigative units so as to enable them to enter into dialogue with the territorial and national state, and to make a bystander forum only the ultimate complementary forum (cf. section 6.5.). After all, for a bystander state, it is cheaper and more efficient to have these crimes prosecuted in the home state. As far as the direct effect of the Rome Statute's provision on complementarity (Article 17) is concerned, while that provision should probably not be given direct effect in the domestic legal order, it has been observed that states are nevertheless willing to do just that (section 6.6.). This testifies to their willingness to carry out a horizontal complementarity analysis.

While states such as Spain and Germany may not consider a horizontal complementarity analysis to be binding (section 6.7.), they clearly do believe that such an analysis is desirable from the point of view of criminal policy. Horizontal complementarity guarantees that their courts do not become overburdened, and that only the cases that deserve to be prosecuted extraterritorially, *are* also prosecuted: these are the cases which the territorial or national state is unable or unwilling to genuinely investigate and prosecute, and in relation to which positive complementarity efforts (aimed at convincing initially reluctant territorial or national states to assume their responsibility) do not bear fruit. Horizontal complementarity also guarantees that the diplomatic fallout of the exercise of extraterritorial jurisdiction remains limited: territorial or national states that apparently shield the perpetrator from responsibility by carrying out sham or no proceedings at all against him or her are unlikely to engender much sympathy and support within the international community. Like complementarity at the ICC, horizontal complementarity may ensure that sovereignty is not used as a shield, while at the same time it ensures respect for and, even better, encourages good faith investigations and prosecutions by the territorial or national state.

54 *E.g.*, Canada, Art. 12.2 of the Crimes Against Humanity and War Crimes Act (c. 24); Art. 23.2 (c) in conjunction with Art. 23.5 of the Spanish Organic Law on the Judicial Power.

Thus, there are strong normative arguments in favour of a principle of horizontal complementarity, although admittedly it may not yet have crystallized as a norm of customary international law given the dearth of pertinent state practice. However, stating that there is such a thing as horizontal complementarity is one thing, implementing it correctly is quite another. A warning may have to be provided here as to an overly policy-based horizontal complementarity analysis. Lacking principled guidance, such an analysis may easily be contorted for political purposes. And because prosecutors are not under a *legal* duty to carry out a complementarity analysis, assuming that there are no administrative guidelines on horizontal complementarity which are binding on them either, they may even believe that they can do wholly *without* a complementarity analysis, or at least carry out a very superficial self-serving analysis without genuinely inquiring into whether the territorial or national state has conducted any relevant proceedings.

6.9. Lessons from Recent Spanish Practice

An example of the glaring lack of attention for prosecutorial efforts in the accused's home state was recently offered by the Spanish indictment of a number of high-ranking Rwandan officials in 2008.[55] In this indictment, investigative Judge Merelles of the Spanish *Audiencia Nacional* remained conspicuously silent on Rwanda's efforts to bring the named suspects to justice.[56] Possibly, he was of the opinion that, because the indictment targeted persons linked to the sitting Rwandan Government, it was not to be expected that the Rwandan authorities would seriously investigate the crimes allegedly committed by the suspects. This may be true, but it would have been more honest if the judge had explicitly shed some light on this issue. If he had taken complementarity seriously and had looked at Rwandan practice, he could have come across the case of Wilson Gumisiriza – who was named in the Spanish indictment – in Rwanda itself. He could have noticed that proceedings were to be initiated against Gu-

[55] *Juzgado Central de instruccion No. 4, Audiencia Nacional, Sumario 3/2.008 – D. Auto*.

[56] See also X., "The Spanish Indictment of High-ranking Rwandan Officials", *JICJ*, 2008, vol. 6, p. 1003, at 1008-1009.

misiriza in Rwanda at the time of the indictment.[57] If he had waited somewhat, he could have noticed that, while Gumisiriza was acquitted by the Military Court of Kigali on 24 October 2008,[58] the prosecution appealed (the appeal case was still pending at the time of writing this contribution).[59] What is clear is that the Rwandan justice system seemed to be working. Regrettably, the Spanish judge passed this over, and drew up the indictment, at least against Gumisiriza, without awaiting the outcome of the Rwandan proceedings (which did not seem to shield the perpetrator from responsibility, at least not at the time of writing this contribution).

A similar lack of attention for local investigations is demonstrated by the *Audiencia Nacional*'s court order of 29 January 2009, which granted leave to proceed in the action brought by the representatives of a number of Palestinian civilians killed as a consequence of the targeted bombing of the house of Salah Shehadeh, an alleged Hamas commander, by the Israeli Defence Forces (IDF) in Gaza in 2002.[60] As far as complementarity is concerned, Judge Andreu limited himself to noting, almost in passing, that 'there is no evidence that any proceedings have been brought to investigate the facts'.[61] This assessment is inaccurate. In fact, the IDF and the Israeli Security Agency had launched an inquiry immediately after the death of Shehadeh. This inquiry showed "that the procedures followed in the IDF operation were correct and professional", and that, while it "found shortcomings in the information available, and the evalua-

57 Arrests were made on 11 June 2008 following joint investigations between Rwanda's prosecution authorities and the Office of the Prosecutor General of the ICTR. See "Rwanda: Four RDF Officers Arrested", 11 June 2008, available at http://allafrica.com/stories/200806120012.html.

58 Hirondelle News Agency Arusha, "Rwanda/Church - Rwandan Military Court Acquits Two Officers and Sentences Two Others", 24 October 2008, available at http://www.hirondellenews.com/content/view/2540/26/.

59 Hirondelle News Agency Arusha, "Rwanda/Bishops - Rwandan Military Court to Rule over Appeals on February 25th", 29 January 2009, available at http://www.hirondellenews.com/content/view/2878/26/.

60 Central Magistrates' Court No. 4, *Audiencia Nacional*, Madrid, Preliminary Report no. 157/2.008-G.A., 29 January 2009, unofficial translation by FIDH, available at http://www.fidh.org/IMG/pdf/admission_order_propery_translated-1.pdf (hereinafter, Audencia National's Order). See also, for a discussion of the *Shehadeh* case, S. Weill, "The Targeted Killing of Salah Shehadeh. From Gaza to Madrid", *JICJ*, 2009, vol. 7, p. 617.

61 *Audencia National's* Order, *supra* note 60, at para. 3.

tion of that information, concerning the presence of innocent civilians near Shehadeh's vicinity, the timing or the method of the action would have been changed, as was done a number of times in the past".[62] Although it is true that no criminal prosecutions were subsequently brought,[63] it is no less true that a number of rulings by Israeli courts, including the Israeli Supreme Court – courts that are known for their independence – were made in relation to the *Shehadeh* case.[64] It is almost superfluous to note that a dismissal of the case does not in itself evidence unwillingness on the part of Israel to genuinely investigate and prosecute. More generally, reference should also be made to the Israeli Supreme Court's momentous 'targeted killings' decision of 14 December 2006. In this decision, the Court, drawing widely on recognized sources of international humanitarian law, held that the death of civilian bystanders as a

[62] Israeli Ministry of Foreign Affairs, "Findings of the inquiry into the death of Salah Shehadeh", 2 August 2002, available at http://www.mfa.gov.il/MFA/Government/Communiques/2002/Findings%20of%20the%20inquiry%20into%20the%20death%20of%20Salah%20Sh.

[63] In 2006, the UN Special Rapporteur on extrajudicial, summary or arbitrary executions called on Israel to explain whether the findings of the inquiry were followed by any disciplinary or criminal proceedings, and, if not, the reasons given as to why not (UN Doc. E/CN.4/2006/53/Add.1, (2006)), but apparently the request went unanswered.

[64] According to the Israeli daily *Haaretz*, immediately upon the judge's order being made public, the Israeli Ministry of Justice sent the Israeli Embassy in Madrid a large amount of documents which included legal rulings and Supreme Court decisions dealing with the targeted killing of Shehadeh. The Embassy would submit those documents to Judge Andreu. *Haaretz*, "Spanish FM: We'll act to prevent war crimes probes against Israel", 3 February 2009, available at http://www.haaretz.com/hasen/spages/1059964.html. The Israeli case is known as *Hess and ors v. Military Advocate General and ors,* HCJ 8794/03. The petitioners before the Israeli Supreme Court demanded that the Attorney General initiate criminal proceedings against the commanders involved in the bombing of Shehadeh, and that the government establish a more independent and more competent investigation committee than the one in fact appointed. On 23 December 2008, the Israeli Supreme Court denied the petition on administrative law and not on international law grounds. It held that the decisions taken by the respondents were not so unreasonable as to justify judicial intervention, and that such intervention would only possibly be appropriate after an independent examination committee concluded its investigation. Thanks to Elad Peled for pointing this out to me. See also I. Rosenzweig and Y. Shany, "Universal Jurisdiction: Spanish Court Initiates an Inquiry of the Target Killing of Salah Shehadeh", available at http://www.idi.org.il/sites/english/ResearchAndPrograms/NationalSecurityandDemocracy/Terrorism_and_Democracy/Newsletters/Pages/3d%20Newsletter/1/SpanishCourtInquirySalahShehadeh.aspx.

consequence of a targeted killing is not necessarily in violation of international law: only to the extent that the collateral damage is disproportionate to the military advantage sought would this be the case.[65] This decision, taken by a presiding judge who is well-known for his liberal, human rights-friendly views,[66] was generally praised in the international law literature for its moderate nature.[67] When after a thorough analysis based on the facts of the case, Israeli legal experts conclude that there has been no violation of the law, prosecutions should arguably not be brought. Rather than an unwillingness to bring a case, there is simply no case to answer in this situation. As a result thereof, complementarity jurisdiction does not come into play at all.[68]

The perception of the judge's insensitivity towards Israel's situation in the *Shehadeh* case is augmented by his holding that the facts "must be considered as a Crime against Humanity, and concerning which the international commitments subscribed by Spain impose prosecution", and that they constitute "an attack against civilian population, already illegitimate from the start" (translation by the International Federation for Human Rights, FIDH)[69] – as if there is no act involved of carefully weighing the protection of the lives of innocent civilians against the military advantage anticipated. The judge's failure to heed, or even discuss, Israel's arguments as to the unlawful character of the targeted killings – arguments that are not extreme, but are crafted on the basis of recognized principles

65 *Public Committee against Torture in Israel and Palestinian Society for the Protection of Human Rights and the Environment v. Israel and others*, Original petition to the High Court of Justice, HCJ 769/02, Oxford Reports on International Law in Domestic Courts, ILDC 597 (IL 2006), paras. 40-46.

66 See E. Peled, annotation ILDC 597 (IL 2006), above note 62, A8 ("The fact that President Barak, whose deep commitment to preserving human rights has been evident, decided to uphold the targeted killings policy, albeit on strict conditions, could be read to signify the uniqueness of the phenomenon of terror, at least from an Israeli perspective, and the acute necessity of confronting it seriously").

67 *E.g.*, A. Cassese, "On Some Merits of the Israeli Judgment on Targeted Killings", 7 *JICJ*, 2007, vol. 7, 339; A. Cohen and Y. Shany, "A Development of Modest Proportions. The Application of the Principle of Proportionality in the *Targeted Killings* Case", 7 *JICJ*, 2007, vol. 7, 310.

68 Compare Rosenzweig and Shany, *supra* note 64 (submitting that "it is unclear whether Spain is particularly well-suited to address [the criminality of the targeted killing of Shehadeh] especially given the fact that proceedings in Israel are still pending (although, admittedly, at a very slow pace)").

69 *Audencia National's* Order, *supra* note 60, at para. 3.

of international law – is highly regrettable; if the judge had taken complementarity seriously, he would have adduced evidence of genuine unwillingness to investigate on the part of Israel. Since, moreover, a bystander state's judge has less expertise and legitimacy than the ICC, a high level of deference under the complementarity principle is required.[70] A high level of deference is all the more warranted in relation to a conflict party's proportionality determinations made in the heat of battle. For such a judge, it is a tall order indeed to second-guess matters that essentially pertain to national military tactics. Only when disproportionality between means and ends is blatant, should a domestic judge initiate investigations on the basis of the complementarity principle.[71] It is open to serious doubt whether such blatant disproportionality was present in the *Shehadeh* case.

After a challenge by the public prosecutor, Judge Andreu upheld his decision to open an investigation on 4 May 2009.[72] This time round he did pay attention to proceedings brought in Israel, but considered them to be insufficient so as to warrant deference on the part of Spanish judicial authorities. Amongst others, he pointed out that the targeted killing of Shehadeh took place in the Occupied Palestinian Territories, and not in Israeli territory. Therefore, in the Judge's view, the complementarity principle would not come into play at all, and Spain would have *primary* jurisdiction over the killing.[73] In any event, although the judge believed that a complementarity analysis was not required,[74] he did perform one, but

70 Cf., Ryngaert, *supra* note 3, at 177.

71 See also Rosenzweig and Shany, *supra* note 64 (stating, in relation to the *Shehadeh* case that "an unprincipled employment of universal jurisdiction by foreign judges with a limited appreciation of the unique dilemmas posed by terrorism and counter-terrorism could produce a 'chilling effect' that could further complicate the fight against terrorism", and that "it is questionable that the exercise of universal jurisdiction can be appropriately exercised in the case of the Shehadeh targeted killing operation, which involves difficult issues of law, fact and procedure").

72 Juzgado Central de Instrucción No Cuatro, Audiencia Nacional Madrid, No. 157/2.008, 4 May 2009.

73 *Ibid.*, second legal argument, at 2. It is noted, however, that at least under ICC law the complementarity principle also requires deference to the primary jurisdiction of the State of which the perpetrator is a national. Apart from that, it is arguable that Israel still exercises effective territorial control over the Occupied Palestinian Territories, so that primacy of Israeli jurisdiction on the basis of territoriality is appropriate.

74 See also *ibid.*, fifth legal argument, at 13 (stating that the Geneva Conventions do not establish a regime of subsidiary universal jurisdiction).

noted, rather predictably, that the Israeli authorities who had conducted investigations were not independent, that its decisions did not motivate or justify the inaction on the Israeli side, and that, in fact, since 2002 Israeli authorities had not initiated proceedings inquiring into the criminal responsibility for the targeted killing.[75] This in turn arguably allowed Spanish authorities to establish jurisdiction. Another oddity of the decision is the judge's observation that the (purported) absence of an Israeli investigation necessarily led to a finding of there being no concurrent jurisdiction (by Spain and Israel) and thus no jurisdictional conflict,[76] as if Israel would not take issue with Spain's jurisdictional assertions.[77] Eventually, after another challenge by the public prosecutor, a Spanish appeals court closed Judge Andreu's investigation.

Complementarity was also given short shrift in a later decision of 29 April 2009 by the renowned Investigating Judge Baltasar Garzon (who had also initiated the investigation into Augusto Pinochet's alleged crimes) with respect to the acts of torture allegedly committed at the U.S. detainee camp at Guantanamo Bay.[78] In this decision, the Judge completely dispensed with a complementarity analysis, and merely limited itself to stating: "... we find ourselves confronted with a situation of Universal Criminal Jurisdiction".[79] At the time, it was well-known however that the Obama administration was undertaking efforts to come clean about the previous administration's torture memos and practices, and to reconsider the detainees' limited rights.

75 *Ibid.*, sixth legal argument, at 13-14.

76 *Ibid.*, sixth legal argument, at 14.

77 This 'vacuum' theory has also been used in order to justify assertions of extraterritorial jurisdiction in the field of antitrust law, notably in the U.S. This theory fails to appreciate, however, that inaction on the part of a state may also amount to a conscious exercise of jurisdiction. It may lead to normative competency conflicts when another state actively exercises jurisdiction.

78 Central Court for Preliminary Criminal Proceedings, Number Five, National Court Madrid, Preliminary Investigations 150/09-N, 29 April 2009, unofficial English translation by the Center for Constitutional Rights.

79 *Ibid.*, at 10. The Judge cited an opinion of a judge at the Spanish Supreme Court who found in 2006 with respect to Guantanamo that "the detention of hundreds of people, among them the appealing party, without charges, without guarantees and therefore without control and without limits, at the Guantanamo based maintained by the United States military constitutes a situation that is impossible to explain, much less justify, from the legal and political reality in which it is found embedded". *Ibid.*, at 9.

It is hardly surprising then that, in the immediate aftermath of Judge Andreu's *Shehadeh* order, Israel reacted furiously, and even called on Spain to amend its universality legislation in order to forestall abuse. The U.S. for its part appeared to be working actively behind the scenes to persuade Spain to limit universal jurisdiction.[80] Spain's political authorities quickly caved in to foreign concerns: the day after Judge Andreu issued his order, Spain's Foreign Minister informed his Israeli counterpart that Spain would indeed amend its liberal universality legislation.[81]

Eventually, Spain did not shed the universality principle altogether, but conditioned its application to situations of the presumed offender being found in Spain (that is, presence-based or secondary universality, as required by many other states providing for universal jurisdiction), or of the victims having Spanish nationality (that is, the passive personality principle), or situations having a relevant connection with Spain.[82] Important for our purposes, the amendment in addition calls for the application of a complementarity analysis, along the lines of German statutory law. Under the new law, jurisdiction does not lie if another state, or an international tribunal, has initiated an investigation or an effective prosecution.[83]

80 Political commentators were more open, however. See, *e.g.*, A.C. McCarthy, "Spain's 'Universal Jurisdiction' Power Play", *The National Review*, 31 March 2009 ("Were [Spain's maneuvering] not camouflaged as legal process, it would properly be regarded as a hostile act: an explicit threat of capturing … American officials for performing their official duties in defense of the United States").

81 *Haaretz*, *supra* note 62. See also El Pais, "Moratinos promete cambiar la ley para frenar al juez, según la ministra israelí", 31 January 2009, available at http://www.elpais.com/articulo/espana/Moratinos/promete/cambiar/ley/frenar/juez/ministra/israeli/elpepunac/20090131elpepinac_13/Tes.

82 Boletín Oficial del Estado, Núm. 266, 4 November 2009, Sec. I, p. 92089, 92091, Art. 1. See also Enmienda núm. 676, 121/000017 Proyecto de Ley de reforma de la legislación procesal para la implantación de la Nueva Oficina Judicial, new Art. 23(4) and (5) of the Ley Orgánica 6/1985, de 1 de julio 2009, del Poder Judicial available at http://www.derechos.org/nizkor/espana/doc/oficinajud.html ("Sin perjuicio de lo que pudieran disponer los tratados y convenios internacionales suscritos por España, para que puedan conocer los tribunales españoles de los anteriores delitos deberá quedar acreditado que sus presuntos responsables se encuentran en España o que existen víctimas de nacionalidad española o constatarse algún vínculo de conexión relevante con España …").

83 *Ibid.*, amendment of Art. 23.4, para. 2, *in fine* ("…para que puedan conocer los tribunales españoles de los anteriores delitos deberá quedar acreditado … en todo caso, que en otro país competente o en el seno de un Tribunal internacional no se ha ini-

The law also clarifies that Spanish proceedings are suspended if another state or tribunal has commenced proceedings.[84]

The Spanish *Shehadeh* case presents a cautionary tale for our purposes of horizontal complementarity. The boomerang constituted by the absence of a serious complementarity analysis and the resultant jurisdictional overreaching inevitably returned to the thrower, that is, the Spanish authorities which condoned the practice of going after any alleged international criminal without paying heed to investigations in the presumed offender's home state. It can now only be hoped that Spain will not become the new Belgium, and that only the bathwater is thrown out, not the baby: it is the failure to conduct a horizontal complementarity analysis that ought to be remedied, not the universality principle itself.[85]

6.10. Concluding Observations

Reflecting on the Spanish universality decisions, one can understand that universal jurisdiction is presented as a European imperialist construct in other corners of the world.[86] For the legitimacy and viability of universal

ciado procedimiento que suponga una investigación y una persecución efectiva, en su caso, de tales hechos punibles").

84 *Ibid.*, amendment of Art. 23.4, para. 3 ("El proceso penal iniciado ante la jurisdicción española se sobreseerá provisionalmente cuando quede constancia del comienzo de otro proceso sobre los hechos denunciados en el país o por el Tribunal a los que se refiere el párrafo anterior").

85 It is recalled that Belgium repealed its universality legislation in August 2003 after intense pressure by the United States. See L. Reydams, "Belgium Reneges on Universality: the 5 August 2003 Act on Grave Breaches of International Humanitarian Law", *JICJ*, 2003, vol. 1, 679. Under the new legislation, the prosecution of violations of international humanitarian law is subject to a nationality requirement (Art. 6, 1*bis*, and 10, 1*bis* of the Preliminary Title of the Code of Criminal Procedure), and the prosecution of international crimes under the universality principle is only possible if international law *obliges* Belgium to prosecute (Art. 12*bis* of the same title). Mere international authorization to prosecute does not suffice. The new regime is set out at length (in Dutch) in: J. Wouters and C. Ryngaert, "De toepassing van de (Belgische) wet van 5 augustus 2003 betreffende ernstige schendingen van het internationaal humanitair recht", special issue *Nullum Crimen*, April 2007, 21 pp. See also (again in Dutch): C. Ryngaert, "De toepassing van het beginsel aut dedere aut judicare in de Belgische rechtsorde", *Tijdschrift voor Strafrecht*, 2008, 346.

86 See, *e.g.*, Assembly of the African Union, Decision on the Report of the Commission on the Abuse of the Principle of Universal Jurisdiction, Doc. Ex. CL/411 (XIII), 1 July 2008, stating: "1) The abuse of the Principle of Universal Jurisdiction is a devel-

jurisdiction, it is crucial that the territorial or national state is accorded the first right of way to prosecute, and that due respect is shown for ongoing local prosecutorial efforts. So-called 'liberal' states such as Spain (or France for that matter, where a principle of complementarity or subsidiarity has never been applied in relation to criminal proceedings under the universality principle, amongst others those brought against Rwandan officials), are therefore well advised to examine prosecutorial activity in the suspects' home state more seriously. As far as Rwanda is concerned, the Rwandan authorities ought to be given at least an opportunity to conduct their own proceedings. This is not so much out of respect for the principles of non-intervention and state sovereignty, but because evidence-gathering, effective history-telling, societal reconciliation, and rule of law entrenchment best take place where the crimes have been committed.[87] Or as Gloria Anyango has noted in respect of French prosecutions of a number of Rwandan officials:

> Rwanda is yearning to close the dark chapter in her history. This can only be possible if the world sincerely holds on to its vow, 'Never Again', by providing us a dignified opportunity to deal with the justice and accountability matters, to do with those responsible for the genocide - in this regard France's pompous role must be tamed.[88]

Accordingly, the home state's first right of way to prosecute cases of mass atrocities does not as a matter of course mean that the home state has the final say as to an eventual prosecution. Complementarity means that another jurisdiction may step in when the primary jurisdiction fails to assume its responsibility. If, for instance, sufficient evidence is adduced as to the lack of good faith prosecutorial efforts by Rwanda, other states (or the ICC for that matter) could step in and commence a prosecution, thereby exercising their responsibility to protect victims on behalf of the

opment that could endanger International Law, order and security; 2) The political nature and abuse of the principle of Universal Jurisdiction by judges from some non-African States against African leaders, particularly Rwanda is a clear violation of their sovereignty and territorial integrity …".

87 See also Ryngaert, *supra* note 27.

88 G. I. Anyango, "Rwanda: France, Country's Genocide and the Principle of Universal Jurisdiction", 14 July 2008, available at http://allafrica.com/stories/200807150261.html. See also Rwandan President Kagame's speech at the UN General Assembly, lambasting the abuse of universal jurisdiction by Western countries, cited above in X, *supra* note 56, at 1009.

international community. They should not wait for home state authorities to have tried or pardoned the accused in suspect circumstances;[89] bad faith can transpire rather early on if the authorities seem to have dismissed the case, or are unjustifiably dragging their heels and seemingly shielding the suspect. But as long as a lack of commitment is not apparent, deference on the part of bystander states, in accordance with the principle of horizontal complementarity, appears to be a wise policy.

If anything, it is precisely a wise complementarity policy that may save universal jurisdiction from the dustbin of history. Ultimately, however, exercising universal jurisdiction over foreign state officials will always be perceived by that foreign state as an affront to its national sovereignty, whether or not a proper complementarity analysis is conducted. Indeed, such an analysis does not automatically lead to deference to the home state, even if one were to apply a standard that is somewhat less strict than the ICC admissibility standard. Some states will already recoil at the mere thought of a foreign state examining whether they are genuinely intent on bringing a perpetrator of international crimes to justice. And most states can hardly be expected to take lightly foreign decisions that establish black on white that they shield perpetrators from responsibility for the most heinous crimes. Since it is deeply ingrained in the national psyche than no other state should be at liberty to pass judgment on a state's national history – situations in which international crimes have been committed typically have historical dimensions (for example,

[89] As noted above in note 21, some States (*e.g.*, Canada) have codified this dimension of the complementarity principle (the exception to the *res judicata* principle), which is codified in Art. 20 of the Rome Statute. In a similar vein, drawing on Rome Statute, Art. 20, the Inter-American Court of Human Rights creatively applied the complementarity principle horizontally in an intra-state context (as opposed to the vertical context in which the ICC operates, and the inter-state context in which bystander states exercising universal jurisdiction operate) in order to clarify the scope of the *ne bis in idem* principle in the *Almonacid-Arellano* case. In relation to the closing of an investigation into a murder, the Court believed "that if there appear new facts or evidence that make it possible to ascertain the identity of those responsible for human rights violations or for crimes against humanity, investigations can be reopened, even if the case ended in an acquittal with the authority of a final judgment, since the dictates of justice, the rights of the victims, and the spirit and the wording of the American Convention supersedes the protection of the *ne bis in idem* principle" (Inter-American Court of Human Rights, *Almonacid-Arellano et al. v. Chile*, Preliminary Objections, Merits, Reparations and Costs, Judgment of 26 September 2006, Series C No. 154, para. 154, citing the Rome Statute in footnote 162).

Rwanda, Yugoslavia) – no complementarity test, however objectively it is designed and applied, can prevent states from taking issue with other states' assertions of universal jurisdiction. Inevitably, the exercise of raw political power play by strong states will ensure that such assertions are scaled back (see Belgium and Spain), even in case impunity is and remains blatant. Also in the 21st century, Kantian idealism will have to give way to realism and pragmatism, and judges and prosecutors pressured by NGOs will succumb to the overwhelming force of diplomatic pressure on the governmental masters whom they serve.[90]

[90] Compare L. Reydams, "The Rise and Fall of Universal Jurisdiction", February 2010, paper on file with the author ("Universal jurisdiction as advocated by true believers belongs to the realm of cosmopolitanism. Trying to reconcile a Kantian idea with the Grotian international legal order is like trying to square the circle.").

7

The Role of Universal Jurisdiction in the International Criminal Court Complementarity System

Christopher K. Hall*

7.1. Introduction

Universal jurisdiction plays a small, but very significant, role in the new and still developing global framework of international criminal law. That global framework consists of conventional and customary international law, enforced by national and international criminal courts.

As discussed below, since the adoption of the 1998 Rome Statute of the International Criminal Court (Rome Statute) more than a decade ago, States Parties to that treaty have expressly recognized that they have the primary responsibility to exercise jurisdiction over three crimes under international law – genocide, crimes against humanity and war crimes. There are two basic forms of the principle of complementarity embodied in the Preamble, Article 1 and Article 17 of the Rome Statute. Under the passive form of complementarity (sometimes called classical complementarity), the International Criminal Court merely complements investigations and prosecutions of these three crimes by national police, prosecutors and investigating judges and it only steps in as a last resort when states fail to fulfil their responsibility under international law to investigate and prosecute such crimes genuinely. Under the positive form of complementarity, which the Prosecutor of the International Criminal Court has adopted, the Prosecutor does not simply wait passively for na-

---

* **Christopher Keith Hall** is Senior Legal Adviser at the International Justice Project, Amnesty International. The author wishes to thank Hugo Relva, Legal Adviser, International Justice Project, and Fátima da Camara e Silva, Lusophone Campaign Adviser, Coalition for the International Criminal Court, for their invaluable assistance in researching parts of this chapter and to acknowledge his debt to Dr. Roy S. Schondorf, Debevoise and Plimpton LLP, and Anthea Roberts, Lecturer in Law, London School of Economics, with whom he developed a more detailed analytical model for interpretation of the Rome Statute summarized in section 7.1.2.1.

tional police and prosecutors to fail to act genuinely, but actively encourages states to enact the necessary legislation to permit them to investigate and prosecute these three core crimes, including through the use of universal jurisdiction, and then to enforce that legislation vigorously.[1]

Universal jurisdiction plays a significant role in the complementarity regime in at least three ways. First, as noted below (section 7.2.), universal jurisdiction can act as a catalyst for investigations and prosecutions, both at the national and at the international level. Second, national courts exercising universal jurisdiction can help to fill a small part of the current enormous global impunity gap, or, rather, abyss, more directly by permitting or requiring states to investigate and prosecute cases not being investigated and prosecuted genuinely by national courts in the states where the crimes occurred or in the state of nationality of the suspect or the victim (section 7.3.). Moreover, national investigations and prosecutions based on universal jurisdiction in the decade since the arrest of former President Augusto Pinochet Ugarte of Chile in London on 16 October 1998 have dramatically changed the way governments, the press and the general public see crimes under international law (section 7.4.).

Before addressing these three consequences of universal jurisdiction and their relationship to complementarity, this chapter addresses two preliminary matters. First, there is a brief discussion of this often misunderstood or misrepresented form of jurisdiction under international law. Second, it is demonstrated that States Parties to the Rome Statute not only envisaged that states exercising universal jurisdiction would be an essential part of the complementarity regime, but they recognized in the Preamble that they had a duty to exercise such jurisdiction.

7.1.1. A Preliminary Brief Note About Universal Jurisdiction

In this chapter, universal jurisdiction means the *ability* of the court of any state to try persons for crimes committed outside its territory which are not linked to the forum state by the nationality of the suspect or of the

1 For further discussion of the scope of positive complementarity, see C. K. Hall, "Developing and implementing an effective positive complementarity strategy", in C. Stahn and G. Sluiter (eds.), *The Emerging Practice of the International Criminal Court*, Martinus Nijhoff, 2009, 219, at 220; C. K. Hall, "Positive complementarity in action", in C. Stahn and M. El Zeidy (eds.), *The International Criminal Court and Complementarity: From theory to practice* (forthcoming 2010).

victims at the time of the crimes or by harm to that state's own special national interests. This definition is essentially the same as the definitions used by the Institut de Droit International, the Special Rapporteur of the International Law Commission's study of the *aut dedere aut judicare* obligation, the International Bar Association Task Force on Extraterritorial Jurisdiction and Amnesty International.[2] Sometimes this rule of international law is called permissive universal jurisdiction. This rule is now part of customary international law, although it is also reflected in treaties, national legislation and jurisprudence concerning crimes under international law (such as genocide, crimes against humanity and war crimes), ordinary crimes of international concern (such as hostage-taking and hijacking of aircraft) and ordinary crimes under national law (such as murder, assault, rape and abduction). When a national court is exercising jurisdiction over conduct amounting to crimes under international law or ordinary crimes of international concern committed abroad, as opposed to conduct simply amounting to ordinary crimes, the court is really acting as an agent of the international community enforcing international law.[3]

Universal jurisdiction should be distinguished from other forms of geographic jurisdiction (*ratio loci*): territorial, active personality (crimes

---

2 Seventeenth Commission, Universal criminal jurisdiction with regard to the crime of genocide, crimes against humanity and war crimes, Institute of International Law, Krakow Session – 2005; Preliminary report on the 'Obligation to extradite or prosecute ('aut dedere aut judicare')', A/CN.4/571, by Zdzislaw Galicki, Special Rapporteur, International Law Commission, Fifty-eighth session, Geneva, 1 May - 9 June and 3 July-11 August 2006, para. 19 (http://daccess-dds-ny.un.org/doc/UNDOC/GEN/N06/379/01/PDF/N0637901.pdf?OpenElement); International Bar Association Legal Practice Division, Report of the Task Force on Extraterritorial Jurisdiction, October 2008, (IBA Report) 151 (http://www.ibanet.org/Publications/publications_books.aspx); Amnesty International, *Universal Jurisdiction: The duty of States to enact and implement legislation*, AI Index: IOR 53/002/2001, September 2001, Introduction, 1 (http://www.amnesty.org /en/library/info/IOR53/002/2001/en).

3 The Supreme Court of Israel in the *Eichmann* case explained:

> Not only do all the crimes attributed to the appellant bear an international character, but their harmful and murderous effects were so embracing and widespread as to shake the international community to its very foundations. The State of Israel therefore was entitled, pursuant to the principle of universal jurisdiction and in the capacity of a guardian of international law and an agent for its enforcement, to try the appellant.

Attorney General of Israel v. Eichmann, *Int'l L. Rep.*, 1962, vol. 36, 277, 304 (Israel Sup. Ct. 1962).

committed by persons who were nationals of the forum state at the time of the crime),[4] passive personality[5] (crimes committed against persons who were nationals of the forum state at the time of the crime) and protective jurisdiction (crimes committed against the forum state's own special interests, such as counterfeiting its currency, treason and sedition.[6]

There is also an important related, but conceptually distinct, rule of international law: the obligation to extradite or prosecute (*aut dedere aut judicare*). Under this rule, a state may not provide a safe haven for a person suspected of certain categories of crimes. Instead, it is *required* either to exercise jurisdiction (which would necessarily include universal jurisdiction in certain cases) over a person suspected of certain categories of crimes or to extradite the person to a state able and willing to do so or to surrender the person to an international criminal court with jurisdiction over the suspect and the crime. As a practical matter, when the *aut dedere*

---

4 IBA Report, 144: "The active personality principle, also known as the active nationality principle, permits a state to prosecute its nationals for crimes committed anywhere in the world, if, at the time of the offense, they were such nationals". For the scope of the active personality principle, see Amnesty International, *Universal jurisdiction: The duty of states to enact and enforce legislation – Ch. One*, AI Index: IOR 53/003/2001, September 2001, Sect. II.B (http://asiapacific.amnesty.org/library/pdf/IOR530032001ENGLISH/$File/IOR5300301.pdf). See also Dapo Akande, "Active Personality Principle", in Antonio Cassese, ed., *The Oxford Companion to International Justice,* Oxford: Oxford University Press, 2008, 229 (criticizing the application of the active personality principle to persons possessing the forum state's nationality at the time of prosecution, but not at the time of the crime, except when it was a crime under international law; seeing prosecution of persons who become residents of the forum state after the crime as analogous to active personality jurisdiction).

5 IBA Report, *supra*, note 2, at 146: "The victim must have been a national of the foreign state, State A, at the time of the crime". For the scope of the passive personality principle, see Amnesty International, *Universal jurisdiction (Ch. One), supra*, note 4, Sect. II.C. See also Dapo Akande, "Passive Personality Principle", in Cassese, *supra,* n. 4, at 452 (justifying the passive personality jurisdiction on the ground that perpetrators "will often select their victims based on this nationality and will know that the state of nationality has an interest in preventing such acts").

6 For the scope of protective jurisdiction, see Amnesty International, "Universal jurisdiction" (Ch. 1)*, supra*, note 4, Sect. II.D. For a somewhat more restrictive definition, see IBA Report, *supra*, n. 2, at 149: "[T]he 'protective principle', … recognizes a state's power to assert jurisdiction over a limited range of crimes committed by foreigners outside its territory, where the crime prejudices the state's vital interests". See also Dapo Akande, "Protective Principle (Jurisdiction)", in Cassese, *supra,* n. 4, at 474 (similar narrow definition).

aut judicare rule applies, the state where a foreigner suspected of responsibility for a crime abroad against another foreigner is found must ensure that its courts can exercise all possible forms of geographic jurisdiction, including universal jurisdiction, in those cases where it will not be in a position to extradite the suspect to another state or to surrender that person to an international criminal court.

There are also some misconceptions about universal jurisdiction which should be dispelled before going any further. First, as is clear from the definition, universal jurisdiction is not based on the nature of the crime. Instead, the term simply describes jurisdiction exercised over crimes committed abroad where there are no links of nationality to the suspect or victim or of harm to the state's own special interests. Indeed, as demonstrated almost a decade ago in a study of universal jurisdiction in approximately 125 states, more than 50 states around the world authorize their courts to exercise universal jurisdiction over ordinary crimes.[7] This point is important since states often have not yet defined all crimes under international law as crimes under national law, but they can exercise such jurisdiction over the conduct amounting to crimes under international law when it constitutes an ordinary crime, such as murder, assault, rape or abduction. For example, courts in Denmark[8] and Germany[9] tried persons

[7] Amnesty International, *Universal jurisdiction: The duty of states to enact and implement universal jurisdiction*, AI Index: IOR 53/002 – 018/2001, September 2001 (http://www.amnesty.org/en /library). That 722-page study is now being updated and expanded to cover both universal and civil jurisdiction in all 192 UN member states. The first six papers in this *No safe haven* series have been published: Bulgaria (http://www.amnesty.org/en/library/info/EUR15/001/2009/en); Germany (http://www.amnesty.org/en/library/info/EUR23/003/2008/en); Solomon Islands (http://www.amnesty.org/en/library/info/ASA43/002/2009/en); Spain (http://www.amnesty.org/es/library/info/EUR41/017/2008/es) (Spanish only); Sweden (http://www.amnesty.org/en/library/info/EUR42/001/2009/en); and Venezuela (http://www.amnesty.org/en/library/info/AMR53/006/2009/en).

[8] In November 1994, the Danish High Court (*Østre Landsret*) in Copenhagen, acting on the basis of universal jurisdiction over grave breaches of the Third and Fourth Geneva Conventions, conferred by Article 8(5) of the Penal Code, convicted Refik Sarić after a jury trial of 14 out of 25 charges of assault and aggravated assault under Articles 245 and 246 of the Penal Code in 1993 of detainees in a detention camp in Bosnia and Herzegovina and sentenced him to eight years' imprisonment. *Public Prosecutor v. N.N.*, High Court (*Østre Landsret*), 3d Div., Judgment, 25 November 1994, *aff'd, Public Prosecutor v. T.*, Supreme Court (*Højesteret*), Judgment, 15 August 1995, *Ugeskrift for Retsvæsen* 1995, 838.

for ordinary crimes based on universal jurisdiction when they had not yet defined grave breaches of the Geneva Conventions as crimes under national law. Similarly, before it amended its Penal Code, Norway sought to exercise universal jurisdiction over a person accused in the International Criminal Tribunal for Rwanda of genocide on charges of ordinary murder.[10] As that 2001 study demonstrates, there is no requirement in international law that a suspect have ever been present in the forum state in order to open a criminal investigation or to seek that person's extradition to the forum state for trial. Indeed, there is no requirement under international law that there be any link between the suspect or the crime to the forum state. In addition, to universal criminal jurisdiction, national courts may exercise universal civil jurisdiction, either in civil cases or through civil claims in criminal proceedings based on universal jurisdiction.[11]

9 For example, on 26 September 1997, Nikolai Jorgić was convicted of 11 counts of genocide and 30 counts of murder in Bosnia and Herzegovina amounting to grave breaches of the Fourth Geneva Convention (at the time, Germany had not defined grave breaches of the Geneva Conventions as crimes under national law) and sentenced to life imprisonment. *Public Prosecutor v. Jorgić,* Judgment, Higher Regional Court at Düsseldorf, 26 September 1997 [*Oberlandesgericht Düsseldorf,* StE 8/96, 26 September 1997] (abstract in English *obtainable from* http://www.icrc.org/ihl-nat/ihl-nat), *aff'd, Public Prosecutor v. Jorgić,* Judgment, Federal Supreme Court, 30 April 1999 [*Bundesgerichtshof, Urteil vom 30. April 1999* - 3 StR 215/98], and a constitutional challenge was rejected. *Jorgić* case, Judgment, Constitutional Court, 12 December 2000. [*Bundesverfassungsgericht* (BverfG), 2 BvR 1290/99 *vom* 12.12.2000, Absatz Nr. (1-49) (obtainable from http://www.bverfg.de)].

10 The ICTR accepted that Norway could exercise universal jurisdiction over a person to face charges of the ordinary crime of murder, but rejected the transfer because a conviction for such a crime would not reflect its gravity and the sentence would be far less than would be appropriate for genocide. *Prosecutor v. Bagaragaza*, Decision on the Prosecution Motion for Referral to the Kingdom of Norway – Rule 11*bis* of the Rules of Procedure and Evidence, Case No. ICTR-2005-86-11*bis*, Trial Chamber, 19 May 2006, para. 16; *aff'd, Prosecutor v. Bagaragaza*, Decision on Rule 11*bis* Appeal, Case No. ICTR-05-86- AR11*bis*, Appeals Chamber, 30 August 2006, para. 16. Norway has since amended its Penal Code to permit its courts to exercise universal jurisdiction over genocide, crimes against humanity and war crimes. Amendment to the General Civil Penal Code, LOV-2005-05-20-28, entered into force on 7 March 2008; See "National implementation of international humanitarian law: Biannual update on national legislation and case law July–December 2008", *Int'l Rev. Red Cross*, 2008, vol. 91, at 185.

11 Amnesty International, Universal jurisdiction: the scope of civil universal jurisdiction, IOR 53/008/2007, 1 July 2007 (http://www.amnesty.org/en/library/info/IOR53/008/2007).

7.1.2. Universal Jurisdiction in the Rome Statute: Inadmissibility and Duty

In a political compromise, state parties at the Rome Diplomatic Conference declined to give the International Criminal Court international jurisdiction analogous to the universal jurisdiction States Parties could exercise on their own.[12] However, they not only envisaged in Article 17(1)(a) and (b) of the Rome Statute that states – both States Parties and non-States-Parties – exercising universal jurisdiction would be part of the complementarity regime, but they also recognized in the Preamble that states had a duty to exercise such jurisdiction. As explained below, when the term "jurisdiction" of states is used in the Rome Statute, it means jurisdiction permitted or required under international law, including universal jurisdiction, except in specific instances in Articles 18 and 19 providing for admissibility challenges, when it is clear from the context that a more restrictive meaning was intended. At least one commentary has suggested that there is some ambiguity about the term "jurisdiction" in the Preamble, certain government officials have suggested that this provision does not include universal jurisdiction and little attention has been devoted to the scope of the term elsewhere in the Rome Statute. Therefore, it may be useful to explain the principles of interpretation applicable to that treaty which make clear that this term is not restricted to any particular form of geographic jurisdiction.[13]

7.1.2.1. Principles of Interpretation

Interpretation of the Rome Statute, apart from the definitions of crimes, is a three-step process: first, looking at the Statute and related rules, in the context of other applicable international treaties and norms, and in the light of the Statute's object and purpose, as required by Article 21(1)(a)

[12] For the history of the proposals by Germany and Republic of Korea which would have provided such jurisdiction, see S. A. Williams and W. A. Schabas, "Article 12 (Preconditions to the exercise of jurisdiction)", in O Triffterer (ed.), *The Rome Statute of the International Criminal Court: Observers' Notes, Article by Article*, 2nd ed., Hart, 2008, 550-553.

[13] O. Triffterer and M. Bergsmo, "Preamble", in Triffterer, *supra*, n. 12, at 1, 11 (concluding that "the only dispute" in paragraph 6 of the Preamble with regard to crimes under international law that states had an obligation to prosecute was whether there was "an obligation to proceed on the basis of universal jurisdiction or on a territorial or national basis. The paragraph was left deliberately ambiguous").

and (b) of the Statute and Article 31 of the Vienna Convention on the Law of Treaties; second, in certain circumstances, the International Criminal Court may have recourse to supplementary sources or means of interpretation, as permitted by Articles 21(1)(c) of the Rome Statute and Article 32 of the Vienna Convention; and, third, the Court must ensure that the interpretation is consistent with human rights law and standards and non-discriminatory, as provided in Article 21(3) of the Statute.[14]

The starting point is the set of rules of interpretation in the Rome Statute. Article 21(1) of the Rome Statute provides that the International Criminal Court must apply, "(a) In the first place, this Statute, Elements of Crimes and its Rules of Procedure and Evidence", secondly, "(b) … where appropriate, applicable treaties and the principles and rules of international law, including the established principles of the international law of armed conflict" and, thirdly,

> (c) Failing that, general principles of law derived by the Court from national laws of legal systems of the world including, as appropriate, the national laws of States that would normally exercise jurisdiction over the crime, provided that those principles are not inconsistent with this Statute and with international law and internationally recognized norms and standards.

Article 21 of the Rome Statute must be read together with the general requirements for treaty interpretation found in Article 31 of the Vienna Convention on the Law of Treaties, which states that "[a] treaty shall be interpreted in good faith in accordance with the ordinary meaning to be given to the terms of the treaty in their context and in the light of its object and purpose.[15] Since the Rome Statute is both a normative treaty and one that establishes an international organization, the interpretation must

[14] Interpretation of the definitions of crimes involves a fourth step, in accordance with Article 21(2) of the Rome Statute, requiring a strict interpretation, resolving any ambiguities remaining after the three previous steps have been taken in favour of the accused. Thus, if the International Criminal Court were to conclude, after following the first three steps that it was settled law that the definition of the crime against humanity of enslavement encompassed all contemporary forms of slavery, there would be no ambiguity in the definition to clarify in a fourth step.

[15] See, for example, Situation in the Democratic Republic of the Congo, No. ICC-01/04-168, Judgment on the Prosecutor's Application for Extraordinary Review of Pre-Trial Chamber I's 31 March 2006 Decision Denying Leave to Appeal, App. Ch., 13 July 2006, paras. 6, 33.

place particular emphasis on the Statute's object and purpose.[16] That object and purpose, as spelled out in the Preamble, includes ensuring that the most serious crimes of concern to the international community do not go unpunished, including through effective prosecution at the national level, and "to put[ting] an end to impunity for the perpetrators of these crimes".

7.1.2.2. Inadmissibility of Cases When States are Exercising Universal Jurisdiction

Articles 17, 18 and 19 of the Rome Statute, when read together, make it clear that when a state is investigating or has investigated or is prosecuting or has prosecuted cases genuinely based on any form of geographic jurisdiction, including universal jurisdiction, the case is inadmissible in the International Criminal Court. Article 17(1) provides that the Court shall determine a case is inadmissible either when (a) "[t]he case is being investigated or prosecuted by a State which has jurisdiction over it, unless the State is unwilling or unable genuinely to carry out the investigation or prosecution" or (b) "[t]he case has been investigated by a State which has jurisdiction over it and the State has decided not to prosecute the person concerned, unless the decision resulted from the unwillingness or inability of the State genuinely to prosecute". These provisions apply to "a State", not just to a State Party, and to states exercising either territorial or extraterritorial jurisdiction. Nothing in the wording or the context suggests otherwise.

In Article 18 of the Rome Statute, however, which governs preliminary rulings regarding admissibility, a different wording is used to make clear that at this preliminary stage the Prosecutor has the duty provide notice that he or she has determined that there would be a reasonable basis to commence an investigation pursuant to Articles 13(c) and 15 of the Statute, not only to States Parties, but also to "those States which, taking into account the information available, would normally exercise jurisdiction over the crimes concerned". This wording clearly implies that other states would have jurisdiction in addition to those who would "normally"

16 See R. Jennings and A. Watts (eds.), *Oppenheim's International Law*, 9th ed., Longman, 1992, vol. 1, 1273, note 13 ("Especially with a treaty of constitutional character, it will often be appropriate to lay particular emphasis on the object and purpose of the treaty when interpreting its provisions.").

do so (that is, in addition to territorial states and states exercising active or passive personality).[17]

Article 19(2)(b) and (c) recognizes that there are two groups of states with concurrent jurisdiction over a case which can make an admissibility challenge:

> Challenges to the admissibility of a case on the grounds referred to in article 17 or challenges to the jurisdiction of the Court may be made by:
>
> …
>
> (b) A State which has jurisdiction over a case, on the ground that it is investigating or prosecuting the case or has investigated or prosecuted; or
>
> (c) A State from which acceptance of jurisdiction is required under article 12.

The phrase "which has jurisdiction over a case" in subparagraph (b) is not restricted to any particular form of geographic jurisdiction. Therefore, this phrase must include all forms, including territorial and extraterritorial (active and passive personality, protective and universal). In contrast, subparagraph (c) does not address the jurisdiction of the state which wishes to challenge the admissibility of the case, but simply whether that state has accepted, pursuant to Article 12(2), the Court's jurisdiction over its territory or its nationals.

7.1.2.3. The Duty of Each State, Recognized in the Preamble, to Exercise Universal Jurisdiction

The conclusion that the Rome Statute complementarity system envisages that the there would be no role for the International Criminal Court when a state was investigating or prosecuting a case on the basis of universal jurisdiction genuinely is reinforced by the Preamble. In the Preamble of

[17] A leading commentator and now Judge of the International Criminal Court gives the example of a state which would "normally" exercise jurisdiction as "one whose national commits one of the crimes within the Court's jurisdiction whilst on the territory of a State Party". Daniel D. Ntanda Nsereko, "Article 18 (Preliminary rulings regarding admissibility", in Triffterer, *supra*, note 12, at 627, 631. The same wording is used in Article 21(1)(c) of the Rome Statute with regard to principles in national laws which may be appropriate to consider when interpreting the Statute, thus recognizing that there were states other than territorial states or states exercising active personality jurisdiction which have jurisdiction over crimes under international law.

the Rome Statute, States Parties recall "that it is the duty of every State to exercise its criminal jurisdiction over those responsible for international crimes".[18] They recognize that every state – not just a state party – has a pre-existing duty, not merely to exercise all jurisdiction permitted or required under national law (for example, under the legality principle), but also to exercise all jurisdiction permitted or required under international law (for example, under an *aut dedere aut judicare* obligation), at least, where feasible. The Preamble to the Rome Statute is an integral part of the treaty,[19] which can be seen as part of an emerging constitutional system of international law involving such core treaties as the 1945 Charter of the United Nations, the 1949 Geneva Conventions and their 1977 Protocols and universal human rights treaties, such as the 1948 Convention for the Prevention and Punishment of the Crime of Genocide, the 1966 Covenants on Civil and Political Rights and Economic, Social and Cultural Rights and the 1984 Convention against Torture and Other Cruel, Inhuman or Degrading Treatment or Punishment. As such, the Preamble and the duties recognized in it take on particular significance with respect to international justice generally, in addition to their significance with respect to States Parties in particular.

The three-step process of interpretation of the Rome Statute outlined above in section 7.1.2.1. confirms that the phrase "its criminal jurisdiction" in the Preamble is any jurisdiction that the state can or must exercise under international, as well as national, law.

The plain meaning of the phrase "its criminal jurisdiction" is that the jurisdiction is not restricted geographically. In contrast to the use of the term "jurisdiction" in certain provisions in Articles 18 and 19, this phrase is not qualified in any way in the Preamble. It would require adding words not in the text to limit the criminal jurisdiction of the state to (1) jurisdiction under national law alone or (2) any one of the five forms of geographic jurisdiction (*ratio loci*) – territorial, active personality, passive personality, protective or universal jurisdiction. Therefore, it follows that the obligation to exercise jurisdiction with regard to crimes under international law is not geographically limited.

The teleological interpretation reflected in Article 21(1)(a) and (b) of the Rome Statute, Article 31 of the Vienna Convention on the Law of

18 Rome Statute, Preamble, para. 6.

19 See Vienna Convention on the Law of Treaties, art. 31(2).

Treaties and the normative and constitutive nature of the Statute favours an interpretation providing the broadest possible protection of victims of crimes under international law over alternative interpretations which would restrict the scope of the obligations recognized by states. An interpretation limiting "its criminal jurisdiction" to jurisdiction as defined under national, as opposed to international, law would lead to the absurd result that each state could define its duty independently of international law and change it at will. A similarly absurd result would arise if each state could determine the scope of its duty by picking and choosing only certain forms of geographic jurisdiction.

Since application of the first step in interpretation does not either leave "the meaning ambiguous or obscure" or lead "to a result which is manifestly absurd or unreasonable", there is no need to take the second step of resort to supplementary sources or means of interpretation pursuant to Article 32 of the Vienna Convention. Finally, the interpretation would not merely be consistent with human rights and non-discriminatory, within the meaning of Article 21(3) of the Rome Statute, but strengthen human rights, the third step in the analysis would be fully satisfied.[20]

7.2. Catalyst for Genuine Investigations and Prosecutions at the National and International Level

The exercise of universal jurisdiction since the arrest of former President Augusto Pinochet Ugarte in London on 16 October 1998 has had a catalytic effect on national investigations and prosecutions in the states where the crimes have been committed and on the enactment or strengthening of universal jurisdiction provisions in national law. It could also have an impact on investigations and prosecutions at the international level.

Soon after the issuance of the arrest warrant against Augusto Pinochet, a number of investigations on gross human rights violations were

[20] As alluded to above, the choice of wording was a political compromise between states which wanted the Preamble to reassert the duty of states to exercise universal jurisdiction over crimes under international law whenever international law permitted or required them to do so and those which wished to restrict the recognition of such a duty to one or more of the other forms of geographic jurisdiction. However, the drafters intended that if there was any dispute about the meaning of the term, ordinary principles of interpretation would apply to resolve the question.

open in states which, until then, had been reluctant to do so for legal or political reasons. Amnesties and statute of limitations, the two main legal bars for prosecutions, but also superior orders, were set aside later by courts in Argentina,[21] Bolivia,[22] Chile,[23] Panama,[24] Peru[25] and Uruguay,[26] among other states.[27]

In certain instances, the exercise of universal jurisdiction by national courts could also have an impact on international courts by encouraging them to act. For example, the likely impact of universal jurisdiction cases when filed involving Afghanistan, Colombia and Georgia on the protracted preliminary examinations of those situations by the ICC Prosecutor could encourage him to request authorization at last to open investigations in those situations. Such cases are almost invariably opened only when territorial states or the suspect's own state has failed to investigate or prosecute genuinely the crimes. Similarly, if national courts were to exercise universal jurisdiction over persons suspected of crimes committed in the Darfur region of Sudan or in Uganda, it might well call into question the genuineness of investigations and prosecutions in those countries and undermine any admissibility challenges in cases in the International Criminal Court.

---

21 Argentina Supreme Court, *Priebke, Erich s/ solicitud de extradición*, case No. 16.063/94, 2 November 1995; *Arancibia Clavel, Enrique Lautaro s/ homicidio calificado y asociación ilícita y otro*, case No. 259, 24 August 2004; and *Simón, Héctor Julio y otros s/ privación ilegítima de la libertad,* case 17.768, 14 June 2005.

22 Bolivia Supreme Court, case of *Masacre de la calle Harrington,* 21 April 1993.

23 Chile Supreme Court, Second Chamber, case Rol N°559-04, 13 December 2006. Santiago Appeals Court, Fifth Chamber, case Rol N° 11.821-2003, 5 January 2004 and case Rol N° 24.471-2005, 10 April 2006.

24 Supreme Court of Panama, *Heliodoro Portugal* case, 2 March 2004.

25 Constitutional Court of Peru, case of Genaro Villegas Namuche, Exp.N° 2488-2002-HC/TC, 18 March 2004; Supreme Court, *Alberto Fujimori* case, 7 April 2009.

26 Uruguay Supreme Court, Sabalsagaray Curutchet, Blanca Stela case, 19 October 2009; and *Gregorio Alvarez case,* 21 October 2009 (First Instance Court, Judge Luis Charles).

27 See also N. Roht-Arriaza, *The Pinochet Effect: Transitional Justice in the Age of Human Rights*, University of Pennsylvania Press, 2005.

7.3. Filling the Impunity Gap

In addition to the catalytic impact of universal jurisdiction in the territorial state and other states, it can make a contribution to ending the impunity gap – the gap between the crimes under international law investigated and prosecuted genuinely by national courts based on territorial jurisdiction or other forms of extraterritorial jurisdiction (active and passive personality and protective jurisdiction) and the limited number of cases which are or even can be investigated and prosecuted by international criminal courts. Before addressing how universal jurisdiction is addressing this gap, it would be useful to indicate its scope.

7.3.1. The Scale of the Impunity Gap

The scale of the impunity gap is immense and there is an air of unreality in much of the discussion by governments and academics about its scope.

Starting from the perspective of the International Criminal Court, it may be helpful to note the crimes it cannot or will not address if states are unable or unwilling genuinely to investigate or prosecute them.[28] First of all, the International Criminal Court has no jurisdiction over: (1) crimes other than genocide, crimes against humanity and war crimes – torture, extrajudicial executions and enforced disappearances not amounting to such crimes are outside its jurisdiction; (2) crimes committed before entry into force of the Rome Statute on 1 July 2002; (3) crimes committed before the entry into force of the Rome Statute for each member state or before the period recognized in an Article 12(3) declaration recognizing the jurisdiction of the International Criminal Court; and (4) crimes com-

[28] There are or were, of course, other international or internationalized courts or chambers with jurisdiction over crimes under international law, including the International Criminal Tribunal for the former Yugoslavia (ICTY), the International Criminal Tribunal for Rwanda (ICTR), the UNMIK international panels for Kosovo, the Special Panels for Series Crimes in Dili, Timor-Leste, the Special Court for Sierra Leone, Section I for War Crimes of the Court of Bosnia and Herzegovina and the Extraordinary Chambers in the Courts of Cambodia, as well as courts or chambers proposed for other places, such as for Timor-Leste and Liberia. However, these courts all have limited geographic and temporal jurisdiction (and some have either gone out of existence or will soon do so) and the percentage of all persons suspected of crimes within their jurisdiction who have been investigated and prosecuted is little different from the percentage investigated and prosecuted by the Prosecutor of the International Criminal Court.

mitted in the territory of states that have not ratified the Rome Statute or made declarations or by their nationals after those dates, unless the Security Council has been considering the situation under Chapter VII of the Charter of the United Nations and has referred the situation to the Prosecutor. Even if none of these exclusions are present, under current budgets, the International Criminal Court lacks sufficient resources to investigate and prosecute more than a handful of those suspected of crimes under international law. Moreover, the Prosecutor made it clear shortly after he took office that his policy would be to focus on those bearing the greatest responsibility.[29] In practice, he seeks to prosecute only a very few people in each situation under investigation.[30]

With respect to national investigations and prosecutions, there has been *virtually complete impunity* for all crimes under international law committed since the outbreak of the Second World War in the 1930s, both in the states where the crimes occurred and in other states able to exercise universal or other forms of extraterritorial jurisdiction. One can quibble about the number of crimes under international law committed around the world since Japan invaded Manchuria in September 1931, Italy invaded Abyssinia in October 1935, the Spanish civil war broke out in July 1936 or a similar event – perhaps as many as 100 million civilians, prisoners of war, detainees and wounded murdered, tortured, raped and "disappeared", whether in armed conflict or peacetime. However, the stark fact remains that, despite the Nuremberg and Tokyo trials and the trials in civilian courts and in military courts and commissions of Axis nationals after the Second World War; trials in states where crimes under international law were committed after the War (such as Argentina, Bolivia, Chile, Central African Republic, Ethiopia, Mali and Peru); investigations and, in some

29 "The Office will function with a two-tiered approach to combat impunity. On the one hand it will initiate prosecutions of the leaders who bear most responsibility for the crimes. On the other hand it will encourage national prosecutions, where possible, for the lower-ranking perpetrators, or work with the international community to ensure that the offenders are brought to justice by some other means." Office of the Prosecutor of the International Criminal Court, Some policy issues before the Office of the Prosecutor, September 2003 (http://www.icc-cpi.int/library/organs/otp/030905_Policy_Paper.pdf), 3.

30 So far, in the first four investigations, the Prosecutor has sought five arrest warrants with regard to Uganda, three for the Democratic Republic of the Congo, four in the Darfur region of Sudan and one for the Central African Republic. He has indicated that he might seek as few as two arrest warrants in his fifth investigation, Kenya.

instances, prosecutions starting in 1994 in more than a dozen of countries based on universal jurisdiction for crimes committed since the Second World War (Argentina, Australia, Austria, Belgium, Canada, Denmark, Finland, France, Germany, Netherlands, Norway, Senegal, Spain, Sweden and the United Kingdom) (see section 7.3.2.2. below); and trials in international criminal courts established since 1993, possibly *less that one tenth of one per cent* of the more than several million individuals suspected of responsibility for such crimes since the 1930s have been investigated or prosecuted in international or national courts.[31]

Long-standing, large-scale impunity exists in all regions of the world in countries where the crimes were committed other than the ones mentioned above (despite some efforts in a few of them), including Algeria, Bangladesh, Bosnia and Herzegovina, Brazil, Burundi, Central African Republic, Chad, China, Cote d'Ivoire, Croatia, Democratic Republic of the Congo, Egypt, Eritrea, Ethiopia, Germany, India, Indonesia, Iran, Libya, Mauritania, Nepal, Niger, Pakistan, Paraguay, Philippines, Russian Federation, Senegal, Serbia, Somalia, South Africa, Sudan, Timor Leste, Uruguay, Uzbekistan, Zimbabwe, or in countries where police or prosecuting authorities failed over the past decade to exercise universal jurisdiction in particular cases for wholly inappropriate reasons, including Australia, Austria, Belgium, Brazil, Bulgaria, Canada, France, Japan, Netherlands, South Africa, Senegal, Spain, the United Kingdom and the United States. Although the investigations and prosecutions which have taken place so far are to be welcomed, and the nature of the discussion of such crimes has certainly changed in the past decade (see section 7.4.), surely it would be a mistake to suggest that they have made more than tiny dent in impunity on a global scale. This is not a counsel of despair, but simply a sober assessment of the scope of the problem of impunity which remains to be addressed.

7.3.2. Universal Jurisdiction as Part of the Complementarity System in Practice

As the discussion above indicates, the impunity gap which exists with regard to genocide, crimes against humanity and war crimes, not to men-

---

31 This figure excludes persons subjected to traditional bodies that were alternatives to competent, independent and impartial courts, such as the more than 100,000 persons processed in *Gacaca* proceedings in Rwanda.

tion other crimes under international law, such as torture, extrajudicial executions and enforced disappearances, is enormous. The role that universal jurisdiction can play in attempting to fill that gap will inevitably be very limited for the foreseeable future for several reasons. First, many states still do not have effective universal jurisdiction legislation. Second, the number of suspected perpetrators who are within reach of foreign national courts because they are present in the forum state or because they are present in countries from which extradition is feasible remains limited.

However, as outlined below, in the past decade since the Rome Diplomatic Conference, states have been enacting new legislation with universal jurisdiction over crimes under international law or strengthening existing legislation states, thereby significantly expanding the scope of universal jurisdiction and potentially limiting the number of safe havens for perpetrators of genocide, crimes against humanity, war crimes and other crimes under international law. In addition, there has been an increase in the number of investigations and prosecutions based on universal jurisdiction around the world. Nevertheless, the total number of suspected perpetrators investigated or prosecuted based on universal jurisdiction remains small, for a variety of reasons. Section 7.4. below notes ways some of these obstacles to universal jurisdiction in practice are starting to be overcome through increased cooperation among states.

7.3.2.1. Legislation Providing for Universal Jurisdiction

It is not well known that most states have legislation that would permit them to exercise universal jurisdiction legislation over some conduct amounting to crimes under international law.[32] It is not always widely

[32] There still is no comprehensive, up-to-date and satisfactory study which has been published compiling and analyzing legislation providing for universal jurisdiction over ordinary crimes, crimes under international law of international concern and crimes under international law. Useful, but dated, information can be found in Harvard Research in International Law, *Jurisdiction with Respect to Crime*, *Am. J. Int'l L.*, supp. 1935, vol. 29, 435, 495 (now three quarters of a century old); Amnesty International, *Universal Jurisdiction*, see *supra* note 7 (covering approximately 125 states, but in the process of being updated and expanded to include universal civil jurisdiction); Jean-Marie Henckaerts and Louise Doswald-Beck (eds.), *Customary International Humanitarian Law*, International Committee of the Red Cross, 2005, vols. I and II (focusing on war crimes); Human Rights Watch, *Universal Jurisdiction in Europe: The State of the Art*, 2006 (focusing on Belgium, Denmark, France, Germany, the Netherlands, Norway, Spain and the United Kingdom); Redress, *Universal*

recognized that all states are parties to four treaties requiring them to extradite or try persons found in their territory suspected of grave breaches of those treaties and that most are parties to other treaties requiring them to do so with regard to other crimes under international law or crimes under national law of international concern.[33]

However, what is particularly significant is that in the decade since the former President of Chile returned from 15 months under house arrest in London to leap out of his wheelchair on the airport tarmac almost every single state that has enacted or drafted legislation defining genocide, crimes against humanity or war crimes as crimes under its national law has retained, strengthened or enacted new provisions permitting their courts to exercise universal jurisdiction over these crimes and torture. Indeed, at least 38 States Parties which have enacted legislation implementing their complementarity obligations under the Rome Statute by defining these crimes as crimes under their national law have provided for universal jurisdiction, including: Argentina,[34] Australia,[35] Azerbaijan,[36] Belgium,[37] Bosnia and Herzegovina,[38] Burkina Faso,[39] Burundi,[40] Can-

Jurisdiction in Europe: Criminal Prosecutions in Europe since 1990 for War Crimes, Crimes Against Humanity, Torture and Genocide, 1999; Redress, *Legal Remedies for Victims of "international Crimes": Fostering an EU Approach to Extraterritorial Jurisdiction*, 2004, Annex D: Country Studies (focusing on countries in the EU).

33 Amnesty International, International Law Commission: The obligation to extradite or prosecute (aut dedere aut judicare), AI Index: IOR40/001/2009, 3 February 2009 (http://www.amnesty.org/en/library/info/IOR40/001/2009/en).

34 ***Argentina:*** *Ley de implementacion del Estatuto de Roma de la Corte Penal Internacional* (2007).

35 ***Australia:*** International Criminal Court (Consequential Amendments) Act 2002 (http://www.austlii.edu.au/au/legis/cth/consol_act/iccaa2002543/), Criminal Code Act 1995, div. 15.4 and 268.

36 ***Azerbaijan:*** 2005 Criminal Code of the Azerbaijan Republic, arts. 12(3) and 13(3) (http://www.legislationline.org/download/action/download/id/1658/file/4b3ff87c005675cfd74058077132.htm/preview).

37 **Belgium:** Loi relative à la répression des violations graves de droit international humanitaire 23 March 1999, Moniteur Belge 9286–87 (http://www.unhcr.org/refworld/docid/3ae6b5934.html).

38 ***Bosnia and Herzegovina:*** 2003 Criminal Code of Bosnia and Herzegovina, art. 12 (www.nottingham.ac.uk/law/hrlc/international-criminal-justice-unit/implementation-database.php).

39 ***Burkina Faso:*** *PROJET DE LOI N° 052-2009 /AN portant détermination des compétences et de la procédure de mise en œuvre du statut de Rome relatif à la cour pénale*

ada,[41] Cape Verde,[42] Colombia,[43] Costa Rica,[44] Croatia,[45] Cyprus,[46] Estonia,[47] Finland,[48] Georgia,[49] Germany,[50] Ireland,[51] Kenya,[52] Korea (Repub-

---

internationale par les juridictions burkinabè, art. 16 (draft approved on 3 December, awaiting promulgation by the President as of 20 January 2010).

40 ***Burundi:*** *Loi portant répression du crime de génocide, des crimes contre l'humanité et des crimes de guerre, Loi 1-0004 du 8 mai 2003,* art. 24 (http://www.icrc.org/ihl-nat.nsf/6fa4d35e5e3025394125673e00508143/7cbad250d785314dc125707300366c6b/$FILE/Genocide%20Repression%20Burundi%20-%20FR.pdf).

41 ***Canada:*** Crimes Against Humanity and War Crimes Act 2000, c. 24, An Act respecting genocide, crimes against humanity and war crimes and to implement the Rome Statute of the International Criminal Court, and to make consequential amendments to other Acts, arts. 6 and 8 (http://laws.justice.gc.ca/PDF/Statute /C/C-45.9.pdf).

42 ***Cape Verde:*** Penal Code, art.4 (http://www.mj.gov.cv/index2.php?option=com_docman&task=doc_view&gid=38&Itemid=66).

43 ***Colombia:*** Ley 599 de 2000 (Penal Code), art. 16(6) (http://www.secretariasenado.gov.co/senado/basedoc/ley/2000/ley_0599_2000.html).

44 ***Costa Rica:*** Law 8.272/2003, amending Penal Code (Ley de represión penal como castigo por los crímenes de guerra y de lesa humanidad), art. 7 (http://www.icrc.org/ihl-nat.nsf/6fa4d35e5e3025394125673e00508143/10d7a03ac8767383c125712600525077!OpenDocument).

45 ***Croatia:*** Law on the Application of the Statute of the International Criminal Court and on the Prosecution of Criminal Acts against the International Law on War and Humanitarian Law, Number: 01-081-03-3537/2, Zagreb, 24 October 2003, art. 10(2) (http://www.nottingham.ac.uk/shared/shared_hrlcicju/Croatia/November_2003_Law_on_the_Application_of_the_Statute_of_the_International_Criminal_Court__English_.pdf).

46 ***Cyprus:*** Law amending the Rome Statute for the Establishment of the International Criminal Court (Ratification) Law of 2002, No. 23 (III)/2006, sect. 6 (http://www.icrc.org/ihl-nat.nsf/6fa4d35e5e3025394125673e00508143/057edec3010b50f1c12572d7002bd9cc!OpenDocument).

47 ***Estonia:*** Penal Code, 6 June 2001, as amended (19 May 2004, entered into force 1 July 2004, RT I 2004. 46, 329), art. 7(1) (http://www.legislationline.org/upload/legislations/07/6a/4d16963509db70c09d23e52cb8df.htm).

48 ***Finland:*** Penal Code of Finland, 39/1889, as amended, sects. 7 and 8 (www.finlex.fi/en/laki/kaannokset/1889/en18890039.pdf).

49 ***Georgia:*** Law on amendments to the Criminal Code, 2003 (adding some crimes against humanity to the Criminal Code) (http://www.icrc.org/ihl-nat.nsf/6fa4d35e5e3025394125673e00508143/7fd1f5a507a2531dc12570fb004f3723!OpenDocument).

50 ***Germany:*** Code of International Crimes, 26 June 2002, sect. 1 (http://www.icrc.org/ihl-nat.nsf/6fa4d35e5e3025394125673e00508143/09889d9f415e031341256c770033e2d9!OpenDocument).

lic of),[53] Latvia,[54] Lithuania,[55] Macedonia (the Former Yugoslav Republic of),[56] Malta,[57] Mexico,[58] Montenegro,[59] Netherlands,[60] New Zealand,[61] Norway,[62] Panama,[63] Portugal,[64] Samoa,[65] Serbia,[66] South Africa,[67]

---

51 ***Ireland:*** International Criminal Court Act, 2006, sect. 12 (http://www.irishstatutebook.ie/2006/en/act/pub/0030/index.html) (modest extension of universal jurisdiction to add war crimes other than grave breaches).

52 ***Kenya:*** International Crimes Act, 2008, Sects. 6 and 8 (http://www.kenyalaw.org/Downloads/Acts/The_International_Crimes_Act_2008.pdf).

53 ***Korea (Republic of):*** 2008 Act on the Punishment on Crimes under the Jurisdiction of the International Criminal Court, art. 3 (http://korea.na.go.kr/abo/zin_read.jsp?cha=34&boarditemid=1000008397).

54 ***Latvia:*** Criminal Law, 2004, Sect. 4 (added 17 October 2002) (http://www.icrc.org/ihl-nat.nsf/6fa4d35e5e3025394125673e00508143/330294bcc1401107c12570fb004fb500!OpenDocument).

55 ***Lithuania:*** Criminal Code, 2000, art. 7 (http://www.icrc.org/ihl-nat.nsf/6fa4d35e5e3025394125673e00508143/2bf3baa62a697704c1257331003fa787!OpenDocument).

56 ***Macedonia:*** Criminal Code of the Republic of Macedonia, art. 119 (www.legislationline.org/legislation.php?tid=1&lid=6272).

57 ***Malta:*** Criminal Code, arts. 5(1)(h) and 328 M (www.legislationline.org/upload/legislations/4a/84/8881d69dda92a96bc8e400db18dd.pdf).

58 ***Mexico:*** *Código Penal*, art. 2(I), as amended in 2007.

59 ***Montenegro:*** Criminal Code ("Official Gazette of the Republic of Montenegro " no. 70/2003, and Correction, no. 13/2004), art. 137 (http://www.legislationline.org/legislation.php?tid=1&lid=6221).

60 ***Netherlands:*** International Crimes Act, sect. 2 (http://www.icrc.org/ihl-nat.nsf/6fa4d35e5e3025394125673e00508143/fb9070f8fc60c047c1256da30032f0b0!OpenDocment).

61 ***New Zealand:*** International Crimes and International Criminal Court Act 2000, sect. 2 (http://www.icrc.org/ihl-nat.nsf/6fa4d35e5e3025394125673e00508143/dfa25b039e214405c12569de004ddab1!OpenDocument).

62 ***Norway:*** New chapter 16-1 in Penal Code adopted in 2008 (http://www.legal-tools.org/doc/a9b7c1/).

63 ***Panama:*** Código Penal de Panamá, Ley No.14, of 18 May 2007, arts. 19 and 20(4) (www.gacetaoficial.gob.pa/pdfTemp/25796/4580.pdf).

64 ***Portugal:*** Lei n.º 31/2004, *adapta a legislação penal portuguesa ao Estatuto do Tribunal Penal Internacional, tipificando as condutas que constituem crimes de violação do direito internacional humanitário – 17.ª alteração ao código penal. Artigo 5.º* (Law No. 31/2004: http://www.legal-tools.org/en/doc/55f68e/).

65 ***Samoa:*** International Criminal Court Act 2007, sect. 13 (http://www.parliament.gov.ws/legislations.cfm).

Spain,[68] Timor-Leste,[69] Trinidad and Tobago[70] and Uruguay.[71] Only a few of the states enacting legislation implementing the Rome Statute have failed to provide for some expansion of existing universal jurisdiction[72] or restricted the scope of universal jurisdiction.[73] One state (Belgium) weak-

66 ***Serbia:*** Serbia and Montenegro 2005 Criminal Code, Official Gazette of RS, Nos. 85/2005, 88/2005, 107/2005, art. 9 (www.osce.org/documents/fry/2006/02/18196_en.pdf).

67 ***South Africa:*** No. 27 of 2002, Implementation of the Rome Statute of the International Criminal Court Act, 2002, 18 July 2002, sect. 4(3)(b) and (c) (http://www.info.gov.za/acts/2002/a27-02/index.html).

68 ***Spain:*** Organic Law of the Judiciary, art. 23(4), as amended in 2009 (while the amendment added crimes against humanity to the list of crimes covered by universal jurisdiction, some limitations were also added thus restricting the scope of universal jurisdiction) (http://www.poderjudicial.es/eversuite/GetDoc?DBName=dPortal&UniqueKeyValue=151089&Download=false&ShowPath=false).

69 ***Timor-Leste:*** Penal Code (2009), art. 8(b) (although there is no link to the legislation, there is a summary in English at: http://www.icrc.org/ihl-nat.nsf/6fa4d35e5e3025394125673e00508143/d0e82f00db41732dc125766500511a7e!OpenDocument).

70 ***Trinidad and Tobago:*** The International Criminal Court Act, 2006, sect. 8 (http://www.icrc.org/ihl-nat.nsf/6fa4d35e5e3025394125673e00508143/2bbdd7c1affd8d7bc1257563005c8833/$FILE/International%20Criminal%20Court%20Act.pdf).

71 ***Uruguay:*** Law 18.026, *de cooperación con la Corte Penal Internacional en materia de lucha contra el genocidio, los crímenes de guerra y de lesa humanidad*. Artículo 4(2).

72 ***Mali:*** Penal Code (2001) (failing to provide for universal jurisdiction over genocide, crimes against humanity or war crimes) (http://www.icrc.org/ihl-nat.nsf/6fa4d35e5e3025394125673e00508143/844b7282e856caf3c1257083002ecfa2/$FILE/Penal%20Code%20-%20Mali%20-%20FR.pdf).

73 Although the United Kingdom provided for universal jurisdiction it was limited to covering "United Kingdom residents" and it was not as expansive as prior universal jurisdiction over grave breaches of the Geneva Conventions and Protocol I. International Criminal Court Act 2001, sects. 51, 52, 58, 59, 67 and 68 (http://www.opsi.gov.uk/acts/acts2001/ukpga_20010017_en_6#pt5-pb2-l1g51); International Criminal Court (Scotland) Act 2001, sect. 6 (http://www.opsi.gov.uk/legislation/ scotland/acts2001/asp_20010013_en_2). However, the United Kingdom government has recently proposed to expand the scope of the definition of United Kingdom resident in some respects and to make the legislation retrospective. Jack Straw, Secretary of State, Written Ministerial Statement on the Coroners and Justice Bill, cited in Joint Committee on Human Rights, House of Lords/House of Commons, Closing the Impunity Gap: UK law on genocide (and related crimes) and redress for torture victims, 24th Report of Session 2008-2009, HL Paper 153/HC 553, 11 August 2009.

ened its universal jurisdiction legislation after political threats by the USA.[74]

The situation is similar with regard to draft legislation. At least nine States Parties which have prepared draft legislation implementing the Rome Statute in the past decade have provided for universal jurisdiction over such crimes, including Benin,[75] Brazil,[76] Central African Republic,[77] Congo (Republic of),[78] Democratic Republic of the Congo,[79] Fiji,[80] France,[81] Switzerland [82] and Uganda.[83] Only a few States Parties have failed to include universal jurisdiction provisions in their draft implementing legislation, such as Comoros.[84] In some instances, the legislation extended the scope of existing universal jurisdiction and in others the provision was entirely new.

---

74 *Loi modifiant la loi du 16 juin 1993 relative à la répression des violations graves du droit international humanitaire et l'article 144ter du Code judiciaire, Apr. 23, 2003 Moniteur Belge 24846, 24853*, art.7, translated in 42 I.L.M. 740, 755 (2003).

75 ***Bénin:*** *Avant projet de loi portant mise en œuvre du statut de la Cour Penale Internationale au Bénin*, art. 13.

76 **Brazil:** *Projeto de Lei, Dispõe sobre o crime de genocídio, define os crimes contra a humanidade, os crimes de guerra e os crimes contra a administração da justiça do Tribunal Penal Internacional* (2008). art. 128. O art. 7o do Decreto-Lei nº 2.848, de 7 de dezembro de 1940 (Código Penal, Parte General).

77 ***Central African Republic:*** *Projet de Code de procédure pénale*, art. 335.

78 ***Congo (Republic of):*** *Avant projet de loi portant mise en œuvre du Statut de Rome de la Cour Pènale Internationale en Republique du Congo, 16 avril 2005,* art. 14.

79 ***Democratic Republic of the Congo:*** *Proposition de Loi de mise en œuvre du Statut de Rome de la Cour pénale internationale – Mars 2008.*

80 ***Fiji:*** ICC Working Group, Discussion Paper on Implementation of the Rome Statute of the International Criminal Court in the Law of Fiji (recommending universal jurisdiction).

81 ***France:*** *Disposition modifiant le Code de Procédure Pénale*, art. 7*bis (nouveau)* (http://ameli.senat.fr/publication_pl/2006-2007/308.html).

82 ***Switzerland:*** Projet du Conseil federal du 23 avril 2008, Loi fédérale portant modification de lois fédérales en vue de la mise en oeuvre du Statut de Rome de la Cour pénale internationale, art. 264m (providing for the obligation to extradite or prosecute with regard to genocide [Titre 12 bis], crimes against humanity [Titre 12 bis] and war crimes [Titre 12 ter]). (http://www.parlament.ch/F/Suche/Pages/geschaefte.aspx?gesch_id=20080034).

83 ***Uganda:*** International Criminal Court Bill, 2004, art. 18.

84 See Amnesty International, *Comoros: Analysis of the draft implementing legislation of the Rome Statute of the International Criminal Court*, AI Index: AFR 21/001/2007, December 2007 (http://www.amnesty.org/en/library/info/AFR21/001/2007/en).

In addition, even non-States Parties to the Rome Statute have been amending existing legislation or enacting new legislation to provide for universal jurisdiction over crimes under international law. For example, the United States has recently enacted legislation providing for universal jurisdiction over genocide and the recruitment and use of child soldiers.[85] Draft U.S. legislation is also under consideration which would provide such jurisdiction over some conduct amounting to crimes against humanity, although it has significant flaws.[86] Nicaragua revised its Penal Code in 2008 to provide for universal jurisdiction over crimes under international law.[87] In addition, the Philippines recently enacted legislation providing for universal jurisdiction over genocide, crimes against humanity and war crimes.[88] Turkey amended its Criminal Code to add genocide and crimes against humanity, making both subject to an existing universal jurisdiction provision.[89]

Unfortunately, despite the incorporation or expansion of the scope of legislation providing national courts with universal jurisdiction, there are numerous and serious flaws in that legislation which will weaken its ability to serve as an effective tool for justice within the complementarity system.[90] These flaws include omission of crimes under international law, such as war crimes not included in the Rome Statute and torture, extrajudicial executions and enforced disappearances not amounting to genocide, crimes against humanity or war crimes; incorporating weak definitions of crimes falling short of the strictest requirements of international law; using the two-level standard of superior responsibility in Article 28 of the

---

85 ***USA:*** Genocide Accountability Act of 2007, Public Law No: 110-151, 21 December 2007, Child Soldiers Accountability Act, 2008, Public Law 110-340, 3 October 2008.

86 ***USA:*** Crimes Against Humanity Act of 2009 (bill).

87 ***Nicaragua:*** Law No. 641 of 2008 (Penal Code), art. 16(d) (http://www.icrc.org/ihl-nat.nsf/6fa4d35e5e3025394125673e00508143/aa586dc20177737bc125746700429ee1/$FILE/Codigo%20Penal%20Nicaragua%20mayo%202008.pdf);

88 ***The Philippines:*** Republic Act 9851, 11 December 2009, art. 17(b) (http://www.lawphil.net/statutes/repacts/ra2009/ra_9851_2009.html).

89 ***Turkey:*** Penal Code, art.13 provides for universal jurisdiction and arts. 76 to 78, as amended in 2004, add provisions on genocide and crimes against humanity (http://www.legislationline.org/ documents/action/popup/id/6872/preview) (unofficial English translation).

90 See Amnesty International, *International Criminal Court: The Failure of States to Enact Effective Implementing Legislation*, AI Index: IOR 40/019/2004, 31 August 2004 (http://www.amnesty.org/en/library/info/IOR40/019/2004).

Rome Statute instead of the stricter single standard applicable both to commanders and superiors in Article 86(2) and in Article 6 of the Draft Code of Crimes against the Peace and Security of Mankind; and including prohibited defences, such as superior orders, or defences which are inappropriate to crimes under international law, such as duress and necessity.

In addition, legislation and draft legislation often contains other serious obstacles to the exercise of universal jurisdiction over crimes under international law, including requiring presence in the forum of the suspect at some point before an investigation can be opened or an extradition request issued; statutes of limitation; dual criminality (requiring that the crime under international law have been defined as such at the time in the state where the crime occurred); recognizing claims of immunities by current or former officials; giving a political official power to stop an investigation or a prosecution; bars to retrospective application of national law when the conduct was criminal under international law at the time it took place; giving preclusive effective to a foreign court judgment of conviction or acquittal even when the previous trial was unfair or a sham which shielded a perpetrator from criminal responsibility; political control over the opening of investigations or commencing of prosecutions; restrictions on the rights of victims and their families to initiate proceedings, to participate in them, to be notified of their rights in a timely fashion at every stage of the proceedings, to have legal assistance, to have support and protection and to have an effective right to obtain reparations in the criminal proceedings or otherwise; and recognizing amnesties and similar measures of impunity for crimes under international law granted by a foreign state.

Another set of problems with national legislation regarding crimes under international law involves serious flaws with regard to extradition and mutual legal assistance.[91] Such obstacles, which limit the ability of states to obtain or to provide cooperation in the investigation and prosecution of such crimes, undermine the horizontal system of state-to-state cooperation in the investigation and prosecution of the worst crimes in the world. Of course, such problems are not limited to universal jurisdiction cases, but they limit the effectiveness of this form of jurisdiction to play an important role in the complementarity system. The impact of such

91 These flaws are often replicated in the system of bilateral and multilateral extradition treaties.

flaws was dramatically demonstrated by the decision of a political official, originally taken in secret, to prevent the extradition of former President Augusto Pinochet Ugarte authorized by a United Kingdom magistrate to Spain to face trial for torture, on the dubious ground that the former President was unfit to stand trial, a determination which should have been made by an independent judge in the requesting state.

Problems with extradition legislation can exist with regard to the ability to request extradition to a country and to grant a request to extradite a person to another country. In some instances, extradition requests can only be made by a political official, not by an independent prosecutor or court. Some countries may permit a request for extradition to be made only if the crime occurred in the forum state or was committed by or against a forum state national. There are also many inappropriate bars to the granting of extradition requests with respect to crimes under international law that can often be found in national law, including: political control over the granting of extradition requests, instead of leaving these decisions to independent prosecutors and judges; bars on the extradition of nationals of the requested state; double criminality; requirements that the requesting state be exercising only territorial jurisdiction; precluding the extradition of a person who was acquitted even when the trial was a sham which led to impunity; prohibitions of extradition for conduct that was not a crime under national law of the requested or requesting state at the time it was committed even when the conduct was a crime under international law at that time; statutes of limitations and amnesties under national law for crimes under international law. It is also a matter of serious concern that many states have omitted human rights safeguards in extradition legislation, including failures to prohibit extradition of persons who risk the imposition of the death penalty, torture and other ill-treatment or unfair trial. In some instances, overbroad provisions prohibiting the extradition of persons for humanitarian reasons, such as occurred in the *Pinochet* case, can be misused for political reasons without effective judicial scrutiny.

Flaws in extradition legislation are sometimes mirrored in legislation providing for mutual legal assistance.[92] These include provisions barring mutual legal assistance in all the same circumstances outlined

---

92 As with extradition treaties, mutual legal assistance treaties frequently have many of the same flaws as does national legislation.

above with regard to extradition legislation. There are often cumbersome and ineffective procedures in place to provide or grant assistance. Legislation frequently omits human rights safeguards.

7.3.2.2. Investigations and Prosecutions Based on Universal Jurisdiction

There still is no exhaustive and up-to-date study which has been published discussing all investigations and prosecutions around the world since the Second World War based on universal jurisdiction of conduct amounting to crimes under international law.[93] Nevertheless, Chapter 2 of this volume provides a comprehensive and very useful overview. It is therefore enough for the moment to reiterate a number of countries where such investigations have taken place and then to note briefly the main problems that such investigations and prosecutions have encountered which have limited their effectiveness in the complementarity system.

The Allies tried a number of persons based on universal jurisdiction for war crimes and crimes against humanity committed by Axis nationals during the Second World War, mostly in military courts and commissions and such courts, even when trying persons under different jurisdictional bases for such crimes spoke of the universal nature of the crimes. However, Allied political directives soon prevented further investigation and prosecutions and trials for such crimes.[94] In addition to territorial jurisdiction cases in Germany and some other countries, there were subsequent sporadic investigations and prosecutions based on universal jurisdiction of crimes committed during the Second World War, most notably the trials of Adolf Eichmann and John Demjanjuk in Israel, a trial in Canada and, attempted prosecutions in Australia.

There was dramatic change in 1994, when Austria and Denmark began the first prosecutions based on universal jurisdiction of persons for

[93] Some information can be found in the post-War studies cited above in footnote 32. In addition, there is a useful recent survey of such investigations and prosecutions, but limited to a few countries in Western Europe and including some cases not based on universal jurisdiction: W. Kaleck, "From Pinochet to Rumsfeld: Universal jurisdiction in Europe 1998-2008", *Mich. J. Int'l L.*, 2009, vol. 30, at 927.

[94] For a brief review of this unhappy history, see Amnesty International, *Universal jurisdiction: The duty of states to enact and implement legislation – Ch. Two – The history of the practice of universal jurisdiction,* AI Index: IOR 53/004/2001, September 2001, sect. III. (http://www.amnesty.org/en/library/info/IOR53/004/2001/en).

crimes under international law committed since the Second World War. Since then there have been investigations and prosecutions in four continents: Africa, Europe, North America and South America based on universal jurisdiction regarding post-War crimes. In Africa, in addition to the long-delayed trial of the former President of Chad, Hissène Habré, expected to take place in 2010, there have been several complaints filed in South Africa, although the police and the National Director of Public Prosecutions have failed to act (this failure is currently the subject of a judicial review). In Europe, there have been investigations and prosecutions in Austria, Belgium, Denmark, Finland, France, Germany, the Netherlands, Norway, Spain, Sweden, Switzerland and the United Kingdom. In North America, Canada completed its first universal jurisdiction trial and began its second. In South America, an Argentine judge recently issued the first arrest warrant in the Americas based on universal jurisdiction alleging that a former President of China was responsible for crimes against humanity.

Despite these successes, the number of persons tried so far remains small and there are numerous problems that are emerging in universal jurisdiction investigations and prosecutions in addition to the flaws in the legislation noted above which seriously limit the effectiveness of universal jurisdiction in the complementarity system. The following is not a comprehensive study discussing each investigation and prosecution, nor is it an exhaustive list of all the problems, but it does provide a number of concrete examples to illustrate the scope of the challenges ahead.

Only a few states have special immigration, police or prosecution units to investigate and prosecute crimes under international law (Canada, Belgium, Denmark, Netherlands, Norway, Sweden and, very recently, the USA).[95] At least one state, the United Kingdom, has disbanded a special war crimes unit to deal with war crimes committed during the Second World War. Resources for such units or for investigations or prosecutions by the regular police and prosecutors are usually limited in comparison to the resources allocated to the investigation and prosecution of terrorist crimes, white-collar crimes, money laundering, trafficking in persons, arms trafficking, drug trafficking and cyber-crimes. There is often a lack of political will to investigate or prosecute. In some instances, this lack of

[95] For a study of some of these units, see Human Rights Watch, Universal Jurisdiction in Europe, *supra*, note 32.

political will has led to inventive reasons for declining to investigate or prosecute which have no basis in national law. Sometimes there is even political interference in decisions whether to investigate or prosecute. For example, Spanish prosecutors routinely challenge all investigations conducted by investigating judges which are based on universal jurisdiction. It has also been claimed that UK officials alerted Israeli authorities that an arrest warrant had been issued for an Israeli general en route to London alleging that he was responsible for grave breaches of the Fourth Geneva Convention, who then ordered him not to get off the plane when it landed at Heathrow Airport.

Investigations procedures and practices are often slow and cumbersome. In 2005, the German Federal Prosecutor did not act with dispatch when informed that the Minister of Interior of Uzbekistan, Zokirjon Almatov, who was alleged to be responsible for crimes against humanity and torture, was present in Germany for medical treatment. When he fled after being alerted to the complaint, the Prosecutor declined to investigate on the ground that the official would be unlikely to return.[96] Perhaps the most notorious delay involves the French investigation of Wenceslas Munyeshyaka, a Rwandan minister accused of genocide. That case has been pending for more than a decade since July 1995.[97] Indeed, the delays led to a finding in 2004 by the European Court of Human Rights that France had denied the right to a hearing within a reasonable time.[98] London Metropolitan police spent ten months investigating allegations against a Rwandan national in the United Kingdom without reaching a decision whether to refer the case to a prosecutor before the International Criminal Tribunal for Rwanda sought his transfer.

Officials have often set extremely high evidentiary standards not warranted by legislation to open investigations and have even placed the burden on the victims or those acting on their behalf to investigate the cases before opening investigations. In the Pinochet case, victims and organizations acting on their behalf filed five separate submissions, with

96 Kaleck, *supra*, note 93, at 952.

97 Trial Watch. See http://www.trial-ch.org/en/trial-watch/profile/db/legal-procedures/wenceslas_munyesh yaka_112.html.

98 *Mutimura v. France*, Judgment, 8 September 2004, No. 46621/99,Eur. Ct. Hum. Rts. (http://cmiskp.echr.coe.int/tkp197/view.asp?item=2&portal=hbkm&action=html&highlight=Mutimura%20|%20France&sessionid=43435200&skin=hudoc-en).

extensive victim and witness testimony and other evidence to the United Kingdom Attorney General or Solicitor General seeking permission to conduct a prosecution in the United Kingdom for torture in the event that extradition to Spain was denied. In 2008, Austrian prosecutors declined to open an investigation of allegations that visiting Chechnya Vice President Ramzan Kadyrov was responsible for torture, after initially even refusing to receive the complaint, on the ground that there was insufficient evidence to proceed, without interviewing any witnesses or conducting any further inquiry.[99]

In some instances, police or prosecutors have recognized extremely broad claims of immunities. For example, the Paris prosecutor refused to act on a complaint that a former US defence minister was responsible for torture on the specious ground that the International Court of Justice had held that former heads of state, heads of government and foreign ministers had immunity from prosecution. The German Federal Prosecutor has declined to open an investigation of a former Chinese President on the same claim of immunity.[100] Sometimes, prosecutors or courts decline to act when an official has been invited to visit, even when that official could not assert a claim that he or she was present on a special mission. For example, the German Federal Prosecutor declined in 2008 to open an investigation when the head of the Uzbekistan secret service, Rustan Inojatov visited Germany.[101]

One particularly disturbing obstacle to the exercise of universal jurisdiction with regard to crimes under international law is the judicially created requirement in a handful of states of the misnamed concept of horizontal "complementarity" or the equally misapplied concept of "subsidiarity" before national courts are permitted to exercise universal jurisdiction. For example, in 2005, the German Federal Prosecutor declined to open an investigation of former US defence minister Donald Rumsfeld, alleged to be responsible for torture of political prisoners at a US-run prison in Iraq, on the ground that US authorities were investigating the

---

[99] Kaleck, *supra,* note 93, at 953-954.

[100] Human Rights Watch, *Universal Jurisdiction in Europe: State of the Art*, 2006, 64 (http://www.hrw.org/sites/default/files/reports/ij0606web.pdf).

[101] W. Kaleck, *supra*, note 93, at 952-953 (citing a Section 20 of the German Judicial Service Act prohibiting the prosecution of state officials invited to visit by the government).

situation as a whole, although there was no evidence that this investigation extended to the former minister or that the investigation was thorough, prompt, independent and impartial.[102] In addition, the Spanish Constitutional Court has held that a requirement to open a criminal investigation based on universal jurisdiction is that the territorial state failed properly to investigate the case.[103]

Independently of the unsuitability of these doctrines for determining whether to permit a national court to exercise universal jurisdiction as an agent of the international community, there is an even more serious objection. There should be no priority for territorial states, states of suspect's or victim's nationality.

In the rare event that more than one state claimed priority to investigate and prosecute a suspect for the same crimes under international law based on the same conduct, the state with custody seeking to exercise universal jurisdiction would normally have a better claim than the territorial state to act on behalf of the international community, since the presence of the suspect outside the territorial state creates a presumption that the authorities of the territorial state are not acting with due diligence to investigate and prosecute. Failure to transmit an extradition request would be compelling evidence that the territorial state was not serious. Such priority for the forum state with custody of the suspect is subject to the proviso, however, that when it seeks to exercise its sovereignty, its judicial system must not conduct sham proceedings and must be able and willing to investigate and prosecute in accordance with international law and standards for fair trial and must not impose the death penalty or other cruel, inhuman or degrading treatment or punishment.[104]

It is often difficult or impossible to seek judicial review of prosecutorial decisions not to prosecute cases on the ground of abuse of discretion. For example, attempts in Germany to seek judicial review of such decisions have failed.

---

[102] See English translation of the decision by the Prosecutor in Germany to dismiss the complaint against Rumsfeld *et al.* filed by the Center for Constitutional Rights, 10 February 2005 (http://www.brusselstribunal.org/pdf/Rumsfeld Germany.pdf).

[103] Ríos Montt case, Const. Ct. (Spain), 26 September 2005.

[104] See Amnesty International, *Universal Jurisdiction: The duty of States*, *supra* note 2, Introduction, 48.

When investigations or prosecutions have begun, often the authorities fail to take effective measures to prevent the suspect or the accused from fleeing. For example, Ely Ould Dah, a Mauritanian soldier charged with torture, fled before his trial in France.

7.4. Changing the Approach to Crimes Under International Law

Investigations and prosecutions based on universal jurisdiction in the decade since Pinochet's arrest have led to a sea change in the way governments, the press and the general public understand crimes under international law. More and more as a result of such cases these crimes are no longer seen as political and diplomatic problems to be resolved by politicians and diplomats, but as serious crimes to be investigated and prosecuted by police and prosecutors.

Perhaps the most important practical aspect of this new perspective has been the beginnings of moves in the international community toward a shared responsibility model to investigate and prosecute crimes under international law which by their very nature are an attack on the international community.[105] As with other serious crimes which threaten the international legal fabric, such as terrorist crimes and trafficking in persons, national police and prosecutors have come to realize that a response based on individual states reacting to the chance presence of suspects on their territory was wholly inadequate to permit effective law enforcement.

Developing an effective shared responsibility model to address crimes under international law should be part of a larger, long-term global action plan to end impunity.[106] One component of that plan should address how to improve the effectiveness of universal jurisdiction as one tool to end impunity for such crimes. There are at least three steps which should be taken as a matter of priority. First, police in each state – without waiting for law reform to correct the flaws noted above – should begin to

[105] The shared responsibility model is discussed in more depth in a statement delivered by the author on behalf of Amnesty International at the Fourth International Expert Meeting on War Crimes, Genocide and Crimes against Humanity of Interpol in Oslo, Norway, 18 to 20 May 2009, published in Amnesty International, *Universal jurisdiction: Improving the effectiveness of interstate cooperation*, AI Index: IOR 53/004/ 2009, October 2009.

[106] Amnesty International, *Ending impunity: Developing and implementing a global action plan using universal jurisdiction*, AI Index Number: IOR 53/005/2009, 1 October 2009.

develop a global crime map of genocide and other crimes under international law. The goal of this mapping exercise would be to lay the foundation for a global cooperative law enforcement strategy permitting police and prosecutors to go on the offensive. Four different maps could be prepared (crime, evidence, resources and law) which could permit police and prosecutors from different countries working together to develop a series of joint, targeted investigations, aimed at building international dossiers, using evidence gathered in more than one country usable in any national court in sealed arrest warrants to ensure that suspects were caught. Second, states need to create immigration screening units designed to identify potential suspects with a view to prosecuting them, not simply excluding them. Third, states should begin drafting an effective international extradition and mutual legal assistance treaty to address the flaws in current bilateral and multilateral treaties. With such steps, states might begin to ensure that universal jurisdiction finally becomes an effective tool of complementarity.[107]

[107] For extensive concrete recommendations for improving such treaties and state-to-state cooperation, see Statement to Interpol in Ottawa, June 2007: *Universal jurisdiction: Improving the effectiveness of state cooperation*, AI Index: IOR 53/006/2007 (http://www.amnesty.org/en/library/info/IOR53/006/2007/en); Statement to European Union, 20 November 2006: *European Union: Using universal jurisdiction as a key mechanism to ensure accountability*, AI Index: IOR 61/013/2007 (http://www.amnesty.org/en/library/asset/IOR61/013/2007/en/dom-IOR610132007en. pdf); Statement to Interpol in Lyon, 16 June 2005: *Universal jurisdiction: The challenges for police and prosecuting authorities in using it*, AI Index: IOR 53/007/2007, June 2005 (http://asiapacific.amnesty.org/library/Index/ENGIOR530072007?open&of=ENG-385).

8

Concurring Criminal Jurisdictions under International Law

Florian Jessberger[*], **Wolfgang Kaleck**[**] **and Andreas Schueller**[***]

8.1. Introduction

8.1.1. The Problems Discussed in this Chapter

The exercise of universal jurisdiction in Europe over the past fifteen years reveals a number of legal and practical problems[1], among the most crucial ones is the problem of concurring criminal jurisdictions, often discussed under the heading of complementarity or subsidiarity. In general, the merits of these principles may not be doubted; however, the danger of their extensive application becomes apparent when a forum state declines to exercise universal jurisdiction over one suspect based on the fact that the home state has shown or has pretended to be willing and able to prosecute lower-ranked human rights violators. Recent cases in Germany and Spain illustrate the results of this false interpretation. In Germany the Federal Prosecutor invoked an analogy to Article 14 of the Rome Statute and declined to open a case against Donald Rumsfeld and other high ranking officials allegedly responsible for the U.S. torture program, based on the fact that the United States had put a number of low-ranking soldiers and agents on trial who were involved in the Abu Ghraib torture incidents.[2]

---

[*] **Florian Jessberger** is Professor of Criminal Law at the University of Hamburg.

[**] **Wolfgang Kaleck** is General Secretary for the European Center for Constitutional and Human Rights.

[***] **Andreas Schueller** is program manager of the ECCHR Universal Justice program.

[1] See, *e.g.*, Wolfgang Kaleck, "From Pinochet to Rumsfeld: Universal Jurisdiction in Europe 1998-2008", Michigan Journal of International Law, 2009, vol. 30, no. 3, 927-980, at 958.

[2] See Florian Jessberger, "Universality, Complementarity, and the Duty to Prosecute Crimes under International Law in Germany", in: W. Kaleck, M. Ratner, T. Singelnstein and P. Weiss (eds.), *International Prosecution of Human Rights Crimes*, Springer, 2007, 213 (221).

Recently, Spanish courts decided in a case on sexual violence and torture against women in Mexico and in another case on the targeted killing of a suspected Hamas-leader with many civilian casualties in Gaza in 2002, that they were not competent to open investigations into the alleged commission of international crimes because investigations were already going on in the territorial state of the crime.[3] The courts argued that by investigating these crimes in the territorial state under its criminal jurisdiction third states were prevented from exercising their criminal jurisdiction under the principle of universality. According to the courts, the hierarchy of jurisdictions gives priority to territoriality over universality. Consequently, as long as a state investigates and is thus exercising its jurisdiction based on the territoriality principle, third states are prevented to exercise their jurisdiction based on the principle of universality. The courts further argued that the investigation does not have to meet certain standards as long as they are conducted by a state based, as a matter of principle, on the rule of law.[4]

On a second line of argument, the courts found that the principle of *ne bis in idem* also does not allow investigations in other states once a state has opened an investigation.[5] Otherwise a perpetrator would have to face being prosecuted twice for the same conduct.

The decisions by the Spanish courts raise fundamental questions of international law and relations. They address one of the key issues of contemporary international criminal justice: how to organize legally an international criminal justice system which involves several actors with, to a large extent, overlapping jurisdictional competences. The Spanish courts seem to push for a quick and uncomplicated closure of highly complex and politically sensitive cases. Focusing on the principles of territoriality and universality, this chapter provides for an in-depth analysis of concurring criminal jurisdictions under international law. Additionally, it analyzes which universal standards of investigation have to be met for there

3 *Atenco* case, Auto of the Sala de lo Penal of the Audiencia Nacional of 14 January 2009 on the Rollo de Apelación nº 172/2008 of Section 2ª, from Diligencias Previas nº 27/08 del Juzgado Central de Instrucción nº 3, pp. 10 and 12; *Gaza* case, Auto 1/2009 of the Sala de lo Penal of the Audiencia Nacional of 9 July 2009 on the Recurso de Apelación nº 31/09 Rollo de Sala de la Sección 2ª Nº 118/09, Diligencias Previas nº 157/08 of the Juzgado Central de Instrucción nº4, pp. 16, 19 and 23.

4 *Atenco* case, *supra* note 3, pp. 10-13; *Gaza* case, *supra* note 3, p. 16.

5 *Atenco* case, *supra* note 3, p. 5; *Gaza* case, *supra* note 3, p. 23.

to be an adequate investigation. Finally, the chapter takes a position on the relevance of the *ne bis in idem* principle in inter-state relations.

8.1.2. Relevant Principles of Jurisdiction

To begin with, it is to be noted that international law recognizes different forms of criminal jurisdiction. In addition to the territoriality principle that connects jurisdiction to the place where a crime was committed, there are several other grounds of extraterritorial jurisdiction. The main forms of extraterritorial jurisdiction are the protective principle, the active personality (or nationality) principle, the passive personality principle and the universality principle.[6]

Whether the passive personality principle can be invoked, that is to say the exercise of jurisdiction based on the nationality of the victim, is a matter of controversy under international law. The principle is established as basis of jurisdiction in numerous domestic laws and in a number of international treaties.[7] Yet some states do not provide for this form of jurisdiction in their domestic legislation. Still, according to the majority view, which is shared by the authors of this article, there is sufficient support for the position that, under international law, the fact that the victim holds a state's nationality forms a firm basis for the exercise of extraterritorial jurisdiction by this state.[8] It should be noted, however, that some cases which from the viewpoint of international law can be regarded as exercise of the passive personality principle may, from the perspective of specific national legislation, be dealt with as exercise of another jurisdictional principle, for example the universality principle.

Unlike the other principles of extraterritorial jurisdiction, the universality principle requires no specific nexus between the crime and the forum state. Jurisdiction is solely based on the nature of the crime, with-

6 See Cedric Ryngaert, *Jurisdiction in International Law*, Oxford: Oxford University Press, 2008, pp. 85-133.

7 *E.g.*, Spanish law established the passive personality principle in Article 23.4 and 5 of the Spanish Law of the Judiciary by the Organic Law 1/2009 on 3 November 2009; according to Article 5(1)(c) of the UN Convention Against Torture and Other Cruel, Inhuman or Degrading Treatment or Punishment, states are authorized but not obliged to establish criminal jurisdiction on the basis of the passive personality principle.

8 See, *e.g.*, Tom Vander Beken *et al.*, *Finding the Best Place for Prosecution*, Antwerp: Maklu, 2002, p. 13: Bundesverfassungsgericht, Juristenzeitung 2001, pp. 975, 979; see also Restatement (Third) of Foreign Relations Law, 1987, § 402.

out regard to where the crime was committed, the nationality of the (alleged) perpetrator, the nationality of the victim, or any other connection to the state exercising such jurisdiction.[9] This principle recognizes the authority of each state to prosecute especially "heinous" crimes, which due to their specific characteristics, affect the international community as a whole. By allowing all states to prosecute those international crimes such as genocide, war crimes, crimes against humanity, and, arguably, torture, the principle of universal jurisdiction protects and upholds fundamental values of the international community. The universality principle for those crimes is rooted in customary international law.[10]

Drawing on this background information, this chapter will address the following questions: Does international law provide for the priority of territorial jurisdiction over extraterritorial, in particular universal jurisdiction? And does the *ne bis in idem* /double jeopardy principle, under international law, bar prosecution in a foreign jurisdiction?

8.2. Does International Law Provide for the Priority of Territorial Jurisdiction over Extraterritorial, in Particular Universal Jurisdiction?

8.2.1. The *Lotus* Case

International law envisions a system of concurrent jurisdictions. There is no rule prohibiting states from establishing domestic criminal jurisdiction on the basis of active or passive nationality, or universality over an extraterritorial situation that is already covered by the jurisdiction of other

[9] See, *e.g.*, Princeton University Program in Law and Public Affairs, 2001 Princeton Principles on Universal Jurisdiction. The steering committee was composed of Professors Macedo, Bass, Falk, Flinterman, Butler, Oxman and Lockwood. See also the definition of the *Institut de Droit international* of 26 August 2005, seventeenth commission, universal criminal jurisdiction with regard to the crime of genocide, crimes against humanity and war crimes, resolution, para. 1; members of the 17th Commission of the *Institute de Droit international* in Krakow 2005 were Professors Ando, Barberis, Bennouna, Caflisch, Cassese, Conforti, Crawford, Dinstein, Lee, Momtaz, Orrego Vicuna, Rozakis, Salmon, Tomuschat, Torres Bernárdez, Vinuesa and Yusuf.

[10] See, *e.g.*, Princeton Principles, *supra* note 9; see also Claus Kress, "Universal Jurisdiction over International Crimes and the *Institut de Droit international*", *Journal of International Criminal Justice*, 2006, vol. 4, 561-585 (566).

states, especially the territorial state.[11] As the Permanent Court of International Justice stated in its famous *Lotus* case:

> It does not, however, follow that international law prohibits a State from exercising jurisdiction in its own territory, in respect of any case which relates to acts which have taken place abroad, and in which it cannot rely on some permissive rule of international law (allowing exercising jurisdiction outside its own territory). (…) The territoriality of criminal law (…) is not an absolute principle of international law and by no means coincides with territorial sovereignty.[12]

Moreover, the Fourth Geneva Convention in its Article 146 even obliges all states to establish their domestic criminal jurisdiction over one and the same act of a grave breach of the Fourth Geneva Convention as defined in its Article 147.

8.2.2. No Hierarchy Between Jurisdictional Principles

International customary law recognizes no hierarchy among the different types of criminal jurisdictions outlined above. In particular, there is no conclusive evidence regarding the existence of a rule of customary international law which may provide for the priority of the territoriality principle. It follows that, under international law, a state which practices universal jurisdiction – the so-called third state – is under no legal obligation to accord priority in respect of investigation and prosecution to the state where the criminal acts were committed.[13]

Equally, the Fourth Geneva Convention in its Article 146 does not establish any hierarchy between jurisdictional principles. This provision simply obliges state parties to provide effective personal sanctions for persons committing any of the grave breaches of the Convention in order to avoid safe havens for perpetrators; it does not establish an order of priority whatsoever among different grounds of jurisdiction.

To conclude, a state exercising extraterritorial jurisdiction by investigating and prosecuting a crime on the basis of one of the acknowledged

---

11 Ryngaert, *supra* note 6, at 129.

12 Permanent Court of International Justice, Series A, No. 10, 7 September 1927, *The case of S.S. "Lotus"*, pp. 18-20.

13 See *AU-EU Technical Ad hoc Expert Group on the Principle of Universal Jurisdiction*, Report (2009), 8672/1/09 Rev 1 Annex, para. 14, at 11.

jurisdictional principles is not violating international law even if the crime is already investigated or prosecuted by the authorities of the state where it was committed.

8.2.3. Territorial Jurisdiction has a Special Role

Notwithstanding the absence of a positive rule of customary international law providing for the priority of territorial jurisdiction, jurisdiction exercised on the basis of the territoriality principle is accorded a special place. This follows not from a firm rule of international law but as a matter of policy. In fact, there is reason to believe that states prosecuting international crimes on the basis of the universality principle should, as a matter of policy, accord priority to territoriality as a basis of jurisdiction.[14] State practice accompanied by what appears to be an emerging sense of *opinio juris* indicates that states consider a prosecutorial effort by the territorial state to foreclose the possibility of a prosecution by states with universal jurisdiction.[15]

There are several reasons for the preference of territorial jurisdiction which are based, *inter alia*, on procedural as well as political considerations and the recognition of a legitimate primary interest of those states that are most directly connected with the crime. While third states act in the interest of and, thus, as agents of the international community as a whole, the territorial state primarily pursues its own interests by prosecuting alleged offenders.

As regards the said priority of territorial jurisdiction, however, three points must be stressed: First, it is to be emphasized that territorial jurisdiction enjoys such priority relative to universal jurisdiction as a *matter of policy* only and not as a matter of international law. Second, the priority of territorial jurisdiction is *not* under discussion *relative to other principles of extraterritorial jurisdiction, such as the passive personality principle*, but only relative to the universality principle where no link whatsoever exists between the crime and the third state. And third, priority is subject to *certain conditions relating to the exercise of jurisdiction* by the

14 See *ibid.*, recommendation R9, at 42.

15 Spanish Constitutional Court Judgment 237/2005, of 26 September, II. conclusions of law, para. 4.; Anthony J. Colangelo, Double Jeopardy and Multiple Sovereigns: A Jurisdictional Theory, 86 Wash. U. L. Rev. (2009), 769 (835).

territorial state and its authorities. These conditions are spelled out in the following paragraphs.

8.2.4. Unsettled, Conditional Subsidiarity

Hence, the position territorial jurisdiction enjoys under international law does not lead to an absolute and unlimited subsidiarity of universal jurisdiction; rather, it is a form of conditional subsidiarity whose nature and content are not yet settled conclusively.

However, there is a widespread view that where the authorities and courts of a third state have serious reason to believe that the territorial state is manifestly unwilling or unable to prosecute the alleged offender, they may initiate criminal proceedings and take the necessary steps to prosecute the crime.[16] In other words: the argument that prosecutorial efforts by the territorial state foreclose the possibility of exercise of universal jurisdiction by third states is dependent on the condition that the territorial jurisdiction is exercised genuinely or in "good faith".[17] Further, it is difficult to assert that the principle of subsidiarity already applies at the initial investigation stage compared to the situation after the conclusion of an investigation.[18] Investigations can be initiated simultaneously in different countries and the results and evidentiary material collected be shared in legal assistance to the forum state of prosecution.[19]

The necessity of imposing the condition of subsidiarity regarding prosecution is rooted in the rationale of universal jurisdiction. Universal jurisdiction is supposed to be exercised only in cases that affect the international community as a whole and in order to prevent gaps of enforcement leading to impunity. In cases where jurisdiction is effectively exercised on other grounds, there is no need for universal jurisdiction. However, the lack of "good faith" investigations and prosecutions in other *fora*

---

16 Compare AU-EU Technical Ad hoc Expert Group, *op. cit.*, recommendation R10, at 43; see also Section 3(c) of the Resolution of the *Institute de Droit international* (2005), *supra* note 9.

17 See Anthony J. Colangelo, *supra* note 15, 769 (835); for a similar approach, see Joint Separate Opinion of Judges Higgins, Kooijmans and Buergenthal, International Court of Justice, Arrest Warrant of 11 April 2000 (*Democratic Republic of the Congo v. Belgium*), Judgment, I.C.J. Reports 2002, pp. 64 – 91.

18 See Claus Kreß, *supra* note 10, at 580.

19 See AU-EU Technical Ad hoc Expert Group, *op. cit.*, recommendation R10, at 43.

means that the exercise of universal jurisdiction by third states is the only chance to avoid impunity.

8.2.5. Assessing Territorial State Prosecutions

To determine the "good faith" of prosecutorial efforts in the territorial state, criteria established in international human rights law regarding universal standards for investigations should be taken into account. As such, not only international human rights courts can determine whether an investigation meets universal standards, but national courts too can apply these universal principles to determine whether the territorial state is investigating genuinely or whether a third state has to step in.

Various decisions of international human rights courts support the universal principles of independence, effectiveness, promptness and impartiality in carrying out investigations.[20] The Inter-American Court of Human Rights found in its *Moiwana Community* case that the State has the obligation to initiate *ex officio* and immediately, a genuine, impartial and effective investigation, which is not undertaken as a mere formality predestined to be ineffective.[21] The European Court of Human Rights found in its *Finucane* decision of 1 July 2003 that certain rights imply some form of effective official investigation to secure these rights of individuals.[22] The Court reaffirmed its jurisprudence that "(f)or an investiga-

---

20 Chamber Judgment of the European Court of Human Rights in the case of *Finucane v. United Kingdom*, 1 July 2003; European Court of Human Rights cases *Hugh Jordan; Kelly and others; Shanaghan v. United Kingdom; Mckerr v. United Kingdom*, 4 May 2001; *Fatma Kaçar v. Turkey*, 15 July 2005; *Isayeva (I) and (II) v. Russia*, 24 February 2005; the Inter-American Court of Human Rights has established similar jurisprudence in the case of *Ituango Massacres v. Colombia*, Judgment of 1 July 2006, Series C No. 148, at 296 and the case of *Mapiripan Massacre v. Colombia*, Judgment of 15 September 2005, Series C No. 134, para. 223. See also Harmen van der Wilt and Sandra Lyngdorf, "Procedural Obligations Under the European Convention on Human Rights: Useful Guidelines for the Assessment of 'Unwillingness' and 'Inability' in the Context of the Complementarity Principle", International Criminal Law Review 9, 2009, at 50 *et seq.*

21 Inter-American Court of Human Rights case of the *Moiwana Community*, Judgment of 15 June 2005, Series C No. 124, paras. 145-146; *Ituango Massacres v. Colombia, supra* note 20; *Pueblo Bello Massacre*, Judgment of 31 January 2006, Series C No. 140, para. 143; and *Mapiripan Massacre*, *supra* note 20.

22 *Finucane v. United Kingdom*, *supra* note 20, p. 67; see, *mutatis mutandis*, *McCann and Others v. the United Kingdom*, Judgment of 27 September 1995, Series A No.

tion to be effective, it may generally be regarded as necessary for the persons responsible for and carrying out the investigation to be independent from those implicated in the events. This means not only a lack of hierarchical or institutional connection but also a practical independence".[23] As for the content of an investigation, the Court further noted that "(t)he authorities must have taken the reasonable steps available to them to secure the evidence concerning the incident, including, *inter alia*, eyewitness testimony, forensic evidence and, where appropriate, an autopsy which provides a complete and accurate record of injury and an objective analysis of clinical findings …".[24] Turning to the requirement of promptness and reasonable expedition, the Court found this "implicit in this context. … a prompt response by the authorities in investigating a use of lethal force may generally be regarded as essential in maintaining public confidence in their adherence to the rule of law and in preventing any appearance of collusion in or tolerance of unlawful acts".[25]

8.2.6. The Standard of ICC Article 17 as a Guiding Principle

On the inter-state level, in determining the "good faith" of prosecutorial efforts in the territorial state the complementarity principle of Article 17 of the Rome Statute of the International Criminal Court (ICC) is a useful reference as it establishes the preconditions that a state has to meet in

324, p. 49, para. 161; *Kaya v. Turkey*, Judgment of 19 February 1998, *Reports of Judgments and Decisions* 1998-I, p. 324, para. 86. The Inter-American Court of Human Rights has established similar jurisprudence in the case of *Ituango Massacres v. Colombia*, *supra* note 20, p. 297.

23 *Finucane v. United Kingdom*, *supra* note 20, p. 68; see, *e.g.*, *Güleç v. Turkey*, Judgment of 27 July 1998, *Reports* 1998-IV, p. 1733, paras. 81-82; *Oğur v. Turkey* [GC], No. 21594/93, paras. 91-92, ECHR 1999-III; see, *e.g.*, *Ergi v. Turkey*, Judgment of 28 July 1998, *Reports* 1998-IV, pp. 1778-1779, paras. 83-84, and the recent Northern Irish cases cited above, *supra* note 20, for example, *McKerr*, para. 128, *Hugh Jordan*, para. 120, and *Kelly and Others*, para. 114.

24 *Finucane v. United Kingdom*, *supra* note 20, p. 69; see, *e.g.*, *Salman v. Turkey* [GC], No. 21986/93, para. 106, ECHR 2000-VII; *Tanrıkulu v. Turkey* [GC], No. 23763/94, para. 109, ECHR 1999-IV; *Gül v. Turkey*, 22676/93, para. 89, 14 December 2000.

25 *Finucane v. United Kingdom*, *supra* note 20, at 70; see *Yaşa v. Turkey*, Judgment of 2 September 1998, *Reports* 1998-VI, pp. 2439-2440, paras. 102-104; *Çakıcı v. Turkey* [GC], No. 23657/94, paras. 80, 87 and 106, ECHR 1999-IV; *Tanrıkulu*, *supra* note 24, para. 109; *Mahmut Kaya v. Turkey*, No. 22535/93, paras. 106-107, ECHR 2000-III; see, *e.g.*, *Hugh Jordan*, *supra* note 21, paras. 108, 136-140.

order to avoid that the ICC exercises its jurisdiction. Notwithstanding that the horizontal relation between two states is different from the vertical relation between a state and the ICC,[26] the standard established by the complementarity principle can be taken into consideration and may be, as a guiding principle, transferred to inter-state relations. However, it has to be emphasized that the complementarity principle itself, applicable to the state-ICC relation, does not exist on a state-to-state level where concurrent jurisdiction with conditional subsidiarity prevails.

Article 17(1)(a) states that a case is inadmissible before the ICC where "the case is being investigated or prosecuted by a state which has jurisdiction over it, unless the state is unwilling or unable genuinely to carry out the investigation or prosecution". According to this wording, and particularly in regard to the element of unwillingness, the lack of efforts to genuinely prosecute the crime needs to be determined positively; it is not sufficient that investigations or prosecutions might merely be conducted more effectively by the ICC or – in the case of third party prosecutions – by other states.[27] References for this interpretation are contained in Article 17(2) of the Rome Statute:

> In order to determine unwillingness in a particular case, the Court shall consider, having regard to the principles of due process recognized by international law, whether one or more of the following exist, as applicable:
>
> a) The proceedings were or are being undertaken or the national decision was made for the purpose of shielding the person concerned from criminal responsibility for crimes within the jurisdiction of the Court referred to in article 5;
>
> b) There has been an unjustified delay in the proceedings which in the circumstances is inconsistent with an intent to bring the person concerned to justice;
>
> c) The proceedings were not or are not being conducted independently or impartially, and they were or are being conducted in a manner which, in the circumstances, is inconsistent with an intent to bring the person concerned to justice.

---

26 Florian Jessberger, "Universality, Complementarity, and the Duty to Prosecute Crimes under International Law in Germany", *supra* note 2.

27 Compare R. Cryer *et al.*, An Introduction to International Criminal Law and Procedure, Cambridge, 2007, pp. 127-128.

Thus, also on an inter-state level a positive determination whether another state is genuinely conducting an investigation or prosecution should be made. A state cannot refuse investigations simply pointing to another state claiming it is carrying out an investigation. A state has to consider whether universal standards of investigations are met by the other state. Only with an affirmative answer to that question can a state invoke the priority of the territorial state's jurisdiction as a matter of policy.

To conclude, international law does not provide for a priority of territorial jurisdiction over extraterritorial, in particular universal, jurisdiction. It is only as a matter of policy that the territoriality principle is favoured over the universality principle once there is an investigation concluded – this conditional subsidiarity requires that international human rights standards for investigations are respected.

8.3. Does, Under International Law, the *Ne Bis in Idem* Principle Bar Prosecution in a Foreign Jurisdiction?

The *ne bis in idem* principle signifies that no one shall be tried twice for the same offence. The principle is incorporated in most national criminal justice systems and contained in many international conventions, both in the area of cooperation in criminal matters as well as human rights.[28] While most states seem to recognize the principle, there are so many qualifications and restrictions to it that it is difficult to describe its status in international law or in comparative criminal law.[29]

The first qualification that needs to be made is in regard to the extent of the *ne bis in idem* principle. With the possible exception of the formulations in the statutes of international criminal courts, it becomes apparent that this principle is usually a safeguard only against double prosecution by entities of the same organized political power, usually the nation state. The formulation of Article 14(7) of the International Covenant on Civil and Political Rights (ICCPR) is a clear example of this:

> No one shall be liable to be tried or punished again for an offence for which he has already been finally convicted or ac-

[28] See, *e.g.*, Article 14(7) ICCPR.

[29] Christine Van den Wyngaert and Tom Ongena, "*Ne bis in idem* Principles, Including the Issue of Amnesty", in A. Cassese, P. Gaeta and J. Jones (eds.), *The Rome Statute of the International Criminal Court*, Oxford University Press, 2002, 705-729 (706).

> quitted in accordance with the law and penal procedure *of each country*. [emphasis added]

This restriction of the *ne bis in idem* principle to decisions by the same sovereign was partly abandoned in the process of European integration, as Article 54 of the Schengen Convention[30] (1990) extends this principle to the decisions of other contracting parties. This development is, however, not indicative of a wider interpretation of the *ne bis in idem* principle in international law beyond the context of the European Union.

The second qualification is that the *ne bis in idem* principle merely protects from double prosecution, once there has been a final decision. Most legal systems will only invoke the *res judicata* principle for judgments on the merits of the case, while interlocutory judgments usually do not have that effect. That means that the *res judicata* effect is generally bound to the condition that the offender has been acquitted or sentenced and that the sentence is currently being served or has already been served. Obviously, the mere opening of investigations or prosecutions carried out by another state does not fulfil these criteria as it does not put an end to a proceeding. Thus it cannot exert a *res judicata* effect since the existence of a judgment, whether convicting or acquitting, is the key rule to consider a double jeopardy situation. As we have already pointed out, a mere investigation or ongoing prosecution will simply create a conflict of jurisdiction or a *lis pendens* which, unlike the *ne bis in idem* principle, does not prohibit another jurisdiction from investigating or prosecuting the same case.

8.4. Summary and Conclusions

International law envisions a model of concurrent jurisdictions. It enables states to exercise their jurisdiction on different grounds without prescribing a hierarchy between those types of jurisdiction.

However, one can recognize a policy rule to accord priority to the principle of territoriality in combination with a model of conditional subsidiarity of universal jurisdiction once an investigation is concluded. The conditionality of the exercise of universal jurisdiction, while not settled

30 Convention of 19 June 1990, applying the Schengen Agreement of 14 June 1985 between the Governments of the States of the Benelux Economic Union, the Federal Republic of Germany, and the French Republic, on the Gradual Abolition of Checks at their Common Borders, *ILM*, 1991, p. 84.

conclusively, may be based on the "good faith" exercise of the primary jurisdiction and may be construed following the case law of human rights courts and the basic concept established by Article 17 of the Rome Statute for the vertical state-ICC relation. It follows that, if the territorial state is unwilling or unable to genuinely conduct investigations or if the investigations or prosecutions are no more than sham proceedings to shield the perpetrator, then the third state must initiate its own criminal proceedings. For an investigation to be considered genuine, it must meet the universal standards of effectiveness, promptness, independence and impartiality.

Finally, it is to be noted that the mentioned policy rule does not extend to the exercise of extraterritorial jurisdiction other than universal jurisdiction. Thus, under international law, states exercising jurisdiction on the basis of the nationality principle or the passive personality principle need not – not even as a matter of policy – accord priority to the jurisdiction of the territorial state.

Domestic courts should not blindly trust that investigations in the territorial state of the crime will be proper. States have a duty to exercise their criminal jurisdiction over those responsible for international crimes, as already mentioned in the preamble of the Rome Statute. They cannot refrain from this duty by merely pointing to investigations in another state, regardless whether these investigations are serious or not. Further, they cannot invoke a hierarchy of criminal jurisdiction under international law or the *ne bis in idem* principle to prevent a third state from opening its own investigations. The investigation of international crimes needs international efforts and cooperation. It is a task for the international community as a whole composed of many single states.

9

The Principle of Complementarity: a Means Towards a More Pragmatic Enforcement of the Goal Pursued by Universal Jurisdiction?

Fausto Pocar* **and Magali Maystre****

9.1. Introduction

In 2003, in a provocative remark, Antonio Cassese claimed that "[i]t would seem that the principle of universal jurisdiction over international crimes is on its last legs, if not already in its death throes".[1]

Although universal jurisdiction is not a new phenomenon, it still faces many challenges and obstacles in its application. After addressing the advantages and limits of the traditional grounds of jurisdiction for core international crimes,[2] this chapter examines the origins and content of the principle of universal jurisdiction and clarifies the basic concept. It also highlights and comments on the diversity and complexity surrounding the implementation of the principle of universal jurisdiction in some national jurisdictions.

Despite a wide acceptance of universal jurisdiction by states due to the serious nature of core international crimes, this principle is not applied homogeneously, nor is its application implemented without difficulty. During the past decades, national and international constraints placed on

* **Fausto Pocar** is Appeals Judge and past President of the International Criminal Tribunal for the former Yugoslavia ("ICTY").

** **Magali Maystre** holds a *D.E.A.* (post-graduate degree) in international law from the *Institut universitaire de hautes études internationales* in Geneva. She currently works as an Associate Legal Officer in the Appeals Chamber of the ICTY. The views expressed herein are those of the authors and do not necessarily reflect the views of the United Nations or the ICTY.

1 Antonio Cassese, "Is the Bell Tolling for Universality? A Plea for a Sensible Notion of Universal Jurisdiction", in *Journal of International Criminal Justice*, 2003, vol. 1, no. 3, p. 589.

2 In the framework of this contribution, the term "core international crimes" is used to refer to genocide, crimes against humanity and war crimes.

states have too often prevailed over their legal obligation to prosecute alleged perpetrators of core international crimes. Has the bell therefore tolled for the end of universal jurisdiction? This contribution argues the contrary and explores how the goal pursued by universal jurisdiction could be better enforced through the principle of complementarity. In conclusion, this contribution develops ideas on how the International Criminal Court's complementarity principle could induce states to abide by their obligations and exercise universal jurisdiction for core international crimes.

9.2. Universal Jurisdiction and its Origins

Although the topic of universal jurisdiction has been heavily debated in academic literature, clarifying the basic concepts may provide a better understanding of the complexity and limits of the principle. Before turning to this main issue, this chapter first describes the traditional grounds of criminal jurisdiction in international law and, subsequently, assesses briefly the efficacy and difficulties arising from their application to the prosecution of core international crimes.

9.2.1. From the Principle of Territoriality to Universal Jurisdiction

As a preliminary remark, it is important to recall two points. First, jurisdiction can be civil or criminal. However, only universal jurisdiction linked to individual criminal responsibility will be considered in this analysis. Second, jurisdiction has two distinct aspects, namely *jurisdiction to prescribe* – or prescriptive jurisdiction – and *jurisdiction to enforce* or enforcement jurisdiction. The first refers to the state's authority, under international law, to declare the applicability of its criminal law to given conduct through legislation or, in certain states, through judicial ruling. The latter refers to the state's authority, under international law, to implement or apply its criminal law either through the courts or through police and other executive actions.[3] In other words, "jurisdiction to prescribe refers to a state's authority to criminalize given conduct, jurisdiction to enforce the authority, inter alia, to arrest and detain, to prosecute,

[3] Roger O'Keefe, "Universal Jurisdiction: Clarifying the Basic Concept", in *Journal of International Criminal Justice*, 2004, vol. 2, no. 3, p. 736.

try and sentence, and to punish persons for the commission of acts so criminalized".[4] Logically, in theory, these two aspects are independent of each other. However, in practice, the prescription of an act and its enforcement are intertwined.[5] Nonetheless, it is worthwhile recalling this distinction when dealing with extra-territorial jurisdiction.

Under international law, each state is free to determine the scope of its criminal law. This liberty rests in its sovereignty.[6] Nevertheless, in exercising their criminal jurisdiction, states must respect international law. In short, the exercise of repressive power can be limited by international law, in particular by the prohibition on interference such as when a state interferes in another state's internal affairs[7] or when a state exercises its competence in violation of a norm of higher rank. Conversely, a state can be under an obligation to exercise its criminal jurisdiction to prosecute certain acts by virtue of a norm in international law.

In 1927, in the celebrated *Lotus* case, the Permanent Court of International Justice stated that "in all systems of law the principle of the territorial character of criminal law is fundamental", although it also added that "[t]he territoriality of criminal law … is not an absolute principle of international law and by no means coincides with territorial sovereignty".[8] It further added:

> … jurisdiction is certainly territorial; it cannot be exercised by a State outside its territory except by virtue of a permissive rule derived from international custom or from a convention. It does not, however, follow that international law prohibits a State from exercising jurisdiction in its own territory, in respect of any case which relates to acts which have taken place abroad, and in which it cannot rely on some permissive rule of international law … Far from laying down a general prohibition to the effect that States may not extend

4 *Id.*, pp. 736-737.

5 *Id.*, p. 741.

6 Gerhard Werle, *Principles of International Criminal Law* (Second edition), TMC Asser Press, The Hague, 2009, p. 66 and n. 375.

7 Article 2(1) of the United Nations Charter provides: "The Organization is based on the principle of the sovereign equality of all its Members."; Gerhard Werle, *Principles of International Criminal Law*, see *supra* note 6, p. 66 and n. 376.

8 Permanent Court of International Justice, *The Case of the S.S. "Lotus" (France v. Turkey)*, Judgment, 7 September 1927, Series A, No. 10, p. 20.

> the application of their laws and the jurisdiction of their courts to persons, property and acts outside their territory, [international law] leaves them in this respect a wide measure of discretion which is only limited in certain cases by prohibitive rules; as regards other cases, every State remains free to adopt the principles which it regards as best and most suitable.[9]

In other words, "the principle of freedom, in virtue of which each state may regulate its legislation at its discretion, provided that in so doing it does not come in conflict with a restriction imposed by international law",[10] also applies with regard to law governing the scope of criminal jurisdiction. Consequently, all that can be required of a state, in these circumstances, is that it does not overstep the limits which international law imposes upon its jurisdiction; "within these limits, its title to exercise jurisdiction rests in its sovereignty".[11] States are therefore free to exercise their criminal jurisdiction under different legal grounds of jurisdiction, unless a rule of international law limits their freedom to extend the criminal jurisdiction of their courts.

The *Lotus* case *dictum* concerns *prescriptive jurisdiction*. In other words, it concerns what a state can do on its own territory when investigating and prosecuting crimes committed abroad, not what a state may do on other states' territory when prosecuting such crimes. Obviously, a state has no *enforcement jurisdiction* outside its territory. Without permission to the contrary, a state cannot exercise its jurisdiction on the territory of another state. While *prescriptive jurisdiction* can be extra-territorial, by way of contrast, *enforcement jurisdiction* is strictly territorial without permission to the contrary.[12]

9.2.1.1. Traditional Grounds of Jurisdiction: Territoriality, Active Nationality and Passive Nationality

In international law, there are a number of traditional grounds of jurisdiction to prescribe, pursuant to which states have asserted the applicability

[9] *Id.*, pp. 18-19.

[10] *Id.*, p. 20.

[11] *Id.*, p. 19.

[12] Roger O'Keefe, "Universal Jurisdiction: Clarifying the Basic Concept", see *supra* note 3, p. 740.

of their criminal law. The first is the principle of territoriality. Pursuant to this principle, the laws of the territory where the act is committed is key.

The principle of territoriality has numerous advantages. First, the *locus commissi delicti* – the place where the crime has allegedly been committed – is usually the *forum conveniens*, that is, the appropriate place of trial since it is easiest to collect evidence and hear witnesses. Second, it is normally the place where the rights of the accused are best safeguarded as he is expected to know the law of the territory, providing he is not a foreigner on a temporary visit. Hence the accused is more likely to be familiar with the criminal law in force as well as with his rights as a defendant in a criminal trial. In addition, he is more likely to know and speak the language in which the trial is conducted. Third, the cathartic process of criminal trials will be more effective if the prosecution and sentence occur on the territory where the crime was committed. Furthermore, the judges, being members of the society where the crimes took place, are conscious of the public's close scrutiny on their administration of justice. Thus, they are more accountable to the community for the manner in which they dispense justice. Finally, by administering justice over crimes perpetrated in its territory, the territorial state affirms its authority over crimes within its boundaries; consequently helping to deter the commission of future offences.[13] The advantages of conducting national prosecutions in the territorial state are of course only valid if they are conducted in an independent, impartial and fair manner.

The principle of active nationality is the other traditional legal ground of jurisdiction, according to which a state may criminalize offences committed abroad by one of its nationals. It is normally implemented in one of two ways. In some states, national courts have jurisdiction over certain criminal conduct committed by their nationals abroad, regardless of whether those offences are criminal under the law of the territorial state. In such cases, the underlying rationale is the will of a state that its nationals comply with its own law, irrespective of where they are and regardless of the laws in the state where the offence is committed. In other states, criminal jurisdiction over crimes committed by nationals abroad is subordinate to the offence being punishable under the law of the territorial state. In these the essential motivation behind the principle is

13 Antonio Cassese, *International Criminal Law* (2nd edition), Oxford University Press, Oxford, 2008, p. 336, n. 1.

the desire of the state of nationality not to extradite its nationals to the state where the crime has been committed. Thus, the state of active nationality must provide for the possibility of trying the accused, so that he does not escape prosecution altogether.[14] On the whole, states of civil law tradition – many of which do not extradite their nationals – tend to exercise their jurisdiction on this basis more frequently than states of common law tradition.[15]

In addition, the principle of passive nationality – for so long regarded as controversial[16] – now appears generally accepted.[17] By virtue of this principle, states may exercise jurisdiction over crimes committed abroad against their own nationals. Plainly, the motivation underlying the principle is grounded on: (i) the need to protect nationals abroad; and (ii) a substantial mistrust in the exercise of criminal jurisdiction by the territorial state.[18] Normally, whenever the accused is abroad, a "double incrimination" is required by many states for prosecuting a crime, namely that the offence be considered as such both in the state where it was committed and in the state of the victim exercising its jurisdiction. The underlying rationale is intended to avoid prosecuting a person for an act that is not considered a crime by the territorial state where it has been performed. The motivation for this prerequisite may be explained by the general principle of legality, *nullum crimen sine lege*, a general principle of international criminal law, in addition to being common to all national legal sys-

---

[14] *Id.*, p. 337, n. 2.

[15] Michael Akehurst, "Jurisdiction in International Law", in *British Yearbook of International Law*, 1972-1973, vol. 46, pp. 152 and 156-157; Dapo Akande, "Active Personality Principle", in Antonio Cassese (ed.), *The Oxford Companion to International Criminal Justice*, Oxford University Press, Oxford, 2009, p. 229.

[16] The passive nationality principle has been considered controversial, for a long time, mostly because it implies that a state's national carries with him the protection of his national laws and because it exposes others to the application of laws without there being any reasonable basis on which those persons might suppose that such laws apply to their conduct. See Dapo Akande, "Passive Personality Principle", in Antonio Cassese (ed.), *The Oxford Companion to International Criminal Justice*, see *supra* note 15, p. 451.

[17] International Court of Justice, *Arrest Warrant of 11 April 2000 (Democratic Republic of the Congo v. Belgium)*, Judgment, I.C.J. Reports 2002, Joint separate opinion of Judges Higgins, Kooijmans and Buergenthal, para. 47; Roger O'Keefe, "Universal Jurisdiction: Clarifying the Basic Concept", see *supra* note 3, p. 739.

[18] Antonio Cassese, *International Criminal Law*, see *supra* note 13, p. 337, n. 2.

tems. Furthermore, for extradition, "double incrimination" is usually also a procedural requirement.[19]

Finally, extraterritorial jurisdiction over the crimes of non-nationals has also been exercised, although only with regard to certain offences,[20] under the protective principle, also known as *compétence réelle*. Under this principle, a state exercises its criminal jurisdiction over crimes committed abroad by foreigners where the offence is deemed to constitute a threat to its security or some vital national interests.[21]

9.2.1.2. Traditional Legal Grounds of Jurisdiction and International Crimes

Determining the benefit and the difficulties arising from the application of the above-mentioned legal grounds of jurisdiction to the prosecution of core international crimes, allows understanding the exponential recourse to the principle of universal jurisdiction – with which we will deal later on – in the second half of the 20th century.

First, in the case of core international crimes, there may be a major obstacle to the principle of territoriality. These crimes are often committed by state officials – or military officials – or with their complicity or acquiescence; for example, war crimes committed by servicemen, or torture perpetrated by police officers, or genocide carried out with the tacit approval of state authorities. It follows that state judicial authorities may be reluctant to prosecute state agents or to institute proceedings against private individuals that might eventually involve state organs. A state might be unwilling or unable genuinely to carry out the investigation or prosecute the alleged perpetrators. Further problems may arise when the alleged perpetrator of a crime is a state official enjoying immunity from prosecution under national legislation, for instance the head of state, the

19 *Ibid.*

20 Currency offences, national security offences – such as espionage and treason – and immigration offences are usually crimes covered by the protective principle, as well as some terrorist offences committed or planned abroad which are intended to affect or influence a state. See Dapo Akande, "Protective Principle (Jurisdiction)", in Antonio Cassese (ed.), *The Oxford Companion to International Criminal Justice*, see *supra* note 15, p. 474.

21 Roger O'Keefe, "Universal Jurisdiction: Clarifying the Basic Concept", see *supra* note 3, p. 739.

head or a senior member of government, or a member of parliament. Clearly, if this is the case, national courts are barred from instituting criminal proceedings against the accused, because the latter enjoys personal immunity. It may also be that the alleged perpetrator, regardless of his official status, is covered by an amnesty law. The national authorities of the state in which the amnesty was granted may be precluded from taking judicial action. By contrast, a foreign court, assuming it has jurisdiction over the crime, may consider that it does not have to recognise the amnesty, particularly if this law conflicts with international rules of *jus cogens*, the peremptory norms of international law. Thus, whereas national jurisdiction based on the territoriality principle may sometimes fail, other grounds of jurisdictions invoked by foreign courts may prove workable and lead to the prosecution of the alleged culprit.

Among the international treaties providing for jurisdiction over international crimes based on territoriality,[22] the Convention on the Prevention and Punishment of the Crime of Genocide of 9 December 1948[23] ("Genocide Convention of 1948") should be mentioned. Its article VI stipulates that "[p]ersons charged with genocide … shall be tried by a competent tribunal of the State in the territory of which the act was committed, or by such international penal tribunal as may have jurisdiction with respect to those Contracting Parties which shall have accepted its jurisdiction". In other words, according to the Genocide Convention of 1948, the territorial state where an act of genocide has been committed has an international obligation to exercise its criminal jurisdiction to prosecute alleged accused charged with genocide. This rule, however, has almost never been applied,[24] except in Rwanda, where national courts

---

22 See, *e.g.*, Article 5(1)(a) of the Convention against Torture and Other Cruel, Inhuman or Degrading Treatment or Punishment, annexed to UN Doc. A/RES/39/46 (10 December 1984) ("Convention against Torture of 1984"). Article 5(1)(a) provides: "Each State Party shall take such measures as may be necessary to establish its jurisdiction over the offences referred to in article 4 in the following cases: (a) When the offences are committed in any territory under its jurisdiction or on board a ship or aircraft registered in that State".

23 Convention on the Prevention and Punishment of the Crime of Genocide, annexed to UN Doc. General Assembly resolution 260 (III) A (9 December 1948).

24 William A. Schabas, "National Courts Finally Begin to prosecute Genocide, the 'Crime of Crimes'", in *Journal of International Criminal Justice*, 2003, vol. 1, no. 1, p. 40, n. 3 stating that: "Cambodia held a show trial for genocide of Khmer Rouge leaders Pol Pot and Ieng Sary in 1979, but under an idiosyncratic definition of the

prosecuted thousands alleged authors of the genocide committed in 1994[25] alongside the international prosecution brought before the International Criminal Tribunal for Rwanda ("ICTR"). This was only possible due to the rare circumstance that the victims of the genocide, the Tutsis, had seized power in Rwanda, and were therefore strongly committed to prosecute those responsible for genocide, not least since the genocide legitimized the minority Tutsi's hold on power.

The second traditional ground of jurisdiction to prescribe is the principle of active nationality. This principle entitles a state to exercise jurisdiction over its nationals even with respect to crimes taking place abroad. The principle of active nationality is normally upheld with regard to war crimes, as well as such crimes as torture. Many states, particularly under pressure from the conclusion of treaties setting out international crimes, have passed legislation providing for jurisdiction based on nationality. The active nationality principle is also laid down in a number of international treaties, which include the Convention against Torture of 1984.[26] Notable application of the active nationality principle are the trials

crimes that corresponds more closely to the concept of crimes against humanity" (internal references omitted).

25 *Id.*, pp. 40, 45-46 and n. 44.

26 Article 5(1)(b) of the Convention against Torture of 1984 provides: "Each State Party shall take such measures as may be necessary to establish its jurisdiction over the offences referred to in article 4 in the following cases: (b) When the alleged offender is a national of that State". Outside the framework of core international crimes, the active nationality principle is also laid down in various treaties against terrorism, see, *e.g.*, Article 3(1)(b) of the Convention on the prevention and punishment of crimes against internationally protected persons, including diplomatic agents, annexed to UN Doc. General Assembly resolution 3166 (XXVIII) (14 December 1973). Article 3(1)(b) provides: "Each State Party shall take such measures as may be necessary to establish its jurisdiction over the crimes set forth in article 2 in the following case: (b) when the alleged offender is a national of that State"; Article 5(1)(b) of the International Convention against the taking of hostages, annexed to UN Doc. A/RES/34/146 (17 December 1979). Article 5(1)(b) provides: "Each State Party shall take such measures as may be necessary to establish its jurisdiction over any of the offences set forth in article 1 which are committed: (b) By any of its nationals [...]"; Article 6(1)(c) of the International Convention for the Suppression of Terrorist Bombings of 25 November 1997, annexed to UN Doc. A/RES/52/164 (9 January 1998). Article 6(1)(c) provides: "Each State Party shall take such measures as may be necessary to establish its jurisdiction over the offences set forth in article 2 when: (c) The offence is committed by a national of that State"; Article 7(1)(c) of the International Convention for the Suppression of the Financing of Terrorism of 9 December 1999, annexed

instituted in 1902 by US Court Martial against American servicemen who had fought in the Philippines,[27] the "Leipzig trials" against Germans in 1921-1922, imposed upon Germany by the Allies,[28] and the various trials before US Courts Martial for crimes committed in Vietnam.[29] However, in principle, the problems associated with the principle of territoriality also apply to the application of the principle of active nationality. When a core international crime is committed by a state (or military) official, the state of the offender might be reluctant to prosecute him. Alternatively, the offender might enjoy immunity from prosecution or be covered by an amnesty law. Thus, when the state of the offender is unwilling to prosecute its nationals, the principle of active nationality is inadequate to prosecute core international crimes.

The third traditional ground of jurisdiction to prescribe is the principle of passive nationality. By virtue of this principle, a state may exercise its jurisdiction over crimes committed abroad against its own nationals. The passive nationality ground of jurisdiction has frequently been deployed to prosecute war crimes, particularly after the cessation of hostilities, by the victorious state against the vanquished former enemies. More recently, courts have relied upon this jurisdictional ground with regard to crimes against humanity and torture. Significant in this respect are some cases tried *in absentia*: *Alfredo Astiz*, a case brought before French courts concerning an Argentine officer who had tortured two French nuns in Argentina, and was sentenced to life imprisonment,[30] as

to UN Doc. A/RES/54/109 (25 February 2000). Article 7(1)(c) provides: "Each State Party shall take such measures as may be necessary to establish its jurisdiction over the offences set forth in article 2 when: (c) The offence is committed by a national of that State"; Article 9(1)(c) of the International Convention for the Suppression of Acts of Nuclear Terrorism of 13 April 2005, annexed to UN Doc. A/RES/59/290 (15 April 2005). Article 9(1)(c) provides: "Each State Party shall take such measures as may be necessary to establish its jurisdiction over the offences set forth in article 2 when: (c) The offence is committed by a national of that State".

27 See Guénaël Mettraux, "US Courts-Martial and the Armed Conflict in the Philippines (1899-1902): Their Contribution to National Case Law on War", in *Journal of International Criminal Justice*, 2003, vol. 1, no. 1, pp. 135-150.

28 William A. Schabas, *An Introduction to the International Criminal Court*, Cambridge University Press, Cambridge, 2001, p. 4.

29 Antonio Cassese, *International Criminal Law*, see *supra* note 13, p. 337, n. 3.

30 Alfredo Astiz was sentenced to life's imprisonment. See Cour d'Assises de Paris, *In Re Alfredo Astiz*, Arrêt, No. 1893/89, 16 March 1990; Ellen Lutz and Kathryn Sik-

well as some cases brought before Italian courts against Argentine officers for crimes perpetrated against Italians in Argentina, such as the *Suàrez Masón and others*.[31] This ground of jurisdiction is stipulated in the Convention against Torture of 1984.[32]

---

kink, "The Justice Cascade: The Evolution and Impact of Foreign Human Rights Trials in Latin America", in *Chicago Journal of International Law*, 2001, vol. 2, no. 1, pp. 10-11; Antonio Cassese, *International Criminal Law*, see *supra* note 13, p. 337, n. 3.

31 Suàrez Masón and Riveros were sentenced to life's imprisonment and the five other defendants to twenty-four years of imprisonment each. See Rome Court of Assizes (*Corte di assise*), *Suàrez Masón and others*, 6 December 2000; Ellen Lutz and Kathryn Sikkink, "The Justice Cascade: The Evolution and Impact of Foreign Human Rights Trials in Latin America", see *supra* note 30, pp. 21, 23; Antonio Cassese, *International Criminal Law*, see *supra* note 13, p. 337, n. 3.

32 Article 5(1)(c) of the Convention against Torture of 1984 provides: "Each State Party shall take such measures as may be necessary to establish its jurisdiction over the offences referred to in article 4 in the following cases: (c) When the victim is a national of that State if that State considers it appropriate". In addition, this ground of jurisdiction has been laid down in national legislation with regard to terrorism, for instance in France, Belgium and the United States. It is also stipulated in a number of international conventions against terrorism. See Robert Kolb, "The Exercise of Criminal Jurisdiction over International Terrorists", in Andrea Bianchi (ed.), *Enforcing International Law Norms Against Terrorism*, Hart Publishing, Oxford, 2004, pp. 246-248. The several anti-terrorist conventions concluded at the international level after 1963 are all based on a similar jurisdictional system, with only slight differences due to experience of shortcomings and emergent political consensus. These conventions provide a series of jurisdictional titles for all the States Parties, among which the principle of passive nationality; see, *e.g.*, Article 5(1)(d) of the International Convention against the taking of hostages, annexed to UN Doc. A/RES/34/146 (17 December 1979). Article 5(1)(d) provides: "Each State Party shall take such measures as may be necessary to establish its jurisdiction over any of the offences set forth in article 1 which are committed: (d) With respect to a hostage who is a national of that State, if that State considers it appropriate"; International Convention for the Suppression of Terrorist Bombings of 25 November 1997, annexed to UN Doc. A/RES/52/164 (9 January 1998). Article 6(2)(a) provides: "A State Party may also establish its jurisdiction over any such offence when: (a) The offence is committed against a national of that State"; International Convention for the Suppression of the Financing of Terrorism of 9 December 1999, annexed to UN Doc. A/RES/54/109 (25 February 2000). Article 7(2)(a) provides: "A State Party may also establish its jurisdiction over any such offence when: (a) The offence was directed towards or resulted in the carrying out of an offence referred to in article 2, paragraph 1, subparagraph (a) or (b), in the territory of or against a national of that State"; Article 9(2)(a) of the International Convention for the Suppression of Acts of Nuclear Terrorism of 13 April 2005, annexed to UN Doc. A/RES/59/290 (15 April 2005). Article 9(2)(a) provides: "A State

The principle of passive nationality has been considered a controversial principle for two reasons. First, it implies that a person carries with him/her the protection of his/her national laws. Second, it exposes other persons to the application of laws without these persons supposing that such laws apply to their conduct.[33] However, in case of core international crimes, these explanations are less justifiable given the need to provide a broad basis for ending impunity of such acts and because persons are supposed to know that core international crimes are prohibited under international law. Still, some scholars find this ground of jurisdiction particularly incongruous in the case of some international crimes such as those against humanity and torture.[34] This is perhaps the reason this ground of jurisdiction is envisaged in international conventions, such as the Convention against Torture of 1984, not as an obligation of contracting states but simply as an authorization to prosecute.[35] Conversely, this ground of jurisdiction may prove appropriate for terrorism as a discrete offence, where the perpetrators will often – but not always – select their victims based on their nationality and will know that the victims' nationality state has a particularly strong interest in preventing such crimes[36] and because the

Party may also establish its jurisdiction over any such offence when (a) The offence is committed against a national of that State".

33 Dapo Akande, "Passive Personality Principle", see *supra* note 16, p. 451.

34 Antonio Cassese, *International Criminal Law*, see *supra* note 13, pp. 337-338, n. 3. According to him, "[b]y definition, these are crimes that injure humanity, […] words our concept of respect for any human being, regardless of the nationality of the victims. As a consequence, their prosecution should not be based on the national link between the victim and the prosecuting state. This is indeed a narrow and nationalistic standard for bringing alleged criminals to justice, based on the interest of a state to prosecute those who have allegedly attacked one of its nationals. The prosecution of those crimes should instead reflect a universal concern for their punishment; it should consequently be better based on such legal grounds as territoriality, universality, or active personality. It follows that, as far as such crimes as those against humanity, torture, and genocide are concerned, the passive nationality principle should only be relied upon as a *fall-back*, whenever no other state (neither the territorial state, nor the state of which the alleged criminal is a national, or other states acting upon the universality principle) is willing or able to administer international criminal justice."

35 Article 5(1)(c) of the Convention against Torture of 1984 provides: "Each State Party shall take such measures as may be necessary to establish its jurisdiction over the offences referred to in article 4 in the following cases: (c) When the victim is a national of that State if that State considers it appropriate".

36 Dapo Akande, "Passive Personality Principle", see *supra* note 16, p. 452.

need to protect nationals' interests and concerns acquires greater relevance.[37]

Finally, it is particularly interesting to recall here the most celebrated case – perhaps because the only one – where the protective principle has been invoked as legal ground to justify the prosecution of core international crimes, the *Eichmann* case.[38] As it is well known, Eichmann was a German national, who had been the Head of the section of the Gestapo charged with the implementation of the "final solution of the Jewish question" during the Second World War.[39] In 1960, he was captured in Buenos Aires by individuals who were probably agents of the Israeli government. After being held in captivity in a private house in Buenos Aires for some weeks, he was taken by air to Israel unbeknownst to the Argentinean government.[40]

Eichmann was subsequently charged under an Israeli statute, the Nazis and Nazi Collaborators (Punishment) Law 5710 of 1950 ("Israeli Law of 1950"), of fifteen counts of crimes against the Jewish people, crimes against humanity, war crimes and membership of a hostile organization.[41] Under Section 1(a) of the Israeli Law of 1950, war crimes were punishable if committed "during the period of the Second World War … in an hostile country"; other crimes were punishable if done "during the period of the Nazi regime in an hostile country".[42]

In the District Court of Jerusalem and on appeal,[43] the Court considered challenges to its jurisdiction based on international law by the

37 Antonio Cassese, *International Criminal Law*, see *supra* note 13, p. 338, n. 3.

38 District Court of Jerusalem, *Attorney General of the Government of Israel v. Eichmann*, Case No. 40/61, Judgment in the Trial of Adolf Eichmann, 15 December 1961, ("*Eichmann* Judgement"). For a discussion of the case, see J.E.S. Fawcett, "The *Eichmann* Case", in *British Yearbook of International Law*, 1962, vol. 38, pp. 181-215; L.C. Green, "The Eichmann Case", in *Modern Law Review*, 1960, vol. 23, no. 5, pp. 507-515.

39 Vanni E. Treves, "Jurisdictional Aspects of the Eichmann Case", in *Minnesota Law Review*, 1962-1963, vol. 47, no. 4, p. 558.

40 J.E.S. Fawcett, "The *Eichmann* Case", see *supra* note 38, p. 182.

41 *Ibid.*

42 *Eichmann* Judgement, see *supra* note 38, para. 4.

43 The Supreme Court of Israel sitting as a Court of Criminal Appeal fully concurred, without hesitation or reserve, with the District Court of Jerusalem's conclusions and reasons, see Supreme Court of Israel, *Adolf Eichmann v. The Attorney General*, Criminal Appeal No. 336/61, Judgment, 29 May 1962, paras. 5, 7, 13.

defence which argued that the Israeli Law of 1950 "by inflicting punishment for acts committed outside the boundaries of the [S]tate and before its establishment, against persons who were not Israeli citizens, and by a person who acted in the course of duty on behalf of a foreign country … conflicts with international law and exceeds the powers of the Israeli legislator".[44]

The District Court of Jerusalem rejected the argument, holding that, in fact, Israel's right to punish had two valid bases of jurisdiction. First, universal jurisdiction – due to the universal character of the crimes in question[45] – which will be discussed later and, second, the protective principle.[46] The District Court held that the protective principle is not limited to only those foreign offences which threaten the vital interests of a state, but also invoke jurisdiction when there is a "linking point"; in other words, when an act or an accused concerns a state more than they concern other states.[47] As a result, the Court held that:

> … The "linking point" between Israel and the Accused (and for that matter between Israel and any person accused of a crime against the Jewish People under this law) is striking in the "crime against the Jewish People," a crime that postulates an intention to exterminate the Jewish People in whole or in part. Indeed, even without such specific definition - and it must be noted that the draft law only defined "crimes against humanity" and "war crimes" … – there was a subsisting "linking point," since most of the Nazi crimes of this kind were perpetrated against the Jewish People; but viewed in the light of the definition of "crime against the Jewish People," as defined in the [Israeli] Law [of 1950], constitutes in effect an attempt to exterminate the Jewish People, or a partial extermination of the Jewish People. If there is an ef-

44 *Eichmann* Judgement, see *supra* note 38, para. 8.

45 *Id.*, para. 11.

46 *Id.*, para. 30 provides: "The State of Israel's 'right to punish' the Accused derives, in our view, from two cumulative sources: a universal source (pertaining to the whole of mankind) which vests the right to prosecute and punish crimes of this order in every state within the family of nations; and a specific or national source which gives the victim nation the right to try any who assault its existence. This second foundation of penal jurisdiction conforms, according to the acknowledged terminology, to the protective principle (the competence réelle)."

47 *Id.*, paras. 31-32.

> fective link (and not necessarily identity) between the State of Israel and the Jewish People, then a crime intended to exterminate the Jewish People has an obvious connection with the State of Israel. …
>
> The connection between the State of Israel and the Jewish People needs no explanation. The State of Israel was established and recognized as the State of the Jews. …
>
> [T]his crime very deeply concerns the vital interests of the State of Israel, and pursuant to the "protective principle," this State has the right to punish the criminals. … [T]he acts in question referred to in this Law of the State of Israel "concern Israel more than they concern other states," and therefore … there exists a "linking point." The punishment of Nazi criminals does not derive from the arbitrariness of a country "abusing" its sovereignty, but is a legitimate and reasonable exercise of a right in penal jurisdiction.[48]

Beside the many problematic issues involved in the *Eichmann* case, it is necessary here to underline how unusual it was to invoke the protective principle in such a case, considering that vital interests of a state, as a ground for jurisdiction, have been always identified with respect to a limited number of criminal offences, such as counterfeiting national currency or planning attacks on a state's security. The District Court of Jerusalem referred to the protective principle and to universal jurisdiction in *dictum*, but relied on Israel's national legislation conferring upon its courts jurisdiction over "crimes against the Jewish people", based on the Israeli Law of 1950 that includes genocide and crimes against humanity whenever committed against the "Jewish people", wherever they may be. Israel's jurisdictional reach is, under its law, universal, but it is based on a nationality connection – it may be more accurate to say on a religious connection – to the victim that places such jurisdictional basis under the principle of passive nationality. Admittedly, that law purports to apply to acts which took place before the establishment of the sovereign state of Israel in 1948, but that does not alter the basis of the theory relied upon. Furthermore, there is no historical legal precedent for such a retroactive application of criminal jurisdiction based on nationality, but that goes to the issue of the law's international validity and the jurisdictional theory relied upon, rather than its jurisdictional basis.

48 *Id.*, paras. 33-35.

9.2.2. Universal Jurisdiction and its Expansion in the Second Half of the 20th Century

During the second half of the 20th Century, following the establishment of crimes under international law, states also started to deal with them under the principle of universal jurisdiction. The *Eichmann* case is just one example in which the principle was invoked, in concert with the principle of protective principle.

9.2.2.1. Definition and Content of the Principle of Universal Jurisdiction

The principle of universal jurisdiction empowers – or requires in certain cases – a state to bring to trial persons accused of certain international crimes, regardless of the place of commission of the crime and irrespective of the nationality of the perpetrator and the victim[49] at the time of the commission of the crime.[50] This principle therefore derogates from the ordinary grounds of criminal jurisdiction requiring a territorial or personal link with the crime, the perpetrator or the victim.[51] While other forms of extra-territorial jurisdiction are grounded in some nexus between the fo-

---

49 Xavier Philippe, "The principles of universal jurisdiction and complementarity: how do the two principles intermesh?", in *International Review of the Red Cross*, 2006, vol. 88, no. 862, p. 377 and references cited therein; Florian Jessberger, "Universal Jurisdiction", in Antonio Cassese (ed.), *The Oxford Companion to International Criminal Justice*, see *supra* note 15, p. 555; Roger O'Keefe, "Universal Jurisdiction: Clarifying the Basic Concept", see *supra* note 3, p. 746; Antonio Cassese, *International Criminal Law*, see *supra* note 13, p. 338, n. 4; Theodor Meron, "International Criminalization of Internal Atrocities", in *American Journal of International Law*, 1995, vol. 89, no. 3, p. 570.

50 This last part is extremely significant. See Roger O'Keefe, "The Grave Breaches Regime and Universal Jurisdiction", in *Journal of International Criminal Justice*, 2009, vol. 7, no. 4, p. 812, n. 2: "The point in time by reference to which one characterizes the head of prescriptive jurisdiction relied on in a given case is the moment of alleged commission of the offence: a foreigner's presence on the prescribing state's territory or his or her assumption of its nationality, etc, after the commission of the offence cannot turn universal jurisdiction into jurisdiction based on territoriality, nationality, and so on".

51 Xavier Philippe, "The principles of universal jurisdiction and complementarity how do the two principles intermesh?", see *supra* note 49, p. 377.

rum state and the crime, universal jurisdiction requires no such nexus.[52] Instead it finds its basis in the notion that certain *jus cogens* and other peremptory norms of international law are so widely and universally endorsed, and that their violations are so harmful, that they constitute a profound attack not just on the immediate victims or to the state community to which victims are related, but on the international community as a whole. As a result of this offence to the international community, the theory of universal jurisdiction asserts that all states have a legitimate interest and are entitled – and even obliged in some circumstances – to bring proceedings against the perpetrators, even if there is no link between the forum state and the crime.[53] Universal jurisdiction allows for the trial of international crimes committed anywhere in the world by and against anybody. In many respects, it is an unprecedented mechanism empowering states to prosecute and try alleged perpetrators of core international crimes.

Traditionally, the *ratio legis* of universal jurisdiction is justified by two main ideas. First, as stated, some crimes are so grave that they harm the entire international community. Second, the gravity of these crimes implies that no safe haven should be available for those who commit them. Although these justifications may not always appear realistic, they clearly explain why the international community or individual states intervene by bringing proceedings and prosecuting the perpetrators of such crimes.[54]

Here, it is important to recall two points. First, that "to the extent that a title to prescriptive universal criminal jurisdiction exists under customary international law, a state that has exercised this title must be presumed to have the jurisdiction title to adjudicate the matter by way of

[52] Roger O'Keefe, "Universal Jurisdiction: Clarifying the Basic Concept", see *supra* note 3, pp. 745-746 and references cited therein.

[53] Xavier Philippe, "The principles of universal jurisdiction and complementarity how do the two principles intermesh?", see *supra* note 49, p. 377.

[54] International Court of Justice, *Arrest Warrant of 11 April 2000*, see *supra* note 17, Dissenting opinion of Judge *ad hoc* Van den Wyngaert, para. 46; Georges Abi-Saab, "The Proper Role of Universal Jurisdiction", in *Journal of International Criminal Justice*, 2003, vol. 1, no. 3, p. 597; Philip Grant, "Les poursuites nationales et la compétence universelle", in Robert Kolb, *Droit international pénal*, Bruylant/Helbing and Lichtenhahn, Bruxelles/Bâle, 2008, p. 454; Florian Jessberger, "Universal Jurisdiction", see *supra* note 49, p. 556.

investigation and, where applicable, prosecution and trial, unless this title is restricted by an applicable international rule stating the contrary".[55] The application of this principle is important for the controversy on the so-called universal criminal jurisdiction *in absentia*, as will be shown subsequently. Second, universal jurisdiction for international crimes is primarily based on customary international law, but can also be established under a multilateral treaty.[56] However, some argue that, by definition, a multilateral treaty-based jurisdiction regime only apply *inter partes* and, therefore, cannot *stricto sensu* be considered universal in nature[57] except for the four Geneva Conventions of 1949,[58] which have been universally ratified. Defining universal jurisdiction as "any" state, or "every" state, having the authority to criminalize international crimes can therefore be unintentionally misleading, "in so far as [the use of these terms] might be mistaken to suggest that universal jurisdiction can never be grounded in treaty law".[59] In fact, the jurisdiction mandated by the relevant treaty provisions is universal jurisdiction; in other words, that is, prescriptive jurisdiction in the absence of any other traditional jurisdictional nexus.

Though its modern application has evolved only recently, historically, universal jurisdiction has its roots in the longstanding criminal law approach to piracy and slavery.[60] Piracy is a crime that takes place in a

55 Claus Kreß, "Universal Jurisdiction over International Crimes and the *Institut de Droit International*", in *Journal of International Criminal Justice*, 2006, vol. 4, no. 3, p. 565.

56 *Id.*, p. 566.

57 *Ibid.*

58 Geneva Convention for the Amelioration of the Condition of the Wounded and Sick in Armed Forces in the Field of 12 August 1949 ("First Geneva Convention of 1949"); Geneva Convention for the Amelioration of the Condition of Wounded, Sick and Shipwrecked Members of Armed Forces at Sea of 12 August 1949 ("Second Geneva Convention of 1949"); Geneva Convention Relative to the Treatment of Prisoners of War of 12 August 1949 ("Third Geneva Convention of 1949"); Geneva Convention Relative to the Protection of Civilian Persons in Time of War of 12 August 1949 ("Fourth Geneva Convention of 1949").

59 Roger O'Keefe, "Universal Jurisdiction: Clarifying the Basic Concept", see *supra* note 3, p. 746.

60 Georges Abi-Saab, "The Proper Role of Universal Jurisdiction", see *supra* note 54, p. 600; Michael Akehurst, "Jurisdiction in International Law", see *supra* note 15, p. 160; Cherif Bassiouni, "The History of Universal Jurisdiction and Its Place in International Law", in Stephen Macedo (ed.), *Universal Jurisdiction: National Courts and the Prosecution of Serious Crimes Under International Law*, University of Pennsylvania

space, the high seas, where there is an absence of territorial sovereignty.[61] This criminal conduct was at its peak during a period in which the vast bulk of commercial activity among nations occurred through maritime operations. The lawless acts of the perpetrators directly impacted that global market, harming states indiscriminately. As such, crimes of piracy were considered crimes against the global community, and thus a concern for all nations "in view of the paramountcy of the perceived common interest in the security of maritime communications since the age of discoveries".[62] For this reason, no nexus between the crime and the forum state was considered necessary to establish jurisdiction and initiate prosecution.

Slave-traders were thought to fall into a similar category. Although the slave trade did not threaten commerce or other interaction among nations in the same way as piracy, the severity of its infringement on individual liberty was considered uniquely atrocious, so much so that it deserved international condemnation as a crime against the global community. Again, a nexus between the crime and the forum state was considered unnecessary to justify the invocation of jurisdiction over slave-traders. However, it was for the slave trade on the high seas that universal jurisdiction was implemented in treaty provisions.[63] We will not dwell on these crimes, although both have recently come to the attention of the international community in different contexts.[64]

Press, Philadelphia, 2004, pp. 48, 49 and n. 62; Cherif Bassiouni, "Universal Jurisdiction for International Crimes: Historical Perspectives and Contemporary Practice", in *Virginia Journal of International Law*, 2001, vol. 42, no. 1, p. 99; Philip Grant, "Les poursuites nationales et la compétence universelle", see *supra* note 54, p. 454; Xavier Philippe, "The principles of universal jurisdiction and complementarity how do the two principles intermesh?", see *supra* note 49, p. 378; Fausto Pocar, "Droit pénal et territoire", in Francis Delpérée *et al.* (eds.), *Droit constitutionnel et territoire*, Académie internationale de droit constitutionnel, 2009, pp. 178-179.

61 Georges Abi-Saab, "The Proper Role of Universal Jurisdiction", see *supra* note 54, p. 599.

62 *Ibid.*

63 Cherif Bassiouni, "The History of Universal Jurisdiction and Its Place in International Law", see *supra* note 60, p. 49.

64 For example, in the contexts of the recent incidents of piracy off the coast of Somalia and human trafficking as a modern incarnation of slave trade. See Douglas Guilfoyle, "Counter-Piracy Law Enforcement and Human Rights", in *International and Comparative Law Quarterly*, 2010, vol. 59, no. 1, pp. 141-169; Fausto Pocar, "Human Trafficking: A Crime Against Humanity", in Ernesto U. Savona and Sonia Stefanizzi

In contrast to the longstanding approach to the crimes of piracy and slavery, the evolution of universal jurisdiction into a mechanism for prosecuting perpetrators of atrocities such as war crimes, crimes against humanity and genocide has been a relatively recent phenomenon. However, unlike universal jurisdiction with respect to piracy, universal jurisdiction in these realms has been grounded in the particularly atrocious nature of the crimes in question, which are prohibited under *jus cogens* international norms. The critical and unifying point with respect to core international crimes that fall within the remit of universal jurisdiction is that the perpetrators are considered *hostes humani generis* or the enemies of all mankind.[65] Precisely because of the nature of this justification, a further expansion of the scope of universal jurisdiction's application to other areas of criminal law is unlikely.

In any event, the implementation of the principle of universal jurisdiction remains controversial.[66] Indeed, as will be shown subsequently, some of the states that have exercised universal jurisdiction, such as Belgium and Spain, have been submitted to substantial international political and legal pressure to curtail their national laws on universal jurisdiction.

9.2.2.2. The 1949 Geneva Conventions and their Historical Legacy for the Expansion of Universal Jurisdiction for Core International Crimes in the Second Half of the 20th Century

The expansion of universal jurisdiction for core international crimes to its contemporary scope has its origins in the dramatic development of inter-

(eds.), *Measuring Human Trafficking: Complexities and Pitfalls*, Springer, New York, 2007, pp. 5-12.

65 Cherif Bassiouni, "Universal Jurisdiction for International Crimes: Historical Perspectives and Contemporary Practice", see *supra* note 60, p. 96 and n. 56.

66 International Court of Justice, *Arrest Warrant of 11 April 2000*, see *supra* note 17, Dissenting opinion of Judge *ad hoc* Van den Wyngaert, paras. 44-45: "There is no generally accepted definition of universal jurisdiction in conventional or customary international law. States that have incorporated the principle in their domestic legislation have done so in very different ways. […] Much has been written in legal doctrine about universal jurisdiction. Many views exist as to its legal meaning and its legal status under international law". See also, *e.g.*, George P. Fletcher, "Against Universal Jurisdiction", in *Journal of International Criminal Justice*, 2003, vol. 1, no. 3, pp. 580-584; International Court of Justice, *Arrest Warrant of 11 April 2000*, see *supra* note 17, Separate opinion of President Guillaume, Declaration of Judge Ranjeva and Separate opinion of Judge Rezek.

national criminal law and human rights consciousness in the aftermath of the Second World War. Through the establishment of the International Military Tribunals and the adoption of conventions containing explicit, or implicit, norms on universal jurisdiction, the idea of universal jurisdiction for international crimes gained ground.[67] Indeed, as the House of Lords recognised in its landmark universal jurisdiction judgement on the extradition of Chilean General and former President Augusto Pinochet:

> Since the Nazi atrocities and the Nuremberg trials, international law has recognized a number of offences as being international crimes. Individual states have taken jurisdiction to try some international crimes even in cases where such crimes were not committed within the geographical boundaries of such states.[68]

Supplementing the legacy of Nuremberg in this respect have been key developments in international human rights and humanitarian law. International law not only recognised the authority but, in certain circumstances, mandated states to prosecute international crimes.[69] Starting with the Genocide Convention of 1948, states have adopted several instruments at the international level that have been widely recognised as contributions to the development of universal jurisdiction.[70] The parties to the Genocide Convention of 1948 undertook to prevent and punish genocide as a "crime under international law".[71] Even though the Genocide Convention of 1948 only provides for territorial jurisdiction,[72] it has been consistently argued that customary international law developed itself in a way to confirm the freedom of states to exercise universal jurisdiction

67 Xavier Philippe, "The principles of universal jurisdiction and complementarity how do the two principles intermesh?", see *supra* note 49, p. 378.

68 House of Lords, *R v. Bow Street Metropolitan Stipendiary Magistrate Ex Parte Pinochet Ugarte (No. 3)*, (HL(E)) [2000] 1 AC, 147, p. 189 by Lord Browne-Wilkinson.

69 Xavier Philippe, "The principles of universal jurisdiction and complementarity how do the two principles intermesh?", see *supra* note 49, pp. 378-379.

70 See the acknowledgement of these developments by the ICJ, in International Court of Justice, *Arrest Warrant of 11 April 2000*, see *supra* note 17, para. 59.

71 Article I of the Genocide Convention of 1948 provides that the "Contracting Parties confirm that genocide, whether committed in time of peace or in time of war, is a crime under international law which they undertake to prevent and to punish".

72 See Article VI of the Genocide Convention of 1948, see *supra* section 9.2.1.2.

with regard to the crime of genocide.[73] The International Court of Justice admitted in a judgement delivered in 1996:

> ... the rights and obligations enshrined by the Convention are rights and obligations *erga omnes*. The Court notes that the obligation each State thus has to prevent and to punish the crime of genocide is not territorially limited by the Convention.[74]

This *dictum* was also recognised by the practice of international tribunals and courts[75] as well as by national courts.[76]

---

73 Gerhard Werle, *Principles of International Criminal Law*, see *supra* note 6, p. 67 and n. 380; Philip Grant, "Les poursuites nationales et la compétence universelle", see *supra* note 54, p. 457, n. 43 and references cited therein. Philip Grant is of the opinion that customary international law developed itself in a way to *authorize* states to exercise universal jurisdiction with regard to the crime of genocide; William A. Schabas, "National Courts Finally Begin to prosecute Genocide, the 'Crime of Crimes'", see *supra* note 24, pp. 42-43, n. 22-23 and references cited therein, see also p. 60 stating that: "Be that as it may, if in 1948 States were generally hostile to universal jurisdiction for genocide, the situation has clearly changed"; Theodor Meron, "International Criminalization of Internal Atrocities", see *supra* note 49, p. 569 and n. 83-84.

74 International Court of Justice, *Application of the Convention on the Prevention and Punishment of the Crime of Genocide, Preliminary Objections*, Judgement, I.C.J. Reports 1996, para. 31.

75 International Criminal Tribunal for the former Yugoslavia, *The Prosecutor v. Duško Tadić a/k/a/ "Dule"*, Case No. IT-94-1-AR72, Decision on the Defence Motion for Interlocutory Appeal on Jurisdiction, 2 October 1995, para. 62 provides: "[...] universal jurisdiction being nowadays acknowledged in the case of international crimes [...]"; International Criminal Tribunal for Rwanda, *The Prosecutor v. Bernard Ntuyahaga*, Case No. ICTR-98-40-T, Decision on the Prosecutor's Motion to Withdraw the Indictment, 18 March 1999, provides: "WHEREAS, that said, the Tribunal wishes to emphasize, in line with the General Assembly and the Security Council of the United Nations, that it encourages all States, in application of the principle of universal jurisdiction, to prosecute and judge those responsible for serious crimes such as genocide, crimes against humanity and other grave violations of international humanitarian law"; European Court of Human Rights, *Jorgić v. Germany*, Application No. 74613/01, Judgment, 12 July 2007, paras. 69-70 provides: "The Court observes in this connection that the German courts' interpretation of Article VI of the Genocide Convention in the light of Article I of that Convention and their establishment of jurisdiction to try the applicant on charges of genocide is widely confirmed by the statutory provisions and case-law of numerous other Contracting States to the Convention (for the Protection of Human Rights) and by the Statute and case-law of the ICTY. It notes, in particular, that the Spanish *Audiencia Nacional* has interpreted Article VI of the Genocide Convention in exactly the same way as the German courts [... T]he principle of universal jurisdiction for genocide has been expressly acknowledged by

Shortly after the adoption of the Genocide Convention of 1948, the adoption of the four Geneva Conventions of 1949 represented a landmark in the evolution of universal jurisdiction for the prosecution of graves breaches.[77] The four Geneva Conventions of 1949 provide that:

> Each High Contracting Party shall be under the obligation to search for persons alleged to have committed, or to have ordered to be committed, such grave breaches, and shall bring such persons, regardless of their nationality, before its own courts.[78]

---

the ICTY [...] and numerous Convention States authorize the prosecution of genocide in accordance with that principle [...]. The Court concludes that the German courts' interpretation of the applicable provisions and rules of public international law, in the light of which the provisions of the Criminal Code had to be construed, was not arbitrary. They therefore had reasonable grounds for establishing their jurisdiction to try the applicant on charges of genocide." Mr. Jorgić, a national of Bosnia-Herzegovina of Serbian ethnicity, was alleging that the German courts had not had jurisdiction to convict him of genocide for acts committed in Bosnia-Herzegovina in 1992.

76 See, *e.g.*, in Germany: *Nikolai Jorgić*, Higher Regional Court (*Oberlandesgericht*), Dusseldorf, 26 September 1997, IV-26/96 (a Bosnian Serb convicted of genocide and sentenced to life imprisonment); *Maksim Sokolović*, Higher Regional Court (*Oberlandesgericht*), Dusseldorf, 29 November 1999, and his appeal dismissed: Federal Court of Justice (*Bundesgerichtshof*), Third Criminal Senate, 21 February 2001, 3 StR 372/00 (a Bosnian Serb convicted of genocide 1992 and sentenced to a nine-year term of imprisonment); *Kjuradj Kusljić*, *Bayerisches Oberstes Landesgericht*, 15 December 1999, 6 St 1/99, and his appeal dismissed: Federal Court of Justice (*Bundesgerichtshof*), 21 February 2001, BGH 3 Str 244/00 (a Bosnian Serb convicted of genocide and sentenced to life imprisonment); in Austria: *Duško Cvjetković*, *Oberste Gerichtshof Wien*, 13 July 1994, 15 Os 99/94-6; *Duško Cvjetković*, *Oberlandesgericht Linz*, 1 June 1994, AZ 9 Bs 195/94 (GZ 26 Vr 1335/94-30); *Duško Cvjetković*, *Landesgericht Slazburg*, 31 May 1995, 38 Vr 1335/94, 38 Hv 42/94 (a Bosnian Serb prosecuted for genocide and eventually acquitted for lack of evidence. Significantly, however, it had been earlier agreed that Austrian courts had jurisdiction to try the case); in France: Cour de Cassation, Chambre criminelle, *Wenceslas Munyeshyaka*, Arrêt, 6 janvier 1998 (ongoing proceedings against a Rwandan accused of genocide); see also William A. Schabas, "National Courts Finally Begin to prosecute Genocide, the 'Crime of Crimes'", see *supra* note 24, pp. 49-50.

77 Roger O'Keefe, "The Grave Breaches Regime and Universal Jurisdiction", see *supra* note 50 , p. 811.

78 Article 49 of the First Geneva Convention of 1949; Article 50 of the Second Geneva Conventions of 1949; Article 129 of the Third Geneva Convention of 1949; Article 146 of the Fourth Geneva Convention of 1949.

The grave breaches regime of the Geneva Conventions of 1949 constitute the first treaty-based incarnation of an unconditional universal jurisdiction applicable to all States Parties.[79] As it was particularly well explained:

> [T]he obligation imposed by the grave breaches provisions is not dependent on any prescriptive nexus of nationality, territoriality, passive personality or the protective principle (or, indeed, any other internationally lawful head of jurisdiction). That is, according to their ordinary meaning, the grave breaches provisions posit an obligation to exercise criminal jurisdiction over persons alleged to have committed, or to have ordered the commission of, grave breaches of the relevant Convention in the absence, where necessary, of any other accepted ground of jurisdiction to prescribe. (*A fortiori*, a [State Party] must exercise criminal jurisdiction in respect of grave breaches allegedly committed on its territory or by one of its nationals.) In short, these identical provisions posit an obligation to exercise, where necessary, universal criminal jurisdiction over alleged grave breaches.[80]

As the Commentary on the Geneva Conventions of 1949 states, the obligation on States Parties to search for persons alleged to have committed graves breaches "imposes an active duty on them. As soon as a [State Party] realizes that there is on its territory a person who has committed such a breach, its duty is to ensure that the person concerned is arrested and prosecuted with all speed".[81] It further adds that "[t]he necessary police action should be taken spontaneously, therefore, not merely in pursuance of a request from another State".[82] Article 85(1) of the Protocol Additional to the Geneva Conventions of 12 August 1949 relating to the Pro-

[79] Roger O'Keefe, "The Grave Breaches Regime and Universal Jurisdiction", see *supra* note 50, pp. 811, 819.

[80] *Id.*, p. 814 (internal reference omitted).

[81] Oscar Uhler and Henri Coursier, "Commentary: Geneva Convention relative to the protection of civilian persons in time of war – vol. IV", in Jean Pictet (dir.), *The Geneva Conventions of 12 August 1949: Commentary*, International Committee of the Red Cross, Geneva, 1958, p. 593.

[82] *Ibid.*

tection of Victims of International Armed Conflicts[83] ("Additional Protocol I of 1977") provides for the same obligation for the graves breaches it enounces. Other international humanitarian law treaties provide for similar obligation.[84] Universal jurisdiction under customary international law for war crimes committed in international armed conflicts is also acknowledged[85] and has been recognised by national courts.[86] With regard

83 Protocol Additional to the Geneva Conventions of 12 August 1949 relating to the Protection of Victims of International Armed Conflicts (8 June 1977) ("Additional Protocol I of 1977").

84 See, *e.g.*, Articles 16(1)(c) and 17(1) of the Second Protocol to the Hague Convention of 1954 for the Protection of Cultural Property in the Event of Armed Conflict, 26 March 1999. Article 16(1)(c) provides: "Without prejudice to paragraph 2, each Party shall take the necessary legislative measures to establish its jurisdiction over offences set forth in Article 15 in the following cases: (c) in the case of offences set forth in Article 15 sub-paragraphs (a) to (c), when the alleged offender is present in its territory". Article 17(1) provides: "The Party in whose territory the alleged offender of an offence set forth in Article 15 sub-paragraphs 1 (a) to (c) is found to be present shall, if it does not extradite that person, submit, without exception whatsoever and without undue delay, the case to its competent authorities, for the purpose of prosecution, through proceedings in accordance with its domestic law or with, if applicable, the relevant rules of international law"; Articles 9(2) and 12 of the International Convention against the Recruitment, Use, Financing and Training of Mercenaries, 4 December 1989. Article 9(2) provides: "Each State Party shall likewise take such measures as may be necessary to establish its jurisdiction over the offences set forth in articles 2, 3 and 4 of the present Convention in cases where the alleged offender is present in its territory and it does not extradite him to any of the States mentioned in paragraph 1 of this article". Article 12 provides: "The State Party in whose territory the alleged offender is found shall, if it does not extradite him, be obliged, without exception whatsoever and whether or not the offence was committed in its territory, to submit the case to its competent authorities for the purpose of prosecution, through proceedings in accordance with the laws of that State. Those authorities shall take their decision in the same manner as in the case of any other offence of a grave nature under the law of that State".

85 International Criminal Tribunal for the former Yugoslavia, *The Prosecutor v. Duško Tadić a/k/a/ "Dule"*, Case No. IT-94-1-AR72, Decision on the Defence Motion for Interlocutory Appeal on Jurisdiction, 2 October 1995, para. 57 provides: "This is all the more so in view of the nature of the offences alleged against Appellant, offences which, if proven, do not affect the interests of one State alone but shock the conscience of mankind. As early as 1950, in the case of General Wagener, the Supreme Military Tribunal of Italy held: "These norms [concerning crimes against laws and customs of war], due to their highly ethical and moral content, have a universal character, not a territorial one. [...] The solidarity among nations, aimed at alleviating in the best possible way the horrors of war, gave rise to the need to dictate rules which do not recognise borders, punishing criminals wherever they may be. [...] Crimes

to war crimes committed in non-international armed conflicts, it has been proved that an *aut dedere aut judicare* international customary rule has recently come into existence[87] or, at least, states are free under international law to adopt universal jurisdiction for these crimes.[88]

against the laws and customs of war cannot be considered political offences, as they do not harm a political interest of a particular State, nor a political right of a particular citizen. They are, instead, crimes of *lèse-humanité (reati di lesa umanità)* and, as previously demonstrated, the norms prohibiting them have a universal character, not simply a territorial one. Such crimes, therefore, due to their very subject matter and particular nature are precisely of a different and opposite kind from political offences. The latter generally, concern only the States against whom they are committed; the former concern all civilised States, and are to be opposed and punished, in the same way as the crimes of piracy, trade of women and minors, and enslavement are to be opposed and punished, wherever they may have been committed (articles 537 and 604 of the penal code)." (13 March 1950, in Rivista Penale 753, 757 (Sup. Mil. Trib., Italy 1950; unofficial translation). […]". *Ibid.*, para. 62 states: "[…] one cannot but rejoice at the thought that, universal jurisdiction being nowadays acknowledged in the case of international crimes […]"; Gerhard Werle, *Principles of International Criminal Law*, see *supra* note 6, p. 67 and n. 380.

86 On 14 October 2005, The Hague District Court sentenced two Afghan asylum seekers for their role and participation in the torture of civilians during the Afghan War of 1978-1992. The Court held in both cases that it had universal jurisdiction over violations of Common Article 3 of the Geneva Conventions of 1949 and that the accused were guilty of "torment" (*foltering*) and torture as a war crime (*marteling*). For a critical comment, see Guénaël Mettraux, "Dutch Courts' Universal Jurisdiction over Violations of Common Article 3 *qua* War Crimes", in *Journal of International Criminal Justice*, 2006, vol. 4, no. 2, pp. 362-371. See also Liesbeth Zegveld, "Dutch Cases on Torture Committed in Afghanistan: The Relevance of the Distinction between Internal and International Armed Conflict", in *Journal of International Criminal Justice*, 2006, vol. 4, no. 4, pp. 878-880; Ward Ferdinandusse, "On the Question of Dutch Courts' Universal Jurisdiction: A Response to Mettraux", in *Journal of International Criminal Justice*, 2006, vol. 4, no. 4, pp. 881-883; Guénaël Mettraux, "Response to the Comments by Zegveld and Ferdinandusse", in *Journal of International Criminal Justice*, 2006, vol. 4, no. 4, pp. 884-889.

87 Christian Maierhöfer, *Aut dedere – aut judicare: Herkunft, Rechtsgrundlagen und Inhalt des völkerrechtlichen Gebotes zur Strafverfolgung oder Auslieferung*, Duncker and Humbolt, Berlin, 2006, p. 217; Claus Kreß, "Universal Jurisdiction over International Crimes and the *Institut de Droit International*", see *supra* note 55, p. 573; Philip Grant, "Les poursuites nationales et la compétence universelle", see *supra* note 54, p. 459 and n. 52 and reference cited therein.

88 Gerhard Werle, *Principles of International Criminal*, see *supra* note 6, p. 67 and n. 381.

With respect to crimes against humanity, it is important to note that there exists no specialized convention. Therefore, one cannot affirm that an international conventional norm providing for universal jurisdiction for crimes against humanity *per se* exists.[89] However, the validity of the principle of universal jurisdiction under customary international law for crimes against humanity is generally acknowledged.[90] Indeed, though not enshrined in treaties with universal jurisdiction clauses, crimes against humanity have now attained clear *jus cogens* status, such that their punishment is similarly mandatory even without explicit codification.[91]

---

89 Cherif Bassiouni, "The History of Universal Jurisdiction and Its Place in International Law", see *supra* note 60, p. 52.

90 International Criminal Tribunal for the former Yugoslavia, *The Prosecutor v. Duško Tadić a/k/a/ "Dule"*, Case No. IT-94-1-AR72, Decision on the Defence Motion for Interlocutory Appeal on Jurisdiction, 2 October 1995, para. 58 provides: "[…] It would be a travesty of law and a betrayal of the universal need for justice, should the concept of State sovereignty be allowed to be raised successfully against human rights. Borders should not be considered as a shield against the reach of the law and as a protection for those who trample underfoot the most elementary rights of humanity. In the Barbie case, the Court of Cassation of France has quoted with approval the following statement of the Court of Appeal: "[...] by reason of their nature, the crimes against humanity [...] do not simply fall within the scope of French municipal law but are subject to an international criminal order to which the notions of frontiers and extradition rules arising therefrom are completely foreign. *(Fédération Nationale de Déportés et Internés Résistants et Patriotes And Others v. Barbie,* 78 *International Law Reports* 125, 130 (Cass. crim.1983).) […]"; Indonesian Ad Hoc Tribunal for East Timor, Human Rights Ad Hoc Court at Central Jakarta District Human Rights Court, Defendant *Eurico Guterres*, No. 04/PID.HAM/AD.HOC/2002/PH.JKT.PST, Judgment, 25 November 2002, provides: "Considering, that the punishment on a perpetrator of the violation against humanity should absolutly [sic] be implemented, so through various instruments of international law, court judgments, or through developed doctrines of international law, the international community has included the international crime within the universal jurisdiction in which each perpetrator can be brought to trial anywhere and anytime regardless the *locus* and *tempus delicti*, and regardless the perpetrator's and the victim's citizenship. It means to show that there are no safe places in the world for a perpetrator of this crime (no safe haven principle)", available at (last visited 30 March 2010): http://www.legal-tools.org/en/doc/bb47f7/; Gerhard Werle, *Principles of International Criminal Law*, see *supra* note 6, p. 67 and n. 380; Theodor Meron, "International Criminalization of Internal Atrocities", see *supra* note 49, p. 589 and n. 82 and references cited therein.

91 Although there is no convention directly addressing crimes against humanity, and thus no textual requirement for punishment, the crimes were first codified at Nuremberg, and have since been codified in each of the international and hybrid criminal tribunals, such that there is now a *jus cogens* norm upholding their universal crimi-

Under the Convention against Torture of 1984, each State Party shall take necessary measures to establish its jurisdiction over acts of torture whenever the alleged perpetrator is present on any territory under its jurisdiction and it does not extradite him to another state.[92] It is an obligation.[93] Article 7(1) further provides for an obligation for the state to submit the case to its competent authorities for the purpose of prosecution, if the alleged perpetrator is not extradited.[94] In addition, according to a common view, the authority to exercise jurisdiction over torture under customary international law has been confirmed in the case law of the International Criminal Tribunal for the former Yugoslavia ("ICTY"). The ICTY recognised that:

> … one of the consequences of the *jus cogens* character bestowed by the international community upon the prohibition of torture is that every State is entitled to investigate, prosecute and punish or extradite individuals accused of torture, who are present in a territory under its jurisdiction. Indeed, it would be inconsistent on the one hand to prohibit torture to such an extent as to restrict the normally unfettered treaty making power of sovereign States, and on the other hand bar States from prosecuting and punishing those torturers who have engaged in this odious practice abroad. This legal basis

nalization. See, *e.g.*, Mark A. Summers, "International Court of Justice's Decision in *Congo v. Belgium*: How has it Affected the Development of a Principle of Universal Jurisdiction that Would Obligate All States to Prosecute War Criminals?", in *Boston University International Law Journal*, 2003, vol. 21, no. 1, p. 74 and n. 55; Gerhard Werle, *Principles of International Criminal Law*, see *supra* note 6, p. 67 and n. 380 and references cited therein; Philip Grant, "Les poursuites nationales et la compétence universelle", see *supra* note 54, p. 460; Florian Jessberger, "Universal Jurisdiction", see *supra* note 49, p. 556.

92 Article 5(2) of the Convention against Torture of 1984 provides: "Each State Party shall likewise take such measures as may be necessary to establish its jurisdiction over such offences in cases where the alleged offender is present in any territory under its jurisdiction and it does not extradite him pursuant to article 8 to any of the States mentioned in paragraph I of this article".

93 Philip Grant, "Les poursuites nationales et la compétence universelle", see *supra* note 54, p. 460.

94 Article 7(1) of the Convention against Torture of 1984 provides: "The State Party in the territory under whose jurisdiction a person alleged to have committed any offence referred to in article 4 is found shall in the cases contemplated in article 5, if it does not extradite him, submit the case to its competent authorities for the purpose of prosecution".

> for States' universal jurisdiction over torture bears out and strengthens the legal foundation for such jurisdiction found by other courts in the inherently universal character of the crime.[95]

This development in the codification of the principle of universal jurisdiction for core international crimes on the back of the Nuremberg trials and the post Second World War flourishing of human rights consciousness has been powerful. Nonetheless, it took some time before state practice started to reflect the international legal developments that had begun in the 1940s. Despite the absence of a general practice of states to exercise universal jurisdiction, many states have adopted legislation permitting their courts to do so.

9.3. Application and Effectiveness of Universal Jurisdiction as a Contemporary Mechanism for Prosecuting Those Responsible of Core International Crimes

This second part highlights and comments on the diversity and complexity surrounding the implementation of universal jurisdiction in some national jurisdictions. The cases of Spain and Belgium are particularly emphasised. Although these states cannot be deemed representative of the entire international community, they have been among the most active in exercising universal jurisdiction. Outlining the obstacles these states have met in so doing allows a better assessment of the challenges and limits states face in their exercise of universal jurisdiction.

9.3.1. Diversity in Implementing Universal Jurisdiction

At the forefront of state action with respect to the expansion of universal jurisdiction have been, *inter alia*, Belgium and Spain. In 1993, Belgium passed the Act Concerning Grave Breaches of International Humanitarian Law,[96] thereby granting Belgian courts jurisdiction over twenty grave breaches of the Geneva Conventions of 1949 and their Additional Proto-

95 International Criminal Tribunal for the former Yugoslavia, *The Prosecutor v. Anto Furundžija*, Case No. IT-95-17/1-T, Judgement, 10 December 1998, para. 156.

96 Loi du 16 juin 1993 relative à la répression des infractions graves aux Conventions internationales de Genève du 12 août 1949 et aux Protocoles I et II du 8 juin 1977, additionnels à ces Conventions, 5 August 1993, Moniteur Belge, 5 August 1993, p. 17751 ("Act of 1993").

cols,[97] irrespective of the nationality of the offender, the nationality of the victim, or the place where the criminal offence had been committed.[98] The Act of 1993 did not require the defendant's presence in Belgium in order to initiate an investigation. Moreover, because of the system of *partie civile*, Belgian courts' universal jurisdiction could be triggered by a victim acting as complainant, regardless of the prosecutor's desire to pursue the case.[99] The Act of 1993 was amended in 1999 to include crimes against humanity and genocide.[100] Additionally, Article 5(3) of the Act of 1999 further denied that immunities could apply to genocide, crimes against humanity and war crimes.[101]

Similarly, Article 23(4) of Spain's *Ley Orgánica del Poder Judicial* (Organic Law of Judicial Power), incorporated into Spanish criminal law in 1985, allows for the prosecution of certain crimes committed outside Spain by non-Spanish nationals which may, according to Spanish law, qualify as genocide, terrorism and any other crimes which under international treaties should be prosecuted by Spain.[102] Like the Belgian law, the Spanish provision at its inception was an example of universal jurisdiction allowing investigations to begin without the presence of the accused in Spain. Also like the Belgian law, Article 23(4) of the Law of 1985 could be invoked by civil parties who, upon convincing the investigating magis-

[97] Article 1 of the Act of 1993. It is interesting to note that the Act of 1993 does not follow the traditional distinction in international humanitarian law between international and non-international armed conflicts for the purpose of defining grave breaches as the Act of 1993 extends its protection to persons or objects protected by Additional Protocol II of 8 June 1977, see Tom Ongena and Ignace Van Daele, "Universal Jurisdiction for International Core Crimes: Recent Developments in Belgium", in *Leiden Journal of International Law*, 2002, vol. 15, no. 3, p. 689.

[98] Tom Ongena and Ignace Van Daele, "Universal Jurisdiction for International Core Crimes: Recent Developments in Belgium", see *supra* note 97, pp. 689-690.

[99] Tom Ongena and Ignace Van Daele, "Universal Jurisdiction for International Core Crimes: Recent Developments in Belgium", see *supra* note 97, p. 692.; Naomi Roht-Arriaza, "Universal Jurisdiction: Steps Forward, Steps Back", in *Leiden Journal of International Law*, 2004, vol. 17, no. 2, p. 376.

[100] Loi relative à la répression des violations graves du droit international humanitaire, 10 février 1999, Moniteur Belge, 23 March 1999, p. 9286 ("Act of 1999"); see Tom Ongena and Ignace Van Daele, "Universal Jurisdiction for International Core Crimes: Recent Developments in Belgium", see *supra* note 97, p. 689.

[101] Article 5(3) of the Act of 1999 provides: "L'immunité attachée à la qualité officielle d'une personne n'empêche pas l'application de la présente loi".

[102] Ley Orgánica 6/1985 del Poder Judicial, 1 July 1985 ("Law of 1985").

trate that a valid case existed, were able to force a full investigation even without the endorsement of the public prosecutor.[103]

Article 23(4) of the Law of 1985 was first used in the context of core international crimes in 1996 in cases against Argentine and Chilean military officers and civilians involved in those countries' respective military dictatorships.[104] Most famously, the Spanish courts attempted to instigate the extradition of General and former President Augusto Pinochet from the U.K. – where he was receiving medical care – to Spain with the intention of prosecuting him for crimes of genocide, terrorism and torture allegedly committed during his notorious rule over Chile and the infamous Operation Condor.[105] The case was initiated by the complaint of a civil party, without the support of the public prosecutor. Indeed, prior to the extradition request, the public prosecutor had appealed to the *Audiencia Nacional*, questioning Spain's jurisdiction to try Pinochet. The *Audiencia Nacional* heard the jurisdictional challenges and in November 1998 found that Spain could properly hear the cases under Spain's universal jurisdiction law.[106] Though there was a case for passive personality jurisdiction, as some of Pinochet's alleged victims were Spanish, the holding did not rest on this basis, but was instead based on an assertion of Spain's universal jurisdiction under Article 23(4) of the Law of 1985.

This put the matter in the hands of the British courts, which needed to determine whether an ex-president could be questioned or prosecuted for crimes committed outside U.K. borders. On 25 November 1998, reversing a decision by the High Court that held that Pinochet was protected by sovereign immunity, a specially constituted Appellate Committee of the House of Lords, acting in its capacity as Britain's highest court of appeal, granted the extradition request on the ground that Pinochet did not enjoy immunity in relation to crimes committed under international

[103] Naomi Roht-Arriaza, "Universal Jurisdiction: Steps Forward, Steps Back", in *Leiden Journal of International Law*, see *supra* note 99, p. 377.

[104] *Id.*, p. 376.

[105] Richard A. Falk, "Assessing the Pinochet Litigation: Whither Universal Jurisdiction?", in Macedo, Stephen (ed.), *Universal Jurisdiction: National Courts and the Prosecution of Serious Crimes Under International Law*, see *supra* note 60, p. 107.

[106] Naomi Roht-Arriaza, "Universal Jurisdiction: Steps Forward, Steps Back", see *supra* note 99, p. 377 and n. 4.

law.[107] This initial judgement by the House of Lords was set aside due to the alleged bias of one of the Lords, Lord Hoffman, who had links to Amnesty International. Nonetheless, on 24 March 1999, a new panel of the House of Lords also reversed the High Court decision, thus endorsing the extradition of Chile's longstanding President to a forum state with no real nexus to the alleged crimes.[108] However, Pinochet was never extradited, because Jack Straw determined in March 2000 that the former President's health, specifically his mental fitness to stand trial, militated against an extradition order.[109] Under a storm of controversy, Pinochet was returned to Chile shortly thereafter.

Though Spain's attempt to assert universal jurisdiction over Pinochet was ultimately frustrated by practical obstacles, it was a landmark case in that universal jurisdiction found judicial support in both Spain and the U.K. Unsurprisingly, then, a number of other complaints under the universal jurisdiction provisions of Spanish law ensued. Adolfo Scilingo, an Argentine naval officer and a member of the infamous Argentinean Naval School of Mechanics ("ESMA"), was accused of participating in 'death flights' in which people who had been abducted were thrown out of the aircraft, naked and unconscious, into the ocean thousands of metres below. Scilingo was arrested when he voluntarily travelled to Spain in 1997 in order to give testimony concerning these events and was eventually convicted on 19 April 2005 for crimes against humanity and sentenced to a 640-year term of imprisonment,[110] increased to 1,084 years on 4 July 2007 by the Spanish Supreme Court. A similar indictment against Ricardo Miguel Cavallo, another ESMA naval officer accused of genocide, terrorism and torture, led to an extradition request to Mexico, where

---

107 Richard A. Falk, "Assessing the Pinochet Litigation: Whither Universal Jurisdiction?", see *supra* note 105, p. 111.

108 *R v. Bow Street Metropolitan Stipendiary Magistrate*, *ex parte* Pinochet Ugarte (No. 3), 24 March 1999.

109 Michael Byers, "The Law and Politics of the Pinochet Case", in *Duke Journal of Comparative and International Law*, 2000, vol. 10, no. 2, p. 438.

110 For a discussion of the case, see Christian Tomuschat, "Issues of Universal Jurisdiction in the *Scilingo* Case", in *Journal of International Criminal Justice*, 2005, vol. 3, no. 5, pp. 1074-1081; Alicia Gil Gil, "The Flaws of the *Scilingo* Judgment", in *Journal of International Criminal Justice*, 2005, vol. 3, no. 5, pp. 1082-1091; Giulia Pinzauti, "An Instance of Reasonable Universality: the *Scilingo* Case", in *Journal of International Criminal Justice*, 2005, vol. 3, no. 5, pp. 1092-1105.

Cavallo was arrested and ultimately extradited to Spain.[111] Further complaints were raised during the ensuing years as a new era of international criminal justice appeared to dawn.

In the late 1990s and into the new millennium, Belgium's universal jurisdiction law was similarly mobilized by civil parties seeking to assert Belgium's jurisdiction over the alleged perpetrators of gross human rights abuses. Investigations were opened against a range of high-profile defendants, including political and military leaders from Chile, Rwanda, Chad, Iran, Ivory Coast, Morocco, Israel, Palestine, Cuba, Iraq, and the United States. Some of these cases were quickly dismissed.[112] On 8 June 2001, the *Butare Four* case,[113] however, led to the first convictions under Belgium's universal jurisdiction law.[114] The case involved complaints against four Rwandan citizens for their participation in a series of crimes committed during the Rwandan genocide in 1994. Vincent Ntezimana, Alphonse Higaniro and the two nuns, Sister Consolata Mukangango and Sister Juli-

---

[111] Naomi Roht-Arriaza, "Universal Jurisdiction: Steps Forward, Steps Back", see *supra* note 99, p. 378. Ricardo Miguel Cavallo was eventually extradited to Argentina on 28 February 2003.

[112] Investigations were opened against high-profiles figures such as Augusto Pinochet (former President of Chile), Paul Kagame (President of Rwanda), Hissène Habré (former Chadian President), Akbar Hashemi Rafsanjani (former Iranian President), Robert Guéï (former Ivory Coast Ruler), Laurent Gbagbo (Ivory Coast President), Emile Boga Doudou (former Ivory Coast Minister of State for the Interior), Moïse Lida Kouassi (former Ivory Coast Minister of Defence), a former Moroccan Minister of International Affairs, Ariel Sharon (former Israeli Prime Minister), Yasser Arafat (former President of the Palestinian National Authority), Fidel Castro (former Cuban President), Saddam Hussein (former Iraqi President) and George Bush Senior (former US President), see, *e.g.*, Tom Ongena and Ignace Van Daele, "Universal Jurisdiction for International Core Crimes: Recent Developments in Belgium", see *supra* note 97, p. 693; Damien Vandermeersch, "Prosecuting International Crimes in Belgium", in *Journal of International Criminal Justice*, 2005, vol. 3, no. 2, pp. 407-408; Naomi Roht-Arriaza, "Universal Jurisdiction: Steps Forward, Steps Back", see *supra* note 99, pp. 383-384.

[113] Assize Court of Brussels (Cour d'Assises de Bruxelles), *Public Prosecutor v. the 'Butare Four'*, Arrêt, 8 June 2001.

[114] On 22 May 2001, the Attorney-General, in his opening statement at trial, made it very clear that he represented the international community who has the right and the duty not to tolerate the commission of barbarous acts such as war crimes, wherever they may be committed, see Tom Ongena and Ignace Van Daele, "Universal Jurisdiction for International Core Crimes: Recent Developments in Belgium", see *supra* note 97, p. 687 and n. 1.

enne Mukabutera, were each accused of having murdered Rwandan citizens in the Butare area or having incited the killings.[115] These crimes were qualified as breaches of the Geneva Conventions of 1949 and their Additional Protocols of 1977 and thus met the requirements of the Act of 1993.[116] The 1999 amendment of the Act of 1993 was not applicable in this case as the acts occurred in 1994. Following a short but thorough jury trial, the "*Butare Four*" received sentences of between twelve and twenty years in prison.[117] The guilty verdicts of the Brussels' Assize Court represented a watershed moment for universal jurisdiction and its advocates.

Despite these impressive strides towards universal jurisdiction in Spain and Belgium, at this early stage, there remained significant questions. Among them were questions surrounding the role of civil parties in initiating such cases, the issue of sovereign and head of state's immunity, and the question of whether universal jurisdiction was tenable. The question arose whether the perpetrator should, at minimum, be within the territory or custody of the forum state in order to be indicted, even in the absence of any other nexus between the forum state and the crime.

It is important to note, in this regard, that Belgium and Spain were not the only states moving towards universal jurisdiction. Others were also advancing in that direction, though not necessarily at the same pace or with the same ultimate ambition. Indeed, a number of states have enshrined in legislation their capacity to assert universal jurisdiction as long as they have custody of the perpetrator. However, some states, such as Germany,[118] do not impose such a requirement. These provisions are de-

---

115 For the detailed official charges, see Luc Reydams, "Belgium's First Application of Universal Jurisdiction: the *Butare Four* Case", in *Journal of International Criminal Justice*, 2003, vol. 1, no. 2, pp. 430-432; Tom Ongena and Ignace Van Daele, "Universal Jurisdiction for International Core Crimes: Recent Developments in Belgium", see *supra* note 97, pp. 693-694.

116 Tom Ongena and Ignace Van Daele, "Universal Jurisdiction for International Core Crimes: Recent Developments in Belgium", see *supra* note 97, p. 694.

117 Luc Reydams, "Belgium's First Application of Universal Jurisdiction: the *Butare Four* Case", see *supra* note 115, p. 433; Tom Ongena and Ignace Van Daele, "Universal Jurisdiction for International Core Crimes: Recent Developments in Belgium", see *supra* note 97, p. 694; Damien Vandermeersch, "Prosecuting International Crimes in Belgium", see *supra* note 112, p. 405.

118 The German Criminal Code (*Strafgesetzbuch*), for example, provides for the application of German law to acts committed by non-nationals abroad against "Internationally Protected Legal Interests" (see Strafgesetzbuch ("StGB"), para. 6.) regardless of

fined and applied in different ways by different states. Some states emphasise international *jus cogens* norms and treaty obligations, such as Belgium in its extradition request for Pinochet[119] and the U.K. in its affirmation of Spain's extradition request with respect to the same individual.[120] Others, however, emphasise domestic implementing legislation, such as Spain in its extradition request for Pinochet.[121] Indeed, different states assert universal jurisdiction with respect to different crimes in various ways. Moreover, some allow civil parties to instigate prosecution, while others limit that right to prosecutors and, in some cases, even require political authorization to proceed.

Interestingly, some states appear reluctant to assert universal jurisdiction without supplementing it with some form of a nexus with the crime even when that nexus is, ostensibly, independently and purely reli-

whether they are criminalized at the place of commission. Such "Interests" include, in much the same form as the Spanish law, "genocide" and "acts which, on the basis of an international agreement binding on the Federal Republic of Germany, shall also be prosecuted if they are committed abroad" (see StGB, para. 6(1) and (9)). Perhaps more importantly, the full range of German criminal law can be made to apply to a non-national who perpetrates a crime that is forbidden at its location, if the perpetrator was later "found to be in Germany and, although the Extradition Act would render such an extradition possible, is however not extradited, because a request for extradition is not made, is rejected, or the extradition is not practicable" (see StGB, para. 7). On the basis of this universal jurisdiction legislation, German courts have convicted several perpetrators of crimes in the war in the former Yugoslavia. In addition, on 30 June 2002, the German Code of Crimes Against International Law (*Völkerstrafgesetzbuch*) entered into force establishing the principle of universal jurisdiction for genocide, crimes against humanity and war crimes in its "pure" form and establishing an obligation – the discretion of the prosecutor being no longer left – to investigate and prosecute for these crimes. The Prosecutor only keeps full discretion whether or not to prosecute when the alleged perpetrator is neither present nor expected to enter German territory; Gerhard Werle and Florian Jessberger, "International Criminal Justice is Coming Home: The New German Code of Crimes Against International Law", in *Criminal Law Forum*, 2002, vol. 13, no. 2, pp. 191-192, 212-213 and 214-223 in Annex for the whole reproduction of the Code of Crimes Against International Law; Steffen Wirth, "Germany's New International Crimes Code: Bringing a Case to Court", in *Journal of International Criminal Justice*, 2003, vol. 1 no. 1, pp. 151-153, 157-160.

119 Richard A. Falk, "Assessing the Pinochet Litigation: Whither Universal Jurisdiction?", see *supra* note 105, p. 109.

120 *Id.*, pp. 113-118.

121 *Id.*, p. 107.

ant on the legal basis of universal jurisdiction. Both France[122] and Spain[123] took this route in making extradition requests for Pinochet during his stay in the U.K. – each including passive personality as an alternative justification for jurisdiction. Thus, even in states that appear to have the capacity for universal jurisdiction, practical or political constraints may sometimes limit its application to cases in which less controversial models of extraterritorial jurisdiction would also apply.

9.3.2. Complexity in Implementing Universal Jurisdiction: the Limits of the Principle

Thus, although the 1990s and early millennium witnessed an impressive growth in the assertion and application of universal jurisdiction in a number of states, serious questions remained with respect to the appropriate limits of the concept. It was not long before Belgium and Spain came under pressure to retreat somewhat from the vanguard of universal jurisdiction.

In Belgium, the pressure came from both legal and political sources. The first major factor in the curtailment of Belgium's universal jurisdiction law came in the shape of a ruling by the International Court of Justice ("ICJ"). A civil party complaint filed in November 1998 by Belgians and Congolese nationals who had sought refuge in Belgium charged Abdulaye Yerodia Ndombasi ("Yerodia"), who was at the time the Minister for Foreign Affairs of the Democratic Republic of the Congo ("DRC"), with grave breaches of the Geneva Conventions of 1949 and crimes against humanity.[124] The civil parties complained that, as part of the efforts of Laurent Kabila's government to expel an ethnically Tutsi rebel force in the eastern part of the DRC, senior officials including Yerodia had publicly called for acts of violence against the "invaders" and incited racial hatred.[125] Following a year of investigation, on 11 April 2000, Judge

122 *Id.*, p. 108.

123 *Id.*, p. 106 and n. 19.

124 Damien Vandermeersch, "Prosecuting International Crimes in Belgium", see *supra* note 112, pp. 406-407; Tom Ongena and Ignace Van Daele, "Universal Jurisdiction for International Core Crimes: Recent Developments in Belgium", see *supra* note 97, pp. 694-695.

125 Tom Ongena and Ignace Van Daele, "Universal Jurisdiction for International Core Crimes: Recent Developments in Belgium", see *supra* note 97, p. 695; Naomi Roht-

Vandermeersch issued an international arrest warrant against Yerodia as the author or co-author of war crimes in violation of the Geneva Conventions of 1949 and their Additional Protocols of 1977 and with crimes against humanity.[126] Judge Vandermeersch noted that "while under the Belgian law there was no reason to preclude the ability of the courts to try the case, the execution of any arrest warrant had to be stayed while the suspect was a state representative on an official visit."[127]

In response to the Belgian international arrest warrant, the DRC filed an application instituting proceedings against Belgium before the ICJ on 17 October 2000, in which it made two core claims. First, it claimed that Belgian universal jurisdiction constituted a violation of the principle of sovereignty of states and of the principle that a state may not exercise its authority on the territory of another state. Second, it asserted diplomatic immunity for the accused.[128] Ultimately, the first claim was dropped and the ICJ decided only upon the issue of diplomatic immunity.[129] In this regard, the Court found, by a majority of thirteen votes to three, that Belgium had violated diplomatic immunity from criminal jurisdiction and the inviolability that Yerodia enjoyed.[130] However, while universal jurisdiction was not officially an issue for determination by the Court, it loomed large in the separate and dissenting opinions of the judges. While most of the judges indicated support for universal jurisdiction's grounding in in-

Arriaza, "Universal Jurisdiction: Steps Forward, Steps Back", see *supra* note 99, p. 384.

126 International Court of Justice, *Arrest Warrant of 11 April 2000*, see *supra* note 17, para. 13; Tom Ongena and Ignace Van Daele, "Universal Jurisdiction for International Core Crimes: Recent Developments in Belgium", see *supra* note 97, p. 695; Naomi Roht-Arriaza, "Universal Jurisdiction: Steps Forward, Steps Back", see *supra* note 99, p. 384.

127 Naomi Roht-Arriaza, "Universal Jurisdiction: Steps Forward, Steps Back", see *supra* note 99, p. 384.

128 International Court of Justice, *Arrest Warrant of 11 April 2000*, see *supra* note 17, paras 17, 41; Damien Vendermeersch, "Prosecuting International Crimes in Belgium", see *supra* note 112, p. 407.

129 International Court of Justice, *Arrest Warrant of 11 April 2000*, see *supra* note 17, para. 21; Tom Ongena and Ignace Van Daele, "Universal Jurisdiction for International Core Crimes: Recent Developments in Belgium", see *supra* note 97, p. 695.

130 International Court of Justice, *Arrest Warrant of 11 April 2000*, see *supra* note 17, para. 78(2).

ternational law,[131] there was considerably more controversy over universal jurisdiction *in absentia*, that is universal jurisdiction asserted despite the absence of the accused from the forum state's territory or custody. President Guillaume, supported in this regard by Judges Ranjeva and Rezek and Judge *ad hoc* Bula-Bula, wrote in his separate opinion that "universal jurisdiction *in absentia* is unknown to international conventional law".[132]

However, treating universal jurisdiction *in absentia* as a distinct head of jurisdiction whose lawfulness is to be proved on its own right is misplaced. Such an approach confuses a state's jurisdiction to prescribe its criminal law with the way of that law's enforcement.[133] As previously shown, universal jurisdiction is a manifestation of jurisdiction to prescribe. Like all grounds of jurisdiction to prescribe, universal jurisdiction may be exercised in a manner with the alleged perpetrator present in court, following his or her arrest in the territory of the prosecuting state. It may also be exercised after the alleged perpetrator is arrested and extradited from a foreign state. As an alternative, universal jurisdiction – like all heads of jurisdiction to prescribe – might as well be exercised without the alleged perpetrator present in court or *in absentia.* In other words, jurisdiction to prescribe is logically independent and distinct of jurisdiction to enforce. "On the one hand, there is universal jurisdiction, a head of prescriptive jurisdiction alongside territoriality, nationality, passive personality and so on. On the other hand, there is enforcement *in absentia*, just as there is enforcement *in personam*".[134] Consequently, as rightly expressed by Judges Higgins, Kooijmans and Buergenthal:

[131] However, President Guillaume argued that "international law knows only one true case of universal jurisdiction: piracy", see International Court of Justice, *Arrest Warrant of 11 April 2000*, see *supra* note 17, Separate Opinion of President Guillaume, para. 12.

[132] International Court of Justice, *Arrest Warrant of 11 April 2000*, see *supra* note 17, Separate Opinion of President Guillaume, para. 12; Declaration of Judge Ranjeva, paras. 6 and 7 stating: "These legal developments did not result in the recognition of jurisdiction *in* absentia"; Separate Opinion of Judge Rezek, paras. 6, 10; Separate Opinion of Judge Bula-Bula, para. 75.

[133] Roger O'Keefe, "Universal Jurisdiction: Clarifying the Basic Concept", see *supra* note 3, p. 749.

[134] Roger O'Keefe, "Universal Jurisdiction: Clarifying the Basic Concept", see *supra* note 3, p. 750.

> Some jurisdictions provide for trial *in absentia*; others do not. If it said that a person must be within the jurisdiction at the time of the trial itself, that may be a prudent guarantee for the right of fair trial but has little to do with bases of jurisdiction recognized under international law.[135]

Accordingly, under international law, if universal jurisdiction is authorized, as a logical consequence its exercise *in absentia* is also authorized. As it has been recognised, "[w]hether it is desirable is, needless to say, a separate question".[136]

Though the ICJ judgement pertained directly only to the issue of sovereign immunity, the Court's ruling reopened a much broader debate in Belgium on the status of the country's universal jurisdiction legislation, and the question of how it should be amended or retracted. At the core of this debate was the lingering question of whether Belgium should remain the "criminal judge of the world".[137]

Pressure on Belgium increased due to the political fall-out following civil party-induced investigations against then-Prime Minister Ariel Sharon and Director-General of the Israeli Defence Ministry, Amos Yaron, for genocide, crimes against humanity and grave breaches of the Geneva Conventions of 1949 allegedly committed at Sabra and Shatilla during Israel's 1982 invasion of Lebanon at the time they were respectively Minister of Defence and Division Commander of the Israeli Army.[138] The General Prosecutor sought an interlocutory ruling on Belgium's ability to proceed and the case's admissibility. In its decision is-

---

[135] International Court of Justice, *Arrest Warrant of 11 April 2000*, see *supra* note 17, Joint Separate Opinion of Judges Higgins, Kooijmans and Buergenthal, para. 56.

[136] Roger O'Keefe, "Universal Jurisdiction: Clarifying the Basic Concept", see *supra* note 3, p. 750.

[137] Tom Ongena and Ignace Van Daele, "Universal Jurisdiction for International Core Crimes: Recent Developments in Belgium", see *supra* note 97, p. 688; It is interesting to note that this question was given particular attention in view of the creation of the International Criminal Court, which many considered a more appropriate forum for the prosecution of core international crimes. Indeed, to some, Belgium's pioneering role at the forefront of universal jurisdiction smacked of neo-colonialism. It was not lost on such critics that universal jurisdiction forums tended to be located in the global north, while the targets of prosecution tended to come from the global south.

[138] Antonio Cassese, "The Belgian Court of Cassation v. the International Court of Justice: the *Sharon and others* Case", in *Journal of International Criminal Justice*, 2003, vol. 1, no. 2, pp. 437-438.

sued on 26 June 2002, the *Chambre de mises en accusation* – the pre-trial Chamber of the Belgian Court of Appeal – reaffirmed the validity of universal jurisdiction, but insisted that courts could only exercise that jurisdiction if the alleged perpetrator was already present on Belgian territory, therefore finding the prosecution not admissible.[139] The court found this requirement in an 1878 criminal procedure code, which remained in effect. Finding no direct contradiction of the provision in the Act of 1993 law or its 1999 amendment, and no obligation to assert universal jurisdiction *in absentia* in Belgium's treaty commitments, the Court of Appeal found no reason why this 1878 limitation should not hold.[140] However, in a never-ending saga, the Belgian Court of Cassation held, on 12 February 2003,[141] that a proper interpretation of the Belgian laws does not require – at the time criminal proceedings are instituted for genocide, crimes against humanity and war crimes – the presence of the alleged perpetrator on Belgian territory.[142]

However, unable to resist the combination of pressures, Belgium's new government – a multiparty coalition[143] – soon modified the law on 23 April 2003.[144] The Act of 2003 creates a dual system "with numerous procedural filters and political exists to thwart 'abuses'".[145] First, it tightens the nexus requirements unless a treaty requires Belgium to exercise

[139] *Id.*, p. 438 and n. 3 (referring to p. 22 of the decision of 26 June 2002).

[140] Naomi Roht-Arriaza, "Universal Jurisdiction: Steps Forward, Steps Back", see *supra* note 99, p. 386.

[141] Cour de Cassation, *Abbas Hijazi et al. v. Sharon et al.*, Decision, 12 February 2003.

[142] Antonio Cassese, "The Belgian Court of Cassation v. the International Court of Justice: the *Sharon and others* Case", see *supra* note 138, p. 438 and n. 4; Luc Reydams, "Belgium Reneges on Universality: The 5 August 2003 Act on Grave Breaches of International Humanitarian Law", in *Journal of International Criminal Justice*, 2003, vol. 1, no. 3, pp. 680-681 and n. 8.

[143] For this reason, the new law has been said to be the result of a compromise, see Luc Reydams, "Belgium Reneges on Universality: The 5 August 2003 Act on Grave Breaches of International Humanitarian Law", see *supra* note 142, p. 681.

[144] Loi modifiant la loi du 16 juin 1993 relative à la répression des violations graves du droit international humanitaire et l'article 144ter du Code judiciaire, 23 April 2003, Moniteur Belge, 7 May 2003 ("Act of 2003").

[145] Luc Reydams, "Belgium Reneges on Universality: The 5 August 2003 Act on Grave Breaches of International Humanitarian Law", see *supra* note 142, p. 684; Damien Vandermeersch, "Prosecuting International Crimes in Belgium", see *supra* note 112, p. 402.

jurisdiction. For the cases with a link to Belgium, a civil party or a local public prosecutor acting on a complaint could initiate criminal proceedings. For the purposes of the Act of 1993, a "link" to Belgium was understood to be the presence of the alleged offender on Belgian territory or the residence of a minimum of three years of a foreign victim.[146] The latter requirement was aimed at ending the practice of "forum shopping" by foreign victims.

Second, the prosecution of cases without any links to Belgium became the prerogative of the Office of the Federal Prosecutor. In principle, upon receipt of a complaint, the Federal Prosecutor has the duty to submit the case to an examining magistrate. However, two exceptions are provided by the Act of 2003, such as a manifestly unfounded complaint and a *forum non conveniens* exception.[147] According to the latter, the prosecutor must not proceed with cases that should be brought either before an international court or – assuming the possibility of a fair and impartial trial – before a national court. Here, a national court could be the one: (i) of the place where the crimes were committed; (ii) where the suspect is found; or (iii) of the state of which the alleged perpetrator is a citizen.[148] In addition, for cases without any links to Belgium, other political and judicial filters are possible. They could involve no less than seven bodies.[149]

146 Antonio Cassese, "The Belgian Court of Cassation v. the International Court of Justice: the *Sharon and others* Case", see *supra* note 138, p. 439 and n. 6; Luc Reydams, "Belgium Reneges on Universality: The 5 August 2003 Act on Grave Breaches of International Humanitarian Law", see *supra* note 142, pp. 681-682. In addition, for the purposes of the Act of 1993, "link" to Belgium was also understood as territoriality, Belgian nationality of the offender or the victim. But in these cases, we cannot speak of universal jurisdiction any more.

147 A *forum non conveniens* decision can be appealed by a complainant before the *Chambre de mises en accusation* (the pre-trial Chamber of the Belgian Court of Appeal).

148 Luc Reydams, "Belgium Reneges on Universality: The 5 August 2003 Act on Grave Breaches of International Humanitarian Law", see *supra* note 142, p. 682.

149 Namely, the Federal Prosecutor, the *Chambre de mises en accusation* (the pre-trial Chamber of the Belgian Court of Appeal), the Minister of Justice, the Cabinet of Ministers, the Court of Cassation, the International Criminal Court and foreign authorities. For more details, see Luc Reydams, "Belgium Reneges on Universality: The 5 August 2003 Act on Grave Breaches of International Humanitarian Law", see *supra* note 142, pp. 683-684.

The final nail in the coffin of Belgium's vanguard universal jurisdiction law came in the form of powerful international political pressure following the filing of civil party complaints in March 2003 against former U.S. President George H.W. Bush, Vice President Dick Cheney, Secretary of State Colin Powell, and retired general Norman Schwarzkopf for bombing an air raid shelter in Baghdad in the first Gulf War.[150] In May of the same year, General Tommy Franks and other U.S. officials were accused in another complaint of war crimes committed during the 2003 invasion of Iraq.[151] Such was American anger at these cases that US Secretary of Defense Donald Rumsfeld even suggested he might remove the North Atlantic Treaty Organization ("NATO") headquarters from Brussels.[152]

Under the pressure of several countries whose leaders had been targeted by complaints filed in Belgium, a new legislative proposal repealing the Act of 1993 was adopted on 5 August 2003.[153] It incorporates the Act of 1993's provisions in ordinary Belgian Criminal Code and Code of Criminal Procedure, while significantly limiting universal jurisdiction with regards to genocide, crimes against humanity and war crimes.[154] The application of the *partie civile* system to universal jurisdiction cases was removed.[155] Belgian courts can now only exercise universal jurisdiction over international crimes if: (i) the alleged accused is Belgian or has his primary residence in Belgium; (ii) the victim is Belgian or has lived in Belgium for at least three years at the time the crimes were committed; or (iii) Belgium is required by treaty to exercise jurisdiction over the case.

---

150 Naomi Roht-Arriaza, "Universal Jurisdiction: Steps Forward, Steps Back", see *supra* note 99, p. 387.

151 *Ibid.*

152 Luc Reydams, "Belgium Reneges on Universality: The 5 August 2003 Act on Grave Breaches of International Humanitarian Law", see *supra* note 142, p. 685; Damien Vandermeersch, "Prosecuting International Crimes in Belgium", see *supra* note 112, p. 403, n. 9; Cedric Ryngaert, "Applying The Rome Statutes Complementarity Principle: Drawing Lessons From The Prosecution of Core Crimes by States Acting Under the Universality Principle", in *Criminal Law Forum*, 2008, vol. 19, no. 1, p. 169.

153 Loi relative aux violations graves du droit international humanitaire, 5 August 2003, Moniteur Belge, 7 August 2003.

154 Damien Vandermeersch, "Prosecuting International Crimes in Belgium", see *supra* note 112, p. 402.

155 Luc Reydams, "Belgium Reneges on Universality: The 5 August 2003 Act on Grave Breaches of International Humanitarian Law", see *supra* note 142, p. 687.

Furthermore, the decision whether or not to proceed with any complaint rests entirely with the Federal Prosecutor. Finally, the latter must reject a complaint if the case should be brought either before an international court, the court of the state of which the alleged accused is a national, the court of the state where the crime was committed or where the alleged accused is found, so long as that court is independent and impartial.[156] Together these reforms represent a significant retreat from the advances of the late 1990s.

Spain eventually also curtailed its universal jurisdiction by legislative amendment after series of judicial decisions. On 2 December 1999, the Nobel Peace Prize winner Rigoberta Menchù and other victims, joined later by more than twenty NGOs, filed a civil party complaint against a number of former Guatemalan officials[157] for crimes against humanity and genocide committed during the civil war in Guatemala between 1962 and 1996 against members of the Mayan ethnic group.[158] In its decision on 13 December 2000,[159] however, the *Audiencia Nacional* decided that "at this moment" the Spanish courts had no jurisdiction over the alleged crimes as Guatemalan law permitted prosecution for genocide, and that the case should be closed.[160] The *Audiencia Nacional* reasoned that the Genocide Convention of 1948 imposes a duty to prosecute only upon the territorial state in which the crime is committed. It therefore inferred that universal jurisdiction ought to be subsidiary to territorial jurisdiction. Hence, the *Audiencia Nacional* implied that an exhaustion of domestic remedies is required to justify the assertion of universal jurisdiction.[161]

156 Naomi Roht-Arriaza, "Universal Jurisdiction: Steps Forward, Steps Back", see *supra* note 99, p. 388.

157 The suspects included five generals, two police chiefs and a colonel; a group that included former presidents and defence and interior ministers.

158 Hervé Ascensio, "Are Spanish Courts Backing Down on Universality? The Supreme Tribunal's Decision in *Guatemalan Generals*", in *Journal of International Criminal Justice*, 2003, vol. 1, no. 3, p. 691.

159 Audiencia Nacional, Sala de lo Penal, Pleno, Asiento no. 162.2000, Rollo apelación no. 115/2000, 13 December 2000.

160 Hervé Ascensio, "Are Spanish Courts Backing Down on Universality? The Supreme Tribunal's Decision in *Guatemalan Generals*", see *supra* note 158, p. 692; Naomi Roht-Arriaza, "Guatemala Genocide Case. Judgment No. STC 237/2005", in *American Journal of International Law*, 2006, vol. 100, no. 1, p. 208.

161 Hervé Ascensio, "Are Spanish Courts Backing Down on Universality? The Supreme Tribunal's Decision in *Guatemalan Generals*", see *supra* note 158, p. 694.

Domestic remedy could be denied *de jure* by a legal impediment to prosecution – for instance where a state had instituted an amnesty law – or *de facto* – where for example state judges were intimidated into denying recourse to the courts. The *Audiencia Nacional* found that there was no *de jure* obstacle and that Guatemala's transition to peace had occurred recently to pass judgment on whether there were *de facto* obstacles to domestic prosecution.[162] As such, Spain had no jurisdiction "for the moment".

The plaintiffs appealed and, on 25 February 2003, the Spanish Supreme Court, acting as a Court of Cassation, overturned in part the *Audiencia Nacional*'s decision by a majority of 8 to 7. However, in so doing, it significantly curtailed Spain's universal jurisdiction law as it held that only cases with clear tie to Spain could proceed.[163] The Spanish Supreme Court reopened the case, but only to pursue investigations in which there were Spanish victims, because they triggered passive personality jurisdiction. However, it did not re-open the case for genocide, terrorism or torture charges, because, even though Spaniards died in the course of these crimes, they were not directed at Spanish victims *per se*. Ultimately, the court held that only cases with a tie to Spain could proceed under Spain's universal jurisdiction law.[164] This did not completely eviscerate Spanish universal jurisdiction, because the court held that the presence of the accused in Spanish territory constituted an adequate tie between the forum and the crime. However, it did mean the preclusion of universal jurisdiction *in absentia*. A year later, on 8 March 2004, a panel of the Spanish Supreme Court reaffirmed this standard in a case involving Chilean General Hernán Brady.[165]

Finally, after the elections of 2004 and the change in the government, on 26 September 2005, in its judgement, the Spanish Constitutional

[162] Hervé Ascensio, "Are Spanish Courts Backing Down on Universality? The Supreme Tribunal's Decision in *Guatemalan Generals*", see *supra* note 158, p. 692; Naomi Roht-Arriaza, "Guatemala Genocide Case. Judgment No. STC 237/2005", see *supra* note 160, p. 208.

[163] Naomi Roht-Arriaza, "Guatemala Genocide Case. Judgment No. STC 237/2005", see *supra* note 160, p. 208.

[164] *Id.*, p. 208.

[165] Tribunal Supremo (Sala de lo Penal), *Hernán Brady Roche*, Judgement No. 319/2004, 8 March 2004; Naomi Roht-Arriaza, "Guatemala Genocide Case. Judgment No. STC 237/2005", see *supra* note 160, p. 210.

Court reversed the previous decision and reinstated the complaint in its entirety, issuing a ringing endorsement of broad universal jurisdiction.[166] It found that "no nexus or tie to Spain – nor the presence of the defendant, the nationality of the victims, or Spanish national interest – was needed to initiate a complaint".[167] The idea that, in order to proceed, plaintiffs needed to show that a trial in the territorial state was not possible was also rejected. Hence, it rejected the prioritization of the grounds of jurisdiction under international law.[168] Accordingly, the exercise of universal jurisdiction by Spanish courts was more likely than ever before. However, it did not last for long. The broad interpretation of the exercise of universal jurisdiction was subsequently curtailed. In 2009, a legislative reform of Article 23(4) of the Law of 1985 limited the exercise of universal jurisdiction to cases where: (i) the alleged perpetrator is present in Spain; (ii) the victims are of Spanish nationality; or (iii) there is some demonstrated relevant link with Spain. In any event, Spanish courts will only have jurisdiction if there is no other competent state or international court where proceedings have been initiated that constitute an effective investigation and prosecution of the same crimes. The criminal process initiated before Spanish courts will be provisionally superseded when there is proof that the same crimes are tried by the state where they were committed or by an international court.[169]

Although the legislation and implementation of universal jurisdiction by Belgium and Spain cannot be deemed representative of the entire international community, they have been among the most active states in exercising universal jurisdiction. However, the enforcement of the principle of universal jurisdiction remains difficult. The way in which the principle of universal jurisdiction is implemented in practice is influenced by the inherent differences between legal systems. International law seems to leave states to determine the means to enforce this principle and does not

---

166 Naomi Roht-Arriaza, "Guatemala Genocide Case. Judgment No. STC 237/2005", see *supra* note 160, pp. 207, 210.

167 *Id.*, pp. 207, 210-211.

168 Naomi Roht-Arriaza, "Guatemala Genocide Case. Judgment No. STC 237/2005", see *supra* note 160, pp. 207, 211; Cedric Ryngaert, "Applying The Rome Statutes Complementarity Principle: Drawing Lessons From The Prosecution of Core Crimes by States Acting Under the Universality Principle", see *supra* note 152, p. 161.

169 Ignacio de la Rasilla del Moral, "The Swan Song of Universal Jurisdiction in Spain", in *International Criminal Law Review*, 2009, vol. 9, no. 5, p. 804.

provide precise guidelines or criteria for its implementation. From a comparative law perspective, the principle of universal jurisdiction is either implemented extensively, narrowly or not at all. In other words, the exact scope of the principle, when it is enforced, is difficult to assess. Its application varies from one country to another. Therefore, universal jurisdiction currently defies homogeneous application and "[i]t is therefore difficult to gain a clear picture of the overall situation".[170] In this regard, it would perhaps be more accurate to refer to multiple grounds of "universal jurisdictions" instead of a principle of universal jurisdiction. Moreover, the principle of universal jurisdiction still remains more theoretical than practical in many states. Notwithstanding positive developments in some states, in practice, several core international crimes remain unpunished despite international obligations to prosecute the perpetrators. Unfortunately, political interests and interference have prevailed over legal arguments in a number of cases.[171] The question therefore arises how universal jurisdiction can gain greater legitimacy and be better and more pragmatically implemented. In other words, through which mechanism might states be encouraged to increase the investigation and prosecution of core international crimes and exercise universal jurisdiction?

9.4. The Principle of Complementarity: an Enforcement Tool of the Principle of Universal Jurisdiction?

9.4.1. The Principle of Complementarity in the Rome Statute and its Relationship with National Courts Exercising Universal Jurisdiction

The Rome Statute of the International Criminal Court ("ICC") is based on the principle of complementarity, which governs the ICC's exercise of jurisdiction. Its Preamble affirms that "the most serious crimes of concern to the international community as a whole must not go unpunished and that their effective prosecution must be ensured by taking measures at the national level and by enhancing international cooperation".[172] It further

170 Xavier Philippe, "The principle of universal jurisdiction and complementarity: how do the two principles intermesh?", see *supra* note 49, p. 379.

171 *Id.*, pp. 376, 380.

172 Paragraph 4 of the Preamble of the Rome Statute of the International Criminal Court (17 July 1998) ("Rome Statute").

recalls that "it is the duty of every State to exercise its criminal jurisdiction over those responsible for international crimes".[173] The duty to prosecute core international crimes is therefore clearly stated.

Paragraph 10 of the Rome Statute's Preamble and Article 1 emphasise that the ICC "shall be complementary to national criminal jurisdictions". According to this principle, further developed by Article 17 of the Rome Statute, the ICC will only exercise its jurisdiction if "a State which has jurisdiction" over a case involving core international crimes is "unwilling or unable genuinely to carry out the investigation or prosecution".[174] Article 17(2) and (3) of the Rome Statute defines in detail when it may be assumed that a state is "unwilling or unable" in a particular case.[175] Thus, contrary to the ICTY or the International Criminal Tribunal

173 Paragraph 6 of the Preamble of the Rome Statute.

174 According to Article 17(1)(a) and (b) of the Rome Statute, the ICC will not conduct proceedings when: "(a) [t]he case is being investigated or prosecuted by a State which has jurisdiction over it, unless the State is unwilling or unable genuinely to carry out the investigation or prosecution; [or] (b) [t]he case has been investigated by a State which has jurisdiction over it, unless the State is unwilling or unable genuinely to carry out the investigation or prosecution". In addition, according to Articles 17(1)(c) and 20(3) of the Rome Statute and in accordance with the principle *ne bis in idem*, the ICC will not exercise its jurisdiction when a domestic jurisdiction has already tried the person concerned for conduct which is the subject of the complaint unless (a) it was done with the purpose of shielding the person concerned from criminal responsibility or (b) the proceedings were not conducted independently or impartially in accordance with the norms due process recognized by international law and were conducted in a manner which, in the circumstances, was inconsistent with an intent to bring the person concerned to justice. Finally, the Court will determine that a case is inadmissible where the case is not of sufficient gravity to justify further action by the Court, according to Article 17(1)(d) of the Rome Statute.

175 Article 17(2) of the Rome Statute reads as follows: "In order to determine unwillingness in a particular case, the Court shall consider, having regard to the principles of due process recognized by international law, whether one or more of the following exist, as applicable: (a) The proceedings were or are being undertaken or the national decision was made for the purpose of shielding the person concerned from criminal responsibility for crimes within the jurisdiction of the Court referred to in article 5; (b) There has been an unjustified delay in the proceedings which in the circumstances is inconsistent with an intent to bring the person concerned to justice; (c) The proceedings were not or are not being conducted independently or impartially, and they were or are being conducted in a manner which, in the circumstances, is inconsistent with an intent to bring the person concerned to justice." Article 17(3) of the Rome Statute provides that: "In order to determine inability in a particular case, the Court shall consider whether, due to a total or substantial collapse or unavailability of its na-

for Rwanda ("ICTR"),[176] primacy responsibility for enforcing criminal liability for violations of core international crimes rests on the national criminal jurisdictions of States Parties to the Rome Statute. In other words, the ICC acts as a safety net. It will only be engaged where states do not fulfil their obligations under international law by exercising effective criminal jurisdiction over the crimes set out in the Rome Statute. In this sense, the principle of complementarity respects the principle of state sovereignty in international law and the principle of primacy of action regarding criminal prosecutions.[177]

In the context of concurrent jurisdictions between the ICC and national jurisdictions over the crimes embodied in the Rome Statute, it seems pertinent to discuss various possible scenarios.

First of all, if there is no doubt that states exercising territorial or active national jurisdiction have primacy of criminal jurisdiction over the ICC, do states also have priority over the ICC when exercising universal jurisdiction? The Rome Statute does not provide an explicit answer. One scholar pointed out:

> [O]ne could indeed argue that the coming into existence of the ICC makes the establishment of universal jurisdiction obsolete with regard to crimes committed by a national or on the territory of a State party to the Rome Statute. In these cases, the ICC would fill the void that underlies the concept of universal jurisdiction. This latter aims at ensuring the enforcement of meta-national values by prosecuting perpetrators if States with a *nexus* based on traditional jurisdictional

tional judicial system, the State is unable to obtain the accused or the necessary evidence and testimony or otherwise unable to carry out its proceedings".

176 Article 9(2) of the ICTY Statute provides: "The International Tribunal shall have primacy over national courts. At any stage of the procedure, the International Tribunal may formally request national courts to defer to the competence of the International Tribunal in accordance with the present Statute and the Rules of Procedure and Evidence of the International Tribunal". Similarly, Article 8(2) of the ICTR Statute reads as follows: "The International Tribunal for Rwanda shall have the primacy over the national courts of all States. At any stage of the procedure, the International Tribunal for Rwanda may formally request national courts to defer to its competence in accordance with the present Statute and the Rules of Procedure and Evidence of the International Tribunal for Rwanda".

177 Xavier Philippe, "The principle of universal jurisdiction and complementarity: how do the two principles intermesh?", see *supra* note 49, p. 388.

> principles are unwilling or unable to do so. As such, the exercise of universal jurisdiction is conceived as an act on behalf of the international community, which, lacking any enforcement organs of its own, relies on national courts. However, since the entry into force of the Rome Statute, the international community has for the first time established a permanent enforcement organ for (some of) the crimes for which universal jurisdiction had initially been developed. An argument can therefore be made that the ICC, rather than national courts exercising universal jurisdiction, would be the proper organ to act on behalf of the international community. In fact, the ICC would probably do so with greater authority than national courts and be better equipped to adjudicate such cases. In contrast, universal jurisdiction over offences that do not fall within the jurisdiction of the ICC, for example because they are neither committed on the territory nor by a national of a State party or committed prior to the entry into force of the Statute, remains crucial in order to ensure that crimes of international concern do not go unpunished. If States were to implement such a jurisdictional regime they could do so by differentiating between cases that are subject to the ICC's jurisdiction and those that are not, confining the establishment of universal jurisdiction to the latter category.[178]

This argument is not tenable as it would lead to impunity gaps through which alleged perpetrators could escape prosecution for various reasons, contrary to the goal of the Rome Statute.[179] Indeed, even though the ICC would have jurisdiction in particular cases, the Court would not be able to investigate or prosecute all core international crimes that are not prosecuted by states with a *nexus* based on traditional grounds of criminal jurisdiction. This is especially true for the prosecution of lower-level perpetrators. In addition, not all cases of core international crimes would meet the gravity threshold embodied in Article 17(1)(d) of the

[178] Jann K. Kleffner, "The Impact of Complementarity on National Implementation of Substantive International Criminal Law", in *Journal of International Criminal Justice*, 2003, vol. 1, no. 1, p. 108.

[179] Paragraph 5 of the Preamble of the Rome Statute stresses the States Parties' determination "to put an end to impunity for the perpetrators" of the most serious crimes of concern to the international community.

Rome Statute for the ICC to find a case admissible.[180] Therefore, many perpetrators of core international crimes would remain unpunished.

The ordinary meaning of the terms[181] of Article 17 of the Rome Statute makes it clear that the Rome Statute gives primacy of criminal jurisdiction not only to the territorial state where the crimes were committed, but to "a State which has jurisdiction". This terminology does not impose any limitation on the criteria to which a state may assert its jurisdiction. This basically leaves the door open to any State Party to the Rome Statute, including states exercising their criminal jurisdiction in accordance with the principle of universal jurisdiction.

The first part of this contribution established that states, under either conventional or customary international law, are free or, in certain circumstances, under an obligation to exercise universal jurisdiction over all the crimes set out in the Rome Statute, namely genocide, crimes against humanity and war crimes.[182] Therefore, if a state has jurisdiction in accordance with the principle of universal jurisdiction, it also has primacy of criminal jurisdiction over the ICC and the ICC must respect it. As a matter of principle, there is no reason why universal jurisdiction exercised by national courts would not fall within the general principle of complementarity. It is worth noticing that, while implementing the Rome Statute of the ICC in their national legislation, some states took the approach to establish universal jurisdiction.[183] In this sense, the principle of

[180] Article 17(1)(d) of the Rome Statute provides that the ICC shall determine that a case is inadmissible where the case is not of sufficient gravity to justify further action by the Court.

[181] According to Article 31(1) of the Vienna Convention on the Law of Treaties (23 May 1969), "[a] Treaty shall be interpreted in good faith in accordance with the ordinary meaning to be given to the terms of the treaty in their context and its light of its object and purpose".

[182] Article 5(1)(d) of the Rome Statute also gives jurisdiction to the ICC for the crime of aggression. However, according to Article 5(2) of the Rome Statute, the ICC will only be able to exercise its jurisdiction over this particular crime once a provision is adopted defining the crimes and setting out the conditions under which the ICC shall exercise jurisdiction with respect to this crime. Considering the framework of this contribution, the crime of aggression is not included in this analysis.

[183] See, *e.g.*, Germany, Canada, New Zealand, South Africa, Australia; Jann K. Kleffner, "The Impact of Complementarity on National Implementation of Substantive International Criminal Law", see *supra* note 178, p. 107, n. 100; Juliet Hay, "Implementing the ICC Statute in New Zealand", in *Journal of International Criminal Justice*, 2004, vol. 2, no. 1, p. 196.

complementarity can be conceived as a means of improving implementation of the principle of universal jurisdiction. Indeed, it places the primary burden of the responsibility to prosecute core international crimes on all States Parties owing to the fact that all states are free or under an obligation, in certain cases, to exercise universal jurisdiction. Similarly, universal jurisdiction can also be regarded as a means to implement the principle of complementarity rather that an obstacle to achieving its goals.

The question may nonetheless arise which state has primary responsibility if both a state exercising universal jurisdiction and having custody over an alleged offender and the state where the crimes were committed (or the state of nationality of the offender) is willing and able genuinely to carry out the investigation or prosecution. Is there an obligation for a state exercising universal jurisdiction to defer to a state with an intimate connection to the crimes? From a policy point of view, there is little doubt that this should be the case. Based on the recognition of a legitimate interest of those states that are directly linked with the crime in question, deference should be exercised towards these states. Whether there is also an international legal obligation to do so is a different question.[184] It is impossible to identify through the current practice and *opinio juris* of states exercising universal jurisdiction an international customary rule obliging those states to defer to the territorial or national state. Nonetheless, states might be under a conventional international obligation to do so, for example because an extradition treaty includes such a requirement.

A more interesting scenario is where the territorial state, or the national state, of the commission of the crimes (state A) is unwilling or unable genuinely to carry out the investigation or prosecution and the state on which the alleged perpetrator is found (state B) has jurisdiction over the crimes under the principle of universality. Would state B in this case be under any incentive to investigate or prosecute the case?

On the one hand, states with jurisdiction under the principle of universal jurisdiction may have a less obvious interest in investigating or prosecuting the case. On the other hand, one can assume that States Par-

[184] On this issue, see, *e.g.*, Cedric Ryngaert, "Applying The Rome Statutes Complementarity Principle: Drawing Lessons From The Prosecution of Core Crimes by States Acting Under the Universality Principle", see *supra* note 152, pp. 153-180; Claus Kreß, "Universal Jurisdiction over International Crimes and the *Institut de Droit International*", see *supra* note 55, pp. 579-580.

ties to the Rome Statute will desire to investigate and prosecute core international crimes for which they have jurisdiction, including under the principle of universal jurisdiction, rather than deferring to the competence of the ICC.[185] Indeed, states in the position of state B might have an interest, political or not, in avoiding the scrutiny of the ICC and the embarrassment of being pigeonholed as "unwilling" to carry out investigation or prosecution[186] or "unable" owing to the absence or inadequacies of substantive national implementing legislation. As such, the principle of complementarity may act as an incentive, first, to enforce criminal jurisdiction for core international crimes, including through the exercise of universal jurisdiction[187] and, second, to adopt adequate national implementing legislation.[188]

9.4.2. Proposal Towards a More Pragmatic Enforcement of Universal Jurisdiction Through the Principle of Complementarity

The fact that states exercising jurisdiction under the principle of universality have priority over the ICC is a positive development in the application of the principle of universal jurisdiction. By recognising such primacy, the ICC gives greater legitimacy to states exercising universal jurisdiction who are, otherwise, under enormous political constraints and

185 Louise Arbour, "Will the ICC have an Impact on Universal Jurisdiction?", in *Journal of International Criminal Justice*, 2003, vol. 1, no. 3, p. 586.

186 If state B is passive in bringing the person concerned to justice, the ICC is competent in this specific scenario pursuant to the complementarity principle and Article 17(2)(b) of the Rome Statute, providing that the other criteria of admissibility are fulfilled.

187 Jann K. Kleffner, "The Impact of Complementarity on National Implementation of Substantive International Criminal Law", see *supra* note 178, pp. 87-89. Kleffner envisages the principle of complementarity as a "carrot-and stick mechanism" where the ICC will retain the stick to take over such investigations and prosecutions if states fail in their endeavour to create and enforce a legislative framework for the effective investigation and prosecution of core international crimes.

188 Jann K. Kleffner, "The Impact of Complementarity on National Implementation of Substantive International Criminal Law", see *supra* note 178, pp. 88-94; Jo Stigen, *The Relationship between the International Criminal Court and National Jurisdictions: The Principle of Complementarity*, Leiden/Boston: Martinus Nijhoff Publishers, 2008, pp. 473-474. However, both authors recognise that the Rome Statute does not provide for an explicit obligation to implement its substantive law.

pressure. Furthermore, if the principle of complementarity acts as an incentive for states to exercise universal jurisdiction in order to avoid the scrutiny of the Court, this development is also welcome.

Nonetheless, more can – and should – be done in order to reduce existing impunity gaps. In this sense, a positive or proactive vision of the principle of complementarity must be implemented and encouraged. A "carrot-and-stick" based understanding of the principle of complementarity, while efficient, is not a sufficient means to enforce the goal pursued by universal jurisdiction. It is fundamental to explore new avenues as to how international criminal justice can interact better and more effectively with national courts.

Whether state B in the above-mentioned scenario will decide to exercise its jurisdiction over a case under the principle of universality will largely depend on the ICC and how its Prosecutor will be successful in encouraging states with universal jurisdiction to proceed on this basis rather than to undertake the prosecution if no state is willing to do so. It will also depend on the ICC's deliberate policy choice to encourage States Parties' expansion of their universal jurisdiction. Cooperation must therefore be seen in two ways; cooperation of states with the Court, but also the ICC's cooperation with domestic jurisdictions. Strengthening a reverse form of cooperation from the Court to national courts should be part of the ICC and its Prosecutor's policy. Promoting legal empowerment of domestic jurisdictions, including those exercising universal jurisdiction, should be encouraged by the ICC and its Prosecutor.

Some scholars have advocated that such a policy direction could come in the Assembly of States Parties, where a consensus could develop if states encourage universal jurisdiction for economic and efficiency reasons rather than fully fund the ICC.[189] Regardless of these reasons, a discussion among States Parties to promote a more harmonized approach towards universal jurisdiction would also be welcome. Indeed, the Assembly of States Parties, in consultation with its members, could develop common criteria or guidelines to improve the implementation of universal jurisdiction. Another proposal would be for regional organization, in consultation with its member states, to foster a better harmonization of uni-

[189] Louise Arbour, "Will the ICC have an Impact on Universal Jurisdiction?", see *supra* note 185, p. 587.

versal jurisdiction among its member states in order to ensure that core international crimes do not remain unpunished.

Another scenario is where an alleged perpetrator is in the custody of the ICC, after an arrest warrant has been issued and enforced, but the ICC does not have the financial or human resources to deal with all cases within its limited funding. The question therefore arises whether the ICC may request that another state with jurisdiction under the principle of universality deal with the case. Encouraging cooperation under the auspices of the ICC to transfer a case to a state more suited to deal with it does not seem to be explicitly addressed by the Rome Statute.[190] As the Court will hardly be able to deal with all cases within its limited available resources, the exercise of universal jurisdiction by states would assist in filling a gap and represent a form of cooperation with the Court in the performance of its functions. Whether such cooperation may already be due under the Rome Statute or would require an amendment is questionable. Although Article 86 of the Rome Statute[191] imposes on States Parties a general obligation to cooperate with the Court, the scope of such cooperation seems limited to the other provisions explicitly listed in the Rome Statute.[192] Thus, an amendment is likely to be necessary. A development in this direction appears highly desirable, and even more desirable if the exercise of universal jurisdiction would occur under the control or coordination of the Court itself. Indeed, the ICC may be entitled by amendment to its Statute to make use of referral procedures to national courts of states that have adopted national legislation on universal jurisdiction, as experienced

[190] If a state which has jurisdiction can challenge the admissibility of a case before the ICC "[i]n exceptional circumstances, […] at a time later than the commencement of the trial" according to Article 19(4) of the Rome Statute, then one must assume that the ICC is empowered to transfer the alleged perpetrator to the a state which successfully challenges its jurisdiction, even if not envisaged explicitly in the Statute. However, this does not give the ICC the right to transfer a person to a state which has not challenge the admissibility of a case before the Court.

[191] Article 86 of the Rome Statute provides: "States Parties shall, in accordance with the provisions of this Statute, cooperate fully with the Court in the investigation and prosecution of crimes within the jurisdiction of the Court".

[192] Claus Kreß, "Article 86 General obligation to cooperate", in Otto Triffterer (ed.), *Commentary on the Rome Statute of the International Criminal Court*, Nomos Verlagsgesellschaft, Baden-Baden, 1999, p. 1053.

by the ICTY and the ICTR under Rule 11*bis* of their Rules of Procedure and Evidence.[193]

Obviously, all these proposals would require closer consideration. Nonetheless, they have the advantage of using already existing mechanisms and the institutions to give concrete effect to the goal pursued by universal jurisdiction, namely that core international crimes do not remain unpunished and that the perpetrators of these crimes are brought to justice.

9.5. Conclusion

Having recourse to traditional grounds of jurisdictions for prosecuting core international crimes has numerous advantages. However, in many cases, this is not always possible due to various political and legal impediments at a national level. The purpose of the principle of universal jurisdiction is to avoid loopholes in the prosecution of core international crimes. Although the principle seems well established both in conventional and customary international law as a ground of jurisdiction to prescribe, its application remains controversial and difficult. Indeed, in theory, states are free, or under a legal obligation, under international law to implement universal jurisdiction in their national legal systems. In practice, however, states exercising such jurisdiction continue to face substantial international political pressure. The gap between the existence of the principle and its application remains quite wide. As a result, national and international constraints placed on states have too often prevailed over their legal obligation to prosecute alleged perpetrators of core international crimes. Does this mean the end for universal jurisdiction? No, however, it does indicate that universal jurisdiction has certain limits.

From both a legal and policy perspective, the implementation of the principle of universal jurisdiction is welcome. This remains true even with the creation of the ICC. Indeed, the concept of "unwillingness" and "inability" should not serve too easily as a pretext for the sole intervention of the ICC. Remedies for dealing with perpetrators of atrocities should come at the domestic rather than at the international level. Justice cannot be

193 Fausto Pocar, "UN Approach to Transitional Justice", Statement given on 2 December 2009 during the Dialogue with Member States on rule of law at the international level organized by the Rule of Law Unit, available on http://www.unrol.org/doc.aspx?d=2917 (last visited on 27 April 2010).

entirely removed from the domestic to the international level; not only for organizational or financial reasons. The primary responsibility for prosecuting core international crimes rests with states and their judiciaries, as affirmed by the Preamble of the Rome Statute. Ensuring the existence and enhancing the operational capacity of independent and impartial domestic courts with a view to establishing a legal framework based on the rule of law remains the main challenge for international criminal justice. States should therefore be encouraged to investigate and prosecute core international crimes and to exercise criminal jurisdiction, by virtue of the traditional grounds of jurisdiction and by recourse to universal jurisdiction as appropriate.

Universal jurisdiction provides for the possibility of decentralized prosecution of international crimes by states, creating a comprehensive framework of jurisdictional claims for core international crimes. This markedly improves the chances of ending, or at least reducing, impunity for such crimes.

Nonetheless, certain risks must not be disregarded. First, the principle of universal jurisdiction can be open to potential abuses, especially if used in a complete discriminatory manner, for revenge or for responding to exigencies of foreign policy. Second, having recourse to universal jurisdiction can create a large number of competing claims from various states exercising their jurisdiction under different grounds, and potentially causing conflict among states. Although these dangers must be taken seriously, the excessive prosecution of core international crimes has not yet occurred. Thus, this is not a reason to relinquish the principle of universal jurisdiction.

The principle of complementarity and the ICC may induce states to abide by their obligations to exercise universal jurisdiction for core international crimes and therefore avoid loopholes in the prosecution of core international crimes. In addition, universal jurisdiction implemented under the ICC's umbrella would likely induce greater legitimacy in the application of the principle.

While the principle of complementarity will not remedy all the inadequacies of the implementation of universal jurisdiction, it may assist its enforcement in a more pragmatic and homogenous manner. The primary responsibility for investigating and prosecuting core international crimes rests with states and their judiciaries. Enhancing a more pragmatic and homogenous implementation of the principle of universal jurisdiction remains the main challenge for international criminal justice. Positive and proactive implementation of the principle of complementarity, as well as cooperation of states with the Court and of the Court with states, must be encouraged and strengthened. A mechanism of transfer of cases from the Court to domestic courts exercising universal jurisdiction should also be envisaged. Only concerted efforts will lead to a better enforcement of the goal pursued by universal jurisdiction; namely to ensure that core international crimes are punished and their perpetrators are properly prosecuted.

INDEX

F

G

H

I

T

U

V

W

FICHL Publication Series

OTHER VOLUMES IN THE FICHL PUBLICATION SERIES

Morten Bergsmo, Mads Harlem and Nobuo Hayashi (editors):
Importing Core International Crimes into National Law
Torkel Opsahl Academic EPublisher
Oslo, 2010
FICHL Publication Series No. 1 (Second Edition, 2010)
ISBN 978-82-93081-00-5

Nobuo Hayashi (editor):
National Military Manuals on the Law of Armed Conflict
Torkel Opsahl Academic EPublisher
Oslo, 2010
FICHL Publication Series No. 2 (Second Edition, 2010)
ISBN 978-82-93081-02-9

Morten Bergsmo, Kjetil Helvig, Ilia Utmelidze and Gorana Žagovec:
The Backlog of Core International Crimes Case Files in Bosnia and Herzegovina
Torkel Opsahl Academic EPublisher
Oslo, 2010
FICHL Publication Series No. 3 (Second Edition, 2010)
ISBN 978-82-93081-04-3

Morten Bergsmo (editor):
Criteria for Prioritizing and Selecting Core International Crimes Cases
Torkel Opsahl Academic EPublisher
Oslo, 2010
FICHL Publication Series No. 4 (Second Edition, 2010)
ISBN 978-82-93081-06-7

Morten Bergsmo and Pablo Kalmanovitz (editors):
Law in Peace Negotiations
Torkel Opsahl Academic EPublisher
Oslo, 2010
FICHL Publication Series No. 5 (Second Edition, 2010)
ISBN 978-82-93081-08-1

Morten Bergsmo, César Rodríguez Garavito, Pablo Kalmanovitz and Maria Paula Saffon (editors):
Distributive Justice in Transitions
Torkel Opsahl Academic EPublisher
Oslo, 2010
FICHL Publication Series No. 6 (2010)
ISBN 978-82-93081-12-8

All volumes are freely available as e-books on the FICHL homepage www.fichl.org. Printed copies may be ordered online at www.amazon.co.uk.

www.ingramcontent.com/pod-product-compliance
Lightning Source LLC
Chambersburg PA
CBHW071337230926
51849CB00006B/509/J
* 9 7 8 8 2 9 3 0 8 1 1 4 2 *